EUROPEAN
DESIGNER JEWELRY

EUROPEAN
DESIGNER JEWELRY

Ginger Moro

Schiffer Publishing Ltd

77 Lower Valley Road, Atglen, PA 19310

Dedication

To those who shaped my sensibilities as a young woman
in Paris: Michel, Muriel, Ahmed, John, Nick, Pierre, and Russ.

Two cast metal brooches with pavé strass: the owl is marked "*Déposé*"
the butterfly with faux turquoises is unsigned. Ca. Fifties. *Courtesy of
Robin Feldman Collectibles, New York, NY. Photo by Robert Weldon*

Half-Title
Brooch with "topaz" and "citrine" rhinestones shading down to gilded
brass tassels, Fifties, marked "Déposé". *Courtesy of private collection,
Milan, Italy*

Frontispiece 1:

Six necklaces by European designers. From the top down:
Italy - Blue and clear crystal beads by Coppola e Toppo, Sixties; Austria
- Enamelled copper necklace by unknown designer, Thirties; Germany
- Chrome gas pipe with Bakelite tips by unknown designer, Thirties;
England - Eastern style necklace of faux pearls and turquoise by
Mitchell Maer for Dior, Fifties; France - Strass and "emerald" necklace,
Twenties by Maison Gripoix (?) unsigned; France - Topaz and citrine
rhinestones form a deep V by Cis, Austro-Hungarian Countess
Zoltowska, Sixties. *Courtesy of the author. Photo by Sandro Moro*

Library of Congress Cataloging-in-Publication Data

Moro, Ginger Hall.
    European designer jewelry / Ginger Hall Moro.
        p.   cm.
    Includes bibliographical references and index.
    ISBN: 0-88740-823-0
    1. Jewelry–Europe–Design–History–20th century. I. Title.
NK7342.M58   1995
739.27'094'0904–dc20   95-2180
                                    CIP

Printed in China
ISBN: 0-88740-823-0

We are interested in hearing from authors
with book ideas on related topics.

Published by Schiffer Publishing, Ltd.
77 Lower Valley Road
Atglen, PA 19310
Please write for a free catalog.
This book may be purchased from the publisher.
Please include $2.95 postage.
Try your bookstore first.

We are interested in hearing from authors
with book ideas on related subjects.

Contents

I would like to thank my photographers for their infinite patience and support: Robert Weldon, Sandro Moro, Christie Romero, Los Angeles; Victor de Liso, Richard Marx, New York; Bruno Pierson, Paris; Helmar Dankl, Vienna; Pierre Higgonet, Venice; and my editor, Nancy Schiffer.

For their personal anecdotes about life and art in Paris in the Twenties and Thirties as recounted to me in the Seventies, I am grateful to: Josephine Baker, Paul Colin, Sonia Delaunay, Jean Desprès, Erté, Janet Flanner (Genêt of the *New Yorker*), Eileen Grey, Denise Poiret, and Béla Voros.

To the artists, curators, dealers, collectors and couturiers in Europe who shared with me their knowledge and artistry: Denise Arnal, Artcurial, Tiany Chambard, Décalage, Dominique Emschwiller for Jean Paul Gaultier, Francine Fontaine, Olwyn Forest, Lili and Daniel Gantarski, Robert Goossens, Josette Gripoix, Guy Rambaldi for Louis Féraud, Laure du Pavillon for Christian Lacroix, Roger Jean-Pierre, Francois Lesage, Lei, Naïla de Monbrison, Jeanne Péral, Denise Rousselet and Jean Claude, Lea Stein and Fernand Steinberger, Sorelle, Jacqueline Subra, Jean-Pierre Thiebemont, Gérard Tremolet, Hervé van der Straeten, Monique Vittaut, Line Vautrin, and M. Zisul in Paris. Centre Culturel Aragon, Oyonnax, France.

Deanna Farneti Cera, Ugo Correani, Dolce & Gabbana, Barnaba Fornasetti, Melissa Gabardi, Franco Jacassi, Rosita Missoni, Anna Rabolini, Sylvie de Michaux for Ken Scott, Donatella Pellini, and Gianni Versace in Milan; Riccardo Cascio, Martha Corsi, Giancarlo Fiaschi, and Emilio Pucci in Florence; Marie-Hélène Laurens Alzetta, Signora Moretti-Giusi, and Rialta of Venice; Luciana de Reutern, Contessa della Noce, and Alberto Andreozzi of Gioielli L.A.B.A. in Rome, Italy.

Gijs Bakker, Onno Boekhoudt, Willemyn Bertrams, Jorge Cohen, Frans Leidelmeijer and Anneke Schat in Amsterdam, Holland.

Butler and Wilson, Barbara Cartlidge, David Gill, Francis della Vita, John Jesse, David and Sonya Newell-Smith, Wendy Ramshaw, The Worshipful Company of Goldsmiths, Jan van den Bosch and Carole Underwood, and the photo research staff at the Victoria & Albert Museum. Christopher St. James, William Wain, Georgina Vogel, Pam and Zance Yianni, Maria Merola, Melanie Coe, Linda Morgan, Monika, Paul Orssich, M & R Glendale's, Beauty and the Beasts, Pruskin Gallery, Didier Antiques, Themes and Variations, N. Bloom & Son, Aalto Gallery, Editions Graphiques, in London.

Dr. Graham Dry, Ulrike von Hase-Schmundt, Osiris, Jan Vichel, Galerie von Spaeth, Brigantine, Mary Sue Packer, Munich; Dr. Merkel of Henry's AuktionHaus, Mutterstadt; Dieter Zühlsdorff of Arnolds'che Verlag, and Suzanne Kiess-Schaad of langani, Stuttgart; Dr. Fritz Falk of the Schmuckmuseum, Harald Hämmerle and Michael Grosse of Pforzheim, Germany. Ewa Möwe and Reiner März, Berlin, Germany.

P. Vanderborght, Aline Goffard, Nicoli, Galerie de Windt of Brussels, Belgium.

In Scandinavia: Bendix Bech-Thostrup of Guldsmedeblat, Christian Hansen, Michael von Essen, Georg Jensen museum in Denmark; Tone Vigeland, Widar Halén at the Kunstindustrimuseet, and Suzanne Minton-Fulbruge and Jon David-Andersen in Oslo, Norway; Helena Dahlbäck-Luttemans at Swedish National Art Musem, Sigurd Persson in Stockholm; Marianne Aav, Tony Parkimma at the Arts and Crafts Museum, Ulla Tillander-Godenhielm, Eva Kuntz and Björn Weckström, Kalevela Koru, Kaunis Koru, and Oppi Untracht in Helsinki, Finland.

Elizabeth Reichel and Johann Kilianowitsch of Wiener Interieurs, Eva Reiter of Hochschule für angewandte Kunst, Dr. Elizabeth Schmuttermeier of Museum für angewandte Kunst, Karl Hagenauer, Wolfgang Bauer of Bel Etage, Anita and Bernd Bayer, Galerie Austria, Galerie bei der Albertina, Ingrid Höfstätter, Sophie Blau, A. D. Meek, and Jacqueline Lillie in Vienna, and Karen Byrne-Laimbock of Innsbruck, Austria.

In America: Elise Misiorowski and Donna Durham of the Gemological Institute of America in Santa Monica, CA; Joan Agajanian, Dharam Damama, Gail Freeman, European Antiques, Gail Gerretsen, Marilyn Hirsty, Kerry Holden, l.a. Eyeworks, Diane Keith, Joanne McPherson, Dena McCarthy, Marc Navarro, Ruby Newman, Lisa Siddens, Connie Parente, Charles Pinkham, Terrance O'Halloran, Linda Rinella, Michael Richards and Christie Romero, Countess Cissy Zoltowska of Los Angeles, and the cultural attachés of the Consulates of Sweden and Finland in Los Angeles; Peregrine Gallery of Santa Barbara and Sara Gabarini, in Tiburon, CA; Davida Baron, Lucille Tempesta of *Vintage Costume and Fashion Jewelry* Newsletter, Glen Oaks, NY; Mark Walsh, Yonkers, NY; Norman Crider, Ilene Chazanoff, Irene Carpelis, Rita Sacks, Susan Meisel, Ward Landrigan of Verdura, Robin Feldman, Harrice Miller, and Audrey Friedman, Leonard Fox Rare Books, New York; Joanne Ball of Avon, CT.; Mario Rivoli of Denver, CO; Ellen Germanos, Rolling Meadows, IL. Rita Goodman of Santa Fe, NM; Fern Simon of Arts 220, Winnetka, Il; Lillian Baker, Gardena, CA.; Carri Priley, St. Paul, MN.

Baudelaire wrote in *L'Art Romantique*: "Every epoch has its gait, glance, and gesture." To that we might add, " and its adornment". Jewelry is both the creation and the mirror of its times. Design is dependant upon cultural changes, art movements, economic vicissitudes, and historical events (like war and its aftermath). This distillation, the spirit of each country's culture, is defined in its applied arts and its jewelry. Noone was working in isolation, yet despite the constant exchange of ideas and techniques among twentieth century European and Scandinavian artists, there is always that essence of national characteristics which distinguishes one country's design aesthetic from another.

The jewelry depicted in this book is divided into three categories: 1) artists'jewelry which was hand-crafted in limited editions; 2) fashion jewelry which was created expressly for haute couture collections and boutiques; and 3) costume jewelry which was mass-produced, intended for department stores and specialty shops. There were many connections and cross-overs among the three.

Costume and fashion jewelry generally are made with non-precious materials (including synthetics), whether copies of the real thing or original designs. Artists' jewelry can be made with gold, silver and semi-precious stones, or alternative materials. Although artisans like to be independant of fashion trends, art and couture remain subliminal sources and the current neckline and hairdo must be considered by all jewelry designers alike. In Europe, artists are often commissioned to design for couturiers and manufacturers who target a wide international clientele.

Silver, which is used by both fine and costume jewelers, is technically a precious metal, but is more democratic than gold. Even if mounted with semi-precious stones, silver jewelry is accessible to a wide market. The term "semi-precious" is a continuing dilemma in the trade. It is an out-dated reference in today's market to all gemstones other than the Big Five precious gems: diamonds, rubies, emeralds, sapphires, and natural pearls. (These gems are outside the scope of this book.) However, it is still in general use, even among some fine jewelers, because noone has come up with a more acceptable term. (In German it was called *halbedelstein*, or "half-precious".) "Semi-precious" in this book pertains to "the more affordable stones" like quartz (crystal, amethyst, citrine), tourmalines, garnets, opals, turquoise, lapis, coral, onyx, agates, (and other hardstones), aquamarines, topaz, as well as amber and blister pearls. (Nothing over the hardness of 7.) This category of gems was used to great effect by the Arts & Crafts artists in England, the *skønvirke* jewelers in Denmark, Art Nouveau artists in France and Belgium, Wiener Werkstätte designers in Vienna, and neo-Renaissance jewelers in Hungary, usually mounted in silver and silver-gilt settings. One great innovation of these artists was occasionally mixing a precious gem with amber, opals or garnets. This has since become common practice in modern times.

Synthetic gemstones, as defined by the Gemological Institute of America (the G.I.A.), have approximately the same physical, chemical, and optical properties as the natural stones. Imitation stones, on the other hand, are stones made from something that doesn't exist in nature, like glass. In Europe, there are different names for what Americans call "rhinestones." *Strass* (named after Georges Frédéric Stras, who invented them in the 18th century) and *simili* (for simulated) are used in France and most of Europe. *Rhinestones* were natural iridescent quartz stones which washed down the Rhine river and were later imitated in glass by the Czechs as clear or colored rhinestones. *Paste* (for high quality vintage strass) and *diamanté* are terms used in England. Whatever we call them, we've come a long way from the 18th century when quartz crystals were thought to be "unripe diamonds!"

There has always been a connection between artist-jewelers and fashion or costume jewelry. In France, Jean Dunand, a superb craftsman in lacquer and copperware, designed lacquered hatpins and buckles for Mme. Agnès, the milliner, in the Twenties. Jean Desprès and Béla Voros made buttons and jewelry for Paul Poiret. The sculptor Gustav Miklos designed in gold for Raymond Templier and in plastic for manufacturers in Oyonnax. Claude Lalanne was known for her art sculptures and furniture as well as cast metal jewelry and belts for Yves St. Laurent. Wendy Ramshaw and David Watkins in England, who now work mostly in gold, began by designing disposable paper jewelry in the Sixties. French jewelers who apprenticed with Cartier in Paris, (Marcel Boucher and Alfred Philippe), emigrated to America where they created costume jewelry using fine jewelry techniques.

Artist-manufacturers like Arthur Liberty in England, Theodor Fahrner in Germany, David-Andersen in Norway, Georg Jensen and A. Michelsen in Denmark, the Wiener Werkstätte in Vienna and Lalique in France serially-produced artist-designed jewelry. In Scandinavia, known for its silversmithing traditions, Denmark turned to making costume jewelry in the Thirties in self defense because so much of it was being imported from Europe. The Nordic countries had their revenge in the Fifties when Europeans, who had no silversmithing tradition, imported vast quantities of silver and enamelled jewelry from David-Andersen and Georg Jensen. Tit for tat.

Because fashion is so closely linked to jewelry design, biographies have been included here of the leading couturiers who were usually intimately involved with the conception though not the execution of the accessories for their collections - from Schiaparelli and Chanel to Dior and Lagerfeld. Fashion models have replaced movie stars as trend setters. Women are more interested in what jewelry Christy, Kate, and Nadja (the Shrimp, Twiggy and Veruschka of the 1990s) are parading, than what Meryl Streep, (etc.) wears to the Oscars.

On the cusp of the 21st century, we look back at the evolution of jewelry in Europe and Scandinavia over the past 100 years. New directions were taken in design which, even though inspired by artistic precedents, seemed fresh and exciting. British Arts & Crafts sprang from Celtic and Medieval themes. In Austria, the Wiener Werkstätte tempered these borrowed, austere aesthetics with Viennese sensuousness for its own revolutionary style. Never had Nature, or a woman's face and form, been so glorified as in French and Belgian Art Nouveau jewelry which was inspired by decorative arts from the Far East. Geometric Art Deco, borrowing from the naively named "primitive" sources of the ancient civilizations of Africa, Egypt, and Central America, embodied the ultimate in sleek sophistication with luxury materials.

What began in France as faux Cartier, originally conceived to deceive in the Twenties, was served up "straight, no chaser" in Germany in the Thirties. Machine Age and Bauhaus designers used "new" metals that had previously been confined to the aircraft and construction industries. Utility Modern chains and bracelets of the Forties were inspired by gas pipes and tank tracks. Fifties necklaces transformed the look of Edwardian pearls or 18th century rose diamond garlands into elaborate costume jewelry with faux stones. Sixties sources were as disparate as the Space Age and mystical India. The Dutch at first drew on their colonies in Indonesia for inspiration, then turned to plastics. The Italians tapped into their immense artistic resources of Etruria, ancient Rome, Venice and the Renaissance. The Czechs produced their own interpretations of the cultural crossroads of Eastern and Western Europe. The Hungarians never strayed far from the Renaissance. The Scan-

dinavians created impeccably modern silver pieces, some of which could be traced back to Viking and Medieval folk costume jewelry and mythology.

For many, the trick was to convert ancient or forgotten cultural motifs into new 20th century styles with a twist. Turning tradition on its ear, jewelers experimented with unusual materials in unexpected ways using modern techniques. The true originals were artists whose inspiration was uniquely their own: aware of the past but defying its influence.

Historically, what we now call antique or vintage jewelry was considered "modern", if not avant-garde in the Old World in its time. The British art publication *The Studio* devoted an entire 1901 issue to the "Modern Design in Jewellery and Fans". Siegfried Bing's Maison de l'Art Nouveau was dedicated to decorative arts "in the modern spirit" in 1900. The 1925 Arts Décoratifs Exposition was open only to "artistic products that showed modern tendancies". *Moderne* was modern. Both the Bauhaus and the Wiener Werkstätte were dedicated to the very modern concept of "creating a new unity by the welding together of many arts." The Italian Futurists, and French Cubists and Surrealists were modern. The British "Mods" of the Sixties were modern. Then came the Postmodern Seventies with a new appreciation of the classical traditions. The designers and artists who created the jewelry and fashions of each era were convinced that their creations were on the cutting edge; of their time, or better yet, ahead of it.

Despite its origins in Europe and Scandinavia, the majority of the jewelry in this book was, and still can be, acquired in America. Costume jewelry was imported by American department stores in vast amounts. Fashion jewelry was sold at the international branches of the couture houses, and the artist-jewelers' creations were available globally at art galleries and specialty shops. Dedicated travelers returned from Europe with their acquistions which eventually wound up at auction; (the Diana Vreeland, Andy Warhol, and Chanel collections fetched high hammer prices). Collectors combed the flea markets, estate sales, or grandma's attic. For the really esoteric antique pieces, however, it is still best to travel to the source and truffle for treasures abroad.

Collecting is a fundamental human drive. What begins as an accumulation becomes a collection, then (after assiduous culling) a selection. When this reaches what in physics is called critical mass, it's time to gear down. Vintage jewelry is like wampum; it can be exchanged for cash, or trading up, and is much more satisfying than money in the bank.

Drilling down through the layers of 20th century Europe, we find that each decade (give or take a year or two) had its capital: **Paris** in the 1900's (The Exposition Universelle, Alphonse Mucha, Sarah Bernhardt, René Lalique, Samuel Bing's Maison de L'Art Nouveau, Toulouse-Lautrec); **Vienna** in the Teens (Wiener Werkstätte, Gustav Klimt, Café Fledermaus, Gustav Mahler); **Paris**, again, in the Twenties (the Exposition des Arts Décoratifs, Josephine Baker, Mistinguett, Maurice Chevalier, F. Scott Fitzgerald, Ernest Hemingway); **Berlin** in the (early) Thirties (Bertold Brecht's *Three Penny Opera*, Marlene Dietrich in the *Blue Angel*, Christopher Isherwood's play *I am a Camera* which became *Cabaret*, the Expressionists, The Bauhaus); post-war **Paris** in the Forties (The Existentialists, Juliette Greco, Christian Dior's New Look); **Rome** in the Fifties (historical epic films and Fellini's films culminating with *La Dolce Vita*, the new Italian fashion collections); **London** in the Sixties (the Beatles, the Rolling Stones, Mary Quant, "The Angry Young Men" in theater and film); **New York** took the art scene lead from Europe (which was in limbo in the Seventies,) with Andy Warhol. and Op and Pop Art (early Seventies); and **Milan** in the Eighties (design leaders Memphis Group, Fornasetti, Italian Couturiers Gianni Versace, the Missonis, Dolce & Gabbana). The Nineties are still up for grabs; what clear leaders have emerged in any country?

This work celebrates the liberation from old constraints and will serve as a navigational guide chronologically through nearly 100 years of jewelry design in 13 countries. *Bon Voyage!*

Ginger Moro
Los Angeles, California

E. Belet designed porcelain cigarette cases, pendants, brooches and belt buckles for the Exposition Universelle in Paris, 1900, for which he won a prize. These sketches of algae and plants show the influence of *Japonisme* in France. Heliotype print from *Modéles & Documents Modernes pour la Porcelaine & la Bijouterie,* ca 1905. *Courtesy of the author. Photo of print by Robert Weldon*

PART I

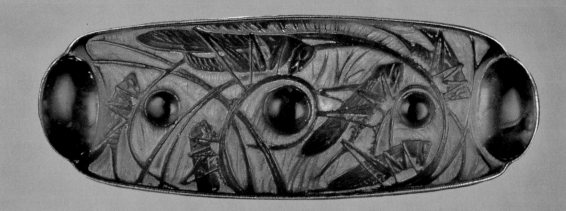

EUROPE

Sauterelles, or grasshoppers, one of Lalique's earliest brooches of deep blue moulded glass, 1911. (This was made in several colors.) Signed R. Lalique in script. *Courtesy of Terrance O'Halloran Collection, Los Angeles. Photo by Robert Weldon, courtesy of the Gemological Institute of America (GIA), Santa Monica, Ca.*

G. BARBIER

falbalas &
fanfreluches

almanach
pour
1923

Chapter 1

France

France & Art Nouveau

Why has France been the arbiter of taste for centuries? What makes Paris so seductive to sybarites? The artists say it's the light; the writers, the stimulating conversation; the couturiers, the innate chic of the Parisiennes; the gourmets, the fine food and vintage wine. It's all of these things, plus a sense of place, a love of beauty, an appreciation of luxury and a deep respect for things well made.

So how did Paris, the home of Cartier, Mauboussin, Boucheron, and Van Cleef and Arpels come to accept costume jewelry? How could the French, used to aged Camembert, be enticed by Velveeta? Because besides quality, they revere value. And if they can't have both, one will do. A fake diamond is better than no diamond at all, provided it is so well set that it fools one's peers.

Jewelry in Gaul is divided into three parts: **costume jewelry** (in series of 50 or more, or mass-produced); **fashion jewelry** (in small runway editions for the privileged few, as well as ready-to-wear boutique jewelry in larger editions for the middle class); and **artists' jewelry** (usually hand-crafted, limited-edition pieces created independently of fashion trends).

Many of the major artists of the 20th century have been French, or people born in other lands who settled in France. They brought the creative seeds of their culture to the nourishing soil of France. Paris was the mulch. She has always been a source of inspiration for artistic endeavours. The cafés are bursting with painters and poets, actors and architects, all exchanging ideas and critically defending or denouncing each other. Designers great and small, whether of ivory sculpture or Bakelite baubles, have always been treated with the same irreverence.

Creative periods in Europe, and France in particular, can be measured between wars. The one most often cited refers to the years between World Wars I and II, but there was another such time of peace between the Franco-Prussian War of 1870 and the outbreak of WWI in 1914. The Art Nouveau movement in France spanned two distinct periods in that time frame. During the *fin de siècle* (end of the nineteenth century from 1880 to 1900), France was recovering from the Franco-Prussian War and her citizens flocked to the theater to admire Sarah Bernhardt and her extravagant Lalique jewelry. The *Belle Epoque* (1900-1914) was the "beautiful period" before World War I when Europe was prospering; Paris and Vienna toasted their beautiful women and the decorative arts flourished. The horse-drawn carriages gave way to the motor car, and the ladies at the Longchamps racetrack, freed of their corsets by the couturier Paul Poiret, replaced their real pearl chokers with faux pearl sautoirs. These were frivolous times and there was

jewelry to match. For the first time, the intrinsic value of an adornment was not the primary consideration. The design was paramount, and jewelers were challenged to use humble materials to stunning effect. The glitter of gold and gemstones was left to fine jewelers Georges Fouquet, Eduard Colonna, Lucien Gaillard, and Vever. René Lalique, who was the master of all materials, gave up gold and gems for horn and *pâte de verre*. This was Art Nouveau... New Art.

The International Exhibitions in 19th and early 20th century Europe had many functions. They were the diasporas of new designs, the catalysts of taste, and a substitute for travel. There was a carnival atmosphere; families made a day of it, lunching and dining on exotic cuisines in foreign pavilions, and admiring or decrying the exhibits. There one could experience Austria, Russia, Siam, Indo-China, or the Belgian Congo without leaving town. Industrial designers, couturiers, artists, architects, and jewelers presented their best and most innovative ideas in the multi-national pavilions. In the days before T.V. and radio, this was the most effective way to reach a wide public. Trade journals, art magazines, and deluxe fashion albums were the only other alternative.

A comprehensive international overview of the applied arts was offered at the Paris Exposition Universelle in 1900. Art Nouveau was called *Jugendstil* (Youth style) in Germany, *Stile Floreale* in Italy, *Style Nouille* (Noodle Style) in France and Belgium, *Liberty Style* in England (named after the London firm), and *Glasgow Style* in Scotland. These labels reflected not only cultural differences, but national attitudes. In France there was common agreement to dub it *Art Nouveau* after Siegfried Bing's gallery. Changing the name of the movement, however, did not alter the distinctive national interpretations. No sooner had they given it a name, than the movement peaked, to expire ten years later. But Art Nouveau had served its dual purposes: to clear the oppressive 19th century derivative clutter out of the overstuffed European drawing rooms, and to welcome in the renaissance of craftsmanship. A lesson had been learned from the direct simplicity of 18th century Japanese woodblock prints which affected every branch of the arts in the West, from Art Nouveau to Art Deco.

The Exposition Universelle was a convenient showcase for the designers and architects of the participating countries, with the French winning the highest acclaim. Among those was Emile Belet, an artist painter at the Sèvres porcelain factory who won a prize

Opposite
Hand colored *pochoir* cover by George Barbier of the 1923 deluxe fashion album *Falbalas & Fanfreluches*, showing the long pendant earrings, bandeau, sautoirs, and shoe buckles fashionable at the time. *Original print courtesy of the author, photographed by Sandro Moro.*

Two blue moulded glass pendants by Lalique: the *Guêpes* (wasps) on the left has holes for tassels and the *Grenouilles* (frogs) leap around the pendant, taken from the Japanese *tsuba* sword-guard. Ca. 1920. Signed "R. Lalique", script. *Courtesy of Marc Navarro, Los Angeles, Ca. Photo by Robert Weldon*

Reverse of blue pendant showing "R. Lalique" script signature. *Photo by Robert Weldon, courtesy of G.I.A.*

for his vases, porcelain cigarette cases, necklaces, and belt buckles which showed the *Japonisme* influence. Delicate designs of plants, algaes, shells, and flowers were worked in Art Nouveau volutes, as illustrated in silver and gold paint for *Modèles & Documents Modernes*, ca. 1905.

A German-born art dealer gave this French movement its name. Siegfried Bing (1838-1905) was born in Hamburg. He moved to Paris in his early thirties, became a naturalized French citizen, and opened a gallery selling Japanese objets, all in rapid succession. Bing parlayed his knowledge of the ceramics business in Hamburg into an immediately profitable Oriental imports business, riding the crest of the Western discovery and appreciation of *Japonisme*. Connaisseur and entrepreneur, he had the conviction and foresight to open a gallery in 1896 called La Maison de L'Art Nouveau, which exhibited the work of international artists who had "the modern spirit" in the decorative arts. The gallery showed Tiffany and Gallé glass, Toulouse-Lautrec posters, Georges de Feure textiles, and René Lalique jewelry. In 1900, this led to his own Art Nouveau pavillion at the Exposition Universelle. But the New Art as envisioned by Bing was not yet commercially viable, so he was forced to return to his profitable Oriental Art dealing. He died in 1905, his avant-garde goal unachieved, but having given an important art movement its name.

René Lalique (1860-1945) was that rare combination of artist-craftsman and manufacturer (of mass-produced jewelry and art glassware). He spanned both the Art Nouveau and Art Deco movements, establishing jewelry as an *objet d'art*. Artist and innovator, his breathtaking gold and enamel necklaces and corsage ornaments of the 1890s, carved horn combs of 1900, and moulded glass pendants of the Twenties were unique conceptions.

Lalique studied at the Ecole des Arts Décoratifs in Paris, setting up his atelier in 1885. He drew inspiration from nature, ranging from the grotesque (the writhing serpents piece of 1900) to the mundane pine cone. He opened his glassworks in 1909, producing cast glass with moulded ornamentation, mostly in monochromatic glass, letting the translucence and form of the material speak for itself. Swans, birds, fish, lizards, frogs, poppies, orchids, grapes, lilies, and the female form graced his pendants, brooches, and necklaces. He made his last piece of metal jewelry in 1912, converting totally to the mass-production of art glass. One of the early brooches, 1911, featured moulded *Sauterelles* (grasshoppers) in colored glass which glimmered against the metal ground. The glass was usually frosted or opaline. His style remained figurative, changing very little in the Twenties.

Lalique was the hit of two Paris Expositions. In 1900, he was acclaimed for his unique gold and enamel creations, and carved horn combs; by 1925 he was the most successful manufacturer of mass-produced glass in France. According to the *Catalogue des Verreries de René Lalique*, 1932, the oval figurine pendants were made in editions of 150-200, and the Art Deco zig-zag motifs were reproduced 1000 times each. In a low bow to *Japonisme* metalwork, he translated the shape of the Japanese sword-guards into cobalt glass, hanging it on a silk cord and adding a tassel. Hundreds of examples of the bracelet elements shaped like glass cherries, fish, ferns, etc. were cast to match Lalique's necklaces, and mounted on elastic cord. These were nothing like the dramatic showpieces he had created for Sarah Bernhardt (in gold or aluminum) in the 1890s, but they reached a large clientele, and were reasonably priced.

Two triangular pendants, *Trefles* (clover) and *Sorbier*, and *Fioret*, a moulded glass brooch mounted on metal. Signed "R. Lalique," ca. 1920. *Courtesy of Marc Navarro, Los Angeles. Photo by Robert Weldon*

"R. LALIQUE" was stamped or etched in block letters to identify most of his jewelry. (Most early pieces were engraved "R. Lalique" in script.) Necklaces and bracelets in colored or clear crystal were in production long after Lalique committed to mass-produced glassware. Colored glass pendants were eventually phased out. For collectors who can't afford the prohibitive prices of gold Art Nouveau Lalique jewelry, his Art Deco glass pendants, still in style after 60 years, can be found in antique stores and at auction.

What of Lalique's early contemporaries who could only dream of such luxury, and yearned for affordable adornment? For these women, shopping habits in the 1890s were forever changed when the large department stores were built. The Printemps and the Galeries Lafayette, with sweeping staircases and stained glass roofs, lured the working class girl to spend her money behind the Neo-Baroque Opéra de Paris. The Bon Marché (meaning "cheap") department store on the Left Bank of the Seine was partly designed by Gustav Eiffel, whose Tower was the object of such Gallic vitriol at the 1900 Exposition. The Samaritaine advertised its wares in huge orange enamel signs across its glass facade in 1905. For the first time, the French could buy their household wares, clothes, accessories, and costume jewelry all under one roof. Salesgirls, hairdressers, and housemaids could gussy themselves up in the latest fashions, with a Piel Frères belt buckle and a Bonaz hair ornament, and go to the theater or cabarets feeling just as chic as the elegant ladies from the Faubourg St.-Germain. The middle class shop owners were challenged to make their exclusive boutiques attractive to their vanishing clientele. The upper class remained faithful to their couturiers and Cartier, until Art Deco designs became so beguiling that they, too, fell for the new designs.

Art Nouveau costume jewelry was created of natural materials like horn, ivory, and tortoiseshell, as well as *pâte de verre* glass, enamel, Celluloid, and base metals with faux stones. These were mainly hair ornaments, hatpins, brooches, pendants, and belt buckles. Bracelets were seldom worn, as sleeves were long. The recurring themes were tendrils of hair (the female and her shape were glorified) and the organic curves of flowers, vines, plants, and insects. Botany was king and entomology was queen. There wasn't a right angle in sight. Women were metamorphosed into bizarre images, becoming part flower or dragonfly. It took getting used to, but with René Lalique leading the way in jewelry, Alphonse Mucha in the decorative arts, Gallé in glass, and Hector Guimard in architecture, this Art Nouveau style dominated France for over 2 decades.

Fin de siècle French women wore carved horn pendants of delicately colored insects. Dragonflies and bees spread their translucent wings across Madame's bodice. Bull or mountain goat horn from the Jura mountains was sliced, heated, bleached, carved, polished, and stained by hand. Lalique was the first to master the art, and Elizabeth Bonté (who also studied at the Ecole des Arts Décoratifs) and George Pierre ("G.I.P." for short) made it their exclusive creative choice. Horn slices were soaked in hydrogen peroxide for translucence, then bathed in chemicals to give a shimmering sheen to the wings, or a dewy gloss to the petals[1]. The pendants, carved and stained with inks, were mounted on silk ribbons, cords, or chains with pastel glass beads repeating the delicate hues. Bonté and G.I.P., at first rivals, pooled their resources and talents and produced horn jewelry until 1936 when Bakelite became the preferred material for costume jewelry.

Carved horn pendant, and a cord with matching petals, of *monnaie du Pape*, a plant with dry translucent leaves that lent itself to Art Nouveau translation in horn or enamel. Ca. 1910. Probably by Bonté, but unsigned. *Courtesy of Peacock Alley, Santa Fe, NM. Photo by Robert Weldon*

Two carved horn pendants; a dragonfly, and pink thistle mounted on pink silk cord and ribbon. Unsigned, ca. 1910. *Courtesy of Peacock Alley. Photo by Robert Weldon*

Unusual horn bracelets of *monnaie du Pape* and a bee, mounted on adjustable silk ribbons. Unsigned, ca. 1900. *Courtesy of Peacock Alley. Photo by Robert Weldon*

Wasp on the wing in tinted horn pendant. Signed "GIP" for George Pierre, ca. 1915. *Courtesy of Peacock Alley, Santa Fe, NM. Photo by Robert Weldon*

Carved horn hair combs and barettes, delicately tinted, of plants, snakes, and a rose with a beetle on its petal by Auguste Bonaz, all signed. Ca. 1900. *Courtesy of Lili Gantarski Collection, Paris, France. Photo by Bruno Pierson*

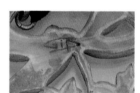

Reverse of "GIP" horn pendant showing signature. *Photo by Robert Weldon*

Auguste Bonaz, well known in the Twenties and Thirties for his Celluloid Art Deco jewelry, produced some hauntingly beautiful Art Nouveau horn hair combs and barrettes in the shape of snakes, dragonflies and flowers, each delicately stained pastel hues. Fine jewelers Lucien Gaillard and Georges Fouquet set horn pieces with gemstones. Other jewelers carved horn brooches and bracelets simulating *monnaie du pape* (Pope's money). This plant has a round (like a coin), white (for the Pope), leaf which when dried becomes translucent, reproducing well in the horn medium. Sycamore seeds and mistletoe were also rendered in horn pendants, but since these were not signed, they shall remain anonymous.

Four different enamel techniques were used for fine and costume jewelry. Enamel is colored vitreous paste which is fused into place. With *champlevé* enamel, the metal "field" (*champ*) is scooped out of the piece, and "raised or filled up" (*levé*) with different colors of enamel. For *cloisonné* enamel, the glass powder is introduced into separate metal cells (*cloisons*) constructed of copper wire which is soldered to the metal ground. These show through the surface of the finished piece when polished, and are an integral part of the design. *Plique-à-jour* is the most exacting technique, requiring the careful removal of the metal backing of the *cloisons* after firing so that the daylight (*jour*) shines thru the translucent enamel. Lalique created gossamer dragonfly wings with this process. With *guilloché* enamel, the machine-etched wavy background is filled with transparent enamel. This technique was frequently used in Edwardian England for belt buckles, and in Norway by David-Andersen.

Faux tortoise shell Celluloid hair combs, gold electro-plated, signed by Auguste Bonaz, 1900-1915. *Courtesy of Lili Gantarski Collection. Photo by Bruno Pierson*

Plique-à-jour enamel dragonfly with opal body and tail set in silver. This one was possibly made in Pforzheim, Germany for the French market. 900 silver mark. *Courtesy of Terrance O'Halloran Los Angeles, Ca. Photo by Robert Weldon, courtesy of Gemological Institute of America, (G.I.A.), Santa Monica, Ca.*

Piel Frères belt buckles, belts, and hair combs were made of both *cloisonné* and *champlevé* enamel on copper, brass, silver plate, or silver gilt. This Parisian firm was headed by Alexandre Piel, who was making costume jewelry as early as 1890. At the 1900 Exposition, Piel Frères received the Grand Prix. Piel collaborated with the sculptor Gabriel Stalin to produce Egyptian revival buckles around 1902-1910. The wings of the sacred Ibis were decorated with matt enamel in several different renderings. An entire belt was made of separate plaques representing Nefertiti, and scarabs with faux turquoises. These pieces are signed "PF' or "P. Fres" with a sword. In 1925 the firm's name was changed to Paul Piel et Fils, (and son) who designed high fashion Art Deco enamel buckles for Jean Patou's dresses and hats.

Art Nouveau belts and buckles were wonderfully flamboyant, working wonders with base metal and strass. Cast into swirling organic shapes, set with marcasites, cut steel, or colored glass, they made the wasp waist a point of interest. Sold separately, or conceived as an integral part of the belt which was leather, suede, or velour, there were buckles both fore and aft, accentuating the fashionably unhealthy "S" curve into which the female shape was tortured in 1900. Belt buckles dipped down in the front and up in the back, with the same motif repeated around the waist. Smaller buckles were also worn on hats, or on velvet ribbons around the neck.

Egyptian revival belt buckle of *cloisonné* enamelled sacred Ibis bird with faux pearls, ca. 1915, by Piel Frères. Signed "P.Fres". *Courtesy of Rita Sacks Collection, New York. Photo by Robert Weldon*

Silver-plated Egyptian revival buckle with *champlevé* motifs and *cloisonné* winged Goddess kneeling in the lotus leaves. By Piel Frères, ca. 1912. Signed "PF." *Courtesy of Linda Rinella Collection, Beverly Hills, Ca. Photo by Robert Weldon*

Elaborate Art Nouveau *repoussé* silver belt buckle inspired by Alphonse Mucha's paintings with the poppies, medieval headdress, and flowing hair an integral part of the fluid design. 1900. *Courtesy of the author. Photo by Robert Weldon*

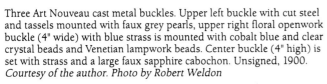

Three Art Nouveau cast metal buckles. Upper left buckle with cut steel and tassels mounted with faux grey pearls, upper right floral openwork buckle (4" wide) with blue strass is mounted with cobalt blue and clear crystal beads and Venetian lampwork beads. Center buckle (4" high) is set with strass and a large faux sapphire cabochon. Unsigned, 1900. *Courtesy of the author. Photo by Robert Weldon*

Grey-green leather belt, (with deep V in front) adorned with two metal buckles fore and aft with cut steel studs riveted to the belt. 1910. *Courtesy of the author. Photo by Robert Weldon.*

Adjustable lime green suede belt with exhuberant Art Nouveau metal buckles (dipping down in front and straight across the back) set with faux emeralds, cut steel and marcasites. 1900. *Courtesy of the author. Photo by Robert Weldon*

Shoe buckles were less elaborate, but sparkled with cut steel or strass. The more facets that were cut on the steel studs, the brighter the effect. Each stud was individually riveted into the metal buckle. Shoe buckles were worn when high vamped shoes were in fashion, into the Twenties. They were slipped over the vamp and held in place by a slide. When the Twenties T-strap shoe became popular, the buckle was abandoned.

Lethal-looking hatpins made of porcelain, jet, silver and marcasite, or molded glass were stuck into enormous wide-brimmed hats until 1910 when the double whammy of Paul Poiret and the Ballets Russes hit Paris, and aigrettes sprouted out of the newly fashionable turbans. The *Belle Epoque* milliners, accustomed to planting mini-gardens, or impaling whole stuffed birds on one chapeau, discarded their hatpins and settled for one feather.

Jewelry and textile designer Edouard Benedictus (1878-1930) sketched hair combs, hatpins, and pendants with stylized flowers, cicadas or scarabs for a design portfolio, ca. 1900. The scarab is a dung beetle which resolutely rolls a ball of dung before it along the ground. In Egyptian lore, the scarab came to symbolize the sun's trajectory across the sky impelled by a mystical force. The Egyptian scarab was reborn many times in Celluloid, Bakelite, ceramic, and enamel throughout the XXth century.

Shoe buckle with cut steel studs in an openwork pattern, marked "Made in France", 1914-1925. *Courtesy of private collection, Los Angeles. Photo by Robert Weldon*

Designs by Edouard Benedictus of floral necklace, scarab and figural hatpins and stylized scarab pendants on finger ring chains, 1900. Pictured with brooches of Celluloid reverse-painted cicadas, and a black Bakelite insect with silver wings, ca. 1920-60's. Heliotype print from the *Document du Décorateur-3e série*, 1900. *Courtesy of the author. Photo of print and brooches by Robert Weldon*

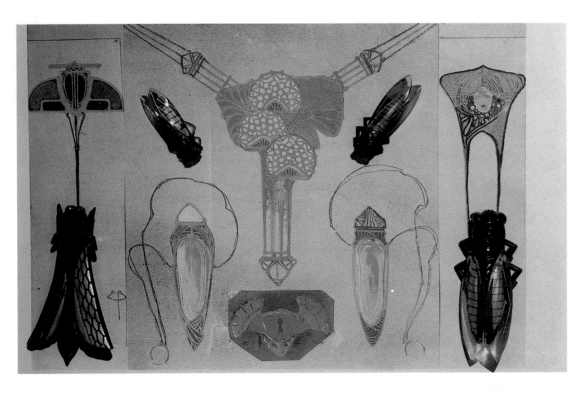

Belle Epoque arts flourished, and wealthy patrons of the arts with a discerning eye like Jacques Doucet, Diaghilev, and Lucien Vogel were defining taste. They were the catalysts who commissioned work and finacially supported the artists. Serge Diaghilev's Ballets Russes, with Leon Bakst's sumptuous costumes and sets for *Shéhérazade* shocked and thrilled Paris in 1910. The choreography (passionately danced by Nijinsky) and the sets of jade green and crimson, or violet and orange seemed outrageous at first, but soon vivid oriental floor cushions were replacing Louis XV chairs in Parisian salons. Diaghilev's impact on all the decorative arts was immediate and far-reaching. Women yearned for harem pantaloons, slave bracelets, and a sultan to woo them on their silken pillows. Pale mauve and dusky rose (the Art Nouveau palette) were *demodé* overnight. The new colors screamed like Stravinski's atonal music. Each of Diaghlilev's audacious productions was a harmonious unit, because he chose artists like Bakst, Benois, Goncharova and Larionov, Picasso, Derain, and Braque who could design costumes, sets, accessories, and posters for his ballets. European interior decorators and artists began to see the value of creating all-of-a-piece designs.

In 1909, Blériot made his first flight across the English Channel. Suddenly the concepts of the machine and speed intruded into the langourous *Belle Epoque*. The Italian Futurist Manifesto was published in Paris in the same year, exalting not only high velocity and the machine, but war. The first two themes didn't impact design until the Twenties, but they had their way with the third.

Jacques Doucet (1854-1932) an elegant couturier, was also a keen art collector who recognized talents like Paul Poiret, (who began designing for him in 1896). He gave young designers Paul Iribe, Pierre Legrain, Jean Dunand, Jean Desprès, Gustav Miklos, and Eileen Gray their first important commissions. They designed his clothes, furniture, silverware and jewelry. His home in Neuilly contained the most extraordinary avant-garde collection of objets and paintings of the early XXth century.

Lucien Vogel published the *Gazette du Bon Ton* from 1912 to 1925, and the *Feuillets d'Art* in 1919-'20. He delighted the fashion and art world with beautiful limited-edition, hand-colored gouache *pochoir* prints by Georges Lepape, George Barbier, Charles Martin, André Marty, and Benito. The latest haute couture fashions, accessories and jewelry were exquisitely illustrated in settings and situations of the period; Poiret, Worth, Doucet, Paquin, Lanvin etc. were all gloriously represented. The *Gazette* was published in Paris, New York, and Buenos Aires, making it perfectly clear that high fashion was terribly chic, and that Paris was the place to buy it. These same artists also illustrated luxury art books, and covers for *Vogue* and other fashion magazines until photography became the favored medium for fashion in the Thirties.

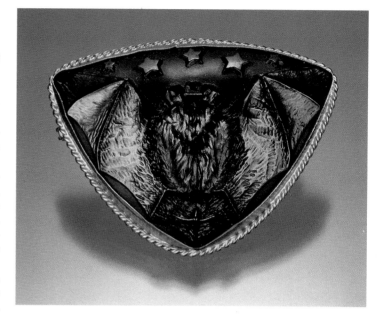

Iridescent green moulded glass bat hat pin (made in Austria for the French market), converted to a brooch. Ca. 1900. *Courtesy of Peacock Alley, Santa Fe, NM. Photo by Robert Weldon*

Original hand-colored *pochoir* print by Georges Lepape from *Les Choses de Paul Poiret*, 1910. Inspired by the Ballets Russes, Poiret dressed sloe-eyed Parisiennes in turbans and jewelled feather aigrettes. *Courtesy of the author's collection. Photo of print by Robert Weldon*

Paul Poiret (1879-1944) was hired by the haute couturiers Doucet and Worth (the "caviar" of fashion houses) to design *pommes frites* or "french fries" fashion for every day wear. He was to remember the commercial viability of a cheaper line, when he commissioned costume jewelry for his own salon which he opened in 1903 on the rue Auber. "Poiret changed the Parisian "S" silhouette which he compared to a woman "pulling a barge against the wind", laughed Mme. Denise Poiret in her country home outside Paris. He abolished the corset, invented the brassiere, lowered the neckline, lifted the waist, and devised the lampshade tunic and the hobble skirt.

He was the "Prince of P.R." In 1908 , he commissioned Paul Iribe (1883-1935) to illustrate his *Robes de Paul Poiret*, and Georges Lepape in 1911 to hand-color *Les Choses de Paul Poiret* in silky pochoir portfolios. He designed the first couture costume jewelry: colored glass pendants which swung on long silk cords, and jewelled tassels made by Maison Gripoix. Sautoirs, two meters long, made of glass beads or faux pearls, hung to the hips. The Oriental influence was apparent in silk turbans with arching feather aigrettes sprouting out of jewelled clips. This fashion decimated the egret population in Europe, whose feathers were surrendered to the cause. Colette and the general public were outraged, so Poiret, always inventive, made them from spun glass.

Poiret founded an art school for young girls, named "Martine" after his daughter. He gave them paints, and instructed them to go into the garden and draw what they saw. They created textile designs and the first couturier perfume bottle, "Rosine", named after Poiret's other daughter. Poiret was an Original, but he was eventually done in by his own extravagance. His clothes were opulent, and so were his tastes. His costume parties were legendary. At the "1002 Nights" Ball, he reigned as the bejewelled Pasha, surrounded by his harem and wild animals. His wife, Denise, wearing an aigrette 30 centimeters high and slave anklets, perched in a golden cage, to be released at the climax of the festivities. "I was his type", Mme Poiret smiled. (Nevertheless, she eventually flew the coop for good, exasperated by his excesses). Poiret decorated three barges on the Seine for the 1925 Exposition des Arts Décoratifs, (one with fabrics designed by Raoul Dufy) but public taste was turning away from his fancy brocades and flamboyant life-style. He refused to compromise his high standards, so his backers pulled out. He was bankrupt in the late Thirties, and died a pauper in the South of France in 1944.

Poiret was a patron in his own right. He hired José de Zamora, and young Romain de Tirtoff fresh from Saint Petersburg in 1913, to design clothes and jewelry for him. Erté,(1894-1991) as he became known (taken from the French pronunciation of his initials) wrapped his models in yards of faux pearls. He wound them into their coiffures, and festooned their arms with pearl sleeves. The traditional Russian head-dress with pearl garlands under the chin was the inspiration for many Erté fantasies (adopted first by actresses, then by café-society women.) Poiret and Erté quarreled, never to speak again. Their two egos were incompatible.

Costume and jewelry design by Erté for Carmel Myers in the 1925 film *Ben Hur*, showing Erté's talent for incorporating the pectoral, head-dress, and bracelets into the cape and costume design. Photo is autographed by Carmel Myers. *Courtesy of the author and Erté.*

For his first M.G.M. film, *Ben Hur* in 1925, Erté designed the costumes and jewelry for the star, Carmel Myers. "She was beautiful with enormous, dark eyes, so I designed for her an enamelled Egyptian pectoral necklace and a cape attached to wide cuffs on the upper and lower arms, perfect for a vamp. She wore long pearl earrings and rings on every finger. Carmel Myers was the only star in Hollywood who knew how to wear my creations." A disagreement with Lillian Gish over his costume designs for her role in *La Vie Bohème* hastened his departure from Hollywood (she would only wear silk against her sensitive skin, and Erté maintained that Mimi was too poor for silk.)

Breaking his contract with Louis B. Mayer, Erté returned to Paris to become one of the most successful costume, set, and jewelry designers of the 20th century. From the Folies Bergère to the Opéra Comique, his theatrical costumes and accessories were applauded. Beginning in 1915 through 1937, he designed 240 covers for *Harper's Bazaar*, illustrating in his inimitable style the latest fashions and costume jewelry out of Paris.

Many of the rings, earrings, and pendants Erté designed in the 70s and 80s in Paris (which were made in America) were taken from the fantasy jewels he painted in the Twenties and Thirties as adornments for his willowy models. These were in turn copied in strass and faux pearls by Parisian costume jewelers. "My jewelry was an extension of my costumes," Erté told the author in his studio in Boulogne-sur-Seine in 1975. "One would have been unthinkable without the other". Erté sketched every day from late afternoon till 2:00 A.M., surrounded by his Siamese cats, right up until his death at 97.

As the *Belle Epoque* came to a close, society was reeling from the impact of new ideas. In 1900, women fell into one of three categories: faithful wives in arranged and often loveless marriages; *demi-mondaines* courtesans and sometime actresses, who were much admired style-setters in fashion and jewelry; or prostitutes. Socialism and Feminism were speaking to women of all classes, who were beginning to speak for themselves.

In his book, *The Flowering of Art Nouveau*, Maurice Rheims describes the "craving for harmony" which brought the Art Nouveau period to life.[2] But having forged new paths, it sank under its own weight of ornamental excesses, and the glut of inferior copies of original designs. Symbolism and Mannerism proved decadent, and were eclipsed by the successive electric shocks of Cubism, Futurism, Fauvism, Surrealism, and the Russian Avant-Garde. But before any of these art movements could be thoroughly digested and translated into the applied arts, World War I cut off all creative juices. France did not come alive again until the early Twenties, in time to host the amazing Exposition des Arts Décoratifs in 1925. This international expo had been planned for 1916, but was cancelled because of the war. It would have been a very different exhibit.

Art Deco, Machine Age, Volutes, and Utility Modern

Europe suffered terribly from the ravages of World War I; France, in particular, as it was fought largely on her soil. So the Twenties, which the French called *Les Années Folles*, the crazy years, were devoted to a frenzied celebration of the end of "the war to end all wars."

It is amazing that France recovered as fast as she did, and that luxury goods were again so readily available. The Art Deco style was a reaction against the ecstatic effusions of Art Nouveau. A new rational, cerebral aesthetic was inevitable. Fuelled by the Futurist "Speedfreaks", animals already streamlined by nature (gazelles, antelopes, cheetahs, borzois and greyhounds) and machines (motor cars, planes, trains, oceanliners, and factories, or any parts thereof) were incorporated into applied art designs.

Cubism and the "discovery" of African art by Picasso and Braque among others, incubated during the war, to resurface as sources for Art Deco painting, sculpture, screens, vases, and jewelry. Dogon masks from the French Sudan, Benin bronzes, and Côte d'Ivoire artifacts inspired a completely new look of stylised African cuffs, necklaces, and pins in ivory, wood, or enamelled metal. (Fouquet and Raymond Templier designed them in silver, Gustav Miklos in gold). Jean Dunand painted Josephine Baker, the American negress who dazzled Paris in 1925, wearing his enamelled copper cuffs and strategic tattoes. The 19 year old chorus girl from the St.Louis slums had to go to Paris to find recognition and her roots, and to prove that Black was Beautiful.

Miroir Rouge, a *pochoir hors-texte* print of an almond-eyed woman with a red enamelled mirror, wearing large cabochon ivory and amber rings (or are they Bakelite?) from *Les Feuillets d'Art*, 1919. Georges Lepape's style shows the *Japonisme* influence, and the jewelry, which is ahead of its time. *Courtesy of the author. Photo of original print by Robert Weldon*

Silver bar pin with pendant brooch of basket bouquet set with strass and faux emeralds. Illegible maker's mark, Art Deco. *Courtesy of private collection, Milan, Italy*

Silver marcasite bow pin with crystal and onyx pendant. *Courtesy of private collection, Milan, Italy*

To add other threads to an already complicated tapestry, Aztec and Mayan stepped temples, and Native American Indian pottery and blanket designs showed up in architecture, wireless radio cases. mantel clocks, brooches and belt buckles. The 1922 discovery of King Tutankhamun's tomb unleashed yet another wave of historical hysteria. An Egyptian revival flood of scarabs, pharoahs, cobras, and sun-worship motifs were produced in both fine and costume jewelry.

The innovations were rectilinear or geometric shapes, a complete rejection of Art Nouveau whiplashes. Yet despite the barrage of ziggurat and zigzag, some traditional designers produced a Twenties version of romantic 18th century Louis XVI-style bouquets, bows, baskets, fountains, and garlands which decorated Süe et Mare furniture and Cartier broches. Costume jewelers followed suit with silver pendant brooches set with strass basket bouquets or marcasite bows with crystal and black onyx.

The French have a national penchant for de luxe quality, craftsmanship, and visual reward. They demand the best, and will pay for it. Mass-produced items did not appeal to the affluent because uniqueness was compromised. So in the early Twenties, the important fine jewelers clustered around the Place Vendôme and the rue de la Paix. Cartier, Boucheron, Mauboussin, and Van Cleef and Arpels, designed classically beautiful "black and white" jewelry which was the fashion for evening dress. Diamonds and frosted crystal with black onyx were mounted in platinum. An unknown designer conceived a magnificent articulated silver collar set with strass and black onyx, which could easily have passed for the real thing. By 1925, polychromatic jewelry of carved Indian gems with Egyptian and Moghul motifs, or baskets of fruit was all the rage. (The Frenchman, Alfred Philippe, translated these themes in faux stones with great success for Trifari in America.)

Costume jewelers and manufacturers quickly seized the opportunity of copying the designs of *Les Grands*, "The Big Boys", into silver or gilded brass, mounted with strass, faux pearls and gems, or marcasites. These, as well as completely original designs were targeted for department stores and speciality shops. "Pearl" sautoirs, "emerald" tassels, and elaborate *parures* (matching sets consisting of necklace, brooch, earrings and bracelet) were produced by supplier/manufacturers like Maison Gripoix and Louis Rousselet who worked with the haute couturiers. Auguste Bonaz supplied the mass market with decorative accessories in horn, Celluloid, and Galalith.

Superb articulated silver collar, set with pavé strass and black onyx in geometric Deco design, Twenties. A "Black & White" Cartier-style masterpiece by an unknown designer. *Courtesy of Lili Gantarski Collection, Paris, France*

The *cocottes* of 1900, dubbed the "*grandes horizontales*," were certainly vertical by the Twenties. Physical activity of a different kind was encouraged, and the vertical line was carried over into fashion and jewelry design. The *Belle Epoque* corsage ornament, (or stomacher) of horizontal garlands across the bodice, yielded to vertical fountain motif pendants. Lalique's enormous illuminated glass fountain for the 1925 Expo was a showstopper.

The new woman was athletic. Strenuous tennis, swimming, and yachting replaced lazy Sunday afternoon croquet and badminton. Coco Chanel leapt off her aristocratic English lover's yacht, the "Flying Cloud", sporting a suntan and bobbed hair, thereby launching a rash of sunburned necks among the young flappers in Deauville and Biarritz. American and English expatriot artists turned the Côte d'Azur into a sun-worshippers' paradise. (Until the Twenties, the French and cosmopolitan aristocrats had reserved the Riviera for winter rendez-vous). Josephine Baker with brilliantined hair and spit curls danced a frenzied Charleston in *La Revue Nègre* which sent Parisians dancing into the streets. Her impact and that of Negro jazz musicians like Sydney Bechet, was nearly as great as that of the Ballets Russes, thirty years earlier. Dancers Loïe Fuller and Isadora Duncan, (both Americans) and Ida Rubenstein popularized flowing garments for freedom of movement. Silver and enamel scatter pins depicting saxophone players and sports were produced in France and Germany for the liberated woman to wear on her blazer.

Adapting to the new active life, hemlines climbed to the knee. Sleeveless dresses fell straight from the shoulder, leaving bare upper arms to be encased in "slave bracelets", and bangles up to the elbow. Long pendant "torpedo" earrings drew attention to the newly exposed neckline, and sautoirs of faux pearls or beads embellished the plunging neckline, both in front and back. These only looked right on the flat-chested, so well-endowed women bound their breasts to affect the *garconne* boyish look. (*Garçonne* is "boy" with a feminine ending. Androgony and homosexuality, both male and female, were not uncommon in the Twenties, partly a product of the war which left France with over a million war widows going home to empty beds.) The heroine of the 1922 novel *La Garçonne*, or "Bachelorette", was a young bourgeoise unwed mother who rebelled against the drugs and sexual decadence surrounding her to defiantly bring up her illegitimate child on her own terms. *Scandaleux!* All over Europe, young women defied men and society's rules, and adopted the androgynous look with bobbed hair.

The large elaborate belt buckles and belts of the *Belle Epoque* shrank to narrow metal or silver belts at the hip embellished with geometric enamel, or *pâte de verre* moulded buckles imported from Czechoslovakia. Bonaz produced them in Celluloid and Galalith. Long cigarette holders in amber and ivory were copied in Bakelite to accompany silver and enamel, or Celluloid cigarette cases.

Four silver and enamel pins celebrating the sports, autocar, and jazz crazes of the Twenties, and a silver portable cigarette ash extinguisher, all marked 935, *Déposé* or maker's marks EH or M. *Courtesy of the author. Photo by Robert Weldon*

Long sautoir of strass rondelles, melon cut crystal beads, and "citrine" crystal dangles. A Twenties necklace flung on a vintage silk and lace Teddy. *Courtesy of the author. Photo by Robert Weldon*

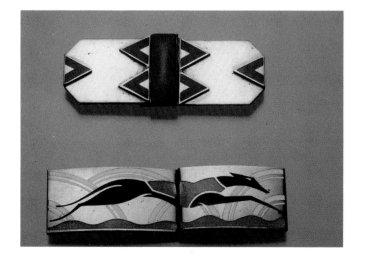

Two Art Deco belt buckles of black and red enamel on chrome-plated metal: the top buckle integrates a red glass stone into a geometric design; and the lower one depicts a racing greyhound, a Twenties symbol of speed. *Courtesy of the author. Photo by Robert Weldon*

Three silver and enamel cigarette cases: two with French silver import marks; the smaller case with the red and black abstract floral spray bears the French Minerva's head silver hallmark and maker's mark "MA*O". Two cigarette holders: one amber and silver gilt enamel; and the other ivory with silver and enamel. Ca. 1925-1930. *Courtesy of the author. Photo by Robert Weldon*

Beaded bag of mauve and orange underwater plants and bubbles with a silver and enamel Art Deco geometric frame with marcasites. French hallmarks. *Courtesy of the author. Photo by Robert Weldon*

Bijou Burma ad (from *Illustration*, Dec. 1932) for faithful reproductions of real jewelry by *Les Grands* jewelers of the rue de la Paix (Cartier etc.) A wide selection of jewelry of faux diamonds and precious stones was offered for 100 Francs, or $5 at the time. *Courtesy of the author's archives*

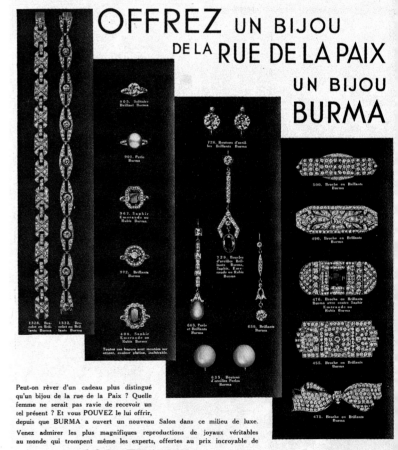

Poiret's silk pouch reticule (derived from the *"ridicule"*, first worn by another Josephine, the fashion-setting wife of Napoleon) was replaced by the *pochette* envelope handbag in leather, crocodile, or silk with Bakelite clasps for day, or beaded for evening with enamelled silver frames set with marcasite. Cloche (or "bell") hats pulled down low over the forehead, and high coat collars up to the ears made identification difficult; only the nose and one eye, heavily made up, were visible. Galalith or enamel clips were sold by the thousands for these hats, and were changed to match the outfit. Costume jewelry was available in boutiques and department stores like the Printemps which (like all the major chain stores) had its own design studio, "Primavera", specializing in Art Deco pottery, textiles, art glass, jewelry, and furniture. ("Printemps" and "Primavera" are the French and Italian words for "spring", symbolizing a birth of new ideas).

"Black and white" jewelry fashions of the Twenties, and the "white" fashion of the Thirties were produced by Cartier in diamonds and platinum, and faithfully copied by the Maison Burma in strass. The Burma Palais de Bijoux was located on the rue de la Paix cheek by jowl with the fine jewelers. Burma had the nerve to offer its faithful copies of diamond brooches, rings, and earrings for the very affordable price of 100 francs each, ($5). Faux pearls by Técla (also on the rue de la Paix) and Richelieu were convincingly made of glass or plastic beads coated with successive layers of *essence d'Orient* made from a fish scale compound. Canvet of Paris produced an unusual metallic pearl, using a metal varnish which gave the bead a strange luster.

Pavé strass copy of real diamond brooch with crystal center stone, à la Burma Bijou. *Courtesy of Diane Keith Collection, Beverly Hills, CA.* and a *tremblant* flower bouquet. *Courtesy of the author. Photo by Robert Weldon*

Metallic pearls by Canvet strung with metal spacers. *Courtesy of Rita Sacks Collection, New York. Photo by Robert Weldon*

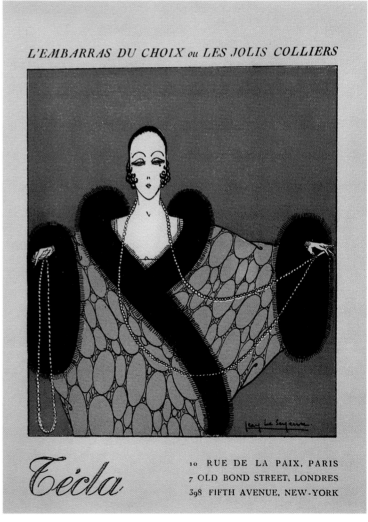

L'EMBARRAS DU CHOIX ou LES JOLIS COLLIERS

Técla

10 RUE DE LA PAIX, PARIS
7 OLD BOND STREET, LONDRES
398 FIFTH AVENUE, NEW-YORK

Vintage Técla advertisement for faux pearls ("An embarrassment of choices or the lovely necklaces"), from *La Gazette du Bon Ton*, 1920. *Courtesy of author's archives. Photo by Robert Weldon*

Five rows of faux amethysts with moulded glass and strass. A Twenties necklace for tea dancing at La Coupole. *Courtesy of private collection, Los Angeles. Photo by Robert Weldon*

Toc or "junk" jewelry was given the stamp of approval by couturiers Coco Chanel, Jean Patou, and Madeleine Vionnet. Manufacturers quickly went beyond mere imitation of real jewelry. Audacious creations were possible because of the low cost of materials, and mass market prices. One could indulge a flight of fancy in glass beads, base metals, plastic, wood, or strass. If the design didn't work, it could be quickly scrapped or altered, which was not a luxury the "Big Boys" could regularly afford with gold and diamonds. Bonaz with Celluloid and Galalith, and Gripoix and Rousselet, both designers/manufacturers of glass beads and faux pearls, were free to take chances. Multi-rows of glass beads were strung with maximum effect for daytime wear and rondelles of strass with melon-cut crystal beads made dazzling evening accessories. Costume jewelers Oréum and Franckie produced enamelled brass, and sparkling strass creations for their shops near the Opera.

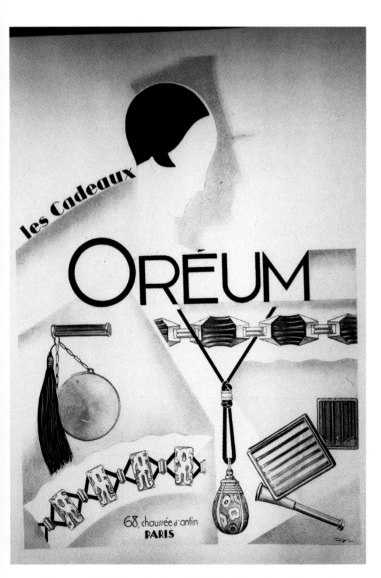

Vintage ad for Oréum jewelry and gift shop from *Pan*, a deluxe album edited by Paul Poiret, 1928. Enamelled bracelets, pendant, *nécessaire de toilette*, and smoking accessories for the Parisian flapper. *Courtesy of the author. Photo of print by Robert Weldon*

Rondelles of strass and graduated "emerald" glass beads, *très chic* for an elegant *soirée* at Maxim's. Twenties, unsigned, possibly by Mme. Gripoix. *Courtesy of the author. Photo by Robert Weldon*

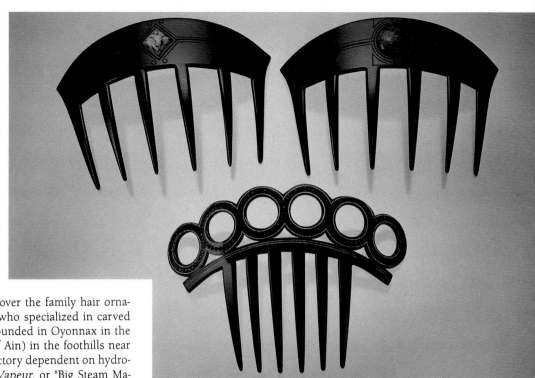

Three Celluloid "mantilla" hair combs, with faux turquoise and lapis stones, and blue strass, signed by Auguste Bonaz. Worn with a chignon, 1925. *Courtesy of Ellen Germanos collection, Rolling Hills, Il. Photo by Robert Weldon*

Celluloid "lace" head-dress with matching pendants for earrings, and Celluloid bandeau with a bird and butterflies among the flowers. Twenties marvels signed by Auguste Bonaz, script. *Courtesy of Lili Gantarski Collection, Paris, France*

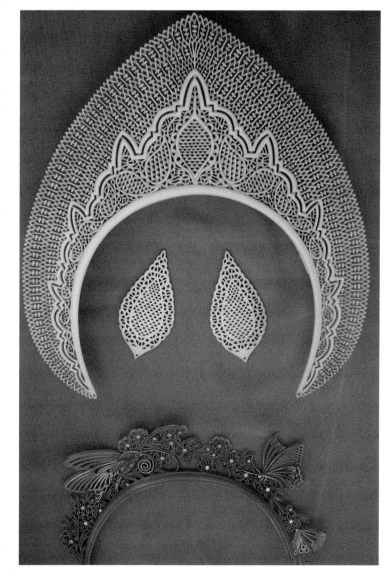

Auguste Bonaz (1877-1922) took over the family hair ornament business from his father, César, who specialized in carved horn combs. The Maison Bonaz was founded in Oyonnax in the eastern part of France (the Province of Ain) in the foothills near the Swiss border. The site of the first factory dependent on hydroelectric power in France, the *Grande Vapeur*, or "Big Steam Machine," was converted to electricity in 1904. Production methods evolved from artisans in family ateliers to more commercially efficient assembly groups. Natural horn plastic was replaced by synthetic plastics like Celluloid and Galalith which imitated ivory, horn, and tortoise-shell convincingly and cheaply, adapting to hand-made products for the mass market. Galalith (pronounced galaleet) was a milk-based casein plastic which took its name from the Greek *gala* (milk) and *lith* (stone). More durable than Celluloid, it was heat-maleable, and was produced in a wide range of colors in Germany and France.

Bonaz produced horn combs until 1910, when he switched to Celluloid for pendants and openwork head-dresses which looked like halos of plastic lace, and were, in fact, inspired by lace designs. In 1924-25 when the hair was worn in a chignon for evening, Bonaz made "mantilla" combs, sometimes as high as 30 centimeters, to be worn Spanish style with silk scarves. The Maison Bonaz stand at the 1925 Exposition des Arts Décoratifs was a great success, showing elaborate painted Celluloid combs and toilet articles for the dressing table, (that being a new piece of boudoir furniture). Faux tortoise-shell combs of oriental design were gilded by an electroplating technique; golden birds and spiderwebs were set with sprinkles of strass. When hair was bobbed, Bonaz quickly diversified with delightful buckles, buttons, and tiny figural pins for the cloche hats as well as bandeaux, barrettes, and scarf pins. Colorful penguins, owls, birds, Negro and Japanese figures, and geometric black and white clips, all hand-crafted, could be worn in clusters. Around 1930, Bonaz turned out bold Modernist necklaces of Galalith sections in contrasting colors which are avidly collected today. The vast Bonaz inventory of jewelry, boxes, and toilet articles was distributed by traveling salesmen to hairdressers, haberdashers, milliners, parfumiers, and department store chains. When Auguste died in 1922, his wife, Marguerite Bailly, directed the business from the Paris atelier until her death 5 years later, when her nephew, Théo Bailly, took charge. The Maison Auguste Bonaz was active until 1940 when the war, and the introduction of injection presses, reduced the economic viability of hand-made products. The factory was abandoned, though a few workers stayed on until 1976. The remaining stock was sold in 1980, some of the best and most representative pieces remaining at the Museum of Combs and Plastic Materials in Oyonnax.

Three gold-plated Galalith barrettes, a black parrot with strass and a "ruby" eye, a scroll barrette with gold trim, and a scarf pin with silver-plate trim, all signed by Auguste Bonaz. Twenties. *Courtesy of the author. Photo by Robert Weldon*

Five gold-plated faux tortoise shell hair combs, and a gold-plated pendant brooch signed by Auguste Bonaz, script. Twenties. *Courtesy of the author. Photo by Robert Weldon*

Winged scarabs and owl eyes are among the Twenties designs by Auguste Bonaz for Galalith belt buckles, signed. *Courtesy of Lili Gantarski Collection. Photo by Bruno Pierson*

Collection of Thirties Galalith brooches and hatpins, silver and gold-plated in geometric designs by Auguste Bonaz. The English £ and American $ signs worn together were especially popular when the franc was devalued. *Courtesy of Lili Gantarski Collection. Photo by Bruno Pierson*

Delightful Galalith figural hatpins and brooches by Bonaz representing Oriental and African heads, an owl, penguin, boats, bird and an Art Deco couple. Twenties, signed "Auguste Bonaz". *Courtesy of Lili Gantarski Collection. Photo by Bruno Pierson*

Pair of black and gold barrettes on original card bearing the Auguste Bonaz script signature. Twenties. *Courtesy of the author. Photo by Bruno Pierson*

Three Thirties Moderne Galalith necklaces: orange and black; blue and ivoirine; and blue and black segments strung on elastic cord. From 1940: a cinnamon Galalith and metal necklace; and a chrome necklace with curved wood segments. All signed "Auguste Bonaz." *Courtesy of Lili Gantarski Collection. Photo by Bruno Pierson*

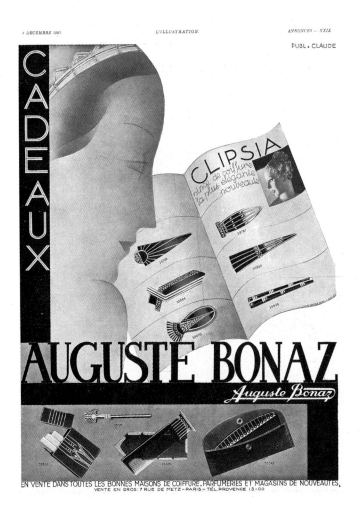

The history of the Bonaz firm is a good example of the XXth century transfer of art to manufacturing. With the changeover from steam to electricity, the passage from artisanal to industrial methods resulted in the specialization of the workers. Grinders, polishers, channelers, and moulders of the plastic material, and faux stone setters were separated into cubicles, as the modification of manufacturing techniques evolved. It was a process which "trained the family workers in the home, while bowing at the same time to the individualist and independent spirit of the employee", according to a brochure from the "Grande Vapeur" Musée du Peigne. Home workers were paid by the piece, depending upon the judgement of the owner of the merchandise produced. (Other firms produced plastic wares in Oyonnax). Industrial promoters of the first factory regrouped a number of home workers together, by renting them individual cubicles and selling them the electrical power necessary for their work. In the new factory, the workers were grouped together in compartments which solved the problem of frequent fires with the highly flammable Celluloid. A primitive sprinkler system connected with a large water reservoir on the roof, dumped water on each cubicle whenever needed, dousing the fire, and the workers.[3]

Several other designers worked in Oyonnax between 1900 and 1940. Marie-Léon Arbez-Carme (1858-1928) invented a process, since lost, of imitating wood or metal in Celluloid. He made combs and pins with classical, Egyptian, or Renaissance themes. Clément Joyard was known for his intricate Celluloid mantilla combs with painted peacock fan tails or a poppy garden.

An ad from *Illustration*, December 1932, showing Galalith hair clips trimmed with marcasite or strass, as well as combs and cigarette cases with geometric designs by Bonaz. These were sold to hair salons, and specialty shops. The inventory #70,647 indicates the vast number of designs available. *Courtesy of the author's archives*

In the center; a silver-plated head by Gustav Miklos, showing Byzantine/African influences for the Maison Azais, 1940, (after his 1927 brooch for Raymond Templier). A Cubist silver-plated mask pendant to the right is unsigned. The seven gilded or silvered Galalith brooches of stylized flower bouquets, hand painted, are by Paul Colomb for Louis Collomb 1940. *Courtesy of Lili Gantarski Collection, Paris. Photo by Bruno Pierson*

Gustav Miklos (1888-1967) was born in Budapest, where he studied at the Royal School of Decorative Arts. He traveled to Paris in 1909, where he showed at the Salon d'Automne. In 1914, he joined the Foreign Legion, and spent several years in Greece where he discovered Byzantine art and mosaics which greatly influenced his style. Returning to France, he became a French citizen, and was commissioned by Jacques Doucet to design his rugs, and silver objets. He took up sculpture in 1923, and exhibited at the 1925 Exposition des Arts Décoratifs, and the 1937 Exposition Internationale. In 1927 he designed a gold brooch for Raymond Templier of a woman's head which showed both Byzantine and African influences.[4] He repeated this stylized head in silver-plated white metal, and gilded Galalith pendants for the Maison Azais, when he moved to Oyonnax in 1940. He remained there till his death, teaching design at the Ecole Nationale des Matières Plastiques.

Louis Collomb (1891-1980) was another Oyonnax designer who manufactured costume jewelry in Celluloid, then Galalith. In 1939 he joined the army. His son, Paul, who studied at the Ecole des Arts Décoratifs in Paris, designed original jewelry for his father from 1939 until 1960 when the firm folded.[5] His bracelets of black Galalith highlighted with silver flowers, and his gilded brooches etched with hand-painted stylized bouquets are some of the most stunning pieces to come out of the Oyonnax factories.

Eight gold-painted brooches and a hand-painted compact, Celluloid, 1930, by the Maison Antonin. *Courtesy of Lili Gantarski Collection. Photo by Bruno Pierson*

Toilette articles, such as portable folding combs and compacts as well as circular brooches were also made of etched, gilded, and hand-painted Celluloid and Galalith. The similarity of design and technique marks these pieces as Oyonnax merchandise, although they are unsigned. Delightfully chic and cheap Celluloid handbags with Bakelite clasps, belt buckles, parrot pins, and necklaces of striped Celluloid flakes, light as air, were produced in other ateliers in Paris and sold in department stores in the Twenties and Thirties. Plastics were all the rage, and affordable. Vast quantities were disseminated throughout Europe, as well as exported to American department stores and Woolworth chain stores. A winged scarab (6" across) pendant made a dramatic statement, while 5" wide belt buckles spanned the waist. Celluloid cigarette cases with clasps in the shape of a hand were, and still are, avidly collected even though they were intended for the short cigarettes of the Twenties. (These were copied by the Japanese.)

Two Celluloid parrot head hat pins, one is moulded, the other has carved ruffled feathers and a gilded beak, marked "Made in France". The original red Bakelite and chrome parrot was copied in the Eighties. *Courtesy of private collection, Los Angeles. Photo by Robert Weldon*

Two red, white, and blue striped Celluloid necklaces and a red and ivory Celluloid pin rolled like a sheet of dough. Twenties. *Courtesy of private collection, Los Angeles. Photo by Robert Weldon*

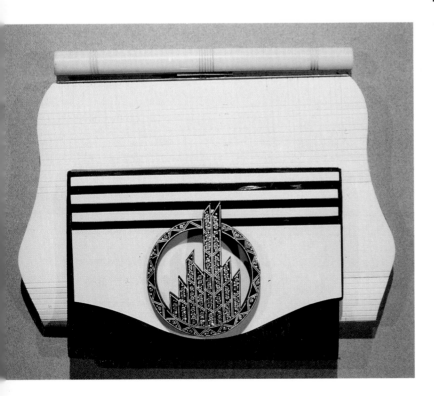

Two Celluloid pochette handbags: one all white with geometric pattern and butterscotch clasp, the other black and white Celluloid with black silk. A black Celluloid pin set with strass is also ca. 1930. *Courtesy of the author. Photo by Robert Weldon*

Impressive tinted Celluloid winged scarab pendant (6" wingspread) with "pearl" dangles and chain. Twenties. *Courtesy of Diane Keith collection, Beverly Hills, CA. Photo by Robert Weldon*

Egyptian revival belt buckle, tinted Celluloid, featuring slaves playing the lyre, and lotus plants. And an "end of day" plastic bow belt buckle (5" wide), studded with strass. Twenties. *Courtesy of Rita Sacks Collection, New York. Photo by Richard Marx*

Six Celluloid cigarette cases with a ringed Celluloid hand forming the clasp. No two alike, from the Twenties (later copied by the Japanese). *Courtesy of the author. Photo by Robert Weldon*

Pair of cobalt blue *pâte de verre* earrings, moulded movement in glass with gold-plated festooned tops. Unknown artist, Twenties. *Courtesy of Ruby at the Landing, Westlake Village, CA.*

Glass workers, inspired by Lalique's success, worked in glass factories in Nancy in Alsace, and in the suburbs of Paris, producing *pâte de verre* vases and light fixtures. They produced oval or circular medallions with holes in them for suspension on silk cords. The *pâte de verre* technique was rediscovered by the sculptor Henri Cros in the factory at Sèvres. Color and form were combined in the mass, not applied separately after the piece was moulded. The semi-opaque glass has a waxy feel to it. Firing was a difficult process since the glass paste did not always melt uniformly, and the mould in which it was fired sometimes dissolved in the high 900 degree heat. Each piece was slightly different, if the mould was destroyed in the process.[6] Gems and hardstones were simulated, and swirling translucent shapes were especially successful for earrings seen against the light.

Gabriel Argy-Rousseau (1885-1953) who studied at the Ecole des Arts Décoratifs in Paris, made *pâte de verre* medallions and earrings using a grey, mauve, rust, and dusky rose palette. His pieces were delicate, usually of flowers in low relief. They were signed "G.A-R."

Alméric Walter (1859-1942) ran the *pâte de verre* workshop for Daum in Nancy. In 1919 he set up his own workshop, collaborating with sculptor Henri Bergé. His medallions, like his vases, were heavier than Argy-Rousseau's. Walter was fond of portraying insects in rust and deep blues, which were in higher relief than Argy-Rousseau's pieces. He signed his initials to his work, AW or AW N. Bergé wittily shaped his "B" initial like a sheep. (In French a "berger" is a shepherd).

Bracelet of faux jade cabochons and amethyst glass, and a pendant brooch with faux "carved" emeralds with amethyst glass. Both were produced with *pâte de verre* moulded glass. Marked *déposé*, France. *Courtesy of Diane Keith collection. Photo by Robert Weldon*

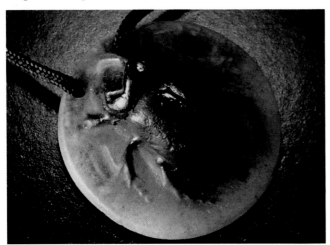

Scarab beetle in high relief *pâte de cristal* moulded pendant by Alméric Walter, Twenties. Walters' naturalistic insects were created in heavy opaque crystal paste. *Courtesy of Terrance O'Halloran, Los Angeles. Photo by Robert Weldon, courtesy of the G.I.A.*

Translucent lavender forget-me-nots captured in low-relief moulded *pâte de cristal* pendant by Gabriel Argy-Rousseau, signed in the mould "GA-R", lower left. Twenties. *Courtesy of the author. Photo by Robert Weldon*

Marcel Goupy (1886-?) was artistic director of Rouard, a shop on the avenue de L'Opéra which specialized in art glass by Decorchement and others. His technique was enamelled glass, using the same designs for his jewelry as for his vases; floral designs in tango orange, acid green, yellow, or Lanvin blue (the cornflower blue that Jeanne Lanvin chose for her extraordinary Art Deco bedroom in 1925). Since these glass medallions were fragile, very few have survived the years without losing their silk cords, or suffering chip damage.

Lalique's work in the Twenties continued along the lines of his pre-war designs, with moulded glass pendants, necklaces, bracelets, and pins in monochromatic animal or floral themes. Lalique's nude or scantily clothed female figures, so effective in his jewelry, vases, and boxes, were inspired by Greco-Roman stone temple friezes or the Pompeian frescos painted on plaster which were preserved under the ash of the Mt. Vesuvius eruption in 79 A.D. (Wedgewood had already adapted these similar silhouettes into his Neo-classical Jasper pottery line in 1800). Tin oxides produced the cloudy "clam broth" opalescence of Lalique's popular moulded glass ornaments. In the Thirties, Lalique phased out jewelry to devote himself to art glass objets and decorative items (including hundreds of millions of designer perfume bottles.) During the war years, the factory at Combs-la Ville was seriously damaged, and glass production was terminated. Lalique died in 1945. The "R." was then dropped, leaving just the "Lalique" signature. The Lalique Verrerie d'Alsace factory at Wingen-sur Moder continued the mass-production of objects.

Lalique's grandaughter, Marie-Claude, revived the jewelry line in 1992 by designing brooches, tie clips, and bracelets of luminous crystal cabochons in 14 colors mounted in silver-plated metal. She brought color back to Lalique. "For me, color is gaiety and life!", she exclaimed. She has also designed a line of silk scarves featuring the most representative of René Lalique's jewelry.

The work of the illustrators Paul Iribe, George Barbier, and Georges Lepape whose exquisite *pochoirs* renderings of couture fashion and accessories appeared in the *Gazette du Bon Ton*, *Falbalas & Fanfreluches*, *Feuillets d'Art*, and the *Bonheur du Jour* design albums, has not been fully appreciated. They both mirrored and invented their times.

Paul Iribe (1883-1935) was picked by Poiret to illustrate his clothes in the 1908 pivotal album *Robes de Paul Poiret Racontées par Paul Iribe*. He followed this in 1911 with *L'Eventail & la Fourrure Chez Paquin* (*The Fan & Fur at Paquin*) with Barbier and Lepape illustrations. He was equally at home in theater, advertising, fashion, jewelry, furniture, and film set design. His versatility was recognized by Jacques Doucet for interior decorating. His advertisements for Maxima, Juclier, and Novelty pearls before the war were followed by fine jewelry for Linzeler, and Gloria Swanson (an amethyst pendant worn in the film *The Affairs of Anatole*). Iribe's geometric rose, symbol of the 1925 Exposition, showed up in jewelry by Boucheron. His 1927 portrait of Jeanne Lanvin and her daughter for the Lanvin perfume bottle is still the couturière's logo. His set design for the original 1920s *Ten Commandments* film by Cecil B. DeMille was recently discovered buried in the sand near San Luis Obispo, California, (there were no mummies). In 1930, for the art brochures for Nicolas wine merchants, Iribe's chic women who perused the *carte des vins* wore a dozen Art Deco bangles on each arm, large cabochons rings on each finger, and three sautoirs around their necks. (How did they find the strength to lift a glass?)

In 1932, at her private mansion, Coco Chanel displayed a truly astronomical diamond collection designed by her lover, Iribe, at

Elegant *garçonne* festooned in faux pearls powders her nose in a *pochoir* print by Paul Iribe illustrating the Nicolas wine merchants' deluxe album, *Blanc et Rouge*, 1930. Signed Paul Iribe. *Courtesy of the author. Photo of print by Robert Weldon*

the request of the diamond industry which was suffering reduced revenues due to the great success of costume jewelry. A comet tail necklace streaked around the neck, stars adorned the ears, crescent moons lit the hair, and sun-ray bracelets blazed on the wrist. Janet Flanner (Gênet of the *New Yorker*), who never missed a trick, wrote in 1932: "With that aggravating instinct to strike when everyone else thinks the iron is cold, Chanel has at the height of the depression returned to precious stones, as having the greatest value in the smallest volume; just as during the boom, she launched glass gewgaws because they were devoid of arrogance in an epoch of too easy *luxe*."[7] Two days after Chanel's diamond show opened in Paris, De Beer's stock jumped 20 points on the London stock exchange. Soon strass copies of the comet and stars appeared as brooches and earrings in specialty shops, completing the cycle.

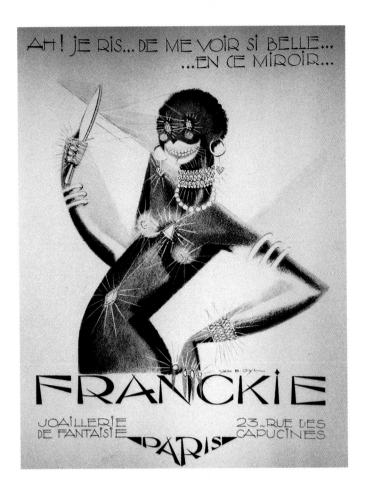

AH! JE RIS...DE ME VOIR SI BELLE...
...EN CE MIROIR...

FRANCKIE
JOAILLERIE
DE FANTAISIE
PARIS
23,RUE DES
CAPUCINES

"Ah! I laugh to see myself so pretty in this mirror" says the black girl in this ad for Franckie's costume jewelry. With pearly teeth and strass eyes, Josephine's look-alike was covered with sparkling faux bijoux. From Paul Poiret's *Pan* deluxe album of advertisements, 1928. *Print courtesy of the author. Photo of original print by Robert Weldon*

George Barbier (1882-1932) set his *pochoirs* interpretations of couture clothes and fashion jewelry in a fantasy world of carnivals in Venice, mythological Greece, and Shéhérazade decor for the de luxe Art Deco fashion portfolios, as well as illustrated books. (He illustrated two volumes of the Ballets Russes stars, Nijinsky and Kasarvina). Torpedo pendant earrings, faux pearl necklaces, shoe buckles, aigrettes, and bangles were delicately drawn for his elegant women. These were created by Barbier's fertile imagination as accessories to complement the couture costumes, and certainly influenced contemporary costume jewelry design. Following Iribe's lead, in 1914, he submitted a design portfolio to Cartier, and was commissioned to design a "Woman with Panther" (with pearls down to her knees) advertisement for the firm. Charles Jacqueau, Cartier's principal designer for thirty years, adapted many of Barbier's design motifs for pendants, aigrettes, and cigarette cases.[8]

Another Georges, named Lepape (1887-1971)) was the artist chosen by Poiret at the age of 24 to illustrate *Les Choses de Paul Poiret* in 1911. This beautifully conceived series of fashion and accessory designs was produced in an edition of 1000 on de luxe paper. There was no text. None was needed to become the most influential pre-war fashion album in Europe as well as North and South America. Lepape had studied at the Ecole des Beaux Arts with fellow artists André Marty and Charles Martin, who also illustrated the major de luxe albums, books, and magazines of the Teens, Twenties and Thirties. These *pochoirs* were faithfully reproduced by hand with stencils; the gouache paint applied with brush strokes gave the drawings a three-dimensional life which was indistinguishable from the original drawing. Besides the *Gazette du Bon Ton*, (1912-1925) Lepape illustrated *hors-textes* for the *Feuillets d'Art* in 1919. His *Miroir Rouge* shows the French passion for *Japonisme*, and Lepape's aptitude for jewelry and accessory illustration. Like Erté, Lepape went on to design sets and costumes as well as covers for *Vogue*, *Harper's Bazaar*, and *Vanity Fair*. The jewelry and accessories were often of his own invention, and served as inspiration for costume jewelry designers.

Visez au cœur, belles dames !

"Aim for the heart, beautiful ladies!". Hand-colored *pochoir* print by George Barbier, for the deluxe album *Le Bonheur du Jour* shows the long pendant earrings and brow-hugging hats worn in 1924. *Courtesy of the author. Photo of original print by Robert Weldon*

José de Zamora, who was assistant designer for Paul Poiret (along with Erté,) in 1913, also designed costumes and accessories for the theater and Music-hall in the Twenties. His illustrations appeared in the *Gazette du Bon Ton*, 1913-14. His dress designs were complete with jewelry (bangles in multiples of seven brought good luck in the Twenties,) and hats.

The purpose of the 1925 Exposition Internationale des Arts Décoratifs et Industriels Modernes had been to celebrate the marriage of art and industry and the superiority of French taste and products. It was open to "all manufacturers whose artistic product clearly showed modern tendencies". Their goal was achieved, and plans were made to follow it with other expos. The timing of the 1931 Exposition Coloniale was less propitious, coming just after the Wall Street Crash of 1929, which devastated European trade and export to America. The frantic gaiety of the Twenties, and the luxury trades which used exotic woods and expensive materials were *démodés* and irrelevant. The cosmic cocktail party was over.

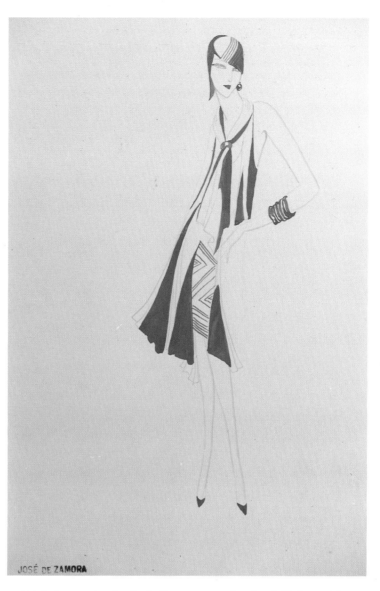

Original watercolor sketch of a bias-cut geometric painted silk dress with asymmetrical dripping hemline and asymmetrical hat tipped over one ear, designed by José de Zamora, ca. 1930. The sloe-eyed model wears one hoop earring and red bangles which were considered lucky in France if worn in multiples of seven. Signed in lower left by the artist. *Courtesy of the author. Photo of the sketch by Sandro Moro*

The Colonial Exhibition was designed to show the art and products of the French colonies in North and West Africa, Madagascar, and Indochina. Pavilions representing each French colony, as well as Dutch Indonesia, the Belgian Congo, and the colonies of Denmark, Portugal, and Italy were scattered all over the Bois de Vincennes. America was represented by Alaska, the Philippines, Puerto Rico, and Hawaii. Ironically, Josephine Baker, a Black American, was named the Queen of the Exposition, even though she wasn't French.[9] Josephine was rarely seen in the "primitive" and "barbaric" accessories that were created by contemporary artists for the Expo; her lovers gave her real jewels, and she walked her cheetah on a solid-gold leash.

Costume jewelry was cast for the Expo by Béla Voros in silver, and carved ivory heads and pendants were made of enamelled masks. Real carved ivory bracelets or tortoise-shell necklaces were popular, but were much cheaper reproduced in Bakelite and Galalith. Large brown, orange, and green wooden beads were strung on window cord by Lelong. Van Cleef & Arpels translated an African chieftain's necklace into ivory cylinders and coral balls. Miklos designed an African/Cubist head in beaten silver for Fouquet. Mauboussin made a brooch of exotic jungle flowers, all enamelled

One of several posters printed for the Paris Exposition Internationale des Arts Décoratifs et Industriels Modernes, 1925. This one by Robert Bonfils displays two of the recurring design themes of French Art Deco: the grace and speed of the antelope; and the stylized flower basket which appeared in jewelry. *Courtesy of the author. Photo of the original poster by Robert Weldon*

An "exotic" silver-plated Galalith brooch (there were male and female versions of this profile,) and a faux "carved jade" brooch inspired by the Exposition Coloniale, 1931. The black and "ivory" Celluloid clip with strass, and Bakelite bracelet of "amber" and "onyx" are further examples of simulating natural materials. *Courtesy of private collection, Los Angeles. Photo by Robert Weldon*

A forever fresh bouquet of white apple blossoms and leaves of *pâte de verre* (called "poured glass" in America.) Unsigned, probably by Mme. Gripoix for Chanel. *Courtesy of Rita Sacks Collection. Photo by Richard Marx*

Necklace of "poured glass" light and dark blue flower petals with a black velvet bow fastening. Thirties, possibly by Mme. Gripoix. *Courtesy of the author. Photo by Robert Weldon*

gold to salute Indochina. Flower petals of glass were strung on metal wire and finished with velvet bows, and enamelled leaves and *pâte de verre* blossoms sprouted on Chanel lapels by Gripoix, as well as in department stores. This pretty fashion survived World War II, when Rousselet and Gripoix produced hundreds of necklaces using floral glass beads and leaves.

There were artist-jewelers who participated in all the International World Fair Exhibitions, but whose aesthetics belong more to the Thirties than the Twenties. Twenties Art Deco jewelry and decorative arts were basically feminine, de luxe, exquisitely crafted for the elite. The Moderne designs of the late Twenties, and early Thirties were broad-shouldered, masculine, and democratic, responding to a wide demand across the social strata. The austere Bauhaus "Less is more" theories had filtered across the border. Furniture, lamps, silverware, rugs, fabrics, and architecture had succumbed to "Mensch Modern". In jewelry, excluding "Les Grands", who clung to platinum and diamonds) luxury materials were used judiciously, if at all, for bold effect. There was a swing to a studied simplicity in the applied arts. Jean Dunand, Jean Desprès, and Béla Voros made valuable contributions to jewelry, objets and sculpture during this period.

Jean Dunand (1877-1942) was born in Switzerland, but lived and worked all his life in France. He was a sculptor who had two successful careers as a coppersmith and lacquer artist. Dunand preferred the arduous process of hand-hammering his copper, pewter, and silver vases, to soul-less industrial methods. In 1912, the technical problem of embellishing the patina of his pieces led him to the study of Japanese vases, and an apprenticeship with Sugawara, the Japanese lacquer artist. Natural lacquer, a sap extracted from the *rhus vernicifera* tree from the Far East, was used in an ancient, exclusively oriental technique, which was both precise and time-consuming. Colors were obtained by mixing the lacquer with pigments, or iron oxide for black. To acquire a perfect mirror-smooth surface, 22 coats were required, each coat polished with pumice after a drying period of 2 to 3 weeks in a humidified room. Lacquer can be decorated by gilding, sculpting or inlaying with ivory, metal, or mother of pearl. Indo-Chinese workers were employed, because the Caucasian skin often was allergic to the process. White lacquer does not exist, so Dunand revived the technique of imbedding crushed egg shells in black lacquer, for texture and stark color contrast. At first he embellished vases and boxes with egg shell, but in 1924 he began experimenting with lacquered Aureum (oroide; a silver and brass alloy,) and red and black lacquered silver jewelry.[10]

Dunand was commissioned to lacquer furniture in collaboration with Jean Lambert-Rucki, the Polish sculptor, for the French Embassy Pavilion at the 1925 Expo. For the couturière Madeleine Vionnet, he created a black lacquer game table inlaid with eggshell. Impressed, she asked him to design lacquer and eggshell pendants. This led to earrings which were gold painted black lacquer on one side and persimmon on the reverse; similar designs were equally as effective as hatpins.

For Madame Agnès, the milliner, he designed eggshell decorated hats and handbags, and hatpins and buckles of persimmon lacquer decorated with geometric black or silver motifs, as well as shoe buckles and bracelets of lacquered wood. Dunand was inspired by primitive African art, and covered 3" wide copper cuffs with incised black and white geometric lacquer for the Modern African Goddess, Josephine Baker. Moderne silver bracelets and

Channel set square-cut crystal clasp with faux emerald cabochons mounted with two rows of pearls, and a crystal clip to match. *Courtesy of the author. Photo by Robert Weldon*

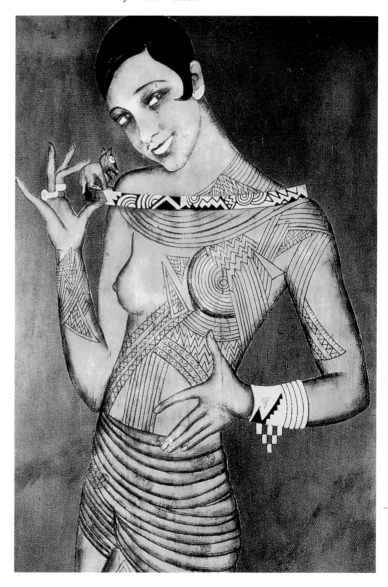

Lacquered wood panel with portrait of Josephine Baker in black, gold, ochre, and silver signed Jean Dunand, 1927. The geometric design of the tattoos is echoed in the silver laquered African cuff and neckpiece supporting the bizarre miniature creature by Lambert-Rucki. *Courtesy of Christie's, New York from the "Important 20th Century Decorative Arts" catalog, December, 1988*

Lacquered pendants with geometric gold and black design on one side, and persimmon lacquer on the reverse. Used for hat pins or earrings (also made in eggshell lacquer). And a persimmon lacquer buckle with black circles, by Jean Dunand, unsigned. Thirties. *Courtesy of the author. Photo by Robert Weldon*

earrings were decorated with red and black geometric lacquer. Mme. Agnès was photographed by D'Ora wearing a hat with eggshell decorations and ivory beads and earrings which had black lacquer abstract designs. Vanity cases, pillboxes, and compacts were black lacquer inlaid with eggshell, (the color varied depending on whether the inside or outside of the eggshell was exposed.) In 1940, when wartime restricted materials, Dunand even lacquered curly wood shavings to decorate Agnès hats!

Dunand collaborated with Lambert-Rucki (1888-1967) who created whimsical animals and characters from an "Alice in Psychedelic Wonderland" for cigarette cases, screens, sculpture, and egg shell lacquer and enamel portraits. The cigarette cases were lacquered fruitwood with inlaid metal. Lambert-Rucki designed a Cubistic African mask bracelet in hammered silver for Georges Fouquet in 1937, but otherwise was not actively engaged in jewelry design.

Dunand survived the Depression, when the *nouveaux riches* became the *nouveaux pauvres*. In 1932, The French government, as part of a policy to encourage crafts and foster French prestige, commissioned Dunand, Jean Dupas, Lalique, and other leading designers, to decorate the most luxurious liner afloat, the "Normandie". Dunand's 6 meter square gold lacquer panels were like Egyptian bas-reliefs. This magnificent ship was not to complete many crossings. Tragically, she caught fire and sank in New York harbor as she was being converted to a troopship. World War II deprived Dunand of his work materials, and his youngest son. This, compounded with the loss of many of his masterpieces, broke his spirit. He died in 1942, only 65 years old.

Jean Després (1889-1980) a native of Burgundy, showed an early aptitude for drawing and was apprenticed to a goldsmith in Avallon at the age of 14. He worked in metal for 5 years, then moved to Paris in 1914, where he shared living quarters in the famous Bateau Lavoir with Matisse and Braque. He designed jewelry for members of the Ballet Russes when they played Paris. During the war he worked in an aircraft factory, and following demobilization, passed exams in aeronautical design.

Waving a well-designed fork over dinner with the author in Paris, in 1974, Després declared: "I admired the clean functional lines of the machines, and the incredible forces at work there. Why not incorporate that precision into my jewelry and objets design?"

Fruitwood cigarette case inlaid with metal and enamel by Jean Dunand. The scene of exotic characters and imaginary animals was designed by Lambert-Rucki, ca. 1930. *Courtesy of the author. Photo by Robert Weldon*

Després' new ideas in silver and semi-precious stones were exhibited at the 1919 Salon d'Automne. The ever-vigilant Jacques Doucet saw that his work was too avant-garde for the general public, and invited him to join his stable of designers. Until 1925, he worked for Doucet, being paid by the piece. Poiret asked him to design clips and ornaments for his clothes, showing him how to drape material on a woman's body. In 1926 he moved into his own atelier, where he concentrated on spartan Machine Age pieces in heavy silver with gold accents. Hardstones like jasper, bloodstone, or lapis adorned his rings and brooches, and enamel or ivory added a note of elegance. He liked the contrast of alternating hammered and burnished surfaces on his silver bracelets and brooches.

Desprès collaborated with Etienne Cournault in 1927, who contributed a delicate etched glass technique (called *verre églomisé*) to his otherwise sober designs. Silver rings and brooches incorporated rectangles of Cournault's reverse etched glass. A necklace of 9 spheres which looked like ball bearings, four lacquered black, was exhibited at both the 1925 and 1937 exhibitions. During the German occupation of Paris, the Nazis admired his work, and asked him to go to Germany to form a school. Desprès refused, and fearing retribution, fled to his home in Avallon. The Nazis destroyed his Paris studio. After the war, he continued working in Burgundy until his death, aged 91.

Silver ring with wavy mounts around a blue jasper stone, signed "Després", by the artist. Ca. 1929. *Courtesy of the author. Photo by Robert Weldon, courtesy of the G.I.A.*

Script signature "Després" on silver and jasper ring, with French silver mark, boar's head. Both Jean Després' letterhead and signature on letters to the author bore the French *accent grave* (è), but he frequently signed his jewelry with the *accent aigu* (é). *Photo by Robert Weldon*

Machine Moderne silver bracelet and two silver rings: one with square-cut crystals; the other with ridged domed element, 1928, by Jean Desprès. *Courtesy of the artist's archives. Photo by Pierre Jahan*

Silver bracelet and brooch with the "ball bearing" motifs, and two silver brooches, one with amazonite, by Jean Desprès. With signature and hallmarks. *Courtesy of the artist, author's archives*

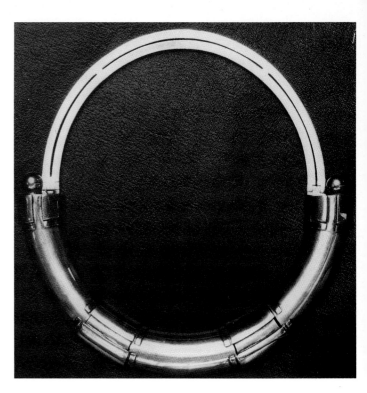

Machine Age necklace of nine silver balls; four lacquered black, and five of hammered silver, with gold links, by Jean Desprès, 1925. This piece was exhibited at both the 1925 and 1937 Paris Expos. With artist's signature and French hallmarks. *Courtesy of Jean Després' archives. Photo by Laurent Sully Jaulmes*

Hinged silver collar with gold knobs by Jean Desprès. With signature and hallmarks. *Courtesy of the artist*

Silver pendant with rough-cut malachite piece and gold bars, and a large jade brooch with the panel sandwiched between two stylized African silver combs, and a jade cabochon brooch mounted on black onyx, and a silver ring with hammered surfaces contrasting with smooth gold spheres, all engraved "J. Desprès. *Courtesy of Christie's, New York: "Important Art Nouveau and Art Deco" catalog, October, 1981*

Silver-plated cast bronze bracelet with classic Art Deco/ Byzantine profiles interpreted by sculptors in 1930. Two cast bronze rings, silver-plated with French Colony (Guadaloupe) native in a turban, and another ring with the squared-off profile, made for the Colonial Exposition, 1931. Unsigned, by Béla Voros. *Courtesy of the author. Photo by Robert Weldon*

Béla Voros (1889-1983) was born in Hungary's oldest village, one of 7 children in a family of modest means. He was an errand boy for a sculptor, who encouraged his interest in the craft. At 17, he enrolled in the School of Applied Arts in Budapest. When the République des Conseils government fell in 1919, many avant-garde artists and writers left the country because the intellectual terror of the counter-revolution denied them free expression. At first, Voros and other students with leftist convictions, were denied higher education, but he finally won a scholarship permitting study in Paris in 1925.

In the lively Montparnasse Café du Dôme, he met fellow countryman, Csaky, a sculptor who worked for Doucet. There was no artistic censorship in Paris, so with Csaky's encouragement, he exhibited at the Salon d'Automne. He worked mostly in bronze, influenced by African art, and the spirit of Cubism. Like everyone else who revelled in Harlem on the Champs-Elysées, he got caught up in the euphoric Negro jazz conquest of Paris. He made bronze busts, and bas-reliefs of jazz bands that were stylised, but always figurative. For the 1931 Exposition Coloniale, he cast rings and bracelets with an African theme in silver-plated bronze.

Voros moved to Nice in 1932, where he began carving heads and nudes in ivory. Poiret saw his work and commissioned him to carve buttons, umbrella handles, pendants, and bracelets for his collections. Poiret's star had descended, but he never stopped designing. "I used the *croute* of the elephant tusk for these small pieces," Voros explained, in a 1975 interview in Sèvres. "That's the hollow "crust" of the tusk which is in the elephant's jaw, usually untouched by sculptors. I scraped it out, and carved lamps and boxes with stylized heads and ebony stands and lids. Poiret and I were both broke, and Nice was cheaper than Paris, but poor Paul was living in miserable circumstances when I left for Sèvres in 1938."

After the war, Voros exhibited his ivory busts in Paris, and belatedly, in his home town, Budapest. In the Fifties, he was forced to give up ivory carving when he developed silicosis of the lungs from breathing the dust. Believing that the elephant would soon be declared an endangered species, he began working in plastic. He died in his atelier in Sèvres outside of Paris, still vigorous at 94.

Jean Dunand, Jean Després and Béla Voros were sculptors and artist/craftsmen who produced *dinanderie* metalwork or ivory sculpture for their private customers, as well as limited-editions for international expos and shops. Fashion jewelry for haute couturiers Poiret, Doucet, Vionnet, and Mme. Agnès was a small but important part of their *oeuvre*. Their work in lacquer, silver, and ivory was an inspiration to a generation of artists. There were Art Deco artists who essayed lacquer boxes, or jewelry à la Dunand, but lacking the expertise, only 2 or 3 layers of lacquer were used, so the effect and the price tag were less dazzling. Others, intrigued by the Bauhaus, or Després' disciplined style, cut their own too-busy designs to the bone. Ivory statues were carved, but mostly in combination with bronze, by chryselephantine sculptors like Chiparus and Preiss. Dunand and Després were lauded in their lifetimes, but Voros only became known to collectors and museums in the Seventies.

Hand-carved ivory box with ebony lids with sculpted heads of five different almond-eyed women. Incised with "VB" signature (In Hungarian the names are reversed), by Béla Voros. One brooch and a pendant, with classic profiles in hand-carved ivory by Béla Voros for Paul Poiret, 1932. *Courtesy of the author, Photo by Robert Weldon*

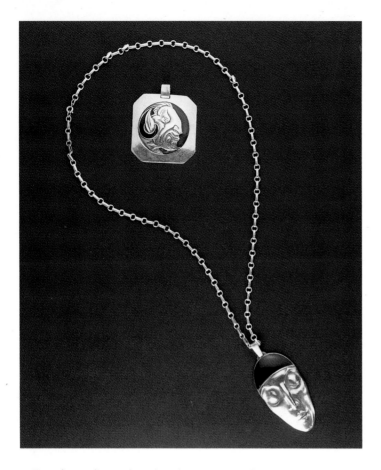

Silver pendant with green and black enamel folds and embossed stylized flowers by Etienne David. Ca. 1925; signed "ED." *Courtesy of private collection, Milan, Italy*

Two silver and enamel pendants by Etienne David: One pendant on a silver linked chain represents a Commedia dell'Arte character with a black enamel cap; the other is a smug Satyr's head with green and black enamel. Signed "ED" (the E is backwards). Late Twenties. *Courtesy of private collection, Milan Italy*

Etienne David, about whom little is known, had a shop on the rue de la Paix along with big names Vever and Mellerio, and designed distinctive silver and enamel jewelry with Art Deco themes. Stylized flowers, geometric planes, and Commedia dell'Arte and mythical figures were worked into his pendants in the Twenties and early Thirties.

The 1937 Exposition Universelle opened in uncertain times. The Führer was revving up for his ignominious Aryan conquests, and Civil War was tearing Spain apart. The Thirties were a time of self-delusion on the part of French (and British) pacifists who believed that appeasement would avert another war. Delusion and illusion went hand in hand, as the applied arts participated in the final fireworks of peace.

This Expo, like the others, celebrated modern art and industry. Sonia and Robert Delaunay decorated the vast French Pavilions for the Railroads, and Aviation with dynamic murals. Never had the machine been so gloriously exalted. Modernism was a *fait accompli*. (Bauhaus artists, who had been so firmly rejected by Hitler, were enthusiastically welcomed in America, while the Swastika flag flew over the German Pavilion.) Moulded *pâte de verre* red, white, and blue bracelets and pins representing the pavilions were especially made in Czechosovakia to commemorate the 1937 Expo, depicting the galleon ship (symbol of the city of Paris, and her motto "Floats, but does not sink"). These souvenirs were transported home by thousands of international travelers, but they are a rare find for contemporary World Fair collectors, because the elastic cords eventually disintegrated, and the glass segments broke.

Unusual ceramic scarabs set in silver bracelet. *Courtesy of private collection, Milan, Italy*

Six moulded glass pieces with *Importé de Tschecoslovaquie*, (Imported from Czechoslovakia) impressed in the mould produced for the 1937 Exposition Universelle in Paris. The bracelets' glass segments are strung on elastic. The gilded galleon is the symbol of the City of Paris. The middle bracelet has a map of Europe with Paris circled. These came in many colors and were made in quantity as souvenirs. The red brooch pictures the U.S.S.R. exhibition building, and the lower brooch has a map of the two hemispheres in red, white and blue. All pieces bear the impressed "Exposition Paris, 1937" trademark which was enamelled in contrasting colors. *Courtesy of the author. Photo by Robert Weldon*

The striking contrast between the styles of the Twenties and Thirties was obvious. Precision, rationalism, and the cold metallic sheen and feel of nickel and chrome infused jewelry and the decorative arts with a different kind of utilitarian elegance. French costume jewelers did inventive things with chrome and Bakelite, and enamelled aluminum. Curved radiator grills inspired Bakelite bracelets.

Compacts and lipsticks were an integral part of Bakelite and brass cuffs by Flamand, providing instant makeup repairs after the long day at the office, or between Foxtrots. Josephine Baker commissioned gift bracelets from Flamand which were presented in commemmorative boxes publicizing her films or songs. "*J'ai Deux Amours,*" referring to her "Two Loves," Paris and America, was inscribed on a box containing a simple black and white Bakelite bangle and ring. Her gift makeup bracelets were boxed to promote her film *Zouzou,* with a photo of Josephine.

Three Bakelite bracelets with the "radio or car grill" 3-D effect mounted with gilded brass grills. *Courtesy of the author.* And two ruffled Bakelite brooches set in chrome, the lower one with Bakelite balls and chains. Thirties. *Courtesy of Diane Keith and the author's collections. Photo by Robert Weldon*

The Flamand (meaning Flemish) Company produced portable makeup bracelets of brass mounted with Bakelite in Paris in the Thirties. This one holds a lipstick container for emergency repairs. (Possibly a gift from Josephine Baker.) Marked "Flamand". *Courtesy of the author's collection. Photo by Robert Weldon*

Reverse of lipstick bracelet showing the manufacturer's marks: "Made in France, Paris. Flamand. *Déposé,*" or registered, was the patent mark used in France, Germany, and Austria. The latter two countries dropped the *déposé* mark after WW I. *Photo by Robert Weldon*

Portable compact cuff mounted with blue Bakelite, marked *déposé* and Flamand, Paris. The bracelet was a gift offered by Josephine Baker to her friends. The box is marked "Zouzou" after the film in which Josephine starred in 1934, directed by Marc Allegret, (with a photo of Josephine). The box is marked "Flamand Paris. *Modéle marquée Présentation déposé.*" (Presentation model registered.) *Courtesy of private collection, Milan, Italy*

Three watches circa 1930. The chrome watch has a black and white enamel design and a chrome mesh adjustable strap. The green Bakelite watch is mounted on a lapel clip. The sterling and marcasite watch has French hallmarks. *Courtesy of the author. Photo by Robert Weldon*

Bakelite lapel watch/clips, and marcasite or geometric enamel faces on silver or chrome watches kept time for the new professional woman. Cocktail rings with flashy faux stones, and articulated strass bracelets imitated Cartier designs. Clips adorned one side of an asymmetrical neckline, or both coat lapels. Pendants took the place of sautoirs, and pins which could not be worn on the fragile bias-cut Vionnet dresses, were worn on hats instead. Men's cufflinks were Deco enamel motifs on silver or brass, and women wore chrome-plated bowties (with or without glass beads) with borrowed men's shirts and cuff links, and tailored slacks.

Wide aluminum cuffs, either in sections or hinged, were enamelled red and white or black or white in geometric designs with a buckle closing. Chrome-plated bracelets, pierced or with matt and shiny contrasts and faux stones, or enamel striped had an industrial chic. Chunky Bakelite spheres and cylinders with chrome balls were strung on metal chains, and chrome and Bakelite pendants hung on slinky snake chains, or chrome and Bakelite cylinder chains. Pendant earrings were made of segments of chrome and Bakelite disks, and Bonaz produced Galalith clips to hold the waves in the "marcelled" hair. Bakelite belt buckles depicted winter sports for the newly fashionable Alpine vacations.

Two enamelled aluminum cuffs ca. 1930. The red and cream enamelled sections of the cuff on the left are mounted on elastic cord. The black and cream scalloped French cuff is hinged and has a chrome buckle. *Courtesy of the author. Photo by Robert Weldon*

Collection of geometric enamelled brass cufflinks, and a lady bug red and black enamelled brass tie clip. The chrome bowtie is decorated with clusters of green glass beads. Thirties. *Courtesy of private collection, Los Angeles*

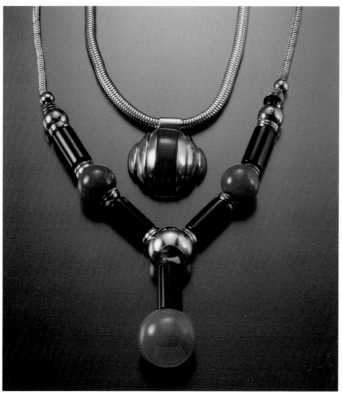

Two Bakelite and chrome necklaces, influenced by the machine aesthetic of Jean Desprès. The black and "amber" Bakelite pieces are mounted with chrome balls on a chrome chain, attached to a chrome snake chain. The crimson Bakelite and chrome pendant is hung on a heavy chrome gaspipe chain. Thirties. *Courtesy of the author. Photo by Robert Weldon*

Two Moderne chrome-plated hinged cuffs set with strass and faux sapphire and coral stones. The third bracelet has different colored striped enamel in the grooves all around the rigid bangle. *Courtesy of the author. Photo by Robert Weldon*

Two chrome and Bakelite pendants on matching chrome and Bakelite cylinder chains: the black pendant with green and white cylinders was a non-precious version of a Fouquet piece, 1927; and the red Bakelite cherry with translucent Bakelite and chrome leaves was a popular Deco motif. *Courtesy of the author. Photo by Robert Weldon*

Chrome and red Bakelite alternating sections are mounted on metal mesh chain. Signed "Paris 820" *Fabrication Française*, (French made.) The brooch is layered green and black carved Bakelite with brass. 1930. *Courtesy of the author. Photo by Robert Weldon*

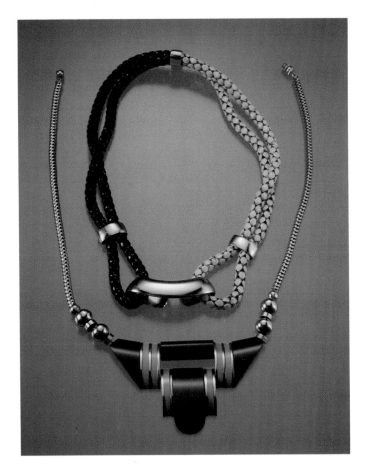

Carved green, orange, and white Bakelite belt buckle with toboggan sportsman, 1930. *Courtesy of the author. Photo by Robert Weldon*

Two Thirties necklaces: light and dark blue Bakelite sections mounted on a chrome-plated snake chain with chrome balls; and black and cream enamelled mesh chains with chrome-plated elements and an illegible maker's mark in a triangle. *Courtesy of the author. Photo by Robert Weldon*

Three hardstone pieces in Art Deco settings: Chrysoprase oval in a chrome brooch marked "EDY"; a malachite cabochon ring set in 18 kt gold, (marked 750 and maker's mark KM); and blue chalcedony mounted in a stepped silver ring with maker's mark in a lozenge, and boar's head silver mark. *Courtesy of the author. Photo by Robert Weldon*

Three chrome and Bakelite pieces: Chrome-plated brooch with black Bakelite; chrome pendant with amazonite green and black Bakelite on a chrome snake chain, and a necklace of five chrome sections, one with red Bakelite on a chrome chain. *Courtesy of Tiany Chambard Collection, Paris, France. Photo by Bruno Pierson*

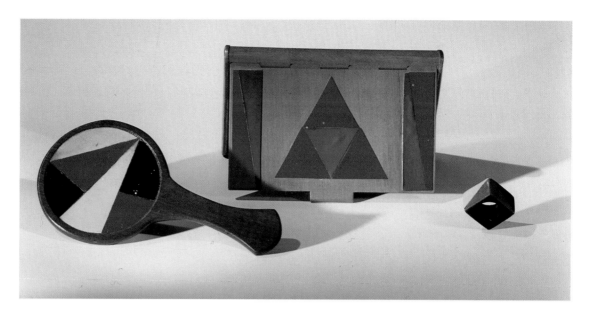

Three inlaid lacquered wood accessories by Vart, 1930, who worked for Poiret. The hand mirror and cigarette case were meant for the purse, and the square wood ring is inlaid in contrasting colors on all four sides. *Courtesy of the author. Photo by Robert Weldon*

Seven pairs of earrings made up of vintage parts: The red Galalith with silver and marcasites earrings are vintage; the black and clear glass pair, and the faux carved jade are vintage French pieces mounted with silver and marcasite tops in the 1980s, and signed "JC" (Jorge Cohen) with Dutch sword hallmark. The four geometric earrings with old Bakelite and new chrome elements have sterling vintage pierced ear wires. The vintage flapper with the embroidered felt hat is sporting Twenties amethyst glass earrings. *Courtesy of the author. Photo by Robert Weldon*

Vart of Paris, who had worked for Paul Poiret, designed precious wood cigarette cases, hand mirrors, necklaces, buckles, and rings inlaid with lacquered wood in abstract designs. The Paris Bureau of *Women's Wear Daily*, August, 1929, photographed Vart's "Modern Art Jewelry" made of ebony and a "composition simulating crystal," as well as buckles of layered precious wood.

The term "Retro" was coined by an auction house appraiser to define a particular style of Forties fine jewelry. This is misleading, because in French, *rétro* is short for *rétrograde*, or looking back to the past, and can denote a revival style of any period. It can also mean "old hat", *démodé*. The Forties-style jewelry was actually created in the mid-to-late Thirties in Paris, and evolved in two different directions: Volutes, like frozen folds of gold; and Utility Modern which wittily turned utilitarian gears and humble mechanical devices into chunky gold jewelry for the privileged few who would not have known what to do with a REAL goose-neck gas pipe, kitchen sieve, or bicycle chain.

The two dimensional geometric surfaces of the Twenties were supplanted by a structural 3-D softer look after 1935. Gold replaced platinum as the precious metal of choice. French sensuousness was now expressed in volume with forms like surging surf; folds, bows, and volutes seemed like fabric dipped in gold. (American costume jewelers designed their own interpretations.) Investment casting and the use of rubber moulds were the new production techniques which contributed to the burgeoning volumes.

Cartier carved or cut crystal not in Art Deco geometrics, but in soft swirls, so costume jewelers carved Bakelite (by machine or by hand) or superimposed figural motifs in layers. Blackamoors with jeweled turbans had faces of carved onyx or black enamel. What had been lacquer or baked enamel accents in the Twenties became cold-painted enamel in the Thirties and Forties.

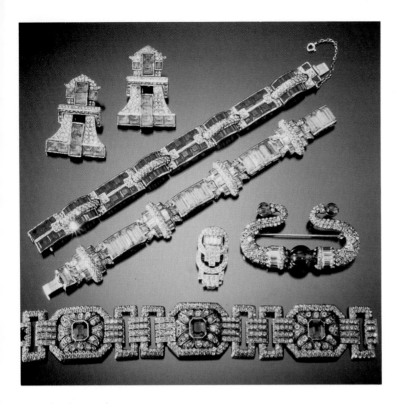

Both fine and costume jewelers were singing "Hooray for Hollywood", as American film stars dressed in Paris labels, with French bijoux to match. When Garbo, Crawford, Dietrich, and Lombard played love scenes wearing multiple strass bangles, or dramatic volute brooches, their fans all over the world rushed out to buy copies to imitate their idols. Offscreen, the stars wore Van Cleef & Arpel, but rhinestones sparkled plenty under studio lights. Cocktail rings with flashy faux stones, and articulated strass bracelets imitated Cartier designs. Clips adorned square necklines or both jacket lapels.

Rings could be worn on any finger. A Frenchman could predict his chances with a woman if he knew the "Ring Code." If the ring is worn on the index finger it means: "I'm available for commitment." On the middle finger: "Too late, I'm in love!" On the ring finger: "I'm taken, or married," and if it's a pinky ring: "Don't insist, I'm a dedicated celibate."

Faux citrine and strass clips and narrow matching bracelet, citrine and ruby with strass, and a wide well-made "emerald" and strass bracelet. Thirties cocktail glamour. *Courtesy of Diane Keith Collection, Beverly Hills, CA.* and a silver *pavé* strass clip, waterfall motif, marked "935", and Cartier-style "doorknocker" silver brooch with melon-cut "emeralds" and crystal, marked "Made in France". Late Twenties. *Courtesy of the author. Photo by Robert Weldon*

Eight cocktail rings to be worn on every finger. The articulated wooden hand on the left displays two bow rings, one silver, one gold with "rubies", and a silver Deco ring with "aquamarine" crystals and a strass silver ring. All with French maker's mark in a lozenge and boar's head (facing left) silver mark. Shown on the wood glove stretcher on the right are two silver rings with faux rubies, sapphires and diamonds, and two gold rings, one with a "ruby" and the other set with real rose diamonds. Bearing French hallmarks. *Courtesy of the author. Photo by Robert Weldon*

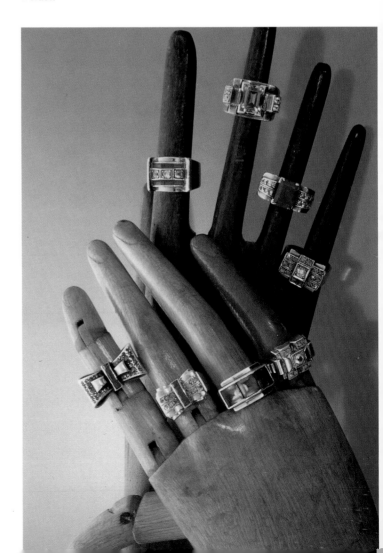

Pochoir print by Paul Iribe of a *garçonne* decked out in several rows of pearls and glitzy Deco bangles from wrist to elbow, and rings on every finger. From *Rouge et Blanc* deluxe wine merchant Nicolas album, 1930. *Print courtesy of the author. Photo by Robert Weldon*

The Forties

Gas pipes, tank tracks, bicycle chains, rat's tails, bed springs, sieves, escalators, gears, and ball bearings - how romantic! Were these motifs designed by plumbers and industrial engineers, or jewelers? They were created by Cartier and Van Cleef & Arpels in 1935 and 1937, but were popular into the late Forties. Costume jewelers picked up the same themes in chrome, or gold plate. (French émigrés Marcel Boucher and Alfred Philippe for Trifari, both of whom had been apprentice designers for Cartier, made volutes and gaspipes chic in America.) Cartier's 1935 *tuyau à gaz* was a flexible solution for the modern Tailored Woman. It could be worn as a simple expandable choker or bracelet, or hung with a pendant or jewelled sections.[11] Since gaspipes were originally made of chrome, it was no big leap for costume jewelers to put it to a second practical use. The rat's tail (called *queue de rat* in France, and *coda di topo*, mouse tail, in Italy) or snake chain was a slender, supple version of the gaspipe.

Other mechanical innovations like tank tracks, "moving staircases", bicycle chains, and gears, were adapted by designers for articulated bracelets, gold or chrome-plated. The kitchen sieve was the inspiration for gold mesh jewelry which was light to wear, and could be very fine mesh or pierced metal combining well with the gaspipe motif (another nod to Utility Modern.)

Utility Modern *tuyau à gaz*, or "gaspipe" necklace, rhodium-plated and slightly extendable, for the chic Tailored Woman. Forties. *Courtesy of the author. Photo by Robert Weldon*

Two gold-plated variations of the Utility Modern machine or tank track motifs, with French marks; and two "moving staircase" style bracelets, gold-plated brass with salmon and espresso Galalith accents. Marked "BF" with a feather, "Paris 725", and *déposé*. 1940. ("Paris 725" and "Paris 820" were trademarks seen in the Thirties and early Forties). *Courtesy of the author. Photo by Robert Weldon*

Reverse of Bakelite piece stamped with *"Fab-on Fse"*, short for *Fabrication Française*, (French-made), "Paris 725" trademark and *Déposé*, (registered).

Gold-plated corrugated heavy mesh bracelet with sculptural decoration of fine "sieve" mesh and stamped metal, alternating shiny and Florentine matt surfaces. Unsigned Utility Modern. (Hattie Carnegie and Schiaparelli pioneered mesh jewelry in the U.S. and Paris.) *Courtesy of private collection, Los Angeles. Photo by Sandro Moro*

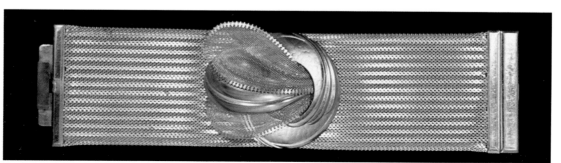

The Tailored Woman preferred her shapes dramatic enough to obviate the use of stones for daytime wear. A bold statement was made without glitz. This was only partly due to post-war necesssity. In the Forties, European women had worked for the war effort from 1939 to 1945, riding bicycles to save gas, or driving ambulances. Practical saddle bags on straps were slung over square padded shoulders by bicyclists, and turbans and snoods were worn to keep the hair neat. The only fashion item that was not controlled by the German Occupation was the *chapeau*, so wonderfully whimsical hats were worn by impertinent Parisiennes, thumbing their noses at the Nazis. If jewelry was worn at all, it had to be simple.

The return to post-war economy found women gainfully employed, (if they had not been collaborators) and sober suits were worn to the office until Christian Dior heralded a return to femininity with his revolutionary "New Look" in 1947. The audacious brooches that had made such a statement at pre-war cocktail parties bowed to the *Femmes* Fifties, only to be enthusiastically revived as Power Jewelry by executive women in the boardrooms of the Eighties.

In 1945, there was a fashion show at the Musée des Arts Décoratifs, where Jacques Fath, Balenciaga, Lelong, and Givenchy contributed short, full skirts, and bateau necklines to the carnival post-war atmosphere. Reconstruction began, politically and artistically speaking. Gold jewelry, which had been hoarded as an "under the mattress" war-time investment, was melted down or remodelled. Bracelets and watches were worn over the gloves, and bird brooches flew on every lapel, a symbol of freedom at last! (During the Occupation, Jeanne Toussaint of Cartier, was interrogated by the Germans for having dared to sell a brooch featuring a nightingale (mute) in a gilded cage. She convinced them that it was not a political statement. After the Liberation, however, a new Cartier brooch designed by Peter Lemarchand showed the cage door open, and the bird joyfully singing.[12])

Other figurals were endless variations of the Big Cats. Leopard, tiger, and zebra skin rugs decorated Hollywood sets, turning wild game hunters into sex symbols, (fuelled by Ernest Hemingway's safari exploits). African wildlife never recovered. The ladies were all panting for panthers, from the Duchess of Windsor, who got them in gold, to the typists who made do with gilded brass. Domesticated animals were popular, and the flamingo, pink in Hollywood and Africa, turned up in diamonds, rubies, and emeralds on the Duchess of Windsor's elegant lapel.

Cocktail rings were enormously popular, in high relief, like the pins of the period. There was a wide variety of designs to choose from: the open book, bow, turban, or bridge motifs were available on the Place Vendôme (sometimes with synthetic rubies) and in department stores with faux stones. The geometric linear look was gone, sumptuous curves abounded.

Pearled and embroidered handbags were frameless and supple for evening. Daytime *pochettes*, or envelope bags over a foot long of leather or crocodile were tucked under the arm by the new career women.

Post-war France, searching for new manufacturing possibilities for plastics, hit on the idea of fantasy frames for eyeglasses. Oyonnax was the natural location for what became a thriving export business in the Forties through the Sixties. Spectacular spectacles became jewelry for the eyes, the tamer versions worn in France by vacationers on the Riviera, while the more outrageous designs were flaunted by Hollywood starlets, Las Vegas showgirls, and Miami Beach matrons. There was a cross-over from sunglasses to prescription glasses, and no frame idea was too fantastic for either.

To see or to be seen? That was the question, and the answer was: both! Visual aids had come a long way since Confucius described the piece of polished quartz that brought sweet and sour pork into focus for the myopic Chinese in 500 B.C. With the invention of the printing press, reading glasses became a mark of respect and proof of literacy, so in 13th century Italy, metal or horn frames were tied to one's head or hat. In the 18th century in England, the temples were invented to support the frames over the ears, and in the 19th century tinted glass was the forerunner of sunglasses.

Red crocodile handbag, (13" long) alternating the large and small scales of the skin, with a chrome and red Bakelite clasp. 1940. *Courtesy of the author. Photo by Robert Weldon*

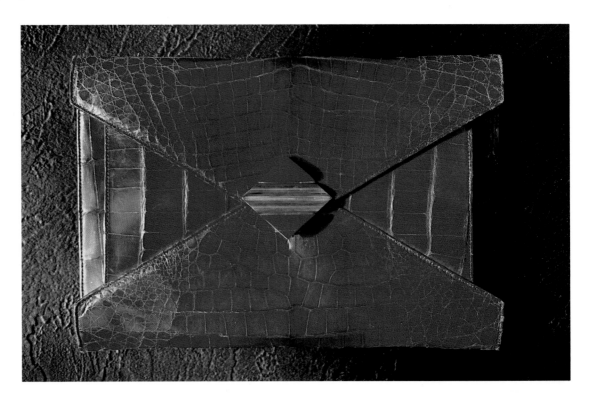

20th century frame designers took advantage of lightweight Celluloid to create crazy confections five inches high studded with rhinestones, or laminated with fabric. Forties and Fifties frames were hand-crafted until the cheaper injection-moulding process was adopted, simulating hand-carving for mass-production. The factories in Oyonnax had evolved in 60 years from manufacturing horn combs to Celluloid hair ornaments and jewelry, then Celluloid jewelled eyeglass frames. These continued to be produced into the Fifties and Sixties, when they were Op Pop Art worn by Rock Stars on and off the concert stage. (Elton John changed glasses several times during a concert, and amassed over 200 different pairs of Celluloid jewelry for the eyes.) The l.a. Eyeworks Collection of Gai Gherardi and Barbara McReynolds in Los Angeles, CA. has the largest collection in the world of these extraordinary glasses which has been shown in museum settings as Optical Art.[13]

Gold-plated cast Volute fur clip with pavé strass accenting the curves designed by French émigré Boucher for Marcel Boucher & Cie in America, ca. 1944. This was one of the two transplanted Cartier styles which flourished Stateside in the late Thirties and Forties. (Boucher had been a Cartier apprentice.) Stamped early "MB" trademark. *Courtesy of the author. Photo by Sandro Moro*

"Kandinsky" artistic frames designed by the French for the Bohemians in Miami Beach. Fifties. *Courtesy of the l.a. Eyeworks Collection. Photo by Tim Street-Porter*

"Serpents and Cats' Eyes" glasses scream " Look at me!" Made in Oyonnax for Hollywood stars, Fifties. *Courtesy of l.a. Eyeworks. Photo by Tim Street-Porter*

France where Faux was born

Bijoux de couture are the most outstanding examples of fashion jewelry in France. The price of producing these magnificent parures is high, as the maximum effect is desired and happily paid for by the elite clientele. The couturier creates twice-yearly collections of models which are made-to-order, to measure, in the couture house's atelier. Jewelry and accessories are an important part of the "look" which is conceived each season, and lengthy consultations with jewelery designers are as important as a choice of fabric or a hat. Both couture, and boutique jewelry (for ready-to-wear clothes, and pattern copies sold to American buyers) are commissioned. The high cost of the original couture prototypes and research spent in developing the multiple variations on a theme of which only a dozen may actually grace the runway each season, is recuperated by the cheaper versions mass-produced for *prêt-à-porter* world-wide. (Perfume sales are an even more important source of revenue, keeping many an haute couture house afloat on the fickle seas of fashion.)

Among the French supplier/manufacturers who executed or conceived these stunning designs through this century are: Maison Gripoix, Louis Rousselet, Francis Winter, and Rose and Joseph Woloch of the supplier/manufacturers. Among the designers who worked closely with the haute couturiers on jewelry were: Robert Goossens; Roger Scemema; Jean Clément; Roger Jean-Pierre; Maison Lesage; Countess "Cis" Zoltowska, Jeanne Péral, Maryse Blanchard, and William de Lillo.

In the heart of the jewelry district on the rue Turbigo, Augustine Gripoix founded la Maison Gripoix in the 1890s. The first of 4 generations, her house specialities were glass buttons and beads in faux copies of real jewelry. Sarah Bernhardt, when she wasn't smothered in Lalique, chose Gripoix to make her shine on stage and off. Madame Gripoix decorated Poiret's tassels before and after the first World War.

Elegant necklace of lattice-work crystal stones with faux pearl drops. Made by Madame Gripoix for Chanel, Twenties. *Courtesy of Jill Spalding Collection. Photo by Richard Marx*

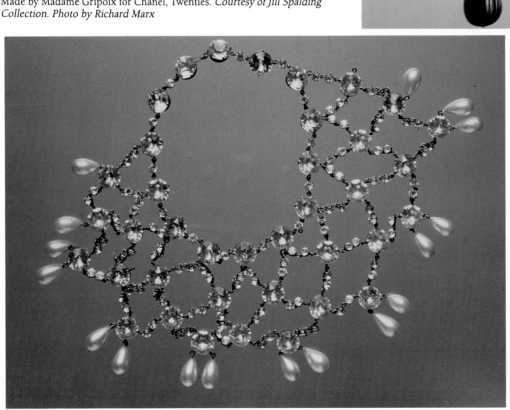

Rows of emerald glass beads with four rectangular elements set with strass and melon-cut "emerald" beads and a drop pendant. Made by Madame Susanne Gripoix for Chanel, Twenties. *Courtesy of Jill Spalding Collection, New York, NY. Photo by Richard Marx*

When Suzanne Gripoix (1895-) was the directrice in the mid-Twenties, her friend, Coco Chanel, asked her to copy some of her elaborate personal jewelry to tempt her clients. These were such a success that a long 40 year collaboration began, using the famous *pâte de verre* pieces and *nacrés* glass pearls (produced in the south of France,) which graced innumerable sautoirs, buttons, and brooches. Daughter Josette was responsible for the jewelry production for Fifties clients Dior, Givenchy, and Balenciaga. Thierry, her son, confers with contemporary designers Isabel Canovas and Pierre Cardin.

Cream-colored pearls with pale "citrines" and "emeralds" with a domed centerpiece and floral drops. Made by Madame Gripoix for Chanel, ca. 1930. *Courtesy of Jill Spalding Collection. Photo by Richard Marx*

Twisted ropes of "emerald" beads with strass spacers, and a knot of "rubies" and pearls with an "emerald" tassel. Made for Chanel when she reopened her House in 1954 by Madame Gripoix. The four fabulous necklaces above were unsigned runway couture pieces which were bought by the owner's mother from Madame Gripoix. *Courtesy of Jill Spalding Collection. Photo by Richard Marx*

Three rows of "ruby" beads with seven large "emerald" drops and gold filigree in a Moghul style necklace. Probably by Maison Gripoix, Fifties. *Courtesy of Rita Sacks Collection, New York. Photo by Robert Weldon*

Production of all the pieces is still carried out in the Maison Gripoix. There are separate ateliers for creating the lampwork beads, for filling the copper *cloisons* with poured glass in a *plique-à-jour* process, for bead stringing, cutting, soldering, and gold-plating of the copper elements, and for mounting the final costume jewelry crosses and bouquets to be worn by a discerning clientele.

Jean Clément (1900-1949) held a degree in chemistry from the University of Paris, as well as an art degree from L'Ecole des Beaux Arts. He was to use both of these when he created plastic jewelry for Schiaparelli, who discovered him in 1927. He also designed her handbags, belts, and buttons, remaining faithful to Schiap (despite tempting offers from Balenciaga and others) until he died in 1949.

Red poured glass and strass ovals with pearl drops made by Maison Gripoix for Maggy Rouff, 1959. *Courtesy of Jill Spalding Collection, New York. Photo by Richard Marx*

Ruby-red *pâte de verre* poured glass in a *plique à jour* technique with gold Venetian lampwork beads set with tiny strass rubies. Maison Gripoix, Fifties. Stamped "Made in France". *Courtesy of the author. Photo by Robert Weldon*

Necklace of pale blue lilies of the valley glass beads strung with pearls and jet bugle beads. This is the favorite flower of the House of Dior, for which Gripoix created appropriate pieces. Unsigned. *Courtesy of Kerry Holden Collection, Santa Monica, CA. Photo by Robert Weldon*

Roger Jean-Pierre (1910-), executed designs for Schiaparelli from 1934-39 when he was director of Roger Modèle, the accessories firm which produced the belts, bags, and buttons for the haute couturiers. Working with Jean Clément, Jean-Pierre claims: "I was a 'mechanic' for the 'locomotive' that produced the fashion accessories at the rue des Gravilliers shop." After the war there was a brief stint as a restaurateur at a Russian restaurant in Montparnasse. From 1947-'58, he was director of the Maison Francis Winter, where he collaborated on jewelry and accessories for Dior, Balenciaga, Grès, Balmain, and Lelong. Sixty craftsmen produced 2500 models a year on the rue du Temple. As was the custom with the best jewelry designers, prototypes were first shown to the haute couturiers who claimed exclusive rights, (these were not signed either Winter or Jean-Pierre.) The rest were sold to smaller couturiers and department stores in Paris and abroad.[14] "At first I was accorded 10% commission on all sales, but when that was reduced to 9% then 7%, I quit and founded my own atelier in 1960 at 11 Place des Vosges in a 17th century environment."

Roger Jean-Pierre's necklaces and brooches were exquisitely fashioned, (inspired by 18th century design and Edwardian workmanship), delicate and lacy with prong-set strass and faux fresh water pearls. Garlands of crystals were hung with graduated drops *en pampille*. Butterflies, buttercups, and florettes of clear or champagne strass encircled the neck in feminine, quintessentially French designs.

His revolutionary elaborate bibs were 4" deep with hand-forged links capping the shoulder. Dubbed Bertha collars (after the 19th century wide lace collars,) these fishnet capes were mesh masterpieces in textured gold and black enamel or encrusted with crystals and featured in *Woman's Wear Daily* in 1960. These were copied by Saks Fifth Avenue and sold for $50. "I showed Balenciaga one collar which was 9" deep, and he said it was the most beautiful necklace he'd ever seen, but he would never buy it. Why not? I wanted to know. Because no one would look at my dress!" was Balenciaga's answer. Later, when I received the Neiman Marcus "Oscar of Fashion Award" (1962), I thanked Schiaparelli for having launched my career. She replied that if she had not been so merciless I would never have won it, but that she almost felt that she had won it a second time through me. I learned a great deal working with these demanding couturiers."

BIJOUX
ROGER JEAN-PIERRE
11 PLACE DES VOSGES
PARIS 4e

*Pierres taillées du Tyrol
Azalée, Cristal et Orchidée
de*
D. Swarovski & C°

Advertisement for Bijoux Roger Jean-Pierre showing two garland necklaces and a brooch with graduated drops (*en pampilles*) in the 18th century style. The Tyrolian-cut stones by Swarovski are named after Azaleas and Orchids. *Courtesy of Roger Jean-Pierre, Paris. Photo by Bruno Pierson.*

ROGER JEAN-PIERRE
MADE IN FRANCE

Paper label of "ROGER JEAN-PIERRE Made in France" which was found on his jewelry made for export. *Courtesy of Roger Jean-Pierre. Photo by Sandro Moro.*

Spray of strass and faux rubies around a glass cabochon make this a distinctive brooch by Roger Jean-Pierre. Ca. Fifties. *Courtesy of Robin Feldman Collectibles, New York, NY. Photo by Robert Weldon*

Jean-Pierre always constructed the prototypes of his jewelry. His Spanish assistant, Olga Rabaneda, copied these originals. Olga's brother, Paco, was studying at the Beaux Arts at the time. "He changed his name to Paco Rabanne, and, inspired by the mesh jewelry he'd seen Olga work on for me, came up with the idea of chain-mail dresses, hanging metal plaques on rings." And the rest is fashion history.

Acting as technical advisor to Dior (until his death), and Manfred Swarovski (1958-73), Roger Jean-Pierre helped with the launching of Aurora Borealis and black *irisé* (iridescent) stones. He was also advisor to Coro in New York for five years, when Vendôme was a subsidiary. (Not to be confused with the Maison Vendôme, which was based in Paris.) His creations were hand-made, not mass-produced. The paper label bearing his "ROGER JEAN-PIERRE MADE IN FRANCE" trademark was found on the pieces sold at Saks Fifth Avenue, Bergdorf Goodman, Neiman Marcus, and Marshall Field in the States, and at Fortnum and Mason in London. In 1976, he lost both his first wife and step-son. "I didn't have the head for designing jewelry any more, and I was 65 years old, so I closed my atelier." Roger Jean-Pierre remarried, and recently celebrated his 84th birthday in fine fettle.

Delicate pastel rhinestone butterflies flutter around the neck as designed by Roger Jean-Pierre in the Sixties. *Courtesy of Roger Jean-Pierre, Paris. Photo by Bruno Pierson.*

Golden buttercups with pearl drops punctuate a blue/green strass collar hand-mounted by Roger Jean-Pierre. Sixties. *Courtesy of Roger Jean-Pierre. Photo by Bruno Pierson.*

Robert Goossens, (1927-) is the son of a foundry-worker who trained with the goldsmith, Monsieur Degorce (Chanel's jeweler in the Thirties.) By 1954 Goossens had his own atelier, and was recommended by the retired Degorce to Chanel, who at 70 had recently made her big comeback. Their collaboration was to last 17 years.

I only did what Mademoiselle wanted. I did not create, I interpreted. She gave me a Russian book on 13th century Georgian enamels, *Les Emaux de Géorgie* as an exchange of references between us. She was besotted with the Byzantine and barbarian. She showed me a gold cross, so I made it in gilded metal with *pâte de verre* stones instead of enamel. She brought me a belt buckle, and I repeated the elements and made a kind of cross interrupted by ruby glass beads. From 1954 to '60s I made bar pins, bracelets, and barrettes of twisted gold with simulated pearls. I contributed my expertise, and "Mademoiselle" brought her taste and preference to the creations. She was very demanding, but it was an exciting challenge.

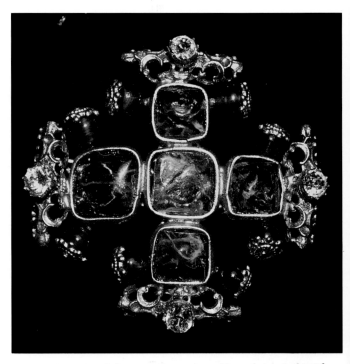

Cross brooch with five *pâte de verre* emeralds, and eight "rubies" for Chanel by Robert Goossens, 1964. *Courtesy of Robert Goossens*

She was, indeed. *"J'ai horreur des amateurs!"* was a frequent statement which kept all her collaborators on their toes. Her credo was that jewelry was not created to make one look rich, but to adorn. "A faux bijou, well-made, can demolish a real one, but it has to be more real than the real, and that is very difficult," Chanel was fond of saying. Goossens adapted many designs based on lions' heads. (Coco was a Leo.) The ancient Persian lionesses stuck out their tongues, so he made a necklace of these heads for her with bright red *pâte de verre* as well as a table ornament with 3 lions supporting an immense crystal ball, which rests on a table in his studio in the Marais.

"When I interpret the ancient civilizations, I take the Scythian, Byzantine, Persian, Celt, Egyptian, and Etruscan techniques and I mix and obtain my own style. The result of this work became the style of Mlle. Chanel after the war", Goossens declares. His Scythian barbarian bracelet of rough gilded metal and multi-colored cabochons looks like an antique relic from a Middle Eastern dig. For a green *pâte de verre* brooch with a faux pearl center, he used an Egyptian technique. Pearl and gold Byzantine crosses in the Fifties were supplanted in the Sixties by crosses made of four terminated rock crystals wrapped together with gold.

"I created jewelry for Mlle. Chanel from 1954 to 1971, executing most of the prototypes in gold and semi-precious stones, and making 10 or 12 copies in gilded bronze," Goossens explains. "Most of the Chanel pieces that come up at auction are the bronze copies."

Robert Goossens also worked for Balenciaga (between 1958 to 1960) but that was a different assignment. "Chanel thought of the jewel first, then the dress. Balenciaga was the opposite; he thought of the dress first, especially with his rigorous cuts. Jewelry played a secondary role, and he wanted it to look real. He often copied the Boucheron or Cartier pieces of his clients." Goossens created pearl necklaces, brooches and a "coat of mail" gold mesh piece edged in strass, and a gold-plated cuff bracelet simulating sharkskin. For his own Goosens Boutique, Av. George V, he used real sharkskin.

For Dior, Goossens made a retro bracelet with red stones, and for Yves Saint Laurent in the '80s a large fan-shaped pin of peacock greens and blues, and red enamelled heart-shaped earrings.

"I'm inspired by Etruscan, Renaisssance, and Baroque motifs and adapt them to modern use. I respect the ancients, and knowing what they did, I do something else." When Goossens began with Chanel, he had 10 workers. Today there are 50 in his factory in La Plaine St. Denis, north of Paris. His son, Patrick, works with him. *"Ma passion, c'est le bijou!,"* he proclaims. Jewelry is his life.

Spanish cross with "ruby" cabochon and faceted jet stones by Robert Goossens for Balenciaga, 1960. *Courtesy of Robert Goossens*

Poster for the Boutique Goossens pictures jewelry by Robert Goossens: On the model's right arm is a chain necklace (Boutique Goossens); an eagle cuff for Chanel (1966); Goossens cuff; and an aqua and blue glass fan for Y.S.L. On her head is a chain mail collar and a brooch for Balenciaga (1962); and earrings, Boutique Goossens. On her left arm is a galuchat (real sharkskin) cuff, and a faux sharkskin gilded brass cuff, a red strass bracelet, chain bracelet, strass and epoxy bracelet, and a gold bracelet; all for the Boutique Goossens. Around her neck are: pearl necklaces for Chanel and Balenciaga, ca. 1960; two lion necklaces for Chanel (one with red enamel), 1966 and 1967; and more pearl necklaces for Chanel and Balenciaga, 1960. *Courtesy of Robert Goossens, Paris.*

Necklace of pastel stones all different cuts, by Robert Goossens for Yves Saint Laurent, Spring 1980. *Courtesy of Robert Goossens*

Cross and earrings of terminated rock crystals mounted with gold-plated brass leaves by Robert Goossens, 80's. *Courtesy of Robert Goossens*

Golden leaves and berries with four rough-cut chunks of rock crystal by Robert Goossens for Yves Saint Laurent, 1989. *Courtesy of Robert Goossens*

Roger Scemama (1898-1989) (pronounced Shaymama) was from a distinguished Florentine family (his grandfather was the surgeon to King Victor Emanuel of Italy.) He created jewelry for the greats of French Couture for 50 years, starting with Schiaparelli in the Thirties, Jacques Fath in the Forties and Dior, Lanvin-Castillo, Balenciaga, and Givenchy in the Fifties. He worked with Jean Dessès, Cerruti, and Yves Saint Laurent in the Sixties. His pieces are often stamped "Made in France," or with the couturier's signature, and occasionally with a black paper label bearing his name and "Paris, France" in gold. Collectors often attribute the "Made In France" label to Chanel pieces, but Scemama, Roger Jean-Pierre, and Louis Rousselet also used that stamp.

Roger began his career by selling buttons from door to door. His style changed from enamelled gilt flower clips in 1930 to elaborate rhinestone and pearl earrings for Jacques Fath in 1949. (He was a prisoner of war until 1945, and upon his release enthusiastically returned to jewelry design.) Scemama was fond of red glass beads, mixing them with black or clear rhinestones. For Givenchy, he made girandole brooches with 3 baroque pendant pearls and rhinestones. A magnificent citrine and topaz glass flower necklace was commissioned by Yves Saint Laurent. In the Sixties, for Saint Laurent, he encrusted a black resin pendant with red strass, or set two large blue and red stones with pearls for a pin. Red strass pops up again with pearls for another pendant. Other pendants for Saint Laurent were of corded gold wire flowers with red glass pendants or brown and green stones. Earrings repeated the flower motif, or were inverted crescents with black stones. Rhodoid plastic hair combs in primary colors were worn with a belt of red wooden beads in 1970 for Saint Laurent. Scemama switched to grey metal pendants with red or black resin and fringes for the late Sixties, and an Indian head for Cerruti. After fifty years of supplying hundreds of couture collections with costume jewelry, Roger Scemama died at the age of 91.

Five strass and ruby glass brooches with pearl pendants by Roger Scemama. The *girandole* piece, lower left and upper right ruby and baroque pearls were for Givenchy, 1954. *Courtesy of the author and Tiany Chambard Collection, Paris, France. Photo by Bruno Pierson*

Gilded brass flower bouquet brooch with red and black enamel by Roger Scemama, 1930. *Courtesy of the Scemama estate, Paris. Photo by Bruno Pierson*

Earrings of strass pendants, and one of a pair with strass and pearls by Roger Scemama for Jacques Fath, 1949-50. *Courtesy of Monique Vittaut Collection, Pontoise, France. Photo by Bruno Pierson*

Black paper label for Roger Scemama, occasionally found on later pieces. *Photo by Sandro Moro*

Black resin encrusted with red strass pendant on red strass and pearl chain by Roger Scemama for Yves Saint Laurent. Signed YSL, 1960's. Brooch with large faux ruby and sapphire stones with pearl pendant by Scemama for YSL, 1962. Ruby strass and pearls pendant set in a black metal on a black metal chain by Scemama, Sixties, unsigned. *Courtesy of Monique Vittaut Collection. Photo by Bruno Pierson*

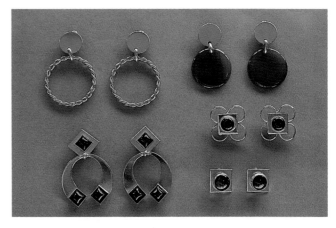

Five pairs of earrings by Roger Scemama, 1960's. *Courtesy of Monique Vittaut, Tiany Chambard, and the author's collections. Photo by Bruno Pierson*

Sparkling collar of light and dark ruby red beads by Roger Scemama, 1965. *Courtesy of Monique Vittaut Collection. Photo by Bruno Pierson*

Three pendants using *pâte de verre* stones and simulated Thirties pressed glass by Roger Scemama, 1965. *Courtesy of Tiany Chambard and Monique Vittaut Collections. Photo by Bruno Pierson*

Four grey metal pendants on chains from the Sixties by Roger Scemama. The "Mayan" head on the left was made for Cerruti.
All of the above Scemama pieces came from his estate, and are not signed. *Courtesy of Monique Vittaut Collection. Photo by Bruno Pierson*

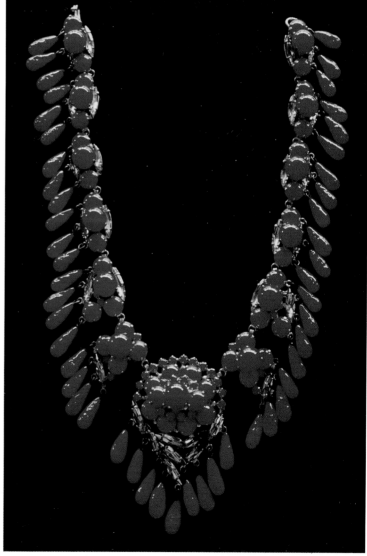

Faux red coral bead necklace with rhinestone navettes by Roger Scemama, 1955. *Courtesy of Monique Vittaut Collection. Photo by Bruno Pierson*

Louis Rousselet (1892-1980) was born in Paris and apprenticed at the tender age of eight to M. Rousseau to master the technique of lamp-work beads. "Before World War I, it was common practice to apprentice young children to a trade. Families needed as many working members as possible," reports Denise Rousselet, Louis' daughter. In 1922, in Menilmontant, Louis began manufacturing glass and Galalith beads as well as imitation pearls (glass beads coated on the outside with *essence d'Orient*, a fish scale compound). Very soon his firm was a major source of handmade beads worldwide, employing nearly 800 workers over the years. A favorite Art Deco item was the Galalith bead, a casein plastic made from a sour milk protein derivative mixed with formaldehyde. Invented in 1897 by Adolph Spitteler, Galalith beads were light and easy to wear in multiple rows. Rousselet produced barrel-shaped or cylindrical beads in a stepped geometric design; fusing royal blue and ivory, or black and ivory together for original results. For spacers he used blue, beige or black stepped cubes. These Galalith beads also came in jade green and black, or a light and dark blue combination which were mounted with brass cylinders. In 1935 these were discontinued, as Bakelite beads with a wider color range became the popular choice. President of the Chambre Syndicale de Fabricants de Perles de Fantaisie (Union of Faux Pearls Manufacturers) Louis Rousselet produced a vast amount of pearls, until the late Sixties when production ceased. His glass beads were manufactured until 1975, and findings for the large stock that remains are still being made.

Unusual hand-made beads by Louis Rousselet, Thirties. The pale yellow beads with black "claws" are glass; the blue, white and beige, and speckled grey with white and black dots beads look like ceramic, but are special glasss beads by Rousselet. *Courtesy of Rita Sacks Collection, NY. Photo by Robert Weldon*

Five necklaces with Galalith beads of barrel, cylinder, or stepped cube shapes from the Twenties mixed with different cylindrical metal beads by Rousselet. *Courtesy of the author. Photo by Sandro Moro*

Galalith beads simulating lapis, ebony, and ivory in stepped or knot geometric designs by Louis Rousselet, 1930. Two are mounted with vintage Galalith pieces. *Courtesy of the author. Photo by Robert Weldon*

During the glory years of the Music Hall Twenties and Thirties, Rousselet bedecked many a bare breast with his pearls and beads; among them Mistinguett, Josephine Baker, and other stars of the Folies Bergère, Casino de Paris and Moulin Rouge. (Mme. Rousselet reports that: "Josephine's daytime jewelry was quite restrained to match her chic couturier clothes. On stage, though, ç'était la folie!") Across town, an altogether different clientele, chastely and expensively robed, purchased Rousselet's faux pearl sautoirs at the House of Chanel. In the Forties, just after the war, Rousselet made "pompom" pendants of metal mixed with enamel beads for Jacques Fath, and necklaces of voluted floral sections with faux pearls and ruby, emerald and amethyst glass beads for Robert Piguet, (100-150 of this model were made in 1948.) Then in 1952, for Balmain, a necklace of pearls and faux emerald beads, flat or pear-shaped was made in a series of 50, with the clasp signed "L.R." in script.

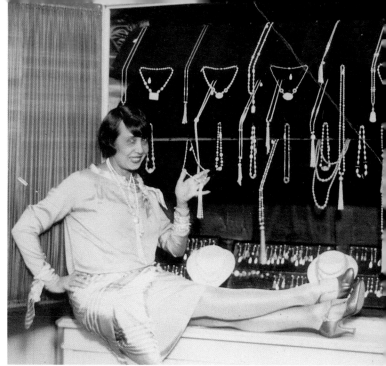

Black and white 1930 vintage photo of the famous Mistinguett wearing and promoting Louis Rousselet tassel sautoirs and earrings. *Courtesy of Louis Rousselet archives*

For Pierre Balmain, Rousselet made this necklace of two rows of pearls with pressed emerald glass beads and pearl drops in 1952. The clasp is stamped "Made in Paris" with the "LR" signature in script. *Courtesy of private collection, Milan, Italy*

Reverse of Balmain necklace clasp showing "LR" signature for Louis Rousselet. *Courtesy of private collection, Milan, Italy*

Le Moulin Rouge, "One of the Pearls of Paris" 1928 poster by Gesmar of Mistinguett, the reigning Music Hall artist who was eventually dethroned by Josephine Baker. Mistinguett, (who saved Gesmar's life and won his lifetime artistic commitment) is shown wearing the Moulin Rouge as a hat with a red jewelled windmill, (*moulin* means windmill). *Courtesy of the author. Photo by Robert Weldon*

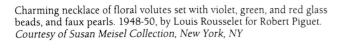

Pearl choker by Louis Rousselet for couturière Maggy Rouff, 1950. *Vintage photo Courtesy of Denise Rousselet archives*

Emerald green glass beads set in gilded brass flower petals with "emerald" drops and gilded chains by Louis Rousselet, 1948, for couturier Robert Piguet. Stamped "Made in France" on clasp. *Courtesy of author's collection*

Charming necklace of floral volutes set with violet, green, and red glass beads, and faux pearls. 1948-50, by Louis Rousselet for Robert Piguet. *Courtesy of Susan Meisel Collection, New York, NY*

Paper label for "Louis ROUSSELET, Modèle Déposé Made in France." *Photo by Robert Weldon*

Two pearl sautoirs by Rousselet designed for Chanel Boutique, 1948-52, restrung. The baroque pearl with strass has a large baroque pearl pendant; the grey and white pearl sautoir has a grey baroque pearl and white pearl tassel tipped with grey pearls. With paper label "Louis Rousselet Made in France". *Courtesy of the author. Photo by Robert Weldon*

Denise Rousselet designed occasional collections for her father from 1943 until 1965, when she took over the exclusive design duties. In 1960 she opened a tiny shop named Jeanne Danjou (her mother's name was Jeanne) on the Ile de la Cité where she sold Rousselet beads separately from trays and boxes piled in every corner. Rousselet beads were all hand-wound and polished. Madame Rousselet reports that it took six or seven years to train workers, an expensive procedure which came to an end when the last trained worker retired in 1975. There was a wide variety of colors and styles of beads: foiled; iridescent; or lamp-wound multicolored swirls were produced in the same way for fifty years.

Rousselet was able to keep his factory functioning through the depression and war years. His beads may be around as long as the Pont Neuf, (the oldest bridge in Paris, called the "new bridge" when it was built in the 17th century) which was at Jeanne Danjou's doorstep. Because his pieces were not always signed (the paper label "Louis Rousselet, Modèle Déposé, Made in France" was easily lost), a number of Rousselet necklaces and earrings have been misattributed to the Maison Gripoix for Chanel in recent publications.

Both Gripoix and Rousselet used double rows of pearls or glass beads, interspersed with separate bouquet elements of pearls and beads in a floral pattern. The designs are always intensely feminine and very French. The delicate necklace of pastel blue and pink beads is the essence of springtime in Paris; this was sold to French department stores as well as to Saks Fifth Ave. These pieces were tagged with the paper label marked "Louis Rousselet, Made in France."

Grey pearl earrings with white and grey pearl tassels, and floral earrings of ruby and emerald glass and pearls with emerald drops 40's designs remounted by Rousselet, marked France. *Courtesy of the author. Photo by Robert Weldon*

Pink, blue, and green pastel glass beads mounted in floral arrangements by Louis Rousselet for spring, 1952. These necklaces were sold to the French Galeries Lafayette, and Saks Fifth Ave. in New York. *Courtesy of Susan Meisel Collection, NY.*

Silver necklace with multicolored *pâte de verre* cabochons. Unsigned, probably French. *Courtesy of private collection, Milan, Italy*

Another baroque pearl and multicolored glass bead choker is of a simpler design, but in the same spirit, and was probably created by someone who appreciated the Gripoix/Rousselet talent for using these materials.

The Maison Lesage is responsible for raising the art of XXth century *bijoux de broderie* to the dazzlingly sumptuous sequin and bead embroidered adornments of 1980s haute couture. In 1900, individual pieces of embroidered jet, usually hung with tassels were sewn on the sleeve or corsage by one's family dressmaker. Albert Lesage (1888-1949) his wife Marie-Louise, and his son, François, (1929-) have collaborated with three generations of couturiers from Madeleine Vionnet to Christian Lacroix on embroidered fashion, accessories, and jewelry.

Albert's entirely sequined chemise dresses were exported to America for the Twenties flappers. After the 1929 crash, the demand was diminished, and an attempt to launch embroidered accessories and jewelry in 1932, was unsuccessful. Schiaparelli came to the rescue in 1934 with an embroidered belt by Lesage which revived the art, thus beginning a long creative relationship. The deep relief (*bourré* or stuffed) embroidery which Lesage created for Schiaparelli's celebrated collections of 1938-1939 are legendary. Their complicity was so close that a phone call of four words sufficed: "Lesage? Elsa Schiaparelli. Circus!" (or "Music!", or "Astrology!") and the magic began. Lesage made Schiap an Egyptian-style necklace in 1938 of embroidered openwork stitches with blown glass coral and jade beads.[15]

Romantic baroque "pearl" necklace with clusters of pastel glass beads and pearls, in the Gripoix/Rousselet style. Unknown maker. *Courtesy of Susan Meisel Collection, NY.*

Trompe l'oeil Murano glass necklaces with real Murano *millefiori* beads decorate an amazing handbag, with matching pendant earrings, cuffs, bandeau, fan and parasol all hand embroidered with beads and tassels. Imaginative accessories by Tremolet for Lesage, Summer, 1991. *Courtesy of Lesage & Cie*

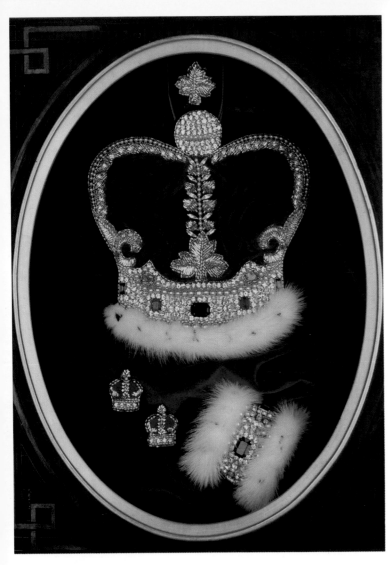

Red velvet handbag with faux crown jewels and "ermine" trim, with matching earrings and a jeweled cuff with rabbit-hair ermine. Designed by Gérard Tremolet for Lesage Winter collection, 1988. *Courtesy of Maison Lesage, Paris, France*

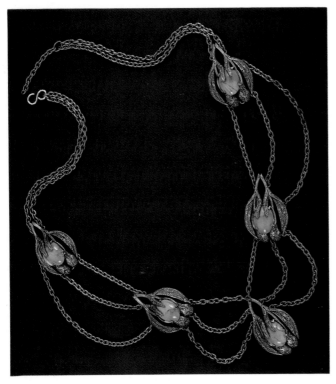

Lesage sailed for New York on the Normandie in 1939 just as the Germans were invading Poland. When he returned to Paris, there were no sequins available to work with so he closed the atelier. (Sequins were made of gelatine from oxen gall mixed with pearl essence until Rhodoid sequins were introduced with Balenciaga in the Sixties.) When Albert reopened, faithful clients Schiaparelli, Balmain, Fath, and Balenciaga were ready to order, and when François took over in 1949 after Albert's death, they were equally willing to help his son over his apprenticeship years. In 1948, François had opened a Lesage Boutique on Sunset Boulevard in Los Angeles. He brought American business know-how to Lesage et Cie, and introduced new materials like Rhodoid sequins to embroidery. The Fifties was a decorative decade, but in the Sixties, opulence was out of fashion with the new youth-oriented society who invented their personal styles, embroidering their own jeans and wrist-bands. Luxury returned in the Seventies with the oil-rich Arab Sheikhs and Persian potentates who bought heavily embroidered gowns with *trompe l'oeil* necklaces for their wives, daughters, and harem favorites.

In 1985 Lesage et Cie diversified its operations with embroidered accessories and jewelry. Gérard Trémolet was hired to design and supervise this exciting new venture. "I had previously designed accessories for Jean-Louis Scherrer, and was now responsible for the creation of Lesage jewelled bags, belts, and scarves as well as sequined earrings, brooches, and cuffs mixed with other decorative materials." Embroidered accessories, *frivolités*, were first created independently from gowns in the 19th century when silk and sequins embellished purses and slippers. Gérard launched elaborate wide cuffs covered with antique sequins in Egyptian or Art Deco designs. Some were decorated with strass or trimmed with fur. Handbags, gloves, headbands, fans, and parasols were created to match necklaces, earrings, and brooches.

In 1988, a Lesage velvet handbag in the shape of a crown studded with strass had matching earrings and an "ermine" trimmed bracelet. Sequinned fish swam on Lucite bracelets for a summer collection. For one delightful tribute to the Muranese glassmakers, Trémolet simulated the *rosetta* and *millefiori* designs in tiny glass beads, and mixed them with the real Venetian beads for a *trompe l'oeil* fantasy. In 1991, "Sophia's lips" appeared in a red sequinned kiss with strass on a bag, brooch, and earrings. The disco revolving glass ball was recreated with mirrored sections for a bag and parure, lending more sparkle to the dance. All these wonders were available at the old Schiaparelli Boutique at 21 Place Vendôme next to the Hotel Ritz, until the shop was closed in 1993. There is a project to reopen another boutique on the Place de la Madeleine in the future. "The Place Vendôme had become a no-man's-land," explained François Lesage. In America, until 1994, Lesage jewelry could be found at Barney's, Saks Fifth Ave., and Henri Bendel in New York as well as specialty stores in Miami, Florida, and Los Angeles.

Rose and Joseph Woloch opened their shop in Paris 1939. Joseph. a skilled goldsmith, was known for his detailed engraving and handwrought metalwork before and after the war. In the Fifties they produced 2 lines: the cheaper one for large volume at the Galeries Lafayette department stores; and more exclusive pieces for French haute couture. A belt of brass chains and leaves with faux turquoise cabochons graced the chemise dresses of the period. After 1966 Rose Woloch changed the name of her firm to Rose Idée, when her son Eric Serge took charge of the business. (This could be the E. Wolloch who made an "onyx" necklace encrusted with glass cabochons for Yves Saint Laurent in 1986.)

Gilded brass chain belt with four "turquoise" cabochons, with sculpted leaves, signed "WOLOCH" in block letters. *Courtesy of private collection, Milan, Italy*

Countess "Cis" Zoltowska was born Maria Assunta Frankl-Fonseca in Vienna, of a Hungarian mother and an Austrian father. She was a true product of the Austro-Hungarian nobility, brought up in a 15th century castle near Vienna, then in a convent. She spent her summers on her grandfather's estate where she raced horses across the Hungarian plains. Only 4'9", weighing 80 pounds, she was and is an intense, fiercely determined woman who survived the Nazi annexation of Austria, only to fly to Switzerland one step ahead of the Soviet "liberation" of Hungary from the Germans in 1945. She left her clothes and jewelry behind in Budapest and had to support herself in Lausanne. Without any formal art training, she began by painting ceramic jewelry, which she successfully sold.

In 1951, having married the Polish Count Zoltowski (Zoltowska is the feminine ending,) she travelled to Paris and was disappointed to find that French costume jewelry mostly imitated the real thing. "I do not like imitations!" Cissy declared, "I eat real sugar, real butter, and drink real Vodka, so I decided to make some "real" fantasy jewelry." Cissy's nickname was derived from her resemblance to the raven-haired Empress Elizabeth ("Cissy") of Austria. She shortened it to "Cis", and began creating her own signature stones. "I painted the reverse sides of glass stones pigeon's blood ruby because the available red stones were too predictably boring, and I sprayed emerald and sapphire glass cabochons with my "gold dust" varnish to give them sparkle", Cissy recalls. In 1951, the Countess hand-painted mother of pearl cufflinks and buttons with miniature horses (her first love) and birds which Pierre Balmain couldn't resist. Jacques Fath designed blouses around her buttons. She designed a faux carved emerald fur clip crowned with imitation rose quartz on long stems, and "turquoises" and "garnets" in 1955. A brooch of grapes made of faux carnelian, malachite, and "crackled" glass cabochons had 22 ct. gold plated leaves and stems. These brooches were stamped "Cis" under the crown.

Helena Rubenstein commissioned Cissy to design a bracelet for her using semi-precious stones. She found emerald, ruby, and sapphire cabochons in Ceylon and Thailand which were prong-set with moonstones and striated agate. On her numerous trips to Bangkok, Countess Zoltowska picked up gemstones which she mixed with Austrian crystals as the spirit moved her. Faux gemstones, however, were her preferred choice for all her elaborate pieces which were always prong-set, and hand-mounted.

Hand-painted mother of pearl cufflinks, earclips, and buttons of horses, fiacres, bird, and a boat by Countess Zoltowska, signed "Cis", 1950-51 for Pierre Balmain, and Jacques Fath. *Courtesy of Countess Zoltowska. Photo by Sandro Moro*

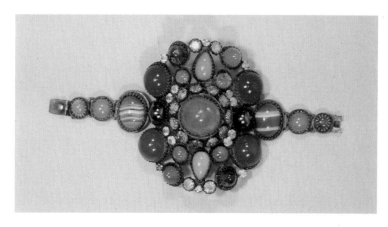

Silver bracelet studded with emerald, sapphire, and ruby cabochons from Sri Lanka, as well as moonstones and agates. This is the proto-type for the piece that was custom-made for Helena Rubenstein in Paris, late Fifties. *Courtesy of Lisa Siddens collection. Photo by Sandro Moro*

Succulent grapes of faux carnelian, emerald, and moonstones with 22 kt. gold-plated grape leaves, Fifties, stamped "Cis". *Courtesy of the author. Photo by Sandro Moro*

Reverse of brooch showing Countess Zoltowska's stamp "Cis" under the crown. *Photo by Robert Weldon*

Cissy worked with Balenciaga for 14 years. He ordered her dandelion pin with multiple blossoms on gold wires in 1955, showing it in several different colors. The subtle combination of grey Mabe pearls bristling with misty pink crystal stones on stems was conceived for Balenciaga's 1960 Fall collection. A pearl pineapple, and a glass pine cone bouquet in fall colors were 1959 brooches. The Countess mixed a row of her crackled pink glass stones with rows of Swarovski crystal daisies and faux moonstones for a delicious necklace and bracelet set for a 1962 couture collection. "My jewelry for Balenciaga bore my signature, not Balenciaga's. Sometimes his fabric designer took his color schemes from my jewelry for the collections."

Cissy's jewelry was also in demand in America. She had a contract with Lord & Taylor, using the "Cis of Paris" signature, and with Bonwit Teller, where her pieces were signed "Countess Zoltowska." B. Altman bought her magenta velvet shoe buckles with pink and green crystal clips. "I made twenty different kinds of dandelion jewelry which I sold to different stores. The model originally shown at Bergdorf Goodman was quickly copied by Bonwit Teller. I was so angry, that my friend Balenciaga promptly banned Bonwit Teller's buyer from viewing his Paris collection. The buyer was so impressed that he asked to meet the woman for whom Balenciaga would do such a thing, and came to Paris to sign me to a contract," the Countess exults. (The lynx-eyed Cissy fulminating in four languages was not to be ignored.) Eventually, orders mounted up by 25 workers filled her atelier in the 16th century apartment (once the gaming rooms of the Prince de Conti) across the Seine from the Louvre. In 1962, she moved to 19, rue Cambon, not far from Chanel whom she never met.

Large star flower brooches and hair ornaments with pearl petals by Countess Zoltowska for Balenciaga, vintage photo 1957. *Courtesy of Cis archives. Photo by Teddy Brauner*

Pearl pineapple with green and aqua glass leaves on gold stems, and a multicolored floral pine cone on oxidyzed metal stems, for Balenciaga, 1958-59. Hand-painted "Cis" signature. *Courtesy of Rita Sacks Collection. Photo by Robert Weldon*

Grey Australian Mabe pearls surrounded by misty pink crystal stones, prong set on wire branches for Balenciaga by Countess Zoltowska, 1960. Later signed "Cis" (hand-painted signature with crown). *Courtesy of Rita Sacks Collection, NY. Photo by Robert Weldon*

Countess Zoltowska playing with her extraordinary jewelry in her apartment/atelier on the Quai Malaquais, Paris, 1960. *Courtesy of Countess Zoltowska archives (photo from German magazine, Elegante Welt)*

In the Fifties and Sixties Cissy was designing 300 models twice a year for France and Germany, as well as for export to North and South America, Australia, and Japan. "I designed two different collections. One for the haute couture, and a more affordable one for the boutiques *de frivolités* in the French provinces as well as the best foreign department stores, because fantasy jewelry should be accessible to every pocketbook." In the early Sixties, an Edwardian-style rhinestone choker (3" high) pictured in *Life* sold at Bonwit Teller's for $143. A long 4" fringed antiqued gold bib sold for $75, and long, dangly earrings for $15 were shown at Lord & Taylor's French Accessories Week according to the *New York World Telegram and Sun* in Sept. 1964.

Rhinestone dandelions with pearl centers thrust high on oxidized metal stems above a pearl studded bouquet, stamped "Cis" with the crown, ca. 1960. This brooch is one of the many variations on the full dandelion brooch designed for Balenciaga. *Courtesy of the author. photo by Sandro Moro*

Two rows of iridescent Swarovski daisies alternating with rows of pink "crackled" rhinestones and faux moonstones with a matching bracelet by Cis for Balenciaga, ca. 1960. *Courtesy of Lisa Siddens collection, Los Angeles. Photo by Sandro Moro*

Jewelry from the Maison Cis is not for the faint-hearted. Her necklaces feature 4 to 10 rows of large Tyrolian-cut crystal or glass stones, often in combinations of fuschia (her favorite color) and chartreuse, or olive green, pink, and yellow. Her earrings demand strong lobes to support tiers of color. (Petite though she is, she sees no reason why small women cannot wear impressive jewelry). Cissy originated oxidized black metal settings so that her colored stones would not be upstaged. "Gold talks too much," she insists. She invented and produced in her atelier *craquelé* "crackled" glass stones to play against the Swarovski "Aurora Borealis", or "rivoli" stones which were faceted concentrically around a central point without a table. "I had a year's exclusivity for the "Aurora Borealis" stones, then they were taken up by everybody else", Cissy claims.

Necklace of five rows of "citrine" crackled and Tyrolean-cut crystals and "amethyst" cabochons by Countess Zoltowska, 1962. *Courtesy of Rita Sacks Collection. Photo by Robert Weldon*

Pink "crackled" stones by Cis, with Aurora Borealis and "rivoli" faceted stones by Swarovski with fuschia "crackled" cabochons surround a large pink mirror-backed cabochon, all prong set in 1964. Signed "Cis" in ink. *Courtesy of the author. Photo by Robert Weldon*

Sapphire, emerald, and aqua glass stones each set separately on oxidized black metal stems for a brooch and pendant earrings. The Countess sprayed the green cabochons with gold dust for a different surface. Brooch is signed in silver ink "Cis". The earrings are stamped "Cis" with the crown. *Courtesy of the author. Photo by Robert Weldon*

When the mini-skirt was the rage in the Sixties, Cissy devised the knee bracelet of multi-colored beads to adorn the space between the hem and knee, and an elongated ankle bracelet which was attached with a ring to the toes. A unique supple collar of silvermesh chain was *tressé*, or braided, then layered with rows of pink, pale amethyst and peridot crystal stones for an early Sixties creation admired by Simonetta of Italy. Seven rows of cabochons and faceted stones shading from lavender to violet were set in a necklace for spring to be worn with a heart-shaped brooch of pearls and lavender stones clustered around an iridescent oval.

Luscious collar of seven rows of lavender shading to violet alternating cabochons and faceted stones to be worn with a heart-shaped brooch of pearls and lavender stones clustered around an iridescent oval for Balenciaga. Sixties. *Courtesy of Lisa Siddens collection, Los Angeles. Photo by Sandro Moro*

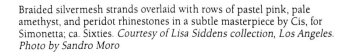

Vintage photo of knee bracelets made of multicolored glass beads for the mini-skirts of 1965, and a dangly wrist bracelet, by Countess Cis Zoltowska. *Courtesy of Cis Archives*

Braided silvermesh strands overlaid with rows of pastel pink, pale amethyst, and peridot rhinestones in a subtle masterpiece by Cis, for Simonetta; ca. Sixties. *Courtesy of Lisa Siddens collection, Los Angeles. Photo by Sandro Moro*

Cissy worked in Paris until 1967, with annual trips to Thailand from 1954 on, where she was enthralled by the infinite variety of the colored silks and semi-precious stones. In no time she was designing jewelry for Queen Sirikit in Bangkok, and Thai silk dresses and tunics for the Parisiennes. Other royal patronage followed: Princess Paola of Belgium caused a minor sensation by choosing a gilded metal tiara by Cis to wear to a Ball rather than the Belgian crown jewels. The Parisian coiffeur, Alexandre, who always coiffed the models for Cissy's fashion shows with nests of false postiches, displayed spectacular Cis hair ornaments of hot pink and amethyst in his salon which ended up on the regal heads of the Duchess of Windsor and Princess Grace, when they tired of Cartier. "Cartier is so stiff!" Cissy declared, never without an opinion. "See those leaves moving on the trees? That is the way my jewelry moves with the body."

For a winter collection, she sculpted and cut metal into enamelled leaves set with green cabochons like dewdrops. Or curled the copper into freeform pins dotted with hot pink and lime green stones. Instead of hugging the wrist, bracelets fell in cascades of pastel panels of Tyrolian-cut stones, with rings to match. Swarowski *carré* square-cut pink and green glass pieces nestled in the hearts of gold metal flowers were made into earrings, pins and necklaces. Cis signature crackled glass stones were silvered fuschia for a necklace with pearls, or tango orange, topaz, amethyst, and olivine flower petals mounted with oxidized metal mesh. A deep V necklace of graduated hues of citrine, topaz, and pale grey-green crystals was a wonderfully subtle combination. Long gold or green enamelled metal links like snake scales (she called them "armadillo" chains) were used in the Sixties for necklaces with pearl drops or medallions of faux malachite and carnelian.

Shoe buckles of magenta velvet and green and pink "rivoli" stones (sold at B. Altman's, NY,) Sixties. And a stunning black metal hair ornament of pink, green, and violet rhinestones to be worn with the elaborate coiffures of the Sixties. This piece can also double as a dog collar mounted on a velvet ribbon. Signed "Cis" in ink. *Courtesy of Rita Sacks Collection, NY. Photo by Sandro Moro*

Green and mauve enamelled metal leaves with emerald green dew drops by Countess Zoltowska, 1960's, photographed on neo-Renaissance bust. With painted "Cis" signature. *Courtesy of the author. Photo by Robert Weldon*

Pastel stones, Tyrolian cut, fall in a cascade from the wrist fastening in this very original bracelet design by Countess Zoltowska, 1960. A matching ring projects stones out from the center. All prong set. Ink signature "Cis". *Courtesy of Rita Sacks Collection. Photo by Robert Weldon*

Lacy necklace of lime-green, apple-green and lemon-yellow crackled pear-shaped stones, rivoli stones, and faux amethysts by Cis. Sixties. *Courtesy of Lisa Siddens collection, Los Angeles. Photo by Sandro Moro*

Square-cut pink and green glass stones by Swarovski set flat or on end, fill the gold-plated petals with color, Sixties. Inscribed with ink "Cis". *Courtesy of the author. Photo by Robert Weldon*

Deep V necklace of subtly shaded topaz, citrine, and grey/green rhinestones, and another necklace with tango orange, topaz, sherry, and olive-green crackled and clear rhinestone petals with oxidized metal stems. Both signed "Cis." Sixties. *Courtesy of the author. Photo by Sandro Moro*

An all metal mesh jacket jewelled by Cis made the double cover of *Harper's Bazaar* in March, 1962, and several French *Vogue* and *Officiel* covers featured her jewelry as well as *WWD* when the Countess brought her collections to America. Bulgari, the famous Italian jeweler, told Cissy: "You are such a success because you have never studied jewelry design with anyone, and you are therefore unafraid of trying something new because you've never been told how not to do it!."

When asked why so many of her pieces are not signed, Cissy explained: "Most of my jewelry was made for shows and collections, and the solderer who was supposed to stamp the pieces with my "Cis" mark under the crown was so rushed, he often forgot to stamp them. In the convent as a child in Austria I was taught to be modest. It was a big mistake. I didn't use the Countess Zoltowska label till the Sixties when I realized what good publicity I could get from my name." Cissy has signed many of her pieces at a later date in indelible gilt or black ink.

Besides jewelry, Cissy also designed lamps, vanity accessories for the purse and dressing table, and jewelled cigarette holders and belts. Cissy moved to California in 1968 where she launched a new career hand-painting canvases for needlepoint. She is currently designing jewelry for the American collections of James Galanos.

Her Lucite and rhinestone pins and earrings, sunglasses, and belt buckles can be found in museum gift shops. Her current cuff bracelets are fashioned out of large slices of gem crystals, and chunks of semi-precious stones.

Jeanne Péral, (1914-) studied design at the Ecole des Beaux Arts in Marseille during the war years. In 1945 she returned to Paris to open her atelier. Jacques Fath was her first mentor and customer, then in 1947 Jean Dessès, Robert Piguet, Balmain, Schiaparelli, Lanvin Castillo and Balenciaga ordered her creations. Dior was her principal client for 20 years.

"I created for the Boutique Dior the most sumptuous gifts. In 1961 I fashioned pendants of seashells from Niger, and rose quartz, or necklaces of coral and turquoise, lapis and pearls. During this period there was no intermediary. You dealt directly with the couturiers who demanded perfection. What a wonderful time it was! Price was no object. They wanted only quality and elegance."

Mme. Péral's atelier drawers were overflowing with antique semi-precious stones, ivory and ebony beads, and exotic woods and seashells collected on frequent trips to Asia in the Fifties. She finally found the artisans capable of mounting all her pieces by hand, as nothing was soldered. In India she was asked to create

French lattice-work jet pendant with French jet drop on a jet beaded collar by Jeanne Péral. 1980. *Courtesy of Jeanne Péral. Photo by Bruno Pierson*

Mother of pearl incised panels from the Orient mounted with pearl, mother of pearl, and porcelain beads for pendant earrings and matching necklace by Jeanne Péral for Jean-Louis Scherrer, 1985. *Courtesy of Jeanne Péral. Photo by Bruno Pierson*

Safari collection necklaces and brooch made with ivory, fur, amber, ebony, turquoise, carnelian, shells, and tiger teeth found in India. Jeanne Péral for Jean-Louis Scherrer and Jean Patou, 1978-79. *Courtesy of Jeanne Péral, Paris, France. Photo by Bruno Pierson*

Delicate necklace with pearls and faux amethysts and turquoises, with matching earrings, ca. 1959, signed "Modèle Maryse Blanchard, Paris." *Courtesy of Sara Garbarini, Tiburon, CA. Photo by Sandro Moro*

models for the Handicrafts Industry, which resulted in 2 decades of collaboration, and the first sucessful merchandising of Indian fantasy jewelry. In 1973 she was invited to Peking to advise on similar projects.

In 1965 she opened her shop, Cassiopée, on the rue des Saints-Pères. Here she displayed her one-of-a-kind jewelry, evening bags, and custom masks on mannequins draped in silk and cashmere shawls. The colors were vivid, but this was not a temple of glitz.

For Jean-Louis Scherrer in 1978, Mme. Péral designed a Safari collection with pendants dripping amber, ivory, ebony, tiger teeth and feathers. For Jean Patou in 1977 she dyed antique ivory beads pastel colors, and made necklaces of straw and feathers, or balls of *passementerie* trimming tassels. For Scherrer's pins and earrings in 1985, she used 19th century engraved mother of pearl pieces

originally intended in the Orient for inlay with precious woods. She liked to mix white on white with mother of pearl, pearl, and porcelain beads. Jeanne Péral wove tiny Venetian jet *conterie* beads into choker necklaces with lacy pendants and drops of antique French jet, accented with an occasional discreet crystal.

Maryse Blanchard, from her atelier on the bld. Haussmann, was designing ultra-feminine jewelry of faux pearls, amethysts and turquoises for Jacques Heim, ca. 1959. In the Sixties, she experimented with alternative materials. Blanchard used Polynacre, a pearlized product that came in many colors, and 2 years later Heloglass, a semi-transparent resin which simulated rock crystals.[16] In the 60s and 70s, Jean Patou and Lanvin showed her jewelry. An oval metal plaque stamped "Modèle Maryse Blanchard, Paris" was affixed to necklaces and earrings.

Coco and Schiap

A telling sketch of Coco Chanel by Cecil Beaton shows her defiantly dripping with her favorite Fulco di Verdura cuffs, Gripoix necklaces, and a Goossens brooch, as well as her couturière scissors, late Sixties.
Courtesy of William Doyle Galleries, New York, "Couture, Antique Clothing, Accessories & Costume Jewelry" catalog, April 27,1994

Coco Chanel and Elsa Schiaparelli were the two counter-weights of French fashion from the Twenties through the Fifties. Consummate professionals, they were passionately devoted to their métier and challenged each other to a *mano a mano* of couture and jewelry innovations, but neither ever had a good word to say about the other.

The most elegant of the French couturières, Gabrielle (Coco) Chanel (1883-1971) was born out of wedlock (in a railroad station waiting room or in a poorhouse - there are two versions of her birth) in Saumur to a peasant family. After her mother died when she was 12, she was left in the care of an elderly aunt by her father, a traveling salesman who emigrated to America. Gabrielle spent her childhood in an orphanage, then a convent boarding school.

Rebellious and determined, Gabrielle left her first job as a seamstress to sing (forgettably) in a music hall, where a wealthy equestrian discovered her and whisked her off to his château in the horse country near the Chantilly race track. There she met the first of several devoted English lovers, Boy Capel, who set her up in 1910 with a milliner's business at 21, rue Cambon in Paris (prophetically, down the street from #31 where she was later to establish her House of Couture.) There followed boutiques in Deauville and Biarritz in 1914, where she reinvented the sailor's jacket and pull-over, adding a little braid, a brooch, and the sailor's beret which launched her career and personal style. In 1919, Boy Capel died in a car accident while shuttling contentedly between his new wife and his mistress, Coco. "Coco" is an affectionate nickname in France, but she may also have taken the name from the titles of the songs she sang on stage.[17]

From the very beginning, accessories were an important integral part of the Chanel Look. In 1920, she was introduced to magnificent jewelry by her Russian lover, the Grand Duke Dmitri (one of Rasputin's assassins). Moving on, in the mid-Twenties she was lured to England by the veddy wealthy Duke of Westminster, where Coco spent several years in the lap of serene luxury, developing a taste for British tweeds and sober tailoring on the one hand, and extravagant jewelry on the other. When Chanel finally settled into her 31 rue Cambon salons, she cultivated aristocratic artists who worked with her through the years on personal and couture jewelry for her collections. In 1924, the Comte Etienne de Beaumont (famous for his fantastic Costume Balls,) began collaborating with her on costume jewelry. He was responsible for the first long chain sautoirs with odd-shaped faux stones and pearls which became a signature Chanel accessory.[18]

The Sicilian, Fulco della Cerda, Duke of Verdura, brought another more Baroque aesthetic to Chanel's attention. (Accustomed as she was to the company of Dukes, it was amusing to have one working for her). Together they transformed the 8-pointed Maltese cross (first worn by the Knights of the military and religious Order of Malta during the Crusades in 1530) into a gemstone fashion statement on a white enamelled gold hinged bracelet. ("There were always problems with the restoration of the chipped enamel," reports Edward Landrigan, owner of Verdura, New York, "and the enamel was always on gold, never copper. Verdura's records show that he may occasionally have used inexpensive gem cabochons, but they were always mounted on gold.")

Photo of Schiaparelli by Piazi, ca. thirties. Fur hat with jewelled eyes.
Courtesy of Musèe des Arts de la Mode, Paris

Black Bakelite hinged cuff bracelet with multi-colored glass gemstones. Unsigned, probably Chanel. *Courtesy of Diane Keith Collection, Beverly Hills, CA. Photo by Robert Weldon*

"Emerald" and "ruby" *pâte de verre* beads mounted with multiple gilded brass chains and filigree elements, and a baroque pearl drop; Robert Goossens for Chanel. "One of 250 different models that I designed mounted in this style," Goossens verified. Made between 1955-1971. Signed "Chanel" in block letters. *Courtesy of private collection, Milan*

Infinite variations were later played on Verdura's 1937 theme; in colored woods, ivory, and hardstone cuffs. Since 1988, Verdura on Fifth Avenue reproduces the black cuffs in onyx, and the white in cocholong, (a white quartz from Russia) with fine gemstones. In the Fifties, there were magenta or orange Bakelite cuffs with Maltese crosses (Diana Vreeland's favorites) or floral motifs of faux gems. *Pâte de verre* emerald crosses by Goossens appeared on white enamelled cuffs in the Sixties, and 1980s interpretations by Kenneth J. Lane were popular in America. Verdura went to Hollywood in 1937 to design for Paul Flato (who became entangled in legal problems,) then to New York in 1939, where he opened his own highly successful shop.

Chanel gleefully mixed the sacred and the profane. Her crosses (Maltese or Byzantine) were hung on gilt chains with glass baubles. Real pearls were worn with the faux. Pilgrimages to the exquisite Byzantine Basilicas of San Vitale in Ravenna, and San Marco and Torcello in the Venetian lagoon, made a profound impression on Chanel. Like the Venetians who triumphantly transported home the spoils of the sack of Constantinople in 1204, Chanel carried the visual, if not the spiritual, splendor back to Paris. The rich colors and jewelled adornments of these Early Christian mosaics turned up time and again in her very secular pearl and glass brooches and pendants. (But rarely in her earclips, which remained classic gilded variations on the pearl or glass bead buttons.) Coco irreverently tumbled many elements together, turning aesthetic values inside out, while maintaining the felicitous proportions necessary to make the piece work. "I am neither retrograde nor avant-garde" Chanel declared. "I am of my own time." (*Rétro* in France is a general term meaning "harking back to the past", as implied by Chanel, but in America it is used in reference to Forties jewelry with gilded volutes.)

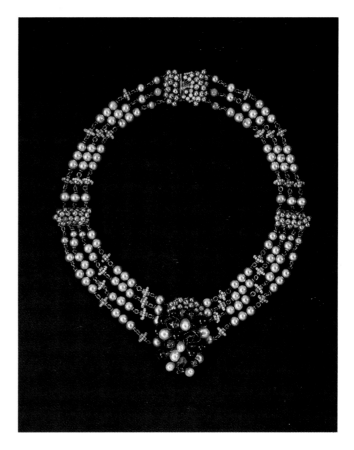

Four rows of pearls with a center cluster of glass beads, pearls and gilded metal flower buds. Unsigned. Possibly Maison Gripoix for Chanel. *Courtesy of private collection, Milan, Italy*

"Barbaric" bracelet of three gilded brass filigree sections with *pâte de verre* beads and pearls, and a tiny jewelled scimitar for the clasp; Robert Goossens for Chanel, ca. Sixties. Unsigned. *Courtesy of private collection, Milan*

A completely different image was exploited in Chanel's figurative floral jewelry, ably interpreted by the Maison Gripoix with poured glass petals and leaves, (from the late Thirties till the present.) These were copied by other firms, but noone quite matched the Gripoix technique with *pâte de verre*. An unknown firm produced a large number of floral bouquets in pot metal and enamel with faux stones with the script signature. The Duc di Verdura executed a gold brooch in the shape of one perfect rose for Chanel in 1935 which was the antithesis of Paul Iribe's (another of Chanel's lovers) geometric stylised rose for the 1925 Expo. The red enamel petals with diamond accents of Verdura's rose were totally naturalistic.

Lovely flowerhead pendant made of *pâte de verre* pink, mauve, and pearl petals with green leaves on a pink and green chain. Signed "Chanel" with three stars, denoting Couture collection. The center red enamelled rose with strass was designed by Fulco di Verdura in 1935 in gold and diamonds. This one is a later version, signed script "Chanel". Three of the other four enamelled floral brooches have simulated *chatoyant* (cat's eye) moonstones or star sapphires and rubies. Signed script Chanel. Ca. Thirties. *Courtesy of Christie's, London South Kensington, England; "Designer Costume Jewellery", April 1992*

Two floral brooches of enamelled white metal: the red and white carnations have strass accents *Courtesy of Sherry Goldman Collection, Sherman Oaks, Ca.*; the blue flower bouquet (5" long), with restored painted enamel, has faux sapphire centers. Both are signed script "Chanel." Ca. Thirties. *Courtesy of the author. Photo by Robert Weldon*

Reverse of blue flower brooch, showing Chanel script signature. *Photo by Robert Weldon*

The war years and the following decade were a murky time for Chanel. When the *drôle de guerre* (the "phoney war") began, Coco closed her couture house, but left her Chanel Boutique open to sell perfumes, accessories, and jewelry. She then embarked on a sinister affair with a dashing German diplomat turned spy with whom she was exiled to Switzerland after the war. Though "banished to Siberia", Coco was still free to return to Paris where she kept her Boutique open selling Chanel No. 5 perfume and jewelry to returning G.I.s after the Liberation.[19] Louis Rousselet supplied her with post-war pearl sautoirs from 1948-1952. After Chanel re-opened her couture house in 1954, she worked with Maison Gripoix and Robert Goossens.

For Coco Chanel, dressmaking was a profession; for Elsa Schiaparelli (1890-1973) it was an art ("a most difficult and unsatisfying art" as she described it in her autobiography, *Shocking Life*.) Elsa (1890-1973) was born and brought up in the Renaissance Palazzo Corsini in Rome. Shy and defiant, she was exposed as a child and young adult to ancient and Modern art (Futurism, Dada, and Surrealism) astrology, and avant-garde photography; all of which shaped her career as a designer. The men she loved did not find favor with her aristocratic parents, and the man she married, the mystic Comte de Kerlor, fell madly in love with Isadora Duncan and abandoned Elsa in New York with her baby, Gogo.

When Elsa settled in Paris in the Twenties, her friends Man Ray and the Dadaists introduced her to Paul Poiret, who generously encouraged her first dressmaking efforts. At the Boeuf sur le Toit nightclub Elsa mixed with the artists who were to design for her fifteen years later (Jean Cocteau, Vertès, and Salvador Dali) as well as the wealthy cosmopolites and actresses who would leave the House of Chanel for Schiaparelli in the Thirties.

Like Chanel, her first successful designs were sporty sweaters for the active woman. Elsa also shared with her rival the ability to uncover fresh talent to design her accessories and jewelry. Here the similarity ends. Coco Chanel's clothes were classic; Elsa's were avant-garde and impudent. Her Italian temperament was expressed in vivid colors, revolutionary new fabrics, amusing buttons, spectacular jewelry, and witty hats.

Arrow brooch with pavé strass and crystal stones. Signed "Chanel." *Courtesy of Sherry Goldman Collection, Sherman Oaks, CA.* Gilded metal floral earrings with "Chanel" (block letters). ca. Fifties. *Courtesy of private collection, Los Angeles, CA. Photo by Robert Weldon*

Lampshade hat by Schiaparelli made of "burnt" bird feathers with Paris label. "Pixie" Celluloid eyeglasses, hand-made in Oyonnax, with twisted green and white decoration and flowers, signed "Schiaparelli", ca. Forties. Modern edition of original eye brooch by Jean Cocteau for Schiap. White and black enamel, and *chatoyant* blue cat's eye glass cabochon and pearl tear drop simulate the original brooch which was made of twisted cord lacquered white in the 1930's. *Courtesy of the author. The Cocteau reissue is from the Musée des Arts de la Mode, Paris. Photo by Robert Weldon*

Front and back of Shocking Pink dress form paper tag for Schiaparelli jewels: "Designed in Paris, Created in America" with style number and price. Over a thousand different styles were executed in America after Schiap licensed her name in 1949. These were used along with, or in place of her stamped script signature.

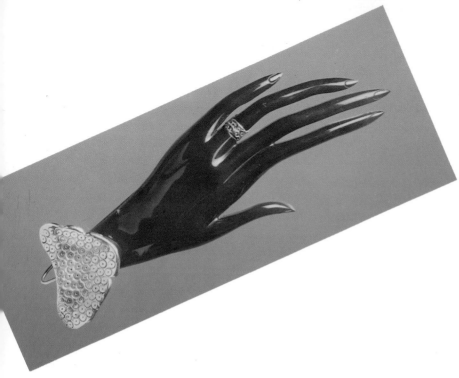

Spectacular long-fingered Bakelite hand brooch with gold-plated brass ring and embossed gilded cuff, Thirties. (attributed to Schiaparelli) Six inches long; unsigned. *Courtesy of Jill Spalding Collection, New York, NY. Photo by Richard Marx*

And now for something completely different! Shocking pink and turquoise blue enamelled four-part pendant brooch decorated with little gold balls and red and yellow glass stones. Thirties. In the style of Schlumberger's creations for Schiaparelli. Unknown maker. *Courtesy of private collection, Milan, Italy*

In 1927, "Schiap" hired young Jean Clément (1900-1949) who designed much of her costume jewelry (called junk jewelry in New York, and *toc* in Paris) over the next two decades. He baked ceramic buttons for Schiap in an electric oven, and made molds for her plastic jewelry. Clément's spinning tops, lollipops, Christmas bells, or veggies in porcelain, aluminum, or Prystal were meant to stand out on a strict black lapel. They would have been noticed anywhere. It was Clément in 1936 who mixed a startling magenta/pink color sample which became Schiap's trademark "Shocking" pink, the inspiration for couture collections, accessories, jewelry, and the perfume which was to be her salvation when her fashion business declined.[20] Clément remained faithful to Schiap until his early death in 1949.

There were other jewelry designers who created for Schiaparelli: Roger Jean-Pierre in the Forties worked wonders with strass and beads; and Coppola e Toppo wove glass-beaded necklaces and bracelets in the late Forties, and early Fifties.

Perhaps the most creative of Schiap's designers was Jean Schlumberger, (1910?-1987) from Mulhouse in Alsace. The son of a wealthy textile manufacturer, he refused the security of the family business to devote himself to his own jewelry atelier. He began by creating contemporary pieces out of antique porcelain flowers and other bits found in the Paris Marché aux Puces. Flotsam from the flea market ended up on the earlobes of English and French aristocrats, which is where Schiap spied them, and pounced. Schlumberger was her answer to the challge of Chanel's Verdura. In 1938, Schlumberger produced delightful three-dimensional cufflinks, brooches, and buttons in figural shapes of enamelled metal or gilt with rhinestones. There were goldfish and sea shells, cupids holding torches, ostriches with pink necks and legs dangling colored glass beads, and tiny feet on roller skates, bagpipes, pink starfish, and for Schiap's famous 1938 "Circus Collection", prancing circus horses and acrobats. For the "Pagan Collection", flowers, vegetables, and vines curled around the wrist and neck, with the occasional insect in the leaves.[21]

Gilded brass cuff enamelled blue with gold leaves, faux moonstones and strass with matching earrings by Schiaparelli, ca. Thirties. Signed in block letters. *Courtesy of private collection, Milan, Italy*

In *Connoisseur* of July 1990, Schlumberger described his breezy style as being "random, organic, in motion. I want to capture the irregularity of the universe." The spontaneity of his creative eye jibed perfectly with Schiap's succession of wildly creative Thirties couture collections. Who knows what further wonders they might have created together if World War II had not abruptly ended their collaboration. Schlumberger was evacuated, and landed in New York in 1940, where he began a long partnership with Nicolas Bongard, a nephew of Paul Poiret's. The two men concentrated on creating spectacular fine jewelry, with Schlumberger, "the pencil", providing the sketches for Bongard's wax models. Diana Vreeland discovered "Schlum", and so in the Fifties, did Thomas Hoving of Tiffany's who made him vice-president of the company with his own department. His signature *paillonné* enamelled gold bangles were soon copied by Kenneth J. Lane in gilded brass.

Schiaparelli enlisted the talents of her Surrealist friends to collaborate on jewelry and couture design. Jean Cocteau made the famous eye brooch out of twisted cord, lacquered white, with a pearl tear drop. This was later reproduced in black and white enamelled metal by the Musée des Arts de la Mode. Disembodied body parts were a favorite Surrealist theme, used by Dali as well, who made a sofa out of "Shocking Pink" lips for Schiap's Boutique. His earrings for her were tiny telephones. Schiap delighted in placing every day mundane objects in a skewed context. Her outrageous hat with a feather chicken in a straw nest, laid an egg. Only the daring socialite, Daisy Fellowes, had the nerve to wear it. The Maison Lesage embroidered Cocteau's profiles on a jacket, as well as slithery snakes, prancing horses, and Sun Gods on capes and opera coats.

Schiap spent most of the war years in America, often doing needlepoint with Diana Vreeland in her "Shocking Pink" living room in the country. When she returned to the Place Vendôme, her adventurous pre-war style was considerably chastened. She flirted briefly with Machine Age motifs, borrowing the belt from the waist and buckling it in metal mesh around the wrist, or stringing red radiators round a necklace. In 1949 she licensed an American company to manufacture her jewelry, stamped with the script "Schiaparelli" oval, or paper-tagged "Designed in Paris, Created in America" with the style no. and price.

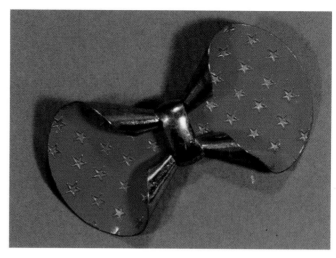

Shocking pink gilded brass bow with gold stars made for the Schiaparelli Paris Boutique as well as Bonwit Teller's, New York (for Xmas, 1938). Signed "schiaparelli" block letters, her pre-war signature. Rare. *Courtesy of the author. Photo by Sandro Moro.*

Reverse of pink bow signed "schiaparelli", lower case block letters, and with 1937 U.S. patent number 2066969. *Photo by Sandro Moro.*

Pavé rhinestone pendants on a slender gold-plated gas-pipe chain, with *pavé* earrings to match. A Tailored gold-plated version of the same asymmetrical gas-pipe necklace, with ribbed pendants without rhinestones. Script "Schiaparelli" signatures, ca. Fifties. Photographed on "Shocking de Schiaparelli" pink silk lingerie case. *Courtesy of the author. Photo by Robert Weldon*

Spectacular bracelets 2" wide were made out of different shaped large unfoiled glass and Swarovski "Aurora Borealis" stones, with necklaces, brooches (3" wide) and earrings to match. Textured "moon rocks" and iridescent stones figured in other designs. Pearl grapes with rhinestone-studded leaves were a popular parure manufactured in sets of beige, grey, or sea-green with the pearls dyed to match. Pineapple pins in subtly shaded stones were sold with matching earrings. Schiap used iridescent glass seashells and pearl peas in a gilded pod for different sets, and mounted multi-colored beads on 13 gilt chains for a wide, supple bracelet. Jewelry for the "Tailored Woman" was produced in gilded brass with chain fringes instead of stones. An enormous openwork silver metal spray set with rhinestones made a dramatic statement on a velvet evening gown. All these pieces were stamped "Schiaparelli" in script, or tagged with the pink paper label in the shape of a dressmaker's dummy. This logo was originally created by Leonor Fini, the Italian Surrealist, from Mae West's measurements for the perfume bottle "Shocking".

(Collectors should be aware that someone has produced jewelry signed "Schaperelli" in block letters, twice misspelled, and obviously not Schiap.)

Schiaparelli closed her couture House in 1954, the same year that her arch rival, Chanel, reopened with new versions of her tried and true formula; soft tweed suits with pearl and glass accessories. Schiap continued to receive income from her perfumes and accessories until 1973, when, without consulting her family, she sold her name and business to a French businessman. Understandably, her daughter, Gogo, would like to buy it back.

Iridescent violet and peacock green glass demi-parure (bracelet, pin, and earrings) mixed with violet/green iridescent textured "moon rocks". Script "Schiaparelli" signature. Sixties. *Courtesy of the author. Photo by Robert Weldon*

Four piece gold-plated brass parure of faux ruby cabochons and Aurora Borealis stones by Schiaparelli, Fifties; script signature. *Courtesy of the author. Photo by Robert Weldon*

Large unfoiled citrine glass set; the bracelet, earrings and pin mounted with Aurora Borealis stones, signed with script Schiaparelli signature. Another link bracelet with large oval "smoky quartz" stones with citrines and strass (2" wide). With script "Schiaparelli". Ca. late Fifties. *Courtesy of the author. Photo by Robert Weldon*

Neo-Renaissance setting for a faux amethyst (mirror backed) and unfoiled citrine link bracelet and necklace with gilded glass navette leaves by Schiaparelli, script signature. Early Sixties. Photographed on a bust of Dante's Beatrice. *Courtesy of the author. Photo by Robert Weldon*

Late Fifties unfoiled faux ruby and Aurora Borealis demi-parure (earrings, pin and bracelet), and a silver-tone necklace with ruby pendants signed with script "Schiaparelli". Photographed with flowered silk bag and shoes, Schiaparelli label; Paris, New York. *Courtesy of the author. Photo by Robert Weldon*

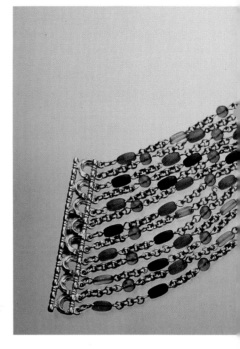

Pink two-tone earrings, unfoiled and satin glass; and a brooch with "pink tourmaline" unfoiled stones separately set with Aurora Borealis stones, pearls, and gilded cast branches. "Smoky quartz" in silver-tone setting, and "green tourmaline" stones with pearls in a gold tone setting are different versions of Schiap's unusual rectangular stones with two triangular cuts on the back. All signed with script Schiaparelli. Late Fifties. Photographed on a silk scarf hand-painted and sewn with sequins, signed "Schiaparelli, Paris", ca. Thirties. *Courtesy of the author. Photo by Robert Weldon*

Supple bracelet of thirteen gilded chains and multicolored glass beads, signed "Schiaparelli", script. *Courtesy of the author. Photo by Robert Weldon*

Pearl grapes and Aurora Borealis strass-decorated grape leaves rendered in four different color combinations: beige and cognac grapes on gold-tone metal leaves; light grey and anthracite pearls with silvered metal leaves; light and dark grey/green pearls with gold toned leaves; and white pearls with silver-tone leaves. The bracelets are either links or a hinged cuff. The earrings are grape leaf clips or grape cluster pendant clips, and the pin is a bunch of pearl grapes mixed with grey/pink Aurora Borealis stones. All signed script "Schiaparelli". Fifties. Photographed on Schiaparelli's "Shocking Pink" hat box. *Courtesy of the author. Photo by Robert Weldon*

Feathery silvered metal pin (5" long) set with ca. 150 glittering rhine-stones, signed script "Schiaparelli". Ca. Fifties. *Courtesy of the author. Photo by Robert Weldon*

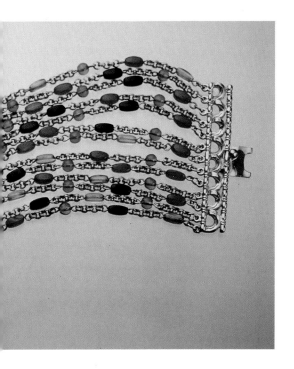

Pineapple set of deep green stones subtly shading up to salmon pink, pistachio, and lime green for the leaves. The earrings have the same shaded leaves. A seafoam green Czech moulded glass bead bracelet with iridescent lime-green shells, Aurora Borealis, and "moonstone" cabochons. All bear the "Schiaparelli" script signature. Ca. 1960. *Courtesy of the author. Photo by Robert Weldon*

Pin of green unfoiled glass stones with Aurora Borealis stones. (These Schiap pins are rarely signed, but earrings, necklace, and bracelet of the parure always are.) Perfume bottle pendant with a flower and bee enclosing a "Mae West" bottle; purple cabochons and unfoiled "amethysts" with iridescent stones; cornucopias terminating in Aurora Borealis stones- this bracelet is part of a set with earrings and necklace; Autumnal colors for the pin and necklace above, part of a four piece parure, some moulded and unfoiled stones. All Schiaparelli, ca. 1960. *Courtesy of Christie's, South Kensington, London, England; "Designer Costume Jewelry catalog, April, 1992*

For the Tailored Woman: a cast gilded brass hinged bracelet with two leaves; a gilded rope chain necklace with center-piece of Florentine volutes and a mesh tassel fringe; and a golden pea pod pin with Florentine cross-hatched finish and five pearl peas. Script "Schiaparelli" signatures. Ca. 1950. *Courtesy of the author. Photo by Robert Weldon*

Bijoux de Couture from other French couturiers (1912-1980)

The Chambre Syndicale de la Couture Française is a judicial and legislative organization unique to France. Half labor union/half guild, the Chambre Syndicale handles labor-management problems as well as foreign relations concerning the bi-annual migration of the international press and buyers to Paris. The elected President must be a diplomat extraordinaire capable of soothing ruffled egos as well as working against style piracy and securing France's supremacy in the couture market.[22] In the 1990s the Haute Couture industry has been on the verge of extinction; only kept alive as a P.R. punch for the more profitable ready-to-wear lines, accessories licenses, and the hugely successful perfumes. The affordable *bijoux de couture* jewelry have continued to be a valuable asset to the runway and Boutique Spring/Summer and Fall/Winter Collections.

The most revolutionary couturière in Madrid in the Teens and Paris of the Twenties was better known as a painter and wife of Robert Delaunay. Sonia Delaunay (1885-1979) was born Sonia Stern in the Ukraine, the daughter of a Russian factory executive. Adopted by a wealthy uncle as a young girl, Sonia lived in St. Petersburg and travelled extensively in Europe, settling in Paris in 1905 to study painting. A "marriage of convenience" to a German homosexual art dealer was amicably dissolved when she fell in love with the painter Robert Delaunay. Together they developed "Simultanism", a style of painting which experimented with the harmony or dissonance of juxtaposed colors. "We were united in art, like other couples are united in alcoholism, crime, or faith," Sonia recalled in a 1975 visit to her studio on the rue Saint Simon.

Robert and Sonia were painting in Portugal and Spain when World War I broke out, and the Russian Revolution cut off Sonia's allowance from her uncle. Sonia realized that they could not live on art alone, so she applied the dynamic Delaunay color theories to costume, and set designs for Serge Diaghilev productions (*Cleopatra* and *Aida*) and Casa Sonia couture clothes for the Spanish high society.

Post-war Paris welcomed the Delaunays back, and soon Sonia's geometrically designed dresses and embroidered coats were hailed at her Boutique in the 1925 Exposition, and worn by Gloria Swanson and Nancy Cunard. "The Founding Mother of European Modernism", as Robert Hughes, art critic of *Time* magazine called her, translated her art into vivid textile and dress designs in *pochoir* portfolios, which she applied to fashion in the Twenties and jewelry in the Seventies. Her clothes (and accessories,) and Robert's sets for the 1926 film *Le Petit Parigot* brought their art to a wide audience. Sonia's projects for industrially produced fashion were cut short by the 1929 Crash, and she happily returned to "pure painting".

In 1937, the Delaunays painted huge murals for the Railway and Aeronautics Pavillions at the International Exposition, and then decamped to the Free Zone in Provence, when the Germans partitioned France. Robert died of cancer in 1941, and Sonia, (who survived the German Occupation despite her Jewish origins,) devoted the next fifteen years to promoting her husband's paintings, ignoring her own career. One-woman shows, and a major retrospective

Still photo of *Le P'tit Parigot* (*The Little Parisian*, starring Georges Biscot), a 1926 film for which Sonia Delaunay designed the costumes and accessories. Her husband, Robert Delaunay, contributed set designs. From the vintage still photo album of the film. *Courtesy of the author's archives*

Two polychrome lacquered brooches by Sonia Delaunay superimposed on a vintage *pochoir* fashion design from her 1925 portfolio *Sonia Delaunay, Ses Peintures, Ses Objets, Ses Tissus Simultanés, Ses Modes*, which was later reproduced in limited edition *Sonia Delaunay, Robes Poèmes*, 1969. On the left: "Flamingo", a bronze brooch with polychrome lacquer was taken from a 1922 costume design, "Rhythm without End". (edition of 500.) On the right: the silver brooch/pendant with polychrome lacquer is also adapted from a Twenties design, (edition of 350.) Photos of the jewelry (available also in vermeil) are *courtesy of Artcurial, Paris. The collage by the author was photographed by Robert Weldon*

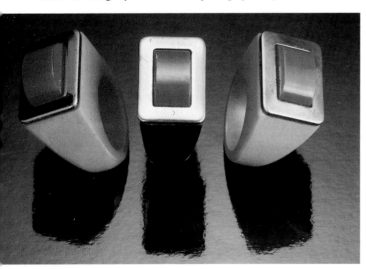

Three high-standing Bakelite rings, butterscotch and black, with orange and plum domed Bakelite segments, and chrome frames. Lanvin, Paris. Ca. Sixties. *Courtesy of the author. Photo by Robert Weldon*

which filled the entire Musée d'Art Moderne in Paris with the work of the Delaunays in 1985[23], assured Sonia her deserved place in the art world. At the age of 93, for the Paris Artcurial Gallery, she produced enamelled brooches and pendants which celebrated the Delaunay themes of vibrating semi-circles of color. Her designs looked as joyfully avant-garde in the Seventies as they had in the Twenties. These limited editions are available to art jewelry collectors (they are, in fact, miniature paintings) as well as long silk scarves reproduced from vintage Delaunay designs.

The House of Lanvin is the oldest continuing couture house in Paris. Jeanne Lanvin invented the chemise in 1914, which was adopted by the new, young *sportives*, and launched "Lanvin Blue", inspired by the stained glass windows of Notre Dame. Her mother and daughter fashions, faithfully illustrated in the *Gazette du Bon Ton* by Pierre Brissaud (from 1912-1924) were romantic and feminine, for those who refused the *garçonne* look. These were worn with necklaces of turquoise and coral beads. As President of the Couture Syndicale, she organised the Pavillon d'Elégance for the 1937 Exposition Internationale, bringing 120 couturiers together under one roof. In the Fifties, the House of Lanvin was still known for its *jeune fille* young and innocent look, displayed with the basic pearl chokers. In the Sixties, there was a drastic makeover, with a less expensive ready-to-wear line, and a new, young designer, Maryl Lanvin. Round, carved Bakelite pendants in red, green, or black hung on chrome-plated or gilded gas pipe chains (1968-72). Large rectangular metal rings were made of cold-painted enamel, or black and butterscotch high-domed Bakelite with chrome. A bright red and blue enamelled cuff completed the neo-Deco look.

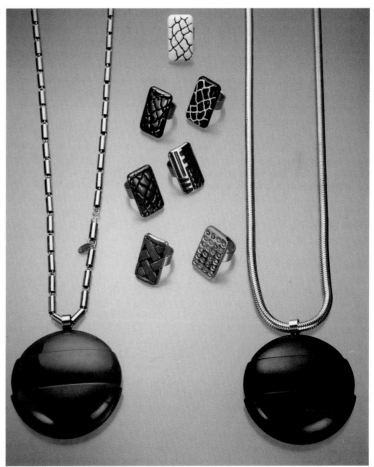

Green and black three-tiered round Bakelite pendants on a chrome-plated chain, and a gilded snake chain, signed "Lanvin Paris" on the reverse, or on an oval tag 1968-'72. Seven rings of different patterns, lacquered or enamelled. Lanvin, Paris, 1960 *Courtesy of the author. Photo by Robert Weldon*

During the Occupation of Paris (1940-44) the Germans proposed moving the French Haute Couture industry to Vienna or Berlin. Lucien Lelong, President of the French Chambre Syndicale, convinced the Nazis that the designers would be unable to function away from the Parisian *ambience*. Twenty couture houses were allowed to remain open, (among them Balenciaga, Grès, Lelong, Robert Piguet, and Jacques Fath) although rationed fabric curtailed production. Amazingly, collections were presented twice a year during the Occupation.

Robert Piguet designed for Paul Poiret (1922-23), who called him his "only disciple". Following time spent with Redfern, Piguet opened his own couture house on the rue du Cirque in 1933. After the war, (1948-'52) Louis Rousselet designed pearl sautoirs and pretty *pâte de verre* necklaces with glass or pearl drops to complement Robert Piguet's discreetly refined collections.

Jacques Fath (1912-1954) is one of those who prospered during the war. Of Flemish/Alsatian origins, Fath attended Business School, which was not to his liking. In 1937 he opened a small shop on the rue la Böetie. By the time the Germans arrived in Paris, he was an established name. (He was briefly taken prisoner in 1940.) During the war, the couture houses relied on the nouveaux riches ladies who had profited from the black market. Dubbed the "B.O.F." (short for *beurre, oeufs, fromage* - the butter, eggs, and cheese which had made them rich), these women and the South American heiresses who were unaffected by the war, kept the couture going, paying for the clothes and jewelry with cash.[24]

Intricately strung bracelet of grey baroque pearls and clear crystal beads with gold-plated brass clasp. Coppola & Toppo for Jacques Fath, 1950. Stamped "Made in Italy by Coppola & Toppo". Courtesy of the author. Photo by Robert Weldon

Vitrine of Jacques Fath Couture House, 39 av Pierre Ier de Serbie, Paris, 1950, showing scarves, accessories, and Coppola & Toppo glass bead and pearl jewelry. *Courtesy of the author's archives. Photo by Maywald*

Fath moved to the avenue Pierre Ier-de-Serbie after the war, launching his young, saucy line with the nipped-in waist worn by Bettina, the mannequin who became Aly Khan's favorite. Among the first to follow Schiap's lead with an accessories Boutique, Jacques Fath sold costume jewelry made by Rousselet (faux pearl cravates, 1948-1950,) Roger Scemama, and Coppola & Toppo (1950-52) as well as scarves, bags, ties, and sunglasses, (Fath cultivated a year-round tan.) Customers and American buyers were invited to his Château de Corbeville where he entertained, like Poiret, at lively costume parties. After he died of leukemia in 1954, his wife, Geneviève kept the house going until 1957. As with all the great fashion houses in Paris, the creative heritage of each label is preserved by the current stylist. Presently, the Jacques Fath couture and ready-to-wear is designed by Tom Van Lingen at the same location.

The acknowledged master of all the couturiers, Cristóbal Balenciaga, was born in 1895 in a Basque fishing village in Spain. In 1915 he opened his dressmaking shop in San Sebastien, learning his trade without any apprenticeship with a French couturier. He opened his Paris salon on the avenue George V in 1937, and was immediately lionized in the pages of *Harper's Bazaar*. A shy and reserved man, Balenciaga believed that the "essence of chic was elimination". His clothes were structured and classical, the product of a dedicated perfectionist, quietly creating trends before they were recognized by the press. (The sack dress of 1957 was his invention, copied by every dress manufacturer in America.)

Balenciaga allowed himself more *fantaisie* in the jewelry department. Robert Goossens designed an openwork "Spanish cross" with a ruby cabochon and faceted black glass stones. Countess Zoltowska of the Maison Cis, designed miniature eggs (pink, green, or turquoise enamel on one side, encrusted with crystals on the other) strung on a sautoir with a pear-shaped pendant in the Sixties. There were earrings and bracelets to match. Her 1955 Balenciaga dandelion pin (over 4" wide) with copper wires and strass was also sold, in another version, at Bergdorf Goodman in New York.

Balenciaga was loyal to his designers and wealthy society clients through the Fifies and Sixties until he abruptly closed his House in 1968. He felt that the astronomically high costs of creating fashion made haute couture an anachronism; a thought shared by the students and radicals who manned the barricades of the May '68 revolution in Paris. All the haute couture houses cut back on their luxury collections. (Among the young people, even wearing a cashmere sweater was considered a bourgeois capitalist sin!) Balenciaga returned to Spain in disgust, where he died four years later.

Hubert de Givenchy, born in 1927, was cut from the same cloth as Balenciaga, who considered him his heir. Although Givenchy was educated at both the Ecole des Beaux Arts and law school, he chose the couture metier, working for Lelong, Piguet and Fath between 1945 and '49, before Schiap asked him to join her stable between 1949 and '51. He opened the House of Givenchy in the following year. His muse, Audrey Hepburn, exemplified his cool, elegant style to perfection in *Breakfast at Tiffany's*. Roger Scemama designed girandole pearl drop pins and earrings for him in the Sixties. A simple gold-plated necklace signed "Givenchy" was typical of the Seventies tailored look.

Magnificent necklace of oval and square-cut "rubies" and pearls by Robert Goossens for Balenciaga, 1961. (Work in progress). *Courtesy of Robert Goossens archives, Paris*

Sleek gold-plated necklace for the Tailored Woman, by Givenchy. ca. 1970. *Courtesy of private collection, Los Angeles. Photo by Robert Weldon*

Pair of crystal earrings with double hoops of strass balls by Maison Gripoix for Christian Dior, 1956. *Courtesy of Jill Spalding Collection, NY. Photo by Richard Marx*

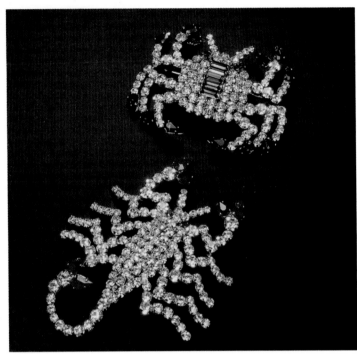

Scorpio and Crab in pavé strass from the Zodiac series, stamped "Christian Dior, 1966." *Courtesy of Robin Feldman Collectibles, NY. Photo by Robert Weldon*

Christian Dior (1905-1957) was born in Normandy to a prosperous family. He spent his youth in Paris of the riotous Twenties, where he opened an art gallery which went belly-up after the Crash of 1929. Dior took art lessons and plucked up the courage to show his fashion designs to the couturier Robert Piguet, who hired him in 1937. During the war, he worked with peasants on a farm in the country, wearing wooden *sabots* shoes and happily growing vegetables. Called back to Paris after the war, he began co-designing collections with Pierre Balmain for Lelong. Then, in 1945, with the backing of the textile tycoon, Marcel Boussac, he opened the Maison Dior on the avenue Montaigne.

In 1946 Dior sent an emissary on a troop ship to New York to announce his opening to New York buyers and the press. They all showed up in 1947 to tout the wildly successful "New Look" collection.[25] (The phrase was coined by the American press.) Dior launched the wasp-waisted, calf-length full skirts which were a welcome relief after war-time austerity. The wasp-waisted *guêpière* corset was introduced to cinch in the waist and push up the breasts. (*guêpe* means "wasp" in French, but the corset was called "Gay Pierre" by the Americans who wore them, little knowing that Pierre had nothing to with it!).

The "New Look" bateau neckline was a perfect frame for elaborate bibs and necklaces of cascading faux pearls and beads. Short hair styles begged for long earrings, and sleeves cut high above the wrist bared arms for bracelets. Dior turned to the Maison Gripoix in Paris, Mitchel Maer in London in 1952, and Henkel and Grossé in Pforzheim in 1955, to design his *bijoux de couture*, and bought the building next to the original salons to house his new jewelry, accessories, and perfume empires.

Necklace of great chunks of "carved" Lucite with chrome-plated balls. Stamped "Christian Dior, 1972." *Courtesy of American Mix, San Francisco, CA. Photo by Robert Weldon*

Necklace of two rows of blue/green iridescent Aurora Borealis beads, plus one row of faux emerald and sapphire pendants marked on clasp "Made in Germany for Christian Dior, 1964". *Courtesy of the author. Photo by Sandro Moro*

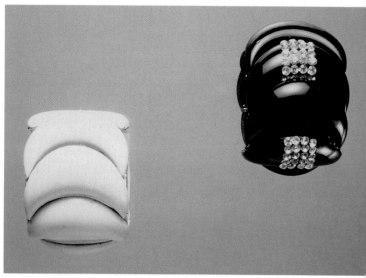

Gold-plated brass ring and earrings with large teal blue faceted crystal stones, mirror-backed for high reflection. All three pieces stamped "Balmain Paris", ca. 1960. *Courtesy of the author. Photo by Robert Weldon*

Two bracelets which are a study in contrasts of color and matières. The pure white leather crescent cuff was worn with the shiny black Bakelite cuff set with strass. Late Sixties, by Emanuel Ungaro. *Courtesy of Rita Sacks Collection, NY. Photo by Richard Marx*

In the mid-Fifties, Dior created the "H", "A", and "Y" lines which freed up the waist, but left plenty of room for elaborate jewelry. When he died suddenly in 1957, Yves St.Laurent, his assistant for four years, designed the "Trapeze" collection, making history again for the House of Dior.

Pierre Balmain was born in 1914 in the mountains of the Haute Savoie. He studied architecture at the Ecole des Beaux Arts in Paris. He was a junior designer for Molyneux before joining the House of Lelong where he and Dior co-designed collections. The two men talked of going into business together, but Balmain decided to go it alone, and opened his own house in 1946. Balmain was a perfectionist, and soon became one of the top couturiers. He especially enjoyed creating fabulous clothes and accessories for actresses, both on and off the stage and screen in the Fifties and Sixties: Kathryn Hepburn and Sophia Loren in the stage and film versions of *The Millionairess*, and Joan Fontaine and Jennifer Jones in *Tender is the Night*, as well as Marlene Dietrich, off stage. Balmain's jewelry is both classic and dramatic, like his clothes. Rousselet's faux pearl and emerald necklace for Balmain (1952) is signed "L.R." on the clasp. The matching ring and earrings pictured are made of large mirror-backed teal blue crystal set in gilded bronze, signed "BALMAIN, PARIS".

The Sixties produced a brand new breed of couturiers and jewelry designers who broke with classical tradition. Courrèges, Ungaro, Rabanne, and Cardin were products of the Space Age, designing revolutionary clothes and accessories for the young women who were eager to express their new freedom. Two of the couturi-

ers studied the basics with "The Master," Balenciaga, and then piloted their own revolutionary rockets into Space Couture.

André Courreges, born in the Basque country of France in 1925, trained 10 years with Balenciaga. In 1964, five years before man walked on the moon, he showed his pure white structural suits and coats worn by tanned, athletic models in his stark white atelier. The girls wore high white Vinyl boots with short skirts (Courregesè claims that he, not Mary Quant, invented the mini) or pantsuits. There was little room for jewelry in his strict aesthetic, but the occasional collar was made of plastic or metal, launching a new futuristic style.

Emanuel Ungaro, was born in Aix en Provence in 1933. His father, an Italian tailor, had fled Fascism and settled in France. Courrèges recommended him to Balenciaga when he left to start his own house, so Ungaro spent six years learning cutting, and an additional year with Courrèges in his atelier. He opened his own house in 1965, (with Sonia Knapp designing the fabrics) showing white bermuda shorts and short skirts with white trim. Ungaro's jewelry in the Sixties and early Seventies was influenced by the dazzling black and white contrasts of Vasarely's Op Art. A perfect complement to his clothes, Ungaro's bracelets were hinged white leather crescents, or black Bakelite with strass. White stacked composition squares with black insets made a stunning optical statement. There were also aluminum necklaces with bras and hip belts to match. In the Eighties, Ungaro was the first to mix four different prints together for one outfit, and the jewelry became more baroque.

Op Art jewelry of superimposed squares of white composition with black metal centers. The necklace is mounted on a chain, and the bracelet is a hinged cuff by Ungaro, Sixties. *Courtesy of Rita Sacks Collection. Photo by Richard Marx*

Cuff of folded chrome-plated metal by Paco Rabanne, for a Sixties runway collection. *Courtesy of private collection, Los Angeles. Photo by Sandro Moro*

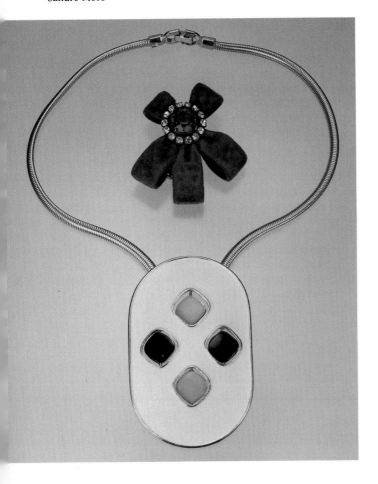

Blue suede stiff bow with faux sapphire and strass by Pierre Cardin, 1965. *Courtesy of Diane Keith Collection, Beverly Hills.* Enamelled white pendant with blue and black swivelling squares that switch colors on a gilded brass snake chain by Pierre Cardin, late Sixties. *Courtesy of Dena McCarthy Collection, Sherman Oaks, CA. Photo by Robert Weldon*

Asymmetric gilded bronze hinged bracelet with multicolored cabochons, ca. 1970. Signed Pierre Cardin. *Courtesy of the author. Photo by Robert Weldon*

It was a Spaniard with a bushy mustache, Paco Rabanne, who took the futuristic fad to the max. An architecture student run amok, he applied his art education to plastic jewelry which at first shocked, then entranced the conservative Balenciaga and Givenchy. For his own house in the mid-Sixties, he designed aluminum chain mail mini-dresses, and aluminum or chrome disc belts by the yard. His hoods, dresses, and jewelry of plastic links were anti-romantic, anti-classical and anti-mode, and were quickly embraced by young clients, then copied for mass-production. In the 90s, *toujours* true to metal, Rabanne enamelled plaques with primary colors for breast-plates and bracelets.

Pierre Cardin was born and brought up in Venice, Italy by his French parents. When his family emigrated, Cardin studied cutting with Paquin and Schiaparelli in Paris in the Forties, then Dior, leaving to form his own house in 1949. Cardin introduced the industrial zipper into his structural haute couture. This was copied in necklace form by costume jewelers. He designed Space Age bracelets and rings made of silver discs decorated with chunks of unfaceted diamond rough. White Vinyl cut into circles were used for collars, and pendants in the Sixties. Breastplates with freeform pendants were cut from metal. Circa 1970, a white enamel pendant on a gilt snake chain had four blue and black diamond-shaped elements which could be spun around for color coordination. A blue suede bow pin sported a faux sapphire center stone. Multicolored glass cabochons adorned an asymmetric gilded bronze bracelet. Cardin is immensely creative on all levels. He was the first haute couturier to open a *prêt-à-porter* boutique, in 1959, for which he was drummed out of the Chambre Syndicale. He stages his couture shows in his own theater, *L'Espace*, and has created industrial as well as fashion designs amounting to nearly 900 different licenses today all over the world.

Karl Lagerfeld (1938-) was born in Hamburg, Germany. His parents were middle-aged, wealthy, and imperious. Karl was "born to be alone," and has always known what he wanted from a very young age. He reads voraciously, popping bright ideas out of his computor brain which is honed in an extensive reference library written in four languages.

"Kaiser Karl" was hired first by Balmain, then Chloé in 1963, where he designed luxurious, young ready-to-wear clothes and accessories. In 1982 he was asked to apply fashion C.P.R. to the geriatric House of Chanel. He enthusiastically revived the patient with an irreverent reconstruction of the Chanel style in couture and *prêt-à-porter* clothes, as well as jewelry. The classic Chanel pearl sautoirs à la Lagerfeld are golf-ball sized. The gilt multi-chained "CC" belts are hung with a fig leaf, meant to be worn exactly where a modest Eve wore hers. Karl designs his own jewelry, as well as hiring freelance designers for couture collections. Ugo Correani in Italy is one of the few who can match his outragous imagination; His shower satire jewelry using the gas-pipe tube (for real,) with plumbing accessories in plastic, pearls, and strass was an amusing innovation in 1982 for Lagerfeld for Chloé.

Christian Lacroix was born in Arles in 1951. As a young boy in Provence, he "learned about Paris from American technicolor musicals." After graduating in Art History, Lacroix went to Paris to look for employment as museum curator. His work for a public relations firm led to designing for Hermès, Guy Poulin, and, finally, Jean Patou in 1981 where he was chief designer for six years. In 1986 he won the Golden Thimble Award in France, and the Oscar of Fashion in America in 1987 which celebrated his first exhuberant collection at his own House on the rue Faubourg St.-Honoré.

Lacroix is passionate about the Opera, and the bullfights (in Arles, the bulls are not killed) as well as Provençal folklore. His gilt brooches for the debut collection were taken from the anchor and trident motif of the Camargue bullfighter's cross, and repeated in gold embroidery by Lesage on his black matador jackets. He mixes different fabrics and bright colors together with the same gaiety as Schiaparelli, whom he admires, and whose Shocking Pink he adopted for his salon. Lacroix's Couture is as saucy and spicy as his beloved Provençal cuisine.

"I'm more interested in *ambience*, in the mood of a dress, than structure, so accessories and jewelry are an important part of creating that mood," Lacroix declares. His favorite motifs, crosses and hearts (he's an avowed romantic) show up in some form in all his collections; textured gold earrings and pendants in 1990, and filigree earrings in 1991. Articulated gold sections with strass made a stunning parure for his winter 1993 collection.

Fig leaf gilded chain belt. Karl Lagerfeld's sly wink at the classic Chanel belt, 1988. *Courtesy of Chanel archives*

Crisscross textured gilded hearts and crosses, and a matching bracelet by Christian Lacroix, 1990. *Courtesy of Christian Lacroix archives, Paris*

Playing with plumbing: Necklace with shower head of strass and pearls and real gas pipe. Three other amusing *tuyau à gaz* and chain pieces with faucet fastenings and nozzles by Ugo Correani for Karl Lagerfeld, 1985. *Courtesy of Ugo Correani, Milan, Italy*

Necklace and bracelet of gilded brass sections set with strass for Fall/Winter 1991/92 collection by Christian Lacroix. *Courtesy of Christian Lacroix*

Shocking pink and faux coral filigree earrings, bracelets, and pins for Spring, 1991 collection by Christian Lacroix. *Courtesy of Christian Lacroix*

Yves Saint Laurent was born in North Africa to a French-Algerian family in 1936. Barely seventeen, he entered a dress design competition held by the International Wool Secretariat, and won first prize (shared jointly with Karl Lagerfeld). Hired by Dior, he worked for him until his death in 1957, introducing his own "Trapeze" collection a year later. "Saint Laurent has saved France!" blared the headlines. It was easier done with a sketch book, than a rifle; the hyper-sensitive young man suffered a nervous breakdown during his compulsory military service in 1961, and was discharged.[26]

Having been replaced chez Dior by Marc Bohan, he opened the House of Saint Laurent (with the help of Pierre Bergé) in 1962, and his ready-to-wear line, Rive Gauche on the Left Bank four years later. Both his practical 1966 pantsuit and "*le smoking*" tuxedo for women were enthusiastically embraced by working women all over the world. Yves later designed dramatic costumes for films, theater, ballets, and the music-hall. A retrospective of his work organized by Diana Vreeland at the Metropolitan Museum of Art in 1983, was the first such accolade for a living couturier.

Jewelry and accessories have always been an important part of the Saint Laurent look. For his first collection in 1962, he showed black jet and baroque pearl earrings with a jet necklace, and in 1969 black Bakelite hoops. Roger Scemama designed a lovely crystal floral necklace for him in citrine and sherry topaz in 1962, as well as pendants mixing ruby strass with pearls or black resin. Flower Power in the late Sixties turned up in red and yellow enamel daisy necklaces, and twisted brass wire flower pendants with resin in red or earth colors. In 1970 Scemama produced Celluloid hair combs in bright colors for spring to wear with a red wooden bead belt. Robert Goossens fashioned a necklace of pastel stones of many different shapes in 1980 for Saint Laurent Couture, and red enamel heart-shaped earrings in 1991 for the Rive Gauche boutiques.

Bright plastic hair combs, and a red wooden bead belt, late Sixties by Roger Scemama for YSL. *Courtesy of Monique Vittaut. Photo by Bruno Pierson*

French jet and baroque pearl earclips by Yves Saint Laurent for his first Winter collection, 1962. Shoulder-sweeping black Bakelite hoops were for his Rive Gauche Boutique, 1969. *Courtesy of the author. Photo by Robert Weldon*

Two Sixties twisted brass wire pendants made with resin, by Roger Scemama for YSL. The red drop pendant is *courtesy of the author.* The brown and green resin set is *courtesy of Tiany Chambard, Paris. Photo by Bruno Pierson*

Persian motif enamelled heart earrings by Robert Goossens for YSL, Rive Gauche, 1992. *Courtesy of Robert Goossens*

Citrine and topaz crystal flowers with floral pendants form this necklace by Roger Scemama for Yves Saint Laurent, 1962. *Courtesy of Monique Vittaut Collection, Paris, France. Photo by Bruno Pierson*

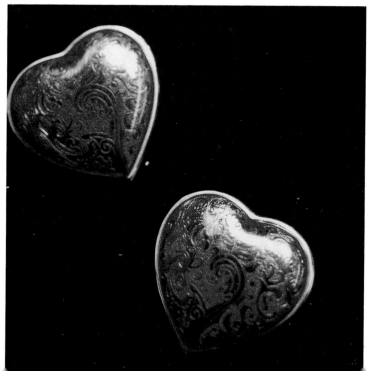

Gilded waterlilies curl around the neck and arm by Robert Goossens for Mme. Grès, 1969. *Courtesy of Robert Goossens*

Mme. Grès (1899-1993), the *Grande Dame* of French couture, who opened her Couture House in 1934, was still open in 1969 to commission a wraparound waterlily parure from Robert Goossens. Trained as a sculptor, Alix, later Mme. Grès, draped fabric like a Greek sculptor on her mannequins. Her contribution was unique and lasting; she continued creating her Classical drapes and pleats into the Eighties. Never without her tightly bound turban, Mme. Grès appreciated a structural approach. The gilded brass waterlily bracelets that Goossens devised for her twined gracefully around the lower and upper arm, with a large waterlily sculpted around the neck. Grès' brass and white metal Sixties pendants were Postmodern. In the Fall of 1994, an exhibition of fifty years of Mme. Grès' timeless fashion was exhibited at the Costume Institute of the New York Metropolitan Museum of Art.

Nina Ricci was another couturière with a long fashion history. Robert Ricci (1905-1988) persuaded his mother who was a dress-maker from Turin, Italy, to open her Haute Couture House in 1932. She began in the post-Depression with 40 dressmakers, building up to 450 by the outbreak of the war. Robert was President of the Chambre Syndicale from 1952-63, and was responsible for the 1948 launching of Ricci's *L'Air du Temps*, one of the great classic French perfumes. Nina Ricci moved to the av. Montaigne, in the "Golden Triangle" of Couture. Robert chose elegant jewelry by Wm. de Lillo, designed in Paris, to show with the 1978/79 collections designed by Gérard Pipart. The Haute Couture's Golden Thimble award was presented to Nina Ricci in 1987.

Rows of faux coral, ranging from angelskin pink to deep red glass beads were strung on a gilded coral branch clasp in the 60s for Ricci. Robert F. Clark and Wm. de Lillo designed outstanding creations for Robert Ricci, using Swarovski crystals and silk tassels. All of these pieces were signed "Wm de Lillo."

Louis Féraud opened his first Couture House in Cannes in 1955, then in Paris on the rue du Faubourg-St.-Honoré opposite the Elysées Palace. In 1957 he designed the wardrobe for several of Brigitte Bardot's films, (she was occasionally clothed!) In 1962, his ready-to-wear line was bought by Saks Fifth Ave., and Harrods in London. For Féraud's 1971 and 1972 collections, langani of Stuttgart, Germany designed a golden bib, and a shiny Space Age collar with contrasting nubby red compostion pendants. Féraud won the Golden Thimble Award for his Spring/Summer 1984 Haute Couture Collection. In 1990, he showed a necklace and hoop earrings of citrus-colored flat glass beads, and in 1992, pearl sautoirs of daisies and pearls to wear with the mini. Louis Féraud has published novels and exhibited paintings as well as designing his Couture and ready-to-wear lines.

L'Enfant Terrible of French fashion, Jean-Paul Gaultier, was born in 1952. From 1970 to 1975, he worked for Pierre Cardin in Paris and Manilla, where he created collections destined for the American market. For two years in between he was assistant to Michel Gomaz at Jean Patou. In 1976 he produced his first electronic jewelry. In 1978, Kashiyama, his Japanese manufacturing partner, backed his first collection. Known as a wild and crazy guy, his accessories for the winter 1981 High Tech Collection were tea bags, tin cans, and faucets. There followed tongue-in-cheek collections inspired by Existentialism, Dadaism, French Gigolos, and Rock Stars. In 1990 he created the costumes for Madonna's "Blond Ambition World Tour." The models on the runway parading the 1994 African Collection wore nose rings attached to the ears with little beaded chains.

Four geometric white metal and brass pendants for a Sixties collection by Mme. Grès. Stamped GRES PARIS. *Courtesy of Jan Vichel Gallery, Munich, Germany.*

After introducing the skirt for men, and hyping androgyny in general, his 1991 *Femme* (Woman) Collection came as a surprise - with a twist. The black "waterfall without diamonds" necklace (*rivière sans diamants*) was mostly unmounted prong settings with occasional strass "diamonds" thrown in, worn by the controversial tatooed model, Eve. Gaultier and his far-out designs can be seen in Robert Altman's 1995 film about Paris fashion *"Prêt-à-Porter"* (*Ready to Wear*) starring Kim Basinger, Julia Roberts, Sophia Loren, and Lauren Bacall.

A necklace with matching double hoop earrings of citrus colored flat glass beads by Louis Féraud. 1990. *Courtesy of Louis Féraud, Paris. Photo by Richard Nourry*

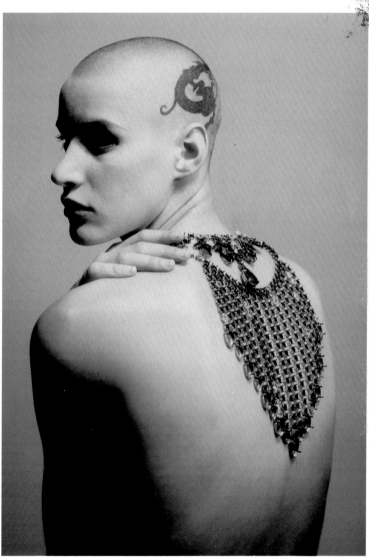

Rivière sans diamants, a graduated black waterfall of mostly unmounted prong settings, with an occasional strass "diamond" thrown in for sparkle, by Jean-Paul Gaultier from his *Femme* collection, autumn/winter 1990-91. *Courtesy of Jean-Paul Gaultier*

Six rows of faux coral ranging from angelskin pink to red. The coral branches are simulated in the gilded clasp signed by Nina Ricci, Paris, ca. 1970. *Courtesy of Dena McCarthy Collection, Sherman Oaks, CA. Photo by Robert Weldon*

Sautoirs of Sixties daisies and pearls to wear with slave bracelets and a mini, 1992, Louis Féraud. *Courtesy of Louis Féraud*

Dramatic necklace and earrings of Bermuda Blue cubes and clear crystal flowers with a 6" long pendant by Robert F. Clark for Wm. de Lillo. Designed and executed in France, these were shown in the 1978 Rothschild Exhibition in Paris. *Courtesy of Wm. de Lillo archives, Phoenix, AZ*

The Haute Couture jewelry of Wm. de Lillo is the creation of two men; Robert F. Clark and William de Lillo. They opened their first successful showroom in New York in 1967, continuing through 1976, when they moved to the south of France, where they experimented with sculpture and designed jewelry for the French aristocracy as well as the Houses of Nina Ricci and Schiaparelli until 1986.

William de Lillo was born in 1925 in Antwerp, Belgium, one of the diamond centers of Northern Europe. In the Forties, he began his association with the jewelry trade as a cleaver of diamond rough. An extended vacation trip to America in 1952 turned into a permanent New York residence, where de Lillo worked as liaison between the design department and the prestigious clientele of the top jewelry houses; Jean Schlumberger, Tiffany, Cartier, and Harry Winston. "For Tiffany, I was part of the designing team which conferred with the ateliers in Valenza, Italy. For Harry Winston, I orchestrated the midnight showing of a $5 million collection of jewelry to Crown Prince Gustav of Sweden," recalls de Lillo. Accustomed as he was to the gold and diamonds of the elite, why did he choose to establish a costume jewelry house in 1967?

De Lillo had long admired the outstanding work of Robert F. Clark. When Clark suggested that they go into business together, following the termination of his highly successful career as head designer for Miriam Haskell (1958-1967), William welcomed the challenge. Robert had been responsible for all the inventive new design ideas with Haskell, but wanted the freedom to create more than the "Haskell Look" in volume. His aim was to establish a high fashion, hand-made-to-order line, so he joined in a collaborative effort with de Lillo, where his imagination could run free. Twenty five jewelry lines for four collections a year were produced by an in-house staff of fifteen. The collections were bought by Neiman Marcus, I. Magnin, and Bonwit Teller, as well as designers Adolfo, Bill Blass, and Norman Norell. Belts, handbags and hair ornaments completed the look. Clark was able, at last, to indulge his ability to design for women who recognized good taste and elegance, and who were willing and able to pay for it.

Although created with Robert Clark, who comes from a distinguished Pittsburgh family (the Clark Candy Bar Magnates), Wm. de Lillo, who advises on the shape, color, and spirit of the jewelry, remains the only name on their trademark.

In 1976, de Lillo and Clark moved to the South of France, where they could concentrate on experiments in bronze sculpture, and the restoration of their historically-classified medieval stone house. While Robert's passion for creating had enticed William into the business partnership, this time it was William's enthusiasm for sculpting which sparked a move in a new direction. Their jewelry gained a new strength in the process.

In 1978, the Baron and Baroness Edmond de Rothschild sponsored, and hosted an exhibition of 400 pieces of Wm. de Lillo jewelry and sculpture, executed in France. Robert Clark designed a dramatic necklace of Swarovski square-cut Bermuda Blue and clear crystals and flowers, with a 6" long pendant. Another spectacular piece was of simulated fire opals, with faceted and cabochons "sapphires" mounted with an elaborate criss-cross of seed pearls.

The same year, Robert Ricci invited de Lillo to design jewelry for the Haute Couture collections at Nina Ricci. These collections required extensive fittings on models wearing the seasonal fashions. De Lillo recalls that one elaborate necklace, six feet long, had to be remade in order to reduce it to order by a quarter inch! The

lyre necklace for Ricci was a more reasonable two and a half inch wide collar of brilliant green Swarovski crystal stones. Robert's original idea of mixing red, navy, and gold silk tassels with red coral fluted glass stones, was designed around the neckline of a Nina Ricci organza evening dress. A butterfly brooch had an antique silver-plated five inch wingspan, and ruby-red cabochons accents.

"We sold a couture collection of prototypes to Ricci for $40,000. A clear crystal ruffle necklace, built on a gallery of wires, was reproduced in about 12 different versions, alternating colors in rows. Ricci made his models parade up and down before mirrors to see the effect. Couture jewelry was priced at about three times boutique jewelry, so it had to be perfect," de Lillo and Clark recall. All of these pieces were signed "Wm de Lillo", an unusual concession for Haute Couture houses in Paris.

Serge Lepage, the stylist for Schiaparelli in 1979, ordered de Lillo jewelry for his collections. Spectacular foot-long brooches were made of 24 kt. gold-plated, hand-hammered shells. Here we see sculptors at work; these are no mere jewels. Robert also designed a floral brooch, four inches across with superimposed layers of faux lapis and jade stones.

Collar of faux fire opals and faceted sapphires with elaborate criss-cross of seed pearls (3" wide), executed in France by Robert F. Clark for Wm. de Lillo, and featured in the Rothschild Exhibition, 1978. *Courtesy of Wm. de Lillo*

"Lyre" collar of emerald green Swarowski crystals by Robert F. Clark for Wm. de Lillo for Nina Ricci, av. George V Boutique, 1978. *Courtesy of Wm. de Lillo*

Silk tassel necklace with red fluted glass cabochons and red, navy and gold silk tassels designed in France for Nina Ricci Haute Couture Collection, 1979, by Robert F. Clark for Wm. de Lillo. *Courtesy of Wm. de Lillo*

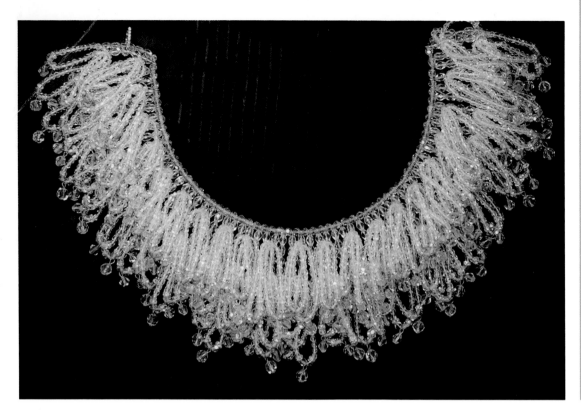

A frothy ruffled collar of clear crystal beads with rhinestone rondelles built on a gallery of crystal beads on wires. This was commissioned by a private client in Monte Carlo, designed by Robert F. Clark for de Lillo, ca. 1980. *Courtesy of the author. Photo by Sandro Moro*

Cascade brooch of 24 ct. gold-plated abstract shells for Schiaparelli Haute Couture Collection, 1979 by Robert F. Clark for Wm. de Lillo. Both these pieces are hand-cut and hammered 12" long sculptures. *Courtesy of Wm. de Lillo*

Cascade of hammered antique gold leaves, 24 ct. gold-plated, for Schiaparelli Haute Couture Collection, Paris, 1978/79, by Robert F. Clark for Wm. de Lillo. *Courtesy of Wm. de Lillo*

Dangling leaves 24 ct. gold plated brooch with matching earrings, and flower brooch of German faux lapis and jade for Schiaparelli Haute Couture Collection, 1979, by Robert F. Clark for Wm. de Lillo. *Courtesy of Wm. de Lillo archives*

Clark and de Lillo have a unique vision. All of their creations are immaculately executed; as impeccable on the back as the front. Robert hand-constructs all of the prototypes himself. When asked where he finds the patience to mount all of those minuscule seed pearls, William admits: "I hear deep sighs coming from Robert on occasion, but his devotion to creating our designs is so deep that he truly enjoys his work." Wm de Lillo jewelry is conceived for and collected by *la crème de la crème*. It can be sumptuous and extravagant. Fortunately, there are numerous pieces available in a medium price range for those women who want to look like a million dollars, even if they don't have it to spend.

De Lillo and Clark moved back to America in 1986. Their medieval house had become too demanding a mistress. In Scottsdale, Arizona, their atelier is devoted to the space and volumes of sculpture; their imaginations challenged by another dimension. The shift from one art to another has been a constant renewal, refining and nourishing each in its turn.

French Costume Jewelry : 1950s thru 1970s

There were many talented designers of costume jewelry in France who were not directly related to the Haute Couture industry, some of whom did not sign their work. Figurals were cast in metal and pavéd with strass. In the Fifties, there was a renewed interest in working with enamel; not the complicated *plique-à-jour* which demanded advanced technique, but the simple process of fusing a translucent layer of enamel, clear or colored, over a base of silver foiled copper. André Bazot and S. Chatenet were two artists who made attractive enamel jewelry in the late Fifties and early Sixties.

Nickel-plated brass or white metal Space Age pendants on neck rings were worn all over Europe by the young who were intrigued first by Sputnik, then the Walk on the Moon in 1969. Metal jewelry was lacquered dead white to match the PVC boots and minis of the pre-Hippy Sixties. Laminated Celluloid was given a new look by a young couple with great imagination and style: Lea Stein, and her husband, Fernand.

Yellow and white foiled enamel necklace and shell earrings signed "André Bazot", ca. late Fifties. *Courtesy of private collection, Milan, Italy*

Collection of colored and clear enamel over silver-foiled copper. The pins and pendants are signed "S. Chatenet, Paris" in gold ink. The earrings are signed "SC". Late Fifties. *Courtesy of the author. Photo by Robert Weldon*

"Flying saucer" matt and shiny nickel-plated pendant with chain fringe on neck ring, Sixties. *Courtesy of the author.* Matt metal cuff with faux aventurine stone in fan. *Courtesy of Arts 220, Winnetka, IL. Photo by Robert Weldon*

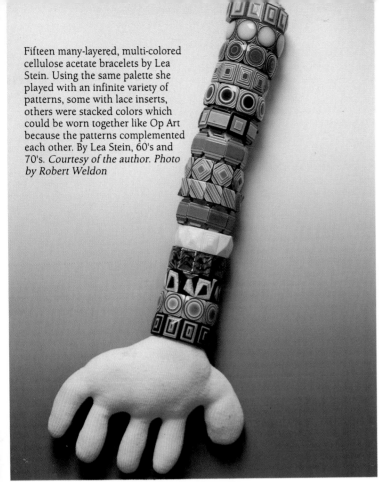

Fifteen many-layered, multi-colored cellulose acetate bracelets by Lea Stein. Using the same palette she played with an infinite variety of patterns, some with lace inserts, others were stacked colors which could be worn together like Op Art because the patterns complemented each other. By Lea Stein, 60's and 70's. *Courtesy of the author. Photo by Robert Weldon*

Lea Stein (1926-) was born in Paris, and studied applied arts with a retired professor in 1950. After marriage to her husband, Fernand Steinberger in 1954, she opened a small atelier in Belleville, a suburb of Paris. Lea supplied the creative ideas, and Fernand the techniques. He invented a laminated Celluloid process whereby up to 20 layers of cellulose acetate sheets were laminated together, sometimes with lace fabric, producing a textured sandwich. A secret component was the "ketchup", and the plastic pie was baked overnight to blend the ingredients. Then the Celluloid layers were cut into patterns for bracelets, pins, earrings, necklaces, and rings, and heated into pliable shapes. One piece could take up to four days to complete. Jewel boxes and picture frames were later added to the vast inventory.

Lea Stein's atelier mass-produced hundreds of figural pins using this process. The most successful model was the 3D fox, with a jaunty tail looped over its head, and shining slanted eyes. The Celluloid was laminated in several layers which were in turn stacked in three layers for the fox's head, alternating lace or moiré patterns. Different colors and iridescent patterns made fascinating eyes. (The eyes and ears of Lea Stein cats are always a point of interest in contrasting colors.) There were other animals and insects: colorful Celluloid cats; swallows; poodles; puppies; owls; ducks; fireflies; panthers; roosters; crocodiles; giraffes; elephants; and lions all paraded across the Parisian lapels in the Sixties and Seventies, as well as in America in the Eighties. Figurals in the shape of 1930s Packard cars, harlequin Pierrettes, bowler hats and canes, fans, shooting stars, hearts, flower pots, bow ties, boys on skateboards, or sporting the *"casquette"* cap, girls in Twenties cloche hats, and plaid

Thirteen French foxes in hot pursuit of three English rabbits. The foxes came in faux ebony, ivory, and tortoise shell as well as pastel shades and bright primary colors. There were plain, lace, *moiré*, or marbled patterns for this three layered design. The eyes was iridescent or pearlized. All signed "Lea Stein Paris" on metal pins, reverse. *Courtesy of the author. Photo by Robert Weldon*

Twenty five bangles: on the model's right arm are combinations of faux ivory, ebony, tiger-eye, and tortoise shell all twisted like taffy or laminated in layers. On her left arm are faux mother of pearl, pink, and fuschia lace snakes, red and olive green bangles and pearlized bangles. On her fingers are a dozen rings repeating the same menu, some high-rise, others are simple concentric pools of color. All by Lea Stein, 1960s and 1970s. *Courtesy of the author. Photo by Robert Weldon*

vests on tiny hangars were all stamped "LEA STEIN, PARIS" in block letters on the metal pin backs. One profile of a woman with wavy hair and 1940s padded shoulders was made in a small edition, because it didn't sell well at the time. (Dubbed "Joan Crawford", she is avidly collected in the 1990s.) Her earrings and eyes varied with each pin.

Seven figural pins: Two fireflies with shimmering wings investigate a 3-D flower pot and edelweiss bouquet; a pastel Pierrette, lad on skateboard, and vest on a tiny red hanger are all examples of "Lea Stein's" imagination. *Courtesy of the author. Photo by Robert Weldon*

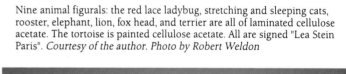

Twelve figural pins: swallow, jungle beasts, butterfly, two flappers with cloche hats, a boy wearing a *casquette* cap, a poodle and beagle, accordion, and two leaves laminated with gilt filigree signed "Lea Stein Paris" *Courtesy of the author. Photo by Robert Weldon*

Nine animal figurals: the red lace ladybug, stretching and sleeping cats, rooster, elephant, lion, fox head, and terrier are all of laminated cellulose acetate. The tortoise is painted cellulose acetate. All are signed "Lea Stein Paris". *Courtesy of the author. Photo by Robert Weldon*

Unsigned bangles with different coordinated hues twisted around each other were produced to complement the pins. Multicolored Celluloid layered sections were mounted on elastic to fit any wrist. Wide translucent cuffs of pink, red, magenta, orange, or black with lace insets were produced for a short time in the Seventies. (The French are small-boned, so the cuffs and bangles can only be worn on narrow wrists.) Ridged cuffs were another alternative. None of the bracelets, cuffs, or bangles are signed, but the palette and style of Lea Stein are instantly recognizable. There was also a small production of earclips in pin wheel, fan, or striped designs, and high rise rings or simple annulars which were cheap and could be worn four or five at a time.

"I have a mad passion for Art Deco motifs, and working with the infinite variety of the cellulose acetate matière. Its visual richness and tactile sensuousness are a constant delight," Lea declares. Her husband, Fernand, had a legitimate excuse to *chercher la femme* queueing for the bus, Métro, or cinema, "provided, of course, that the girls were wearing Lea Stein!," she laughs. Fernand was proud to relate his part in creating the Stein designs to any collector he could find. In 1980, crushingly high production costs forced the closure of the factory, and the inventory was dispersed in Europe and America.

In 1991, Lea Stein put together 2nd editions (from old and new stock) of the famous fox, the cat face hair clips, and assorted cats and dogs (in different colors from the first editions.) These were sold at the Galeries Lafayette in Paris and New York, and have resurfaced in flea markets. They are either signed "Agatha" (a jewelry shop in Paris where they were sold,) or "Lea Stein Paris." The pin fastening with "Lea Stein" signature is riveted on the back in the new editions, (it was heat-mounted in the earlier editions,) but the vivid colors and amusing designs are the same.

Sixteen laminated celluose acetate bracelets by Lea Stein: five bangles of colored lace in Deco patterns over white lace; six transparent bangles of gumdrop colors with lace swirls; three bangles of graduated multicolored or faux tortoise shell; and two layered cuffs. 1960s and 1970s. *Courtesy of the author. Photo by Robert Weldon*

Three "carved" pinwheel earclips, two maroon and olive green earclips, and two fan earclips showing only two of the many colors produced, by Lea Stein. *Courtesy of the author. Photo by Robert Weldon*

Bar pins, autocars, bowties, Pierrettes, "Joan Crawford" (with shoulder pads), a sailboat, and pyramid-layered lapel pins. A wondrous variety of simulated mother of pearl, tiger-eye, or tortoise shell. Signed "Lea Stein Paris". *Courtesy of the author. Photo by Robert Weldon*

The most enduring change in Parisian fashion was brought about by the mushrooming of talented ready-to-wear designers, (called *stylistes*) whose shops clustered around the Left Bank in St.-Germain-des-Prés in the Sixties. Dorothée Bis, Marie Martine, Sonia Rykiel, Emmanuel Khan, and Daniel Hecter brought affordable fashion to the people. Fabrice, on the rue Bonaparte, displayed chic costume jewelry of gilded metal or resin. Scooter carried fun jewelry like oversized *créoles* hoop earrings for the Sorbonne students.

Antiques shops reflected the new appreciation for 20th century art movements. On the Rive Gauche, several tiny boutiques specializing in vintage jewelry, accessories, clothes, and *objets d'art* opened: Tiany, Sorelle, and Aventurine in St.-Germain-des-Prés; and Philomène, Jacqueline Subra, and Aux Trois Grâces in Montparnasse. By the late Sixties, Art Nouveau horn pendants and silver brooches had crowded out the Victoriana in the Left Bank minuscule *vitrines*, only to be replaced in the early Seventies by geometric enamel brooches, and chrome and Bakelite necklaces. The Art Déco craze took off, fuelled by the 1966 *Les Années '25* Expo at the Musée des Arts Décoratifs, and by couturiers/collectors Karl Lagerfeld and Yves Saint Laurent who combed the Marché aux Puces for treasures. The weekly fashion magazine *Elle* (more hip than *Vogue*) featured vintage jewelry from these antiques bou-

tiques in its layouts, alerting young models and collectors who rushed to buy Twenties *robes perlées* and vintage accessories to go with them. (All of the above antiques stores still exist except for the last which closed when the author, the 3rd "Grace," returned to America.)

The dread blue jean invasion followed by the equally boring gold chains fad of the late Seventies put a damper on Decomania, though prices continued to climb as supplies diminished. Neo-Deco Galalith (post-WW II) was beautifully designed. Inevitably, the geometric enamelled brooches, and chrome and Bakelite necklaces were copied. A move to a more romantic style inspired a completely different look with glass necklaces of antique and modern beads from Czech, Venetian, and French sources in the Eighties.

Two glass bead necklaces using Czech and German press-moulded beads, and antique Venetian beads with pendants. Late 1970s, early 1980s. *Courtesy of private collection, Los Angeles. Photo by Robert Weldon*

Artist-jewelers: Line Vautrin and Claude Lalanne

Two auctions in 1986 at the Salle Drouot in Paris brought to light the extraordinary creations of an artist-jeweler who had been forgotten for twenty years. Line Vautrin had no training in making jewelry, and only scant knowledge of the basics; casting, and gilding. But there was metal-forging in her background (both her father and grandfather had been *forgeurs*), so when she was twenty she began forging gilded bronze bracelets like napkin rings (this, in the Thirties when chrome-plated jewelry was all the rage.) "At first I made tiny jewelry. Then a trip to Egypt changed all that. I saw King Tut's tomb and came back to Paris with ideas for massive cuffs and chokers like in Africa," Mme. Vautrin remembers.

She rented a stand at the Paris Exposition Internationale in 1937 which brought her a following, making it possible to open a tiny boutique ("no bigger than a closet, really!") on the rue de Berri in 1939. After three years, she built up a clientele and moved to the rue du Faubourg St.-Honoré, where she sold her jewelry, all-metal belts and belt buckles, cigar boxes, compacts, embroidered wedgies, and hundreds of custom-made buttons of gilded bronze, glass, or ceramic.

"During the Occupation, Parisian women bought jewelry and wore outrageous hats to thumb their noses at the Germans. We wore our platform shoes, and crazy hats, and changed accessories alot to lift our spirits, and when we walked by the Nazis we refused to look at them. That was our *luxe de la guerre*. It was our way of defending ourselves against the Occupation." Petite, peppery, and witty, Line Vautrin is the quintessential Parisienne. She felt that her profession was irrelevant, materials being scarce, but nevertheless the demand grew in the provinces in the gift shops (called *magasins de luxe* at the time.) "By 1946 my atelier/showroom in an 18th century *hôtel particulier* in the Marais employed 40-50 artisans. There were 26 rooms to play with. I displayed my enamelled necklaces (of lamp-wound baroque glass beads) on a 17th century painted wood statue of Venus, or on antique cherubs." (This was the closest she came to conventional costume jewelry.) It was a magical place to live and to work.

Vautrin plunged enthusiastically into experiments with bronze, ceramic, blown and frosted glass, and wire to create unique *bijoux fantaisie*. In the Forties and Fifties she made a series of cast bronze gilded crosses, rebus (puzzle pictographs) compacts, necklaces, bracelets, buttons, earrings, brooches, and boxes, all of which told a story. Line Vautrin is a skilled *raconteuse en métal* who sculpts myths, fables, and brain-teasers in bronze. (The Giacometti brothers were sculpting a similar aesthetic with their bronze furniture and lamps, but they never met. "It was in the air!, Vautrin explains). An intimate knowledge of French proverbs, poetry, and myths is required to unravel the Vautrin mysteries. Compacts and cigarette boxes were inscribed with poems by Paul Verlaine and Jacques Prévert. In the Forties, there were black lacquered brooches depicting the healing saints of Brittany, and compacts with verse in pictographs, and symbolic belts. Chubby crosses of many different denominations were made into gilded or silvered bronze pendants. All this at a time when: "*Bijoux de couture* were in fashion, but that wasn't my thing at all!" Line Vautrin laughs.

The artist's designs were first modelled in plasticine intended for plaster moulds, then cast, chased, and gilded or enamelled; all the usual steps for gilded bronze objets, except that this jewelry was most unusual with fairytale names. One brooch (1955) named *Saute-moutons* (or leap-sheep) is a play on leap-frog, with a ram's head at the bottom of six leaping sheep. Another brooch created in the Forties shows a woman in a crescent moon swinging between a heart and the stars.

Reverse of moon and star brooch with Line Vautrin signature and monogram. *Courtesy of Robin Feldman. Photo by Robert Weldon*

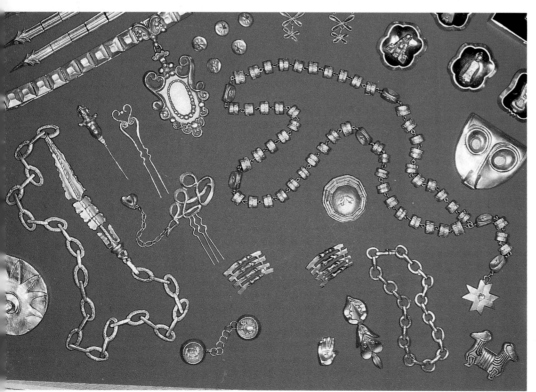

Collection of gilded cast bronze jewelry and compacts by Line Vautrin: Upper right corner clockwise are black lacquered brooches of the healing saints of Britanny; below these are a compact, "Cross my heart" necklace with a Maltese cross; enamelled rams; chain necklace, brooch; button "Apple in the hand of love"; Fat and Lean cow buttons, "Ferrets running" brooches, and articulated aglet belt; shell compact; hair pins, stick pin; belt with pendant, and star buttons, top center. By Line Vautrin, 1945-50. *Courtesy of David Gill Gallery, London, England*

Collection of "Talosel" resin jewelry encrusted with colored mirror-glass: necklaces, bracelets and brooches by Line Vautrin, 1960-65. *Courtesy of David Gill, London*

Six gilded sheep and a ram's head form a cast bronze brooch named *Saute-mouton* (or "Leap-sheep" rather than leap-frog); and a woman in a crescent moon gliding between her heart and the stars. Both gilded brooches were signed "Line Vautrin", 1950-55. *Courtesy of Robin Feldman Collectibles, NY. Photo by Robert Weldon*

There was an abrupt switch in the early Sixties to experiments with resin. "I invented and patented a process called "Talosel" (a synthetic resin based on wood with cellulose lactate) which I embedded with thin slivers of softly shaded oxidized mirror-glass, mounted with nickel-silver wire." Line moved from the Marais to St.-Germain-des-Prés, where she sold her Talosel necklaces, brooches, bracelets, and earrings. This led to dramatic Talosel sun mirrors, frames, and sculptures. After she turned 50, in the Seventies (in another of her 10 year life cycle changes,) she gave up her business and turned to teaching students how to create with resin. Since Vautrin's work has been rediscovered, resin and glass jewelry by her students has come on the market, some bearing their signatures. Not all Vautrin Talosel pieces are engraved "LV" in the resin, but the subtle color nuances of her oxidized mirror-glass, and original design distinguishes the artist's work from that of her students. When asked how she would characterize her work. Line Vautrin smiled: "In the old days we were called *parurières* (designers who created decorative accessories and jewelry), but that's obsolete now. I think *bijoux fantaisie* (fantastic costume jewelry) was apt, then it was art jewelry, but now they call it artists' jewelry. Whenever I take part in a retrospective exhibition, I go along with whatever the fashionable phrase is at the moment."[27] "Unique" about covers it. Vautrin winks at the world.

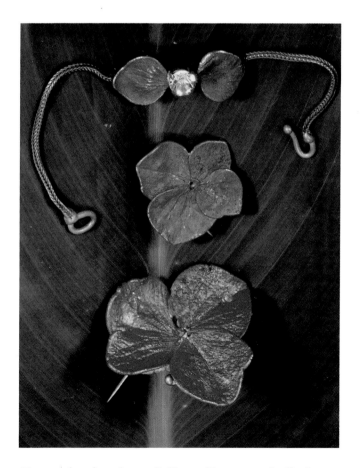

Hortensia bracelet and enamelled bronze blossoms cast by Claude Lalanne, 1980s. *Courtesy of Joan Agajanian Quinn Collection, Beverly Hills, CA. Photo by Robert Weldon*

Another talented artist/jeweler who is also a sculptress is Claude Lalanne. Claude and her husband, François Lalanne (b.1927) are renowned artists who have created furniture, sculpture, and décors for Schiaparelli, Dior, and Yves Saint Laurent, as well as table settings for Salvador Dali. Claude studied architecture at the Beaux Arts and the Arts Décoratifs Schools in Paris. The Lalannes discovered their metal-working technique through the American sculptor, James Metcalf.

Claude applied this art to couture jewelry; gilded bronze belts, necklaces, earrings, and hair combs of various leaf designs with a blackened patina were created for Yves Saint Laurent in the Seventies. Organic necklaces, earrings, and brooches in gilded bronze or silver as well as handbags and *objets extraordinaires* have been shown at the Paris Artcurial Gallery since 1978. The gilded bronze pieces are in editions of 250-350, silver or vermeil versions are available in editions of 150. All are signed and numbered.

"Like a plant twining 'round an arm or a neck, or a petal delicately joining its stem, so should jewelry hold its charm. One never knows for sure when it will open or close, or where it will begin or end,"[28] Claude Lalanne gently explains. She has made exquisite art jewelry of ginkho leaves, dogwood blossoms, mistletoe, lilacs, hortensia, and orchids. She models these fragile things directly in metal. "What can I say, since I love simple lines, and often create quite complicated shapes. In sculpture as in life, one must be stable and above all not too sentimental."[29]

By Claude Lalanne for Yves Saint Laurent: blackened gold metal *monnaie du pape* choker mounted on six strands of black and gilt metal beads; earrings of blackened silver metal leaves with black, grey, and gilt beads; blackened gilt metal leaves decorating two hair combs; and a necklace of bronze, black, and grey beads with leafy clasp. Ca. 1970s. *Courtesy of Wm. Doyle Galleries "Couture, Antique Clothing, Accessories & Costume Jewelry" catalog, April 27, 1994.*

French Jewelry: 1980s & 1990s

Hervé Van Der Straeten (1965-) studied painting at the Ecole des Beaux Arts where he began creating jewelry for his fellow students of twisted gold wire. In 1985 Thierry Mugler hired him to make runway pieces for the couture collection. These were followed the next year by jewelry for Balmain and Karl Lagerfeld, and buckles for Louis Vuitton. Christian Lacroix tapped his creative juices for fantasy jewelry to be shown with his opulent clothing for his 1988-90 Haute Couture.

"When I work with a designer, I try to catch the essence of what he's doing in his collection. I do not design Van Der Straeten for Lacroix; I try to match the spirit of his clothes. I try to create something different for each designer."

Finished prototypes are shown to the designer for approval. For Lacroix, he produced jewelry with an Indian, Thirties, and a sculptural Calder look in 1988-90, as well as pieces for Yves Saint Laurent Couture and Rive Gauche in 1989, and Lanvin in 1990. With gusto, Van der Straeten attacks heavy brass sheets with an electric saw, producing a primitive, rough outline which he hand-finishes or hammers.

Van Der Straeten decided to strike out on his own, but found the French were reluctant at first to buy his jewelry in retail boutiques independent from couture houses. "The French like classical designs", Hervé sighs. (Where have we heard that before!) The British, however, were less timorous, and Van Der Straeten jewelry sold very well at Harrod's and Liberty's in London, and in New York City at Jaded. The French have recently caught up; Jeanne Moreau has worn his jewelry in three films since 1990.

Van Der Straeten does with cut-out brass sheets what Matisse did with cut-out paper. His necklaces are reminiscent of the Master's famous "Dancing", as gold-plated brass nude silhouettes cavort around the wearer's neck. A sun brooch is three-dimensional sculptural, as is all his jewelry. He has designed stage jewelry for artists as diverse as Jessye Norman, and Prince.

A sun brooch cut from brass and gilded by Hervé Van Der Straeten, 1980s. *Courtesy of Hervé Van Der Straeten Collection, Paris, France*

Cavorting nudes dance around the necklace of this gilded brass piece signed Hervé Van Der Straeten. *Courtesy of Hervé Van Der Straeten Collection*

Isabel Canovas was born in Paris in 1945. Her Spanish father, Blas Canovas, (as well as her brother Manuel) designed Haute Couture fabrics so high fashion design was a part of her life. She was accessories designer for Dior between 1972 and 1980, except for one year (1976) when she was accessories director for Louis Vuitton. In 1981 Isabel founded her own company with her husband, Michael Grunelius, to market and create her own couture jewelry and accessories. Her first boutique was on the avenue Montaigne, surrounded by many of the Haute Couture Houses. She opened other boutiques on Madison Ave. in New York, (1985) and in Madrid, (1988.)

Isabel was the first independent designer to launch a complete line of luxurious accessories which included bags, gloves, umbrellas, belts, shoes, hats, scarves, shawls, and hair ornaments as well as her very distinctive jewelry. Her taste is lavish and extravagant using fringes, tassels, fur, and feathers in unexpected places.

"Women like jewelry that swings and clanks, so our best sellers are charm bracelets and pendant earrings with masses of faux stones. Outrageous pins are fun to travel with and versatile; worn one day on a hat, the next on a belt."

Canovas jewelry is gold-plated brass, rich looking and sumptuous. Necklaces of ethnic or Commedia dell'Arte masks have earrings and charm bracelets to match. A multi-chainlink bracelet is

nearly 4" wide, and another wide cuff represents playing cards. Her Circus collection earrings were tigers leaping through hoops, with a charm bracelet of clown faces made of glass. Isabel also designed Byzantine brooches with *pâte de verre* and pearls which were executed by the Maison Gripoix. Individual lampwork glass beads of irregular shapes were specially made for her. Canovas handbags and shoes are custom-made of silk and lizard with matching motifs for her numerous stunning accessories.

French women are geniuses at accessorizing. "The same simple black dress worn with a different shawl and jewelry not only looks completely different; it makes a woman FEEL completely different."[30] That statement is the essence of French femininity and chic, and the key to Isabel Canova's success.

Unfortunately, after building up an international clientele for ten years, Isabel Canovas closed all her boutiques in early 1993, following a serious car accident. She will be missed.

Other talented designers have followed the Canovas total fashion accessories theme. Maud Frizon (who began by designing extravagant shoes), Paloma Picasso (only jewelry, at first, for Tiffany's), Frances Patiky Stein, and Dominique Aurientis are among those who now design a full line of accessories, including jewelry; complementary parts to make the whole woman feel and look special. And French.

Wide (4") chain-linked bracelet of gilded brass by Isabel Canovas, 1990. *Courtesy of the author. Photo by Robert Weldon*

1. Vivienne Becker, *Rough Diamonds*, New York, Rizzoli, 1990, pg.19.
2. Maurice Rheims, *The Flowering of Art Nouveau*, New York, Harry N. Abrams, n.d.
3. *La Grande Vapeur*, Musée du Peigne et des Matières Plastiques, Oyonnax, France, 1987.
4. Melissa Gabardi, *Art Deco Jewellery, 1920 to 1949*, Suffolk, England: Antique Collectors' Club, 1989, pg. 52.
5. Melissa Gabardi, "Flights of Fancy: The Frivolous Years, France 1920-1939" from *Jewels of Fantasy, Costume Jewelry of the 20th Century*, Deanna Farneti Cera, editor. Ruth Peltason, editor, English edition. New York, Harry N. Abrams, Inc.,1992, pg. 144
6. Alain Lesieutre, *The Spirit and Splendour of Art Deco*, London and New York, Paddington Press, Two Continents Publishing group, 1974, pg. 219.

Commedia dell'Arte gilded masks adorn bracelets, handbags, necklaces, and earrings, as well as a fan, late 1980s, by Isabel Canovas. *Courtesy of Isabel Canovas Collection, Paris. Photo by Jean-Louis Bloch Lainé*

7. Janet Flanner (Genêt), *Paris Was Yesterday, 1925-1939*, ed. by Irving Drutman, New York, Viking Press, Inc, 1972, pg. 86.
8. Hans Nadelhofer, *Cartier, Jewelers Extraordinary*, New York, Harry N. Abrams Inc. 1984, pg. 188.
9. Jean-Claude Baker and Chris Chase, *Josephine Baker, the Hungry Heart*, New York, Random House, 1993, pg. 174.
10. Lacquer techniques gleaned from 1975 conversations in Paris with the designer Eileen Gray (who also studied with Sugawara in the Twenties) and Dunand jewelry details and provenance from Felix Marcilhac, *Jean Dunand: His Life and Works*, English edition, New York, Harry N. Abrams, 1991, pp. 101-279.
11. Gabardi, *Art Deco Jewelry*, pg. 203.
12. Nadelhoffer, *op. cit.*, pg. 232.
13. Georges Perec, Yves Hersant, Tim Street-Porter, "Hollywood on Eyes", *FMR* No. 3, Franco Maria Ricci, editor, Milan, Italy, August, 1984.
14. Gabardi, *Jewels of Fantasy*, pg. 51.
15. Palmer White, *Haute Couture Embroidery: The Art of Lesage*, New York, Vendome Press, 1988, pp 61-65.
16. Gabardi, *op. cit.*, pg 250.
17. Amy Fine Collins, "Haute Coco" from *Vanity Fair*, June, 1994, pg. 137.
18. Patrick Mauriès, *Jewels by Chanel*, Canada, Little, Brown & Co., 1993, pg. 34.
19. Collins, *op.cit.*, pg. 144.
20. Palmer White, *Elsa Schiaparelli: Empress of Paris Fashion*, New York, Rizzoli International, 1986, pg. 81.
21. Gabardi, *op. cit.*, pp. 234-237.
22. Marjorie Dunton, "La Chambre Syndicale", *Couture*, Garden City, N.Y., Doubleday & Co. 1972, pp. 40-49.
23. *Delaunay, Robert et Sonia*, exhibition catalog, Musée d'Art Moderne de la ville de Paris, Paris, 1985.
24. André Ostier, "Jacques Fath Recalled", *Couture*, pg. 169.
25. *Ibid.*, pg 147.
26. *Ibid.*, pg. 228.
27. Line Vautrin and Patrick Mauriès, *Line Vautrin, Sculptor, Jeweller, Magician*, London and New York, Thames and Hudson, 1992, pg.14.
28. *Bijoux de L'Art*, Aura, Cahiers d'Artcurial, Paris, 1992.
29. *Les Lalanne*, Aura, Cahiers d'Artcurial, Paris, 1991.
30. Elsa Klensch, "The Finishing Touches," *Connoisseur*, New York, December, 1988, pg. 109.

A winning hand of cards is dealt for this hinged cuff bracelet by Isabel Canovas, ca. 1990. *Courtesy of Isabel Canovas Collection. Photo by Jean-Louis Bloch Lainé*

Neo-Deco hinged cuffs: two of plastic simulating jade and lapis with black layers; and one with Bakelite and black wood, chrome-plated. Two red and black Galalith chrome-plated high standing rings of asymmetric design. *Courtesy of Joanne McPherson and private collection, Los Angeles. Photo by Robert Weldon*

Chapter 2:

Germany

The Darmstadt Experiment

The Munich art publication *Jugend*, meaning "youth," coined the phrase *Jugendstil* for the German version of Art Nouveau style. This magazine published the *fin de siècle* naturalistic and floral designs peculiar to Munich tastes in 1890. The motifs became increasingly controlled and abstract in 1900. Hatpins and belt buckles of silver or Alpacca peacock feathers studded with "eyes" of Czech blue/green foiled glass were not in the wildly exhuberant French style. The trail of the doomed tendrils leads to Darmstadt and Pforzheim, 100 miles apart from each other, where the abstract German character of *Jugendstil* was firmly established.

The Grand Duke Ernst Ludwig Hesse, Queen Victoria's grandson, was anything but Victorian in his tastes. Well acquainted with the English Arts and Crafts and Vienna Secession artists, he was an enthusiastic supporter of avant-garde ideas and had the power and initiative to establish an artists' colony in 1899 near his palace in Darmstadt. He combined the roles of art patron and royal head of his Duchy to further his ideal of a cohesive design style in arts and crafts which could be produced and marketed in Darmstadt, bringing his subjects a successful commercial enterprise. He succeeded in gathering together some formidable talent, all young and full of hope and dedicated to the idea of *Gesamtkunstwerk*, the total art work. The 1901 exhibition of their architecture and objets, however, was neither a financial nor a critical success.

The Grand Duke's stable of artists was lead by the Austrian architect Joseph Maria Olbrich (1867-1908) whose jewelry was as pure and structural as his buildings. Other architects who eventually turned their considerable energies to jewelry design were Patriz Huber (1878-1902) and Peter Behrens from Munich (1868-1940). Sculptors Ludwig Habich (1872-1949) and Rudolf Bossett (1871-1938) and the painter Hans Christiansen (1866-1945) also contributed jewelry designs. Circles were squared, and whiplashes restrained, and the Darmstadt publication, *Deutsche Kunst und Dekoration*, spread the word. Unfortunately, the colony's artistic endeavours as an entity were terminated in 1902, although some artists continued their participation until World War I stopped all activity. Another patron with business acumen and daring ideas was needed. Enter Theodor Fahrner of Pforzheim.

Notturno, from *Stil*, tafel 1, heft VII, issue 7, 1922. Evening coat by Hermann Gerson. *Pochoir* print with silver ink by Offterdinger. *Print courtesy of the author. Photo by Robert Weldon*

A fine Art Nouveau metal belt buckle; the restrained design of the peacock feathers is enlivened with luminous blue-green "eyes" of crystal over silver-foil cabochons from Gablonz, Bohemia. *Courtesy of Rita Sacks Collection, NY. Photo by Robert Weldon*

Theodor Fahrner, the Artists' Manufacturer

Theodor Fahrner (1859-1919) was a man with a mission. He sought designers with innovative ideas whose sketches could be transformed into partly or wholly machine-made jewelry in his Pforzheim factory. He demanded high artistic quality for mass-production; something previously unattainable with the technology and artists available. The Darmstadt Colony was the perfect source. The designers eagerly entered into a mutually beneficial cooperative effort with Fahrner who was more than a business man. He was a creative manufacturer with an infallible eye who had the imagination to hire free-lance artists in addition to his in-house designers.

Architects and interior designers, Joseph Maria Olbrich, Max Gradl and Patriz Huber joined with painters Julius Müller-Salem, Bert Joho, and Ferdinand Morawe, and sculptors Ludwig Habich and Franz Boeres. Georg Kleemann was originally a graphic designer, before he signed on. Fahrner gave his artists free rein and the latest technology with which to express their ideas in silver and gold. Max Gradl (1873-1934) was the first free-lance designer to join the Fahrner firm. His designs won a silver medal for Fahrner at the 1900 Paris Expo. His silver brooch of 1903 with the typically restrained *Jugendstil* curves was decorated with chrysoprase, and green rhinestones, the latter an unusual addition. Gradl remained with Fahrner until 1910 as artistic consultant.

Fahrner's free-lance designers had distinctive styles. Franz Boeres (1872-1956) used matt enamel pyramids, triangles and open-work grills for his pendants designed between 1905 till Fahrner's death in 1919. Patriz Huber's belt buckles and brooches were full of organic curves and chrysoprase stones. He designed prolifically only 2 years for Fahrner, committing suicide in Berlin in 1902, aged 25. Georg Kleemann (1863-1932) mixed matt enamel with opals or garnet cabs, in a distinctive rectilinear style. (He also designed for Heinrich Levinger.) Joseph Olbrich (1867-1908) designed pieces of great refinement with dangling fresh water pearl pendants. Unknown staff artists produced hundreds of designs with matt enamel and agate until c. 1910 when marcasites were added for the subtle reflections that these faceted pyrite stones produced. Fahrner formed an important pre-WW I export business with Murrle, Bennett & Co. in London (see the chapter on England) which supplied that company with 80% of its merchandise.

When Theodor Fahrner died after a long illness in 1919, Gustav Braendle bought the firm from his widow, with the proviso that he retain all former employees. The name was changed to Gustav Braendle-Theodor Fahrner Nachfolge. Braendle and his staff designed hundreds of marcasite and stylised leaf or floral pieces in the Twenties, and striking geometric silver (or silver-gilt) pendants and pins with predominantly coral or black agate stones, colorful matt enamel, and, of course, the ever popular marcasite.

Striking silver pendant with black onyx, coral and marcasites in a geometric design. Probably Gustav Braendle for Theodor Fahrner, c. 1930, stamped "TF". *Courtesy of Sherry Goldman Collection, Sherman Oaks, CA. Photo by Robert Weldon*

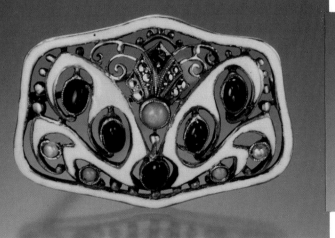

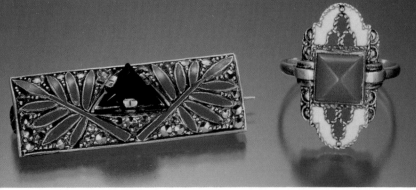

Silver pin with matt white enamel, decorated with coral, pearls, and marcasites. Signed TF, linked in a circle, circa 1910. *Courtesy of Gail Freeman Antique and Estate Jewelry, Los Angeles, CA. Photo by Robert Weldon, courtesy of the G.I.A.*

Silver pin with red enamelled leaves nestling in a marcasite ground, flanking a black onyx triangle, ca. 1920. Signed "TF". *Courtesy of Gail Freeman Antique and Estate Jewelry.* Silver-gilt ring with corded wire, and coral and white mat enamel. Made in Germany in the style of Theodor Fahrner, no signature; ca. 1930. *Courtesy of private collection, Los Angeles. Photo by Robert Weldon, courtesy of the G.I.A.*

Parure of necklace, bracelet, pin, ring, and earrings of silver filigree with turquoise(?) stones and marcasites, signed "TF." *Courtesy of Charles Pinkham, Pomona, CA. Photo by Robert Weldon*

In the Thirties and Forties, filigree jewelry provided a change from the usual inventory. *Filum-granum*, or string and knot, was a traditional folk jewelry technique. Silver wire could be twisted, granulated, beaded or corded by hand and then soldered to the piece. This was an expensive process, and the result was fragile, but both Fahrner and Braendle made good use of it.[1]

Two silver rings in a classic Art Deco design with chrysoprase and marcasites, stamped "Sterling, Germany", attributed to T. Fahrner; c.1930. *Courtesy of Diane Keith collection, Los Angeles.* Silver bracelet with alternating links of marcasites, and six opals, 1931, stamped "TF." *Courtesy of Rosebud Gallery, Berkeley, Ca. Photo by Robert Weldon*

Top center: a silver pin with multicolored matt enamel and hard stones, ca. 1930. Signed "TF." Center right: a silver ring and pendant set with chrysoprase stones and marcasites, signed "TF", ca. 1930. Bottom center: a silver pin with white and coral enamel, and corded wire, c. 1930. Signed "TF." Bottom left: brick-red and cobalt blue porcelain earrings with gold accents by Rosenthal, with silver and marcasite tops, ca. 1930. *Courtesy of Wiener Interieur, Vienna, Austria. Photo by Helmar Dankl*

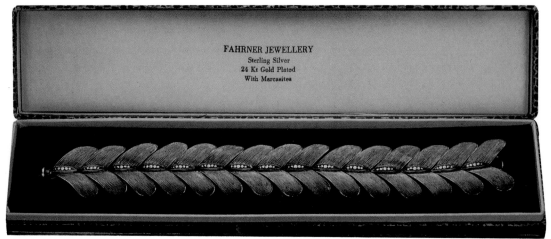

FAHRNER JEWELLERY
Sterling Silver
24 Kt Gold Plated
With Marcasites

Sterling silver bracelet of corded wire, 24 kt. gold plated, with marcasites, in original box. This delicate filigree style was first produced in the Thirties, and reprised in the Fifties. Signed "TF". *Courtesy of Thanks for the Memories, Los Angeles. Photo by Robert Weldon*

Gustav Braendle was an entrepreneur worthy of the Fahrner succession. He ran full page color ads in the German fashion magazines of the Twenties and Thirties (*Die Dame, Der Querschnitt,* and *Die Schaulade*) and increased export trade to Europe and North and South America. He had the chic line for the well-to-do pampered elite, and a cheaper line for the *hausfrau*. In 1931 Braendle registered the Fahrner seal (*mit der plombe,* with the metal tag) to assure authenticity in the wake of cheap copies. The "Original-Fahrner" stamp was used from the middle to the end of the Twenties, while "DEA *Schmuck*" was registered in 1932.

Braendle lost 2 sons in action in World War II, and in 1945 his firm and all the archives were destroyed by the bombing raid which leveled Pforzheim. Undaunted, after the war with his remaining third son he rebuilt his business until he died in 1952. Herbert Braendle produced filigree jewelry with marcasites or translucent, rather than matt enamel, using bird or animal designs or just plain classics that had proved successful before the war. The decision to expand into gold jewelry in the Seventies came too late to save flagging sales. When Herbert Braendle died in 1979, the Fahrner firm closed its doors, having spanned nearly a century of remarkable jewelry design.

An interesting footnote in Theodor Fahrner history was provided by Graham Dry, an art consultant in Munich, when he was asked what has become of the thousands of Fahrner pieces produced before World War II. "In Nazi Germany, when Hitler began his ethnic cleansing campaigns, any jewelry which looked too elegant was probably of foreign origin, and therefore not to be tolerated; so masses of Fahrner jewelry were destroyed because it looked "too French", even though produced by a German firm." This woeful fact, along with the devastation of war, explains the relative rarity in the 90s of 30s German jewelry and artifacts.

Because of the extensive export of German-manufactured jewelry to England by Murrle, Bennett and Fahrner, as well as the importation of British Arts & Crafts, and Liberty & Co., and French Art Nouveau to Germany, exact provenance is difficult to establish. Silver brooches, buttons, and pendants were produced in Pforzheim in the restrained German Art Nouveau, or Celtic Liberty style, and exported to London. An early silver sautoir, with the elongated oval link chain and mauve enamelled oval segments with spirals and pin-head bumps, was typical of a 1902 German (Darmstadt?) design, but is not signed. The 15th century Spanish galleon set sail on numerous Northern European Arts & Crafts pins and was stamped *"hand-arbeit"* (hand-crafted) in Germany.

There were many Pforzheim manufacturers who produced silver Art Nouveau designs from 1900 to 1914. Heinrich Levinger, was a silversmith who executed *plique-à-jour* pieces by the Viennese

Three Art Nouveau pieces probably made in Germany for the English market: silver brooch with spinel and glass stones, a silver pendant and chain with moonstones (marked 800), and a silver (marked 925) pendant with entrelac design around a turquoise (faux?). (This piece was pictured in a Liberty of London catalogue of the period.) *Courtesy of Gail Gerretsen Collection, Los Angeles. Photo by Robert Weldon*

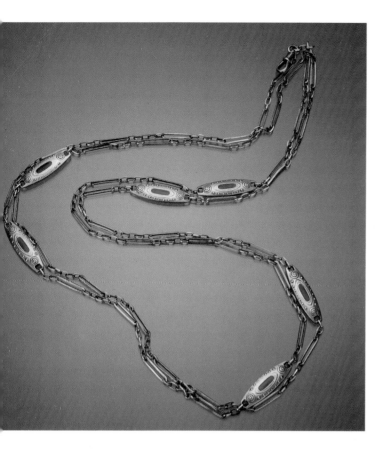

A silver sautoir with mauve enamelled sections with scrolls and pin-head bumps, and a Darmstadt-style chain with elongated links. *Courtesy of Gail Gerretsen Collection, Los Angeles. Photo by Robert Weldon*

artist, Otto Prutscher, as well as Kleemann. Carl Hermann made delicate enamelled dog collars and brooches. Victor Mayer, Mayle & Mayer, Wilhelm Kreiss, and Gebrüder Falk are less well known names who produced inexpensive jewelry before the war.

During World War 1, fine metals were at first curtailed, then forbidden for jewelry, so only glass, cast-iron, ivory, and porcelain were used. At first, ivory pendants and buttons were painted with cherubs and flowers. Eventually, a cheap substitute was needed, so white porcelain medallions, simulating ivory, were hand-painted over the glaze.

Porcelain jewelry in the form of medallions and buttons has been popular in Germany since the 18th century. The Rosenthal factory, founded in 1879 in Selb by Philip Rosenthal (1855-1937) was the first factory after World War 1 to produce heart-shaped porcelain pendants in a diluted Jugendstil motif. Glossy, round medallions were painted with gold scrolls, signed Rosenthal AG, Marktredwitz, Bavaria. Kurt Wendler (1893-) launched his expressionistic style of spiky foliage, Alp wild flowers, and exotic birds in tiny jungle scenes, accented with gold. Silver or brass mounted plaques were overglaze painted in bright yellow, orange, and blue; the pointed leaves reminiscent of the Austrian artist, Dagobert Peche. Other firms followed suit; Deusch & Co. in the town of Lorch, enamelled clover-shaped pendants cobalt blue, and trimmed them with galvanic silver-plate.[2]

Wendler decorated the gold ground of Rosenthal porcelain bracelets with blue, red, and white Deco zigzags in 1923. These were gilded on the interieur as well. Earrings painted from the same spectacular palette were set with marcasites. By the Thirties, modern necklaces of simple enamelled porcelain spheres were the fashion. In 1932, Rosenthal bought a Munich-based porcelain factory and produced thousands of beautifully sculpted statues and china until the company went out of business in 1963.

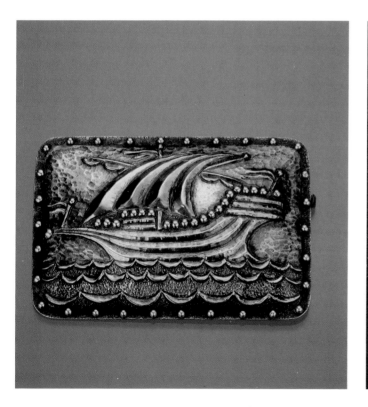

The galleon, (a frequent Arts & Crafts theme), sails across a choppy sea in this silver (.900) pin marked "HANDARBEIT," hand-crafted, with an illegible benchmark shaped something like a Roman centurion's helmet. *Courtesy of Gail Gerretsen. Photo by Robert Weldon*

Pendants and a brooch from the Rosenthal Porcelain AG, overglaze painted. The center pendant, and lower left pendant are attributed to Kurt Wendler, ca. 1924. The others are ca. 1930. Reproduced from "Porzellanschmuck" by Graham Dry from *Die Kunst und das schöne Heim*, July 1982. *Courtesy of Graham Dry, Munich, Germany*

A hand-painted overglaze porcelain pendant, unknown manufacturer, 1920s. *Courtesy of the author. Photo by Robert Weldon*

An overglaze gold-painted pin, signed Rosenthal, Marktredwitz, ca. 1930, and a pendant from Hertel, Jacob & Co., Rehau, overglaze painted with galvanic silver plating by Deusch & Co., Lorch, ca. 1925. *Courtesy of the author. Photo by Robert Weldon*

Manufacturers' marks on verso of Rosenthal (under a crown,) and Deusch (under a pitcher) with silver mark. *Photo by Robert Weldon*

From Jugendstil thru the Machine Age

The extent of Naum Slutzky's influence on modern design has not been fully appreciated. An expatriot in the three countries where he worked and taught, Slutzky's style in the applied arts remained true to the minimalist ethos he acquired at the Weimar Bauhaus. Born Nachman Slucky in Kiev, the Ukraine, in 1894, the son of a Fabergé goldsmith, his family was forced into exile by a Jewish pogrom in 1905. Settling in Vienna, he was apprenticed to the Wiener Werkstätte at the age of eighteen. There he executed the heart-shaped silver leaves of Professor Josef Hoffmann, and mounted stones for Otto Czeschka and Eduard Wimmer.[3] He also learned enamelling, a craft he used to great effect years later in England. That he is not mentioned in Wiener Werkstätte literature is not surprising, since the jewelry that he executed (along with other students of the Viennese Kunstgewerbeschule) was signed by the original artists. Active with the workshop in 1912-13, he voluntarily gave up his post when he recognized their financial difficulties.

The Werkstätte policy of the separation of sketch and execution was common practice at the time, but Slutzky wanted a hands-on realization of his own designs, so when Johannes Itten formed his private art school in 1917, teaching the realization of the idea with the material, the young artist signed up for two years. This eventually led to his apprentice post with the Metalwork workshop at the Bauhaus in Weimar, Germany in 1919.

Since jewelry was not a major concern of the Bauhaus, being technically a decorative art, Slutzky had a separate private workshop within the Metalwork division, where he designed and finished jewelry, becoming a Mastercraftsman by 1922. In all the 600 plus pages of the *Bauhaus- Weimar, Dessau, Berlin, Chicago* history by Hans Wingler, there is only one small mention of a separate precious metal (jewelry) private workshop. Yet the term "Bauhaus-style" which is applied to Twenties and Thirties chrome or nickel-plated jewelry (unadorned, or decorated with Bakelite or enamel) has stuck. This is due as much to the uncompromising austerity of the Bauhaus metalwork techniques, as to Slutzky's creative experiments which were wearable art.

If the Russian Constructivists had designed jewelry, it might have looked like Slutzky's. Kandinsky taught at the Bauhaus in 1922, and the Russian Avant-Garde exhibition in Berlin in that same year, installed by El Lissitsky, was a revelation to the Germans, who knew nothing of Russian art since the outbreak of World War I and the Russian Revolution. The work of Malevich, Tatlin, and Lissitsky was certainly a formidable influence on the Bauhaus, and being of Russian birth, Slutzky surely absorbed from his countrymen the Constructivist credo which emphasized technique at the expense of style. (The artists themselves, referred to their art as "Production Art" before an art critic named it "Constructivist".) So Slutzky's concentric circle pendants were not the Krishna wheel of the Theosophists, or the erotic female symbols of Gustave Klimt's Viennese portraits, but a precursor of the Machine Age. One pendant (1920) looked like a white-walled tire with a quartz cabochon hubcap. (His wheel pin shapes were echoed in his ceiling lights of frosted glass disks of 1927.) When Moholy-Nagy took over the Metalworkshop, the emphasis was more on the spatial relationships of the Hungarian Constructivists, so Slutzky left the Bauhaus in 1924, finally settling in Hamburg in 1927.

Here he spent six fruitful years as an interior designer, exhibiting with the Hamburg Secession in 1928. The Museum for Arts and Crafts bought his modern objects and jewelry, including a chrome pendant which looked like an asymmetrical bottle opener, and a wide chrome-plated bracelet with a rectangular hematite plaque inset. These pieces were not signed or stamped, being nei-

A wide chrome-plated bracelet with a rectangular faceted hematite plaque, by Naum Slutzky, 1929. *Courtesy of the Victoria and Albert Museum, London, England*

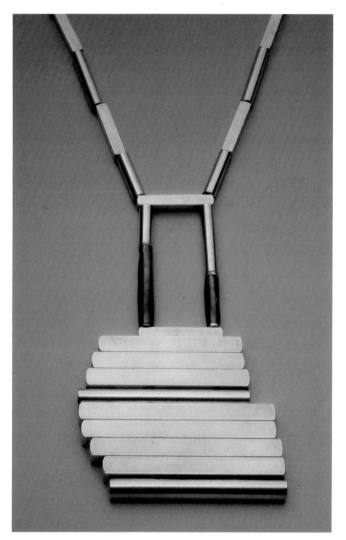

An extraordinary asymmetrical pendant of parallel silver bars with translucent blue enamel by Naum Slutzky. The light reflects differently off the round and rectangular "pipes and sticks" surfaces of the pendant and the chain, 1961. *Courtesy of the Worshipful Company of Goldsmiths, London, England*

Naum Slutzky's take on the artist's palette; silver brooch with perforated holes and enamel glossy green and blue enamel "paint", 1961. *Courtesy of the Worshipful Co. of Goldsmiths, London*

ther silver nor gold. His work of this period, bearing the fruit of his Bauhaus experience, influenced the designs of the manufacturing centers of Pforzheim, and Hanau thru the Thirties and Forties.

In 1933 Slutzky emigrated to London. (Hitler was to include Slutzky's abstract cat sculpture in the infamous "Degenerate Art Exhibition" of 1937 which ridiculed every major artist in Germany whose art was beyond the Führer's limited comprehension.) Though speaking very poor English, he was hired (through Walter Gropius' recommendation) to teach metalwork at the Darlington School in Devon. From 1946-1950 he was professor of Jewellery Design at the Central School of Arts and Crafts in London, then switching back to Industrial Design at the Royal College of Art (1950-57.) (He exchanged ideas on mass-production methods and matières with Charles and Ray Eames in California.[4]) From 1957 to 1964, he was head of the department at the College of Arts and Crafts in Birmingham, the jewelry center of England, where he could indulge his design ideas, up to a point. Slutzky wanted to mass-produce jewelry but his clients preferred hand-crafted pieces, and his time was taken up with teaching metalwork classes.[5] His later work was not executed in quantity, but costume and artist/jewelers of the Sixties in England and Northern Europe were certainly inspired by Slutzky's original ideas.

Slutzky's designs remained relentlessly pure and Modern, translated into silver, and refined with elegant touches of enamel, which softened the hard chrome machine-edge of his early pieces.

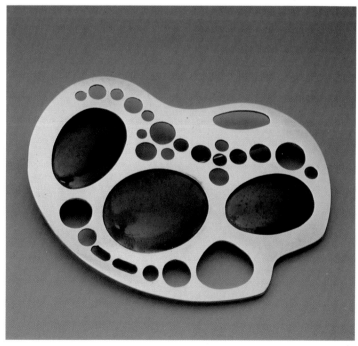

An unusual necklace of opaque black pebbles and translucent red enamel connected with silver loops; a study in contrasts by Naum Slutzky, 1962. *Courtesy of the Worshipful Company of Goldsmiths, London*

The 1961 pendant of parallel silver bars and asymmetric clear blue enamel supports, was hung on a chain of long alternating round and rectangular links which reflected the light differently. Another original design used black pebbles caressed by the sea, alternating with free-form red enamel "pebbles"; the contrast of matt and glossy, rough and smooth, translucent and opaque, all held together with silver loops. His take on the popular artist's palette shape of the Sixties was a brooch perforated with oval and circular holes and three large dabs of enamel "paint" in green, violet and blue. Slutzky played expertly with light, surface, and texture in both his jewelry and industrial design.

Marianne Brandt (1893-1983) was the only woman studying in the Bauhaus Metal Workshop under Moholy-Nagy in 1923-25. By 1929, she was teaching there, and had designed plexiglas earrings decorated with tiny gearwheels and a bell, a chrome-plated neckring and globe pendant, and steel belt buckles. It is not known how many examples were made. Plexiglas was the trade name for a transparent Acrylic resin popular in Germany in the Thirties. A thermoplastic, it was heat maleable many times. Brandt was better known for her utilitarian metal utensils and lamps, which were designed without consideration of conventional aesthetics and were industrially produced by German firms in the thousands.

Mass-production vs. artists' conceptions

"The Bauhaus was not an institution with a clear program- it was an idea", declared Mies Van der Rohe.[6] "Only an idea, not propaganda or organization" could have spread the Bauhaus tenets around the globe. There was a free flow of ideas between the Bauhaus *meisters* who lectured at jewelers' conventions, and professors at Crafts Schools who studied the techniques of the ateliers at Weimar and Dessau.[7]

In the Thirties, the small factories in the towns of Swäbisch Gmünd, Geislingen, and Idar-Oberstein produced vast amounts of low-priced *Modeschmuck*, or fashion jewelry. These were usually made of nickel or chrome-plated copper with Bakelite, Celluloid, Galalith, or Acrylic accents. They were turned out cheaply by unknown designers and manufacturers in time to follow the changing trends of the latest collections. The best ones to survive were strung on metal wire mesh chains. Different colored plastic sections could easily be changed with the seasons, and attached to the chrome elements and chains. The metal was either woven in a webbed brickwork mesh, or echoed the Cartier "gaspipe" sections so popular in France. (It is quite possible that the German chrome version came first). Cotton mesh ropes hung with corrugated chrome disks and Bakelite mixed the soft with the hard, the opaque with the shiny. Another popular treatment was the enamelling of chrome necklaces and bracelets with red, blue, or green geometric designs. These were typically German mass-production items, exported to France, Belgium, and England. When the fashion jewelry went "uptown", it became couture jewelry, and faux pearls and strass were added.

4 "gaspipe" necklaces: all chrome-plated with green or red Bakelite sections. The large one on the bottom row looks heavy, but snakes quite comfortably around the neck; typical of the bold German Thirties style. The red Bakelite are *courtesy of Arts 220, Winnetka, IL.* The green Bakelite are *courtesy of the author. Photo by Robert Weldon*

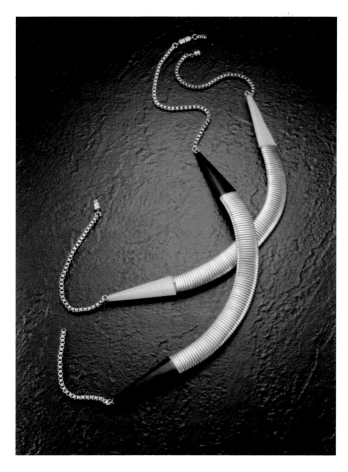

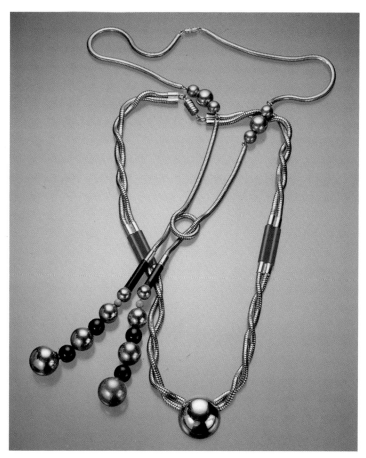

2 flexible chrome-plated gaspipe chokers with navy blue and yellow Bakelite tips on the ends, ca. 1930. *Courtesy of the author. Photo by Robert Weldon*

Two long Thirties necklaces: one chrome-plated with red Bakelite; and the other nickel-plated strung on mesh wire with yellow and green Bakelite beads. *Courtesy of the author. Photo by Robert Weldon*

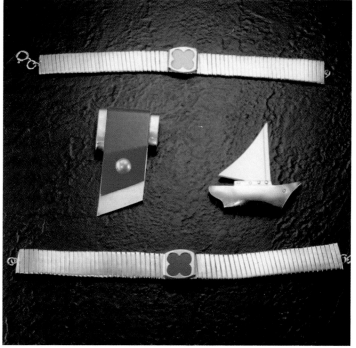

Two chrome bracelets with red or yellow cord interieur. *Courtesy of private collection, Los Angeles. Photo by Robert Weldon*

2 chrome bracelets with four leaf clover Bakelite inserts, one red, one yellow; and a snappy red Bakelite dress clip with a faux pearl, and a chrome sailboat with a Celluloid sail, ca. 1930. *Courtesy of private collection, Los Angeles. Photo by Robert Weldon*

Variations on the cotton mesh cords: bottom row necklace is combined with a chrome "ribbon" tying the Bakelite blue bow; the red thick cord is hung with a snazzy chrome pendant; and the black cord in the top row supports red Bakelite crescents and chrome circles, Thirties style. *Courtesy of Arts 220, Winnetka, IL, (the red and black cord) and the author. Photo by Robert Weldon*

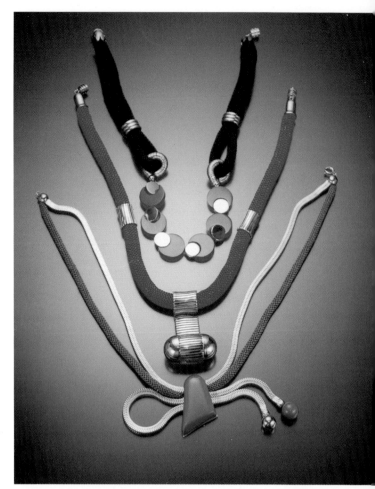

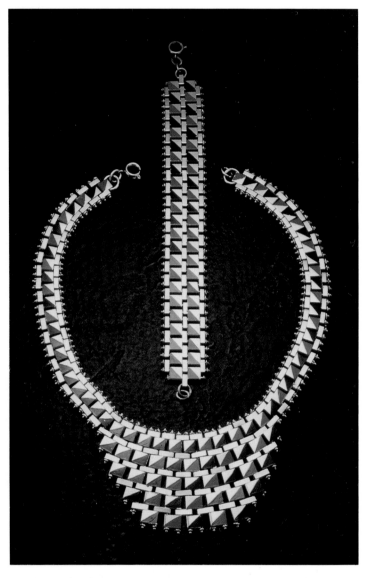

Chrome-plated chainmail mesh necklace and bracelet with geometric design cold-painted in red and black enamel. *Courtesy of the author. Photo by Robert Weldon*

Four chrome-plated necklaces: the bottom two cold-painted red and black enamel; and the top two of brickwork design, one with red Bakelite insets, 1930's. *Courtesy of Arts 220, Winnetka, IL. and the author. Photo by Robert Weldon*

Fine pieces were produced in silver in the Twenties and Thirties. Silver clips bore the "DRGM" patent mark. Stylish silver link bracelets were set with marcasites, agates, coral, or quartz faceted stones. Rolled gold mesh bracelets with glossy enamel wings and faux Chinese carved carnelian were distributed and stamped by the wholesaler, L.S. Mayer. Chrysoprase was mounted in silver and marcasite rings. These pieces came mostly from Pforzheim or Hanau where "serious" silver and goldsmiths plied their trade. Rodi & Wienenberger produced *doublé*, gold-plated link bracelets with Deco designs in Pforzheim in the Twenties and Thirties stamped "RW" with an anchor.

Three chrome and Bakelite watch fobs, with "nickel chrom" tag, Germany, 1930s. *Courtesy of the author. Photo by Sandro Moro.*

A stylish silver bracelet with alternating links of rock crystal and black onyx, with marcasite. Marked "Sterling, Germany." 1930. *Courtesy of Ruth Sofaer Collection, Los Angeles, Ca.*, and a silver Deco dress clip set with faux emeralds and clear rhinestone, together with a slim silver link bracelet with sapphire and clear rhinestones, both stamped "KP". 1920's. *Courtesy Diane Keith Collection. Photo by Robert Weldon*

A silver clip, alternating smooth and textured surfaces, with an onyx stone. Reverse stamped "DRGM", ca. 1920. *Courtesy of author's collection. Photo by Robert Weldon*

Reverse of clip with "DRGM" German patent and business model protection mark (*Deutsches Reich Geschmack Muster*) used from 1891 until World War II. *Photo by Robert Weldon*

A large domed piece of chrysoprase simply and effectively mounted in a Deco design of silver and marcasites. Stamped 935, and signed "AL", ca. 1930. *Courtesy of private collection, Los Angeles. Photo by Robert Weldon*

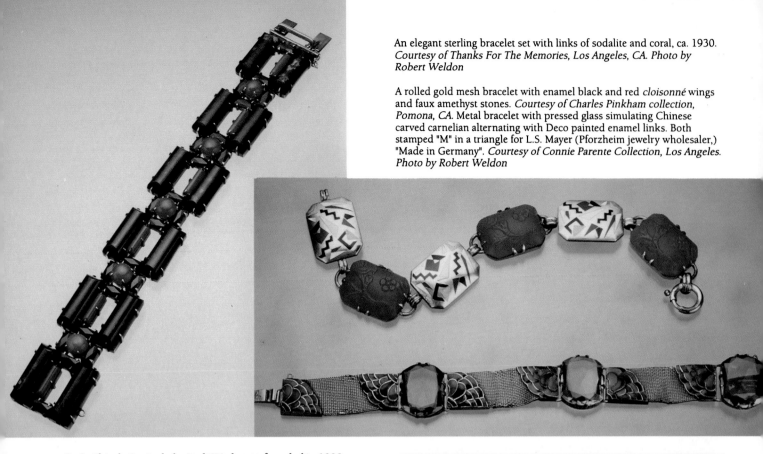

An elegant sterling bracelet set with links of sodalite and coral, ca. 1930. *Courtesy of Thanks For The Memories, Los Angeles, CA. Photo by Robert Weldon*

A rolled gold mesh bracelet with enamel black and red *cloisonné* wings and faux amethyst stones. *Courtesy of Charles Pinkham collection, Pomona, CA.* Metal bracelet with pressed glass simulating Chinese carved carnelian alternating with Deco painted enamel links. Both stamped "M" in a triangle for L.S. Mayer (Pforzheim jewelry wholesaler,) "Made in Germany". *Courtesy of Connie Parente Collection, Los Angeles. Photo by Robert Weldon*

In Swäbisch Gmünd, the Perli-Werkstatt, founded in 1922, was known for metalwork, either unadorned, or of *cloisonné* enamel, matt or translucent. In 1933 there was a hammered silver line of bracelets, brooches, and necklaces decorated with a discreet Perli "pearl". Wood and glass beads were also used. The enamel designs were Thirties Moderne, using circles or rectangles of alternating colors. The reverse side was usually a glossy black enamel, overstamped with "Made in Germany" in white. Bar pins were made to match enamel bracelets, and cufflinks were worn by the men. These were marked hand-made, *handarbeit*, and were a step up artistically from the mass-produced chrome and Bakelite lines. Similar designs were also produced post-war. Perli jewelry was exhibited at the German Pavillion at the 1937 Paris Expo. The company continued producing well-made metal and enamel pieces until 1993 when Perli Werkstatte went out of business, destroying all its records.

Kollmar & Jourdan in Pforzheim was another firm which manufactured dramatic geometric enamelled jewelry in the Thirties, although the metal foundation was silver or silver-gilt rather than copper. A large factory, established in 1885, it closed its doors in 1977.

The leading manufacturers in Pforzheim, apart for Fahrner, were Henkel and Grossé. In 1982, this company celebrated its 75th year as a major source of costume jewelry to the fashion industry in Europe. Founded by Heinrich Henkel (1876-1941) and his brother-in-law, Florentin Grosse (1878-1953), in 1907, it was decided early on that "design would take precedence over the materials used." (There were sculptors in the three generations of the firm's leadership who upheld this statement.) Their Twenties and Thirties designs using various forms of plastic with metal were popular mass-produced necklaces and bracelets.

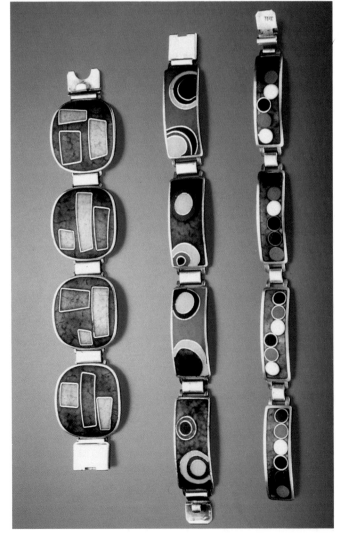

Three metal bracelets with geometric matt *cloisonné* links in subdued browns and black, or bright yellow and green. All stamped "Perli". This style was produced prior to, and following the Second World War. The rhomboids are probably 1960. *Courtesy of Charles Pinkham, Pomona, CA. Photo by Robert Weldon*

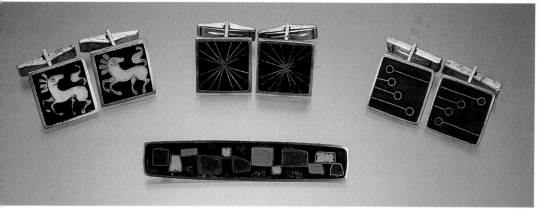

Galalith, the patented name for casein, was invented in Germany in 1899 by Spitteler and Krische. Casein (the dried curds of milk mixed with dough) was widely used for jewelry and buttons, especially in the Twenties in France. Bakelite, a heavier weight thermoset phenolic plastic which could be heated and shaped only once, was preferred in Germany. It's not surprising that the first overseas factory of the Bakelite Co. was established in Berlin. Henkel and Grosse mounted it with the grey-toned metals, like aluminum, Platinin (a H. & G. trade name), Alpacca (called "German silver" although no silver is present in the alloy), and chrome and nickel-plated chains. In the Twenties, a Galalith red and black pendant necklace was worn by the flappers in Germany. In the Thirties, influenced by the Bauhaus aesthetic, Henkel and Grossé worked red, black, or green Bakelite or Galalith with alternating sections of shiny chrome or nickel segments to form flexible bracelets and necklaces. (The photos shown here are of the only pieces salvaged by Frau Grosse from the ruins of the Allied air attack on Pforzheim in 1945.) In 1937 the firm was awarded the *Diplôme d'Honneur* at the Paris Exhibition. Red and blue enamel on folded gilded metal was another choice offered as a change from the white metals in the Thirties. Adalbert and Artur Grosse carried on their father's application of new technological advances in jewelry design and manufacturing.

A 1920s Galalith red and black pendant necklace on a chrome chain by Henkel and Grosse. *Courtesy of Henkel and Grosse, Pforzheim, Germany*

Henkel & Grosse Trademarks

Fabrik ⟨IGI⟩ Marke

until ca. 1938

ℋ𝒢

until ca. 1953

𝕲

until ca. 1979

Grossé®

to present

A fine collection of Henkel and Grosse bracelets and necklaces from the Thirties; the only ones rescued by Frau Grosse from the ruins of the Allied Air Raid of Pforzheim. Chrome and Bakelite at its straightforward best. The two bracelets in the upper right hand corner complement the necklaces in style and color. *Courtesy of Henkel and Grosse*

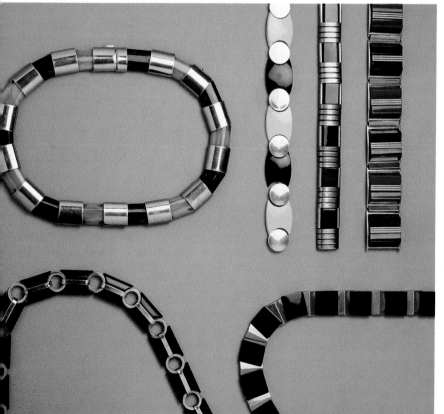

Also from the Thirties, a different approach by Henkel and Grosse; a necklace of enamelled gilt metal, folded over gilded links. *Courtesy of Henkel and Grosse*

The firm's versatility in producing designs for the French taste, very different from the chunky Teutonic Bakelite and chrome, was exploited by the Parisian couturiers. The Houses of Schiaparelli and Jeanne Lanvin both used Henkel and Grossé as a resource before the war, but the really important exclusive Paris connection for the firm was with Christian Dior, beginning in 1955 with four collections annually, and continuing today. Dior's "New Look" of 1947 and subsequent collections demanded extravagant jewelry for plunging or boat necklines, cocktail hats, and elbow-length gloves. Henkel and Grossé took their inspiration from 18th century jewelry, and produced lavish pieces using multi-colored crystals. The gallicized accented é had earlier been added to Grosse, because it "wasn't a very nice word in French", and there had been some criticism in Paris of Dior's choice of a German manufacturer of French Haute Couture jewelry so soon after the war. This gradually subsided as Henkel and Grossé supplied romantic and ethnic looks in the Sixties, and "retro" designs drawn from all the styles of the Twenties thru the Sixties, simultaneously, by their present designer Michael Grossé. Today, the Deco "gas-pipe" is back in contemporary necklaces. "*Plus ça change!*". The initials "HG" were used on Henkel and Grosse pieces until 1955. The crowned "G" until 1979, and "Grossé" alone is still valid. Jewelry made for Dior was marked "Ch. Dior" with the date in an oval tag.

In the Sixties, a complete change of style for the French couturier, Christian Dior. An elaborate sapphire blue and clear crystal necklace created for a strapless ballgown. *Courtesy of Henkel and Grosse*

A budding flutist is wearing a set of black enamelled gilt and rhinestone jewelry by Grosse, 1980s. *Courtesy of Henkel and Grosse*

Sapphire and clear rhinestone pin with a high dome of prong-set stones, signed "Ch. Dior", 1960. *Courtesy of private collection, Los Angeles, CA.* Earrings of ruby and sapphire glass stones with a pearl pendant. Signed "Ch. Dior", dated 1966. *Courtesy of Sherry Goldman Collection, Sherman Oaks, CA. Photo by Robert Weldon*

Glossy enamel links in yellow, red, brown, and blue geometric patterns on a 1925-30 bracelet recall avant-garde art movements. By Irmgard Fuss. *Courtesy of Arnolds'che Verlagsanstalt GmbH, Stuttgart, Germany*

Kirchgaessner and Kraft were Pforzheim manufacturers of Alpacca (nickel-silver) belt buckles, or waist clasps (as they were quaintly advertised), circa 1905. These were of grotesque heads or simple Darmstadt School design, electro-plated in Alpacca, and chased. Robert Kraft was the sole signature from 1909 to 1920 on striking buckles with a hammered surface, and discreet use of enamel and stones in bold, disciplined shapes. Alpacca, originally a trade name invented by Alexander Schoeller in 1854 for his nickel alloy (probably taken from *paktong*, a Chinese alloy) was ideal for inexpensive articles and jewelry with the sheen and look of silver though not its feel and patina.[8] This did not escape the notice of Liberty & Co. which, from 1909, imported Kraft's buckles and hat pins, gave them the name "Nola" and claimed a more exotic "Viennese" provenance. (See Chapter 3, English jewelry.)

Karl Karst, from 1910 thru the Twenties and Thirties, produced openwork silver brooches and pendants signed "KARST". His Deco matt enamel jewelry with geometric motifs and lapis and coral stones was often mistaken for Fahrner's.

There were two talented women designers in pre-WW II Germany who took the art of enamelling beyond the ordinary: Irmgard Fuss; and Erna Zarges-Dürr. Irmgard was born in 1909 and showed a precocious ability at 16 at the Trade School in Schwäbisch-Gmünd. She worked in Albert Holbein's workshop from 1927-29, and for one year in Pforzheim with the Georg Lauer firm. She did outstanding work with enamel on silver or copper, and even some eggshell and lacquer bracelets, à la Jean Dunand.[9] She was conver-

sant with the work of the Expressionists and Russian Constructivists and conceived abstract designs which made very attractive enamel bracelets and pins. Her pendants were *cloisonné* family portraits with metal geometric frames incorporated into the design. Her sudden death in 1930, at the age of 21, cut short what would most certainly have been an illustrious career.

Erna Zarges-Dürr (1907-) apprenticed with a silversmith in Heilbronn, then attended the Kunstgewerbeschule in Pforzheim from 1927-1930. Sketches she made of jewelry with contrasting geometric sections of rock crystal and onyx (executed later) were a sophisticated concept for an eighteen year old. She learned goldsmithing techniques with E. Treusch in Leipzig in 1932, when she became a Mastercraftsman. Erna had her own atelier in Stuttgart until 1939 where she made original contributions to modern design. Her early Thirties bracelet with a plaque of *cloisonné* enamel mounted on flexible metal bead chains anticipated the circle, triangle and rectangle motifs which were seen later in the decade in enamel bracelets from the Perli workshop.[10]

Matt blue enamel plaque using circle, square, and triangle motifs for a bracelet by Erna Zarges-Dürr. Also an opal pendant mounted in gold, a bracelet with topaz stones, and two rings. 1932/33. *Courtesy of Arnolds'che Verlagsanstalt GmbH, Stuttgart, Germany*

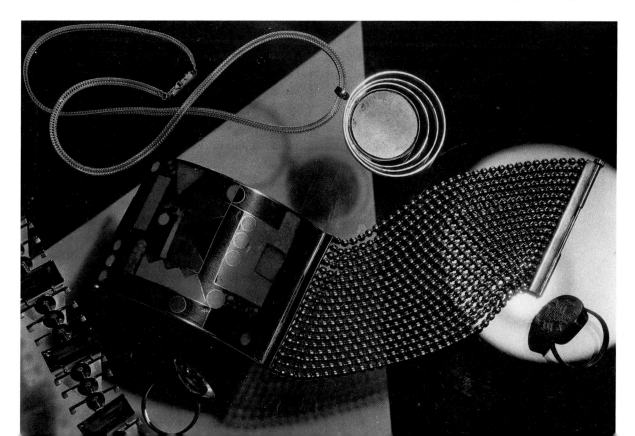

A classic Deco masterpiece by Siegfried Männle: silver pendant with matt glass and green agate disks, 1920's, signed "SM". *Courtesy of Arnold'sche Verlagsanstalt GmbH*

A silver-plated stamped metal necklace in the style of late Twenties IKORA jewelry. *Courtesy of private collection, Los Angeles. Photo by Robert Weldon*

Four unusual Ikora-Kristal glass pendants simulating opal, amber, and aventurine, 1932. *Courtesy of Gallery Von Spaeth, Munich, Germany*

Siegfried Männle (1912-) another talented goldsmith and enameller, attended the State Zeichenakademie in Hanau between 1928-'33. A Mastercraftsman, he had his own atelier from 1945 to '49, and freelanced until 1952, when he was appointed Professor at his old alma mater, the Zeichenakademie. Männle's work was of the highest quality and craftsmanship. The influence of Jean Desprès' structural machine age techniques is evident in his elegant silver rings. Without having attended the Bauhaus, he embraced its functional tenets. His pendants of matt glass disks (Naum Slutzky's fief) were mounted on shiny chrome, or silver with alternating elements of agate or ebony. Balls and cylinders in various materials were an essential part of his Thirties designs.[11]

In Geislingen, south of Schwäbisch- Gmünd, the metalwork factory of Württembergische Metallwarenfabrik, "WMF," was founded in 1853. In the late Twenties, inexpensive jewelry of Bakelite, glass, and metal, followed by ceramic in 1939, was mass-produced. Metal was silver-plated and oxidized in stamped sections which simulated hand-hammering for IKORA Schmuck, the jewelry department of this large factory, which also produced household articles in ceramic and glass.

In 1932, IKORA-Kristal, a new line of glass jewelry was launched. Revolutionary techniques introduced colored incrustations into the glass, obtaining "every conceivable nuance of fantasy through the flux of the glowing mass", according to a contemporary article. A rich variety of colors was offered: "saucy yellow and burning orange set in the minor key of matt silver, or old gold; each piece an individual achievement, never to be repeated. And the price is right (2 Marks) so every woman can afford to have an IKORA pendant matching every blouse and dress, lending an emphatic, artistic note to her wardrobe." IKORA made a remarkably successful attempt at simulating black opal, rutilated quartz, amber, and aventurine for large chunky glass pendants.

Besides the *Modeschmuck* line there were ceramic handbags (which doubled as lunchboxes) with abstract designs produced in the Twenties, all stamped "WMF".

Heinrich Levinger was a Pforzheim firm which manufactured and wholesaled costume jewelry. Established in the 19th century, there was a brief period before WW 1, when a partner, Bissinger, was involved. The firm was known for good quality product, and successfully produced the enamelled jewelry (*plique à jour*, called "window enamel" in German) of the Viennese artist, Otto Prutscher, as well as numerous unknown German designers. The trademark initials "HL" were connected, and sometimes the *déposé* mark was used.

Three different protected patent marks can be found on German jewelry. "D.R.G.M." (for *Deutsches Reich Geschmacksmuster* or German Reich Taste Design, literally) was not regulated by law (though there was expanded model protection by law in 1891) and was voluntarily stamped on jewelry by many German firms. In the case of jewelry, where aesthetics were protected, the "G" stands for *Geschmack*. When applied to technical inventions or novelties, "DRGM" was the abbreviation for *Deutsches Reichs Gebrauchsmuster*, or registered (use) design. Jewelry thus protected from imitation was deposited in the Muster register in the relevant court where it was protected for 1-3 years, which could then be extended to 15 years for a 60 Mark fee. "DRGM" is often mistaken for a maker's mark, and can be found on a wide range of pieces, from silver clips and brooches to strass expandable bracelets. The mark was used until 1945 when the Deutsches Third Reich ceased to exist. (The first two Reichs were those of Charlemagne and Kaiser Wilhelm.)

Déposé, the French patent mark (for *modèle déposé*) was used as a translation of *geschützt* (registered) by German manufacturers on jewelry destined for export, not necessarily to France, but to countries like England where the French word was better understood than "DRGM" and *ges. gesch*. (In France, both "é"s are accented, meaning "deposited or registered". The German stamp often retained only the final "é".) The *déposé* stamp was dropped by Theodor Fahrner, Henry Levinger, Victor Meyer, Carl Hermann, and other German firms around 1915 when all French accents became anathema.

Ges. geschützt ("protected by law") is another abbreviation for *gesetlich*, or the legal registered trade mark used in Germany, sometimes further shortened to a "ges. gesch." (or "ge. gsch.") stamp. This could be found on jewelry and designer's models as well as inventor's utensils.[12] This mark was used after WW I, taking the place of the French *déposé*. (*Gesetlich geschützt* has been seen on the "langani" trademark paper label, established 1952.) The identification of all the above marks is useful to collectors seeking the provenance or production years of their treasures.

A further complication is the use of the "Made in France" mark. Dr. Merkel, appraiser for Henry's AuktionsHaus, reports that quantities of jewelry, Bakelite and otherwise, were made in Pforzheim for the French market, and stamped "Made in France".

Since 1884, silver ware over a fineness of .800 should bear the fineness and the German mark, the crescent moon and the crown. This is only occasionally found on jewelry, however. There are no date letters in Germany.

Post-war Germany rose slowly from the ashes. Pforzheim was completely rebuilt on the banks of the Enz River, where costume jewelry was again produced in the '50s. (Hanau, the goldsmiths' center, and Schwäbish Gmünd were not far behind.) The designs, signed "P", were clean, uncluttered silver, gold, or black metal with press-moulded glass simulating turquoise, moonstones, or onyx. These brooches were one of the inexpensive alternatives in Germany to the higher-priced Dior line by Henkel and Grosse.

Enamel of a modern style surfaced in the Fifties and Sixties in Germany. Enamelled grapes and grape leaves in fall harvest colors were set in silver with a silver link chain, stamped "Germany", 900. Karl Schibensky, from Saarbrücken on the French border, designed pendants, pins, and cufflinks, with matt *cloisonné* enamel on copper. The reverse side was translucent enamel with his "S." signature in a circle.

A.G. Bunge worked in Munich at the Metalwerkstätte in 1960, producing large rectangular linked bracelets, and pendants in silver and enamel, all in the same spirit as Schibensky's pieces.[13] Bunge's pieces had a notched clasp, and were signed "Bunge" in upper or lower case letters. Also in the Sixties, matt enamel bracelets depicting nocturnal street scenes were simply stamped "Made

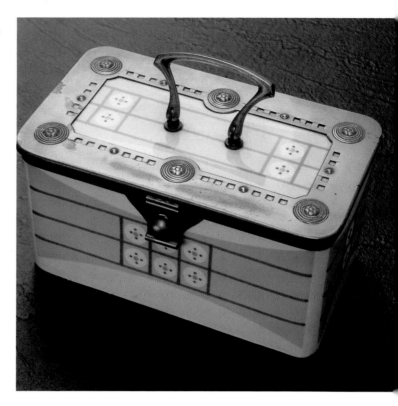

WMF porcelain box/handbag, ca. Twenties. The monogram for Württembergische Metalwarenfabrik signed on porcelain and metal frame. *Courtesy of Marilyn Hirsty Collection, Sherman Oaks, CA. Photo Robert Weldon*

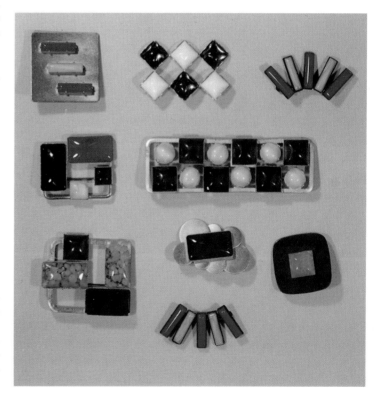

Nine brooches with molded glass simulating turquoise, chalcedony, coral, onyx, jade, and moonstone, discovered in pristine condition still mounted on their sample cards, signed "P". Post-war, ca. 1950. *Courtesy of Mary Sue Packer Collection, Munich, Germany. Photo by Sandro Moro*

in Germany" on the reverse side which was a speckled grey and white enamel.

Another designer who fused *cloisonné* enamel on copper in subtle blues and maroons signed his name "WL". Pendants and link bracelets were enamelled a deep royal blue on the back. If a piece is not signed, the best way to determine provenance is by the color of the enamel on the reverse, which is consistently the same for each artist.

There's is a popular misconception that jewelry made in post-war Germany was automatically stamped "West Germany". There was no law to that effect; it being at the maker's discretion. Some countries insisted on this mark to prove that the pieces were imported. Generally, manufacturers intent on exporting stamped their jewelry either "West Germany" or "Germany" from the Fifties till 1990 when East and West Germany were joyously joined at the fallen Berlin Wall.

Cloisonné enamel grape leaves with grapes pendant and bracelet, in Fall harvest colors on silver, with a silver chain. Signed with intersected "M", (unknown wholesaler's mark) and Germany 900. Ca. 1960, (the wrought silver chain seems earlier.) *Courtesy of Charles Pinkham. Photo by Robert Weldon*

Maker's marks "S" for Karl Schibensky, and unknown mark "M" with horizontal line for 1960 enamel pieces. *Photo by Robert Weldon*

Two *cloisonné* geometric matt enamelled copper link bracelets signed "W.L.", Sixties. And polka dot blue and white glossy enamelled links, unsigned. *Courtesy of the author. Photo by Sandro Moro*

Reverse of blue enamelled bracelet signed "W.L."

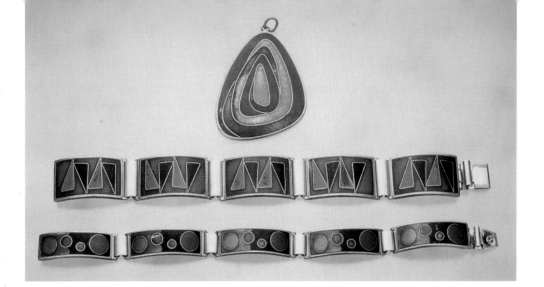

Green and blue matt enamel on copper pendant, a matt enamel bracelet with terracotta and black triangles, and a bracelet with green and blue enamel circles, all by Karl Schibensky, about whom nothing has been published as yet. Ca. 1960. Signed "S" in a circle on the reverse in translucent enamel. *Courtesy of Carri Priley Collection, St. Paul, MN. Photo by Robert Weldon*

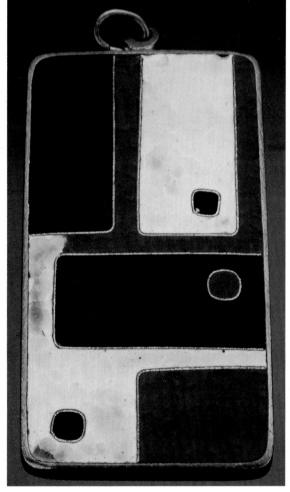

A group of 4 matt enamel bracelets: The top and bottom pieces depicting night street scenes with street lamps and closed shutters, ca. 1960. Unknown maker. *Courtesy of Charles Pinkham Collection, Pomona, CA.* Silver bracelet with abstract matt enamel designs and a notched clasp, attributed to A. G. Bunge, ca. 1960, and a silver bracelet with blue and green enamel circles, maker unknown. *Courtesy of Carri Priley Collection. Photo Robert Weldon*

A striking matt *cloisonné* enamel pendant in brown, black and white enamel by Karl Schibensky, 1960, with "S". *Courtesy of the author. Photo by Robert Weldon*

Tripping the light fantastic with langani

Anni Lang (1911-1988) was born in Stuttgart, Germany, where she studied at the School of Arts and Crafts in 1929-30. Then she went to Vienna where her professor was Josef Hoffmann at the Kunstgewerbeschule, until 1934. The next two years were spent in Munich at the State School for Applied Art, where she studied textile design. In 1935 she married Rudolf Schaad, a film cutter, with whom she had four children in the ensuing years. In 1952, she transformed her maiden name into the trade name "langani" with a small "l", and established her workshop for costume jewelry.

From 1952 to 1965, Anni Schaad used only glass beads; either Venetian or Bohemian. From Neu-Gablonz, she ordered special beads with large holes like donuts, the inner layers were colored glass, or painted with gold or silver foil. In her workshop she produced hand-wound lampwork beads of her own design, which were not available on the open market. The glass beads were mounted on transparent nylon thread and seemed to float around the neck.   Her necklaces were so successful that copies began to appear, forcing her in 1958 to register the trademark black glass bead which always discreetly appears somewhere near the fastening. Langani participated in local and international Arts and Crafts shows in Germany, the Triennale in Milan, and touring shows worldwide.

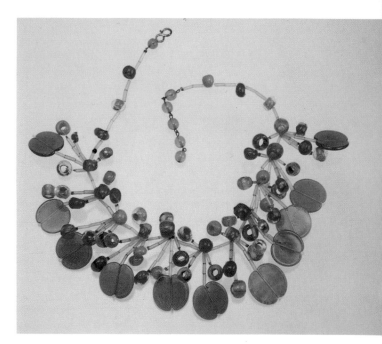

Almost edible donut and cherry glass beads in oranges and pinks, with the black trademark bead by langani, 1962. *Courtesy of Rita Sacks Collection. Photo by Robert Weldon*

Necklace of clear Lucite blossoms with rhinestone petals, and the black bead by langani, 1961. *Courtesy of Rita Sacks Collection, New York. Photo by Robert Weldon*

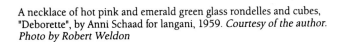

A necklace of hot pink and emerald green glass rondelles and cubes, "Deborette", by Anni Schaad for langani, 1959. *Courtesy of the author. Photo by Robert Weldon*

In 1959 Anni designed "Deborette"; two long 6 strand rows of criss-crossed green, blue and hot pink beads which ended in glass cube tassels. In 1960 she invented "Carrousel", a necklace of dozens of large rings of beads in pink, terra cotta and white. In 1962, "Estrella" made its bow with langani-designed mauve and lilac oblong beads strung with a jointed technique so the necklace moved with the wearer, falling softly around the neck. In 1963 there was a grey and gold brooch of donut beads and flat cherry-shaped segments which she also used in a necklace of pink and apricot. The "Gold Moth" necklace was photographed at a Paris café, turning heads in 1962. Crystal dangly earrings were popular in 1965, as well as earrings with square glass hoops, or a spray of glass petals. For Independence Day, there was a necklace of red glass tube "fire crackers" to light up a July outfit in America or France. A necklace of balls of bright colored glass beads goes with any outfit.

"Estrella" necklace in shades of lavender and lilac glass beads mounted on jointed tube beads for maximum movement, with the langani trademark black glass bead, and paper tag, 1962. The reverse of the tag reads *mit der schwarzen Perle, and gesetlich geschützt. Courtesy of the author. Photo by Robert Weldon*

The "Gold Moth" necklace; all gold glass beads worn with a come-hither look in a Paris café. 1962, by langani. *Courtesy of langani, Stuttgart, Germany. Photo by Relang*

A spectacular explosion of scarlet, jointed glass tubes for a 1960's necklace. *Courtesy of langani. Photo by Relang*

A pair of square colored glass hoop earrings, Sixties, and a pair of multicolored glass flower petal earrings, Sixties. *Courtesy of langani. Photo by Relang*

In 1970, langani began a long association with the Paris couturier Louis Féraud, with exclusive jewelry for his runway models. "Bandura" in 1971 was a metal collar with glass and gold metal sections. "Hannibal" in 1972 had a large Acrylic cube mounted on a plastic collar. A Space Age metal collar for Féraud had a pectoral with red resin pendants; these were the first in a new series in a different style for langani.

Suzanne Kiess-Schaad, Anni's daughter, who joined in the direction of the design atelier for Paris fashion shows and German ready-to-wear, recalls: "In the Seventies, the spectrum was extended by a multiplicity of products from Nature: wood; seashells; ivory; bone; ostrich eggshells; leather and feathers; silk thread; Acrylics; sequins, and even embroidery from old fabric.. any material which could be worked up into a piece with fantasy and charm. Hand-rolled beads, however, have always remained an important element. My mother loved Nature, especially the mountains and the sea, and surrounded herself with flowers from which she drew inspiration for her textiles and jewelry. Her job was her vocation and her hobby at the same time. She had a highly sensitive feeling for colors associated with her love for the abundance of Nature's forms."

"Bandura" necklace for Louis Féraud by langani. A gold metal bib with
glass and gold metal sections. 1971. *Courtesy of langani. Photo by
Relang*

A change of style, Space Age shiny metal collar with
opaque contrast of red resin pendants in relief. For Louis Féraud, Paris,
1972. *Courtesy of Iangani, Stuttgart, Germany. Photo by Relang*

1. Ulrike von Hase-Schmundt, Christianne Weber, Ingeborg Becker,
   Theodor Fahrner Jewelry, between Avant-garde and Tradition. Translated by Dr. Edward Force, English edition. West Chester, PA. Schiffer
   Publishing Ltd., 1991, pg. 55.
2. Graham Dry, "Porzellanschmuck," *Die Kunst und das schöne Heim*, July,
   1982.
3. Monika Randolph, *Naum Slutzky, Meister am Bauhaus, Goldschmeid
   und Designer*, Stuttgart, Arnoldsche, 1990, pg. 25.
4. *Ibid.*, pg. 69.
5. Graham Hughes, *Modern Jewelry, 1890-1963*, London, 1963, pg. 247.
6. Hans Wingler, *Bauhaus, Weimar, Dessau, Berlin, Chicago*, English edition, translated by W. Gabs and B. Gilbert. Cambridge, MA. and London, England, 1969, pg. VII.
7. Gerda Buxbaum, "The Opulence of the Poor Look. Austria and Germany"
   from *Jewels of Fantasy, Costume Jewelry of the 20th Century*, edited
   by Deanna Farneti Cera. English edition, edited by Ruth Peltason.
   German translated by Jurgen Riehle. New York, Harry Abrams Inc.
   and Daniel Swarowski Corporation, pg. 77.
8. Graham Dry, "Liberty & Co.'s "Nola" Metalwork," *Decorative Arts Society, Journal #14*, Eastbourne, England, pg. 37.
9. Christianne Weber, *Schmuck der 20er und 30er Jahre in Deutschland*,
   Stuttgart, Arnoldsche, 1990, pg. 178.
10. *Ibid.*, pg. 94.
11. *Ibid.*, pg. 249.
12. Ulrike von Hase-Schmundt, *op.cit.*, pg. 71.
13. *Deutsche und Osterreichische Schmuckarbeiten*, 1900-1960, Auction
    catalog, November, 1991. Munich, Ketterer Kunst AG.

Necklace of fourteen colored glass balls by langani, ca. 1980s.
Courtesy of langani. Photo by Relang

BOVRIL

FOR Health and Beauty

Chapter 3

Great Britain

Arts & Crafts, and Crafts Revival

Great Britain, though a small country, was of immense importance as the catalyst and cradle of the Arts & Crafts Movement which spread through Northern Europe and Austria in the late nineteenth and early twentieth century. More than an art movement, it was a philosophy. The seeds were sown by William Morris (1834-96), whose horror of the sordid lives and working conditions of factory workers was equalled only by his contempt for the product they turned out. The romantic attachment to the Middle Ages and its methods fostered the formation of guilds among the working class where craftsmanship was encouraged, though artisans were often self-taught. There ensued the battle of the medieval guild system vs. dehumanizing industrialization; hand-crafted pieces vs. machine-made objects. Craftspeople were meant to derive more pleasure from the creative process than from the commercial product. These were the first environmentalists, passionately devoted to saving the landscape from the advancing ravages of industrialization. To live and work together in the country making hand-hammered jewelry from one's own design sketch nurtured the soul. When it was eventually conceded, around 1909, that the machine could indeed be useful if high volume and smart economics were to be realized, the ultimate irony of machine-stamping the hammer marks on jewelry for a faux hand-crafted look was grudgingly accepted. Entrepreneurs and manufacturers like Arthur Liberty, W.H. Haseler, Charles Horner, and Murrle, Bennett & Co. successfully adapted the hand-crafted look for mass-production before World War I.

Discretion was the keynote of British jewelry of the early XXth century. Stones could shimmer and gleam, but not brilliantly blaze. Cabochons opals, moonstones, garnets (called carbuncles), rose quartz, chalcedony, coral, and turquoise were mixed with pastel semi-precious stones like tourmalines and amethysts, which when faceted were unostentatious. (John Ruskin had railed against gem and diamond cutting because he believed that stones should be as close as possible to their natural rough state.) Rubies, sapphires, and diamonds were spurned, though the pale, flawed emerald was acceptable. Silver, pewter, and Alpacca (nickel-silver) were the preferred metals; gold was indiscreet. The soft glow of enamel and baroque pearls were characteristic additions.

Many architects who had a feel for volume and proportion were successful self-trained silversmiths. Charles Ashbee (1863-1942) founded the Guild of Handicrafts in 1888 which produced jewelry and metalwork in London until 1902, when he transferred his workshop to the village of Chipping Camden in the bucolic Cotswolds. Ashbee hoped to convert the whole village into a guild,

One of several versions of the peacock by Charles Ashbee, ca. 1900. This necklace is silver with coral and mother of pearl. *Courtesy of John Jesse, London, England and the G.I.A.*

Opposite
Pre-Raphaelite damsel with auburn hair in a Bovril ad wearing a French jet hat ornament and jewelry by Horner, Murrle Bennett, Ruskin, and an unsigned silver and paste lizard. Lithograph and jewelry *courtesy of the author, except for Ruskin, courtesy of Gail Gerretsen. Photo by Robert Weldon*

Silver grapes pendant set with moonstone and semi-precious cabochons by John Paul Cooper. *Courtesy of Terrance O' Halloran, and G.I.A., Santa Monica, CA. Photo by Robert Weldon*

Card case by Wm. Hasseler, and a silver and turquoise pendant which appeared in a Liberty catalog but was possibly a German import. *Courtesy of Gail Gerretsen Collection, Los Angeles, Ca. Photo by Robert Weldon*

but this proved impractical, and the venture foundered six years later. Ashbee was more successful in spreading the Arts & Crafts aesthetic abroad, and was invited to exhibit at the Vienna Secession in 1900. (Josef Hoffmann subsequently formed the Wiener Werkstätte along the Arts & Crafts lines in 1903.) However, it took respected American architect, Frank Lloyd Wright, to convince Ashbee that the machine was not entirely anathema and could be put to practical use without negating the Arts & Crafts ideals. Ashbee made several versions of a peacock necklace with feathers of opal or abalone shell, and a lovely bodice ornament of oxidised silver with garnet carbuncles and mother of pearl for the Guild of Handicraft in 1900.

John Paul Cooper (1869-1933) trained as an architect but switched to metalwork, studying with fellow architect Henry Wilson who had also converted to jewelry design. He worked in silver, gold, and mixed metals, and became very highly skilled, teaching at the Birmingham School of Art. The most prolific of all the craftsmen of the period, he turned out objets in shagreen, boxes, and table ornaments, as well as jewelry for his own atelier, and the Artificer's Guild. His pendant of silver grape clusters and moonstone and semi-precious (chalcedony) cabochons shows fine craftsmanship and graceful proportions.

The formation of Liberty & Co. in London in 1894 by Arthur Lasenby Liberty (1843-1917) was a mixed blessing for the Arts & Crafts and Art Nouveau artists. Liberty was a shrewd businessman who understood that avant-garde jewelry if well-made and reasonably priced was commercially viable. However, he violated the ideals of the guild members by altering their designs and mass-producing them, anonymously, for his Liberty & Co. shop.

Once a design was proven a commercial success, it could be reproduced in fabrics, buttons, pendants, brooches, cloak and waistclasps, or silver bottle tops; a custom which continues today at Liberty's of London.

Like Siegfried Bing in Paris, Liberty had begun by importing Oriental objets, jewelry, and silk for his shop on Regent St. Indian Mogul jewelry sold there was an inspiration for Arthur Gaskin and other Crafts designers. Liberty expanded his operation to include continental metalware from Germany, and finally Celtic-inspired jewelry made exclusively for Liberty under the "Cymric" label in 1900. (The "Cymric", pronounced "Koomric", silverware and "Tudric" pewter lines were invented marketing names, though Cymric has Celtic/Welsh origins). W.H. Haseler, a Birmingham manufacturer, produced the "Cymric" silver jewelry designs by Jessie M. King and Arthur Gaskin, as well as enamelled card cases and objets. These bore the "W.H.H." hallmark. Liberty's Art Nouveau style was so pervasive, in fabrics and metalware as well as jewelry, that the period was called *Stile Liberty* in Italy, (the second time an art movement was named after a retail establishment; Bing's Maison Art Nouveau being the first.)

Pre-World War I Liberty jewelry was often not hallmarked, but post-War jewelry bore the assay town mark and date letter. The "L & Co." mark in overlapping diamonds was not always stamped because the jewelry was merchandised in fitted boxes with the Liberty logo. Pieces stamped "Sterling silver" (with no English assay marks) and "Liberty and Company" were exported to Liberty retail outlets in America. The actual edition numbers of Liberty's jewelry is unknown, but they were certainly in large enough numbers (over 100 of each piece) to warrant advertisement in the Liberty brochures and gift catalogs. Some pieces are found with the "MB & Co." mark of the London wholesaler for German firms, Murrle, Bennett, who may have wholesaled them in Europe. Answering a new demand for antique designs, Liberty reissued some of its most popular period designs in the 1970s and 1980s which can be identified by the corresponding date letters.[1]

Three silver and enamel brooches by Wm. Hasseler after Knox, for Liberty & Co. *Courtesy of Terrance O'Halloran Collection. Photo by Robert Weldon courtesy, of the G.I.A.*

Art Nouveau pewter belt buckle with blue/green enamel by Liberty & Company. *Courtesy of Terrance O'Halloran Collection, Los Angeles, CA. Photo by Robert Weldon, courtesy of the G.I.A.*

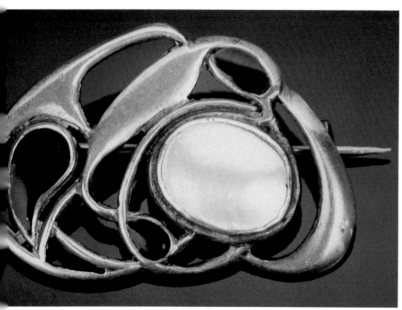

Archibald Knox (1864-1933) from the Isle of Man in the north of England, had long been intrigued by the ancient (300 B.C.) Celtic jewelry and artifacts unearthed on this island. The Celtic *entrelac,* interlaced, forms enjoyed a revival in the Middle Ages, and were born again in the late nineteenth century in Britain and Scandinavia. The Art Nouveau whiplash in France, and the curvilinear treatment of Knox's silver "Cymric" belt buckles and brooches can be traced to the Celtic connection. These were embellished with the blue-green enamel accents popular at the time. It is now known that many Liberty pieces of Knox design were actually produced in Pforzheim, Germany at the Fahrner factory, and imported through Murrle, Bennett & Co.

In the 1909 Liberty & Co. catalogue of "Yule-Tide Gifts", "Nola" Metal-work was illustrated; waist-clasps, hatpins, and brooches of powerful, assertive design "resembling old silver and enriched with Viennese stones and enamel". Neither Viennese nor silver, these were in fact designed and produced by Robert Kraft (?-1933) of electroplated Alpacca in Pforzheim. The simulated silver pieces were enhanced by faux hammer marks, and real enamel. Kraft was happy to provide a strong substitute for "flimsy silverware". The Kirchgaessner and Kraft Co., founded in 1904, was one of the first companies to utilise the Alpacca alloy of copper, nickel, and zinc (called *neusilber*, or new silver) for jewelry and metalware. In 1909, when Robert Kraft established his own factory, Liberty & Co. commissioned him to supply British customers with a cheap, attractive substitute for silver accessories until 1914.[2] Kraft adapted motifs from 7th century Germanic tribal belt buckles for his modern woman, and decorated the surface with bars and spirals, discreet enamel touches, and inset hardstones.

Murrle, Bennett & Co. were both competitors and collaborators with Arthur Liberty. Ernst Mürrle was German, though he dropped the *umlaut* in his English partnership with John Bennett. The workshop was in Pforzheim, but the wholesale showrooms were at Charterhouse St. in London. The company sold jewelry through Liberty & Co, as well as a separate line stamped "MB&Co". Murrle, Bennett designs incorporated the restrained German Jugendstil linear grills with tiny raised "pin-heads", simulated hand-beaten surfaces, and turquoise matrix stones or imperfect blister pearls. The "stitch" elements, simulating handcrafted sewing in metal of one part to another, was borrowed from a Crafts motif. Murrle, a German citizen, was interned in 1915 for a year on the Isle of Man, and his business was confiscated by the British Government. When he was repatriated, the company's name was changed, and German merchandise fell into disfavor in Britain.

Silver and enamel brooch with blister pearl, Liberty & Co. *Courtesy of Terrance O'Halloran. Photo by Robert Weldon courtesy of the G.I.A.*

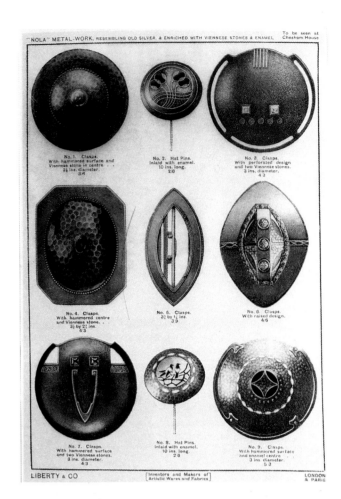

Waist-clasp of Alpacca set with hardstones, borrowing from 7th century Germanic tribal motifs, by Robert Kraft for Liberty & Co., Nola metal-work, 1909. *Courtesy of Tadema Gallery, Islington, London*

Lithograph from the Liberty & Co, 1909, catalog advertising the "Nola" metal-work (Alpacca) resembling silver with "Viennese" stones. All the hatpins and clasps were made by Robert Kraft in Pforzheim, Germany. From an article on Liberty & Co.'s "Nola" metalwork in the *Journal of Decorative Art Society* , #14, Brighton, England. *Courtesy of Graham Dry. Photo by Robert Weldon*

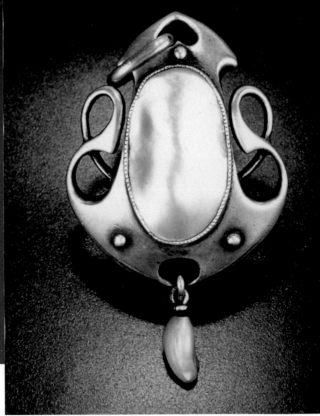

Silver and turquoise matrix brooch with pearls by Murrle Bennett. Ca. 1910, stamped MB&Co. *Courtesy of Terrance O'Halloran Collection. Photo by Robert Weldon, courtesy of the G.I.A.*

Reverse of Murrle Bennett brooch with hallmarks. *Courtesy of Terrance O'Halloran. Photo by Robert Weldon*

Silver pendant with blister pearls and raised "pin-heads" stamped MB& Co. *Courtesy of Terrance O'Halloran. Photo by Robert Weldon, courtesy of the G.I.A.*

In Halifax, Yorkshire, Charles Horner was the first British firm to mass-produce Art Nouveau jewelry between 1905 and 1910. Simplified whiplash and insect motifs were turned into inexpensive silver hatpins, pendants, and tiny knot brooches enamelled in peacock blues and greens. Unique in Britain, Horner jewelry was made from scratch at the family factory; everything including the silver strips and chains were manufactured in Halifax.[3] The silver is of lighter weight and the enamel thinner, lacking the hand-finished look of Liberty's jewelry. Horner's successful production formula was thus free of both the high ideals and high costs of the Arts & Crafts movement. The winged scarab and butterfly in enamelled silver pendants and pins were among the pieces produced in large numbers at affordable prices.

Silver buttons were a popular Art Nouveau accessory. The six pictured here, (one was made into a ring) are well travelled indeed. They were certainly made in Pforzheim, (the design is typically Jugendstil) and exported to France, then England. They bear the French swan import mark as well as the British "RF" import mark (for Robert Friedrich, a Pforzheim manufacturer and importer of foreign wares in London) and date letter for 1904. The buttons probably graced an elegant Edwardian gentleman's velvet waistcoat before being transported to America (embellishing the author's jacket in the Seventies). When jewelry was imported into England at this time, the rule was to stamp the import marks visibly on the front rather than the back of the piece, to encourage customers to buy English, not foreign products. But this policy backfired, because before the Great War, people actually preferred buying foreign merchandise.

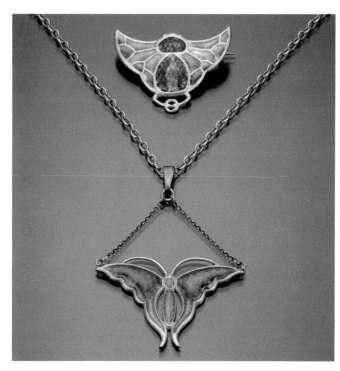

Two silver and enamel pieces by Charles Horner with blue/green enamel and chain made in the Halifax factory. The winged scarab and butterfly were favorite Horner motifs. Stamped "CH" with silver hallmarks. *Courtesy of the author. Photo by Robert Weldon*

Five well-travelled silver Art Nouveau buttons and one ring made in Pforzheim, Germany, imported by Robert Friedrichs to England ("RF" stamp, with 1904 date letter), subsequently exported to France (bearing the French swan import mark.) *Courtesy of the author. Photo by Sandro Moro*

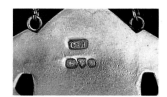

Reverse of a Horner pendant showing "CH" and hallmarks. *Courtesy of G.I.A. Photo by Robert Weldon*

The Ruskin pottery workshop was opened in 1898 by William Howson Taylor in West Smethwick, a suburb of Birmingham. Ceramics provided a cheap substitute for center stones in jewelry. Colorful round glazed plaques were mounted into simple, attractive brooches by Edward Jones, a Birmingham jeweler, combining the hand-beaten look with smooth surfaces in pewter or silver. The pink ceramic brooch pictured is stamped "S & Co." and "PLATANDOR", which may be the name of a metal alloy. These round ceramics were set in buttons, or studded Arts & Crafts mirrors and boxes. Unmounted ceramic plaques were impressed with the "RUSKIN" mark, and MADE IN ENGLAND.

Pink ceramic Ruskin plaque in metal alloy mount (Platandor?) marked "S & Co.", and a Murrle Bennett style rainbow enamelled pendant with stitched sections, 1905, marked "S&E". *Courtesy of Gail Gerretsen, Los Angeles. Photo by Robert Weldon*

Charming silver pendant brooch with black opals and marcasites, and silver chains by Sibyl Dunlop, ca. Twenties. *Courtesy of Terrance O'Halloran, Los Angeles. Photo by Sandro Moro*

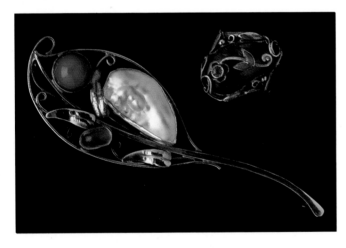

Green tourmaline ring with a silver enamelled floral motif; and a silver leaf brooch set with a blister pearl, moonstone, and opal by George Hunt, ca. 1930. *Courtesy of Van Den Bosch Decorative Arts, London*

Silver openwork clip with semi-precious cabochons and a faceted amethyst by Bernard Instone. *Courtesy of Tadema Gallery, London*

Up until the turn of the century, women were relegated to polishing stones in jewelry shops, but rarely designed jewelry. With the Arts & Crafts movement, designers worked with their wives; Arthur with Georgina Gaskin; and Nelson with Edith Dawson. Scotland was fertile ground for women jewelers: the MacDonald sisters who married Charles MacIntosh and Herbert MacNair; Jessie King, who designed for Liberty; and Sybil Dunlop, who had her own shop in London, all successfully crashed the male artists' barrier.

Sibyl Dunlop (1889-1968) studied jewelry techniques in Brussels, Belgium, and opened her workshop in the Twenties in Kensington Church Street in London. Her pieces were hand-crafted in the Crafts revival tradition, but she incorporated Art Deco tassels into her necklaces and floral elements into her rings. Bold geometric Deco was not for her. Her designs were feminine and delicate, using opals, moonstones and pastel tourmalines and amethysts. Her ties with Belgium continued with a Belgian enameller who decorated her brooches and rings. Dunlop's shop was closed during the war, but was reopened in the late Forties by W. Nathanson, who ran the workshop until her death. She fashioned an unusual pair of earrings out of tiny semi-precious cabochons and upside-down heart-shaped tourmaline drops, specially cut for her in Idar-Oberstein. Dunlop's predilection for pastel stones and openwork settings was one of the inspirations for attractive costume jewelry in America: Hobé in the Thirties; and Hollycraft in the Fifties.

Another British artist who kept the Crafts aesthetic alive into the Thirties, was George Hunt (1892-1960). Born in Birmingham, George contracted diptheria, which left him deaf at the age of five. His early artistic ability was encouraged and inspired by Bernard Cuzner and Arthur Gaskin, who taught at the Vittoria Street School in Birmingham. In 1912, Hunt registered his first punch (benchmark). He was impressed by the Wiener Werkstätte, so Hoffmann's plump heart-shaped leaves and filigree silver swirls are echoed in Hunt's work. His individual style was marked by delicate enamel portraits on Limoges china, surrounded by moonstones and other semi-precious stones or pearls. Like his contemporary, Sibyl Dunlop, his work was untouched by French Art Deco geometrics. He did execute some remarkable Egyptian revival enamel plaques after the 1922 King Tut tomb discovery. His pieces were one of a kind; entirely conceived and hand-crafted by him, including the enamelling and stone setting.[4] This was the normal procedure then, becoming increasingly rare as the century progressed. A green tourmaline cabochon ring inset with an enamelled silver flower, and a graceful brooch featuring a blister pearl with a moonstone, opal and silver leaves are his personal interpretation of the Wiener Werkstätte style.

Bernard Instone (1891-1987) knew what he wanted very early, winning a scholarship to the London's Central School at the tender age of 12. He studied with the best available teachers: Arthur Gaskin at the Vittoria Street School in Birmingham; and perfected his enamelling techniques in Berlin with Emile Lettré. In the Twenties, he designed enamelled silver tableware and the silver clip pictured of semi-precious cabochons and a faceted amethyst set in lacy silver leaves.

Omar Ramsden (1873-1939) was born in Sheffield, the silver electro-plating center of England. He apprenticed with a hometown silversmith, and formed a partnership with fellow art student Alwyn Carr in London which lasted from 1897 till 1919. They produced silverware and jewelry which mixed Art Nouveau and neo-Gothic elements, and since mechanical methods were used on some ostentatious pieces and their atelier staff executed most of their work, they cannot be considered Arts & Crafts jewelers.[5] A silver pendant with drops, and Gothic ogives supporting a bright red enamel plaque, was made before the war.

The emancipated women of early XXth century Britain wore long sleeved blouses with full skirts which were cinched in by a wide belt. This costume accounts for the many elaborate belts and belt buckles produced between 1890 and World War I in silver, silver and enamel, Alpacca, marcasite, Czechoslovakian glass, and pewter. (Some worn by hospital staff, were dubbed nurses' belts)

Child & Child produced enamel jewelry and belt buckles for the Edwardian woman until 1916. Their Art Nouveau pendants were rather flamboyant, brightly colored peacocks etc, but their silver buckles could be a serene pastel pink *guilloché* enamel over a mechanically engraved ground. These bore the "HC" hallmark (for Harold Child, who ran the company after 1900) and the date letter for 1909.

Silver belts were made in flexible sections of Art Nouveau design, (the all silver belt pictured was hallmarked Chester in 1902.) The buckles were either all silver or pastel *guilloché* enamelled silver. These examples are hallmarked London 1918, and Birmingham 1909. The British assay hallmarks for the towns of Chester, London, and Birmingham, are: the three wheat sheaves and a sword; the leopard's head; and the anchor. The letter marks indicate the dates.

An unusual belt of gilded brass sections alternating with oval agate plaques was probably made post World War I.

Red enamel pendant with neo-Gothic interlacing and three pendants by Omar Ramsden. *Courtesy of Van Den Bosch Gallery*

Silver link belt with Chester and 1902 silvermarks; silver clover buckle with London, 1918 hallmarks, and a turquoise *guilloché* enamelled silver buckle hallmarked Birmingham, 1909. *Courtesy of the author. Photo by Robert Weldon*

Silver buckle with pink *guilloché* enamel by Harold Child, 1909. *Courtesy of the author. Photo by Robert Weldon*

Reverse of pink enamel buckle with "Child & Child", "HC" and silvermarks for 1909. *Photo by Robert Weldon*

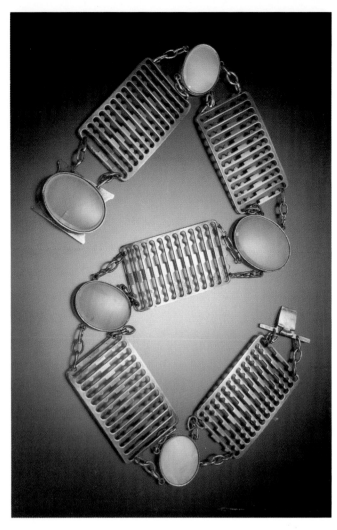

Belt of gilded brass links and five oval agate plaques. *Courtesy of the author. Photo by Robert Weldon*

Silver linear-styled ring set with tiny pearls and rubies and an amethyst by Charles Rennie Mackintosh; and an elongated silver brooch set with pearls and turquoise and a heart pendant with rubies on a long silver chain by Margaret MacDonald Mackintosh. Mixing a precious stone with the semi-precious was a Crafts innovation. *Photo from The Special Winter Number of The Studio, 1901-1902, Modern Design in Jewellery and Fans.*

Scotland

The metalwork of the "Glasgow Four" (plus One), architect Charles Rennie Mackintosh (1869-1929) and his wife, Margaret MacDonald Mackintosh (1865-1933), and Herbert McNair (1868-1955) and his wife, Frances MacDonald McNair (1874-1921) was far too avant-garde for the conservative Scots, but was enthusiastically embraced by Frank Lloyd Wright and Greene and Greene in America, and the Wiener Werkstätte in Vienna. Mackintosh's serene all white interiors marked by an original verticality were a shock to his countrymen who preferred their dark oak unpainted and their decoration traditional. His jewelry designs were rare but arresting; a silver ring with pearls and amethysts was pictured in *The Studio, Modern Design in Jewellery and Fans,* 1901, alongside a very vertical silver pendant brooch by his wife, Margaret. These, and the beaten silver jewelry of the McNairs, as well as the hammered aluminum, copper, or silver buckles of the fifth Glasgow designer, Talwin Morris (1865-1911), were dismissed by *The Studio* with a sniff as "quaint mannerism". Tragically, both Mackintosh and McNair, depressed by the lack of appreciation for their work, gave up the applied arts for the Scotch bottle, unaware how much their design legacy would influence not only Scottish fellow students at the Glasgow School of Art in their lifetime, but foreign artists in the future.

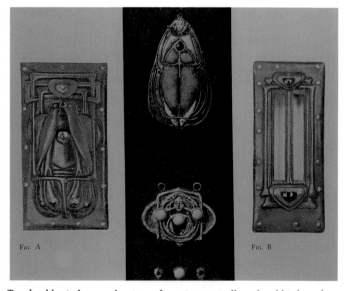

Two buckles in beaten aluminum featuring vertically stylized birds and plants by Talwin Morris; and two silver pendants designed around female heads, the upper with enamels, and the lower set with turquoises by Frances McNair. From *The Special Winter Edition of the Studio, 1901-1902.*

Sir Walter Scott's 19th century crusade to restore Scottish Highland culture to favor brought about a demand for Scottish folk jewelry to be worn with the newly fashionable tartan kilts and shawls. Targe brooches (derived from the ancient shield) that had once been worn by ruddy-complected thanes with stout calves and muttonchop whiskers were adopted by fragile Victorian and Edwardian damosels. Variegated agate, citrine, and smoky quartz were set into silver daggers, (dirks), and clan badges, and dubbed Scottish "pebble" jewelry. Native "cairngorm" (smoky quartz from the Cairngorm mountains of central Scotland) provided center stones for agate slices set in patterns simulating tartan plaid. The strap and buckle motif was popular, a tribute to Queen Victoria who was Head of the Order of the Garter.

From 1860 to 1912, Edinburgh and Birmingham produced quantities of circular brooches with intricate designs in grey or brown striated agate in chased silver (selling for one sixth the price of a single pearl), as well as vaguely Celtic designs made into earrings and bracelets which had certainly never been worn by the rugged Highland clansmen, (who were once referred to as the "aborigines of Britain"![6]). This was the first Scottish folk/costume jewelry which became sacred family heirlooms. There was a Victorian Scottish revival in the Sixties, (Queen Victoria's favorite retreat was Balmoral castle) and again in the Eighties.

In the 60 s as part of the ethnic jewelry revival, an English company called "Miracle", flooded the market with faux Scottish jewelry, simulating the agate, turquoise, malachite, and citrine quartz with glass stones mounted cheaply in white metal. This contribution to the the tourist trade in Scotland, Ireland, and the romantic Lake District was the product of a Birmingham company, A.Hill & Co, established in the Thirties. A second revival of real "pebble" jewelry in the 80 s initiated by British designers, Butler & Wilson, brought Miracle back to life again. (What does the Scotsman wear over his kilt? Is it real or faux?) The faux brooch pictured is also a pendant, and the pistol even has simulated chased silver gun mountings; both are signed "Miracle".

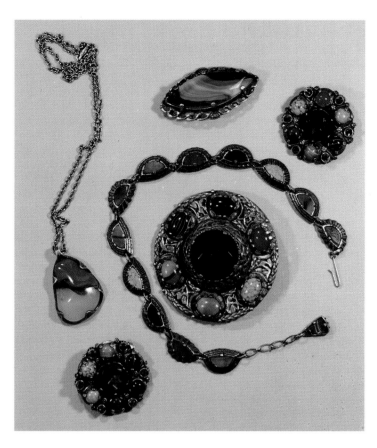

Four brooches, one necklace, and a pendant, each with glass simulating different hardstones by Miracle, Fifties and Sixties. The largest cast metal brooch/pendant with openwork animals cavorting around a faux amethyst is 3 1/4" wide and is signed "Miracle" "Britain". *Courtesy of the author. Photo by Sandro Moro*

Scottish striated agate brooch with chased silver strap and buckle motif of the Order of the Garter. Popular in Britain from 1880-1910. *Courtesy of the author. Photo by Robert Weldon*

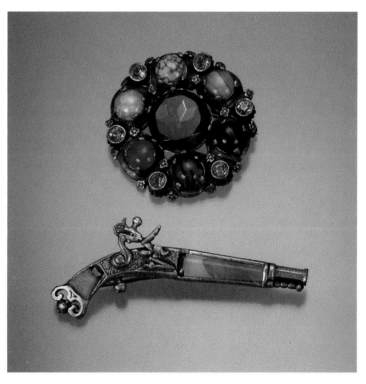

Faux Scottish jewelry manufactured by English company Miracle, in the Sixties, (and again in the Nineties) with glass simulating the smoky quartz, agate, and citrine of Scotland in mass-produced pendant/ brooches. Even the chased silver on the pistol brooch is simulated. *Courtesy of private collection, Los Angeles. Photo by Robert Weldon*

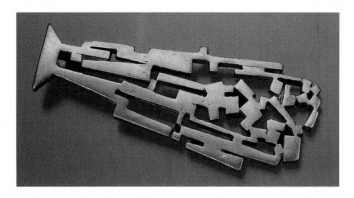

White metal pendant signed "Ceard Fantasy" and "Made in Scotland", of uncertain vintage. *Courtesy of Richard Trader collection, Los Angeles. Photo by Robert Weldon*

Other ceramic companies such as Poole Pottery and Carlton Ware, and designer Susie Cooper, designed Art Deco tableware and the occasional piece of ceramic jewelry. Cooper (born 1902), worked for A.E. Gray & Co. in the Twenties before she struck out on her own for Crown Works in 1931. Pastel floral plaques with pin backs were unsigned Thirties designs with the identifying Poole glaze on the back.

A Scottish company stamped CEARD FANTASY and MADE IN SCOTLAND on a white metal pendant of distinctive modernist design, is probably of Glasgow origin.

English ceramics in the Twenties and early Thirties were innovative and joyous. The most outstanding artist was certainly Clarice Cliff (1899-1972) who, fortuitously, was born smack in the middle of Staffordshire, Britain's pottery country. One of eight children from a working class family, she was apprenticed at 13 to a pottery enamelling firm. Still a talented teenager, she joined the decorating department of the A.J. Wilkinson factory and its subsidiary Newport Pottery. The owner, Colley Shorter, had a professional and personal interest in Clarice, which made rapid advancement possible. By 1928 Clarice was painting her own designs and teaching a staff of hand painters how to imitate her brushstrokes and vivid colors. Freeform landscapes, floral themes, and geometric styles decorated tableware, vases, and flower pots. Ceramic pendants, relatively rare, because infrequently produced in the Thirties, were possibly miniature versions of the popular "Bizarre" face masks which hung on every English bedroom wall. The breezy girl wearing a Thirties hairdo and a plaid scarf must have been a unique pendant design, since Cliff's "wall medallion" face masks were usually full face, not profile.[7] She is stamped "Clarice Cliff", and "Wilkinson Ltd".

Gaily painted ceramic plaque mounted as a brooch, photographed with Thirties Poole sugar bowl. The brooch is unsigned, probably Poole, judging by the glaze on reverse. *Courtesy of the author. Photo by Robert Weldon*

Rare ceramic pendant by Clarice Cliff of a girl with a Thirties hairdo and scarf. Signed "Clarice Cliff" and Wilkinson Ltd. *Courtesy of the author. Photo by Robert Weldon*

Reverse of Clarice Cliff pendant with signatures. *Photo by Robert Weldon*

Thirties - Sixties

English plastics had their own style. Thirties tableware and household plastics under the Bandalasta label were produced in marbled colors, and the jewelry was just as colorful. Carved Bakelite frogs and birds were usually mounted on brass. Moulded Celluloid scotties with movable heads, groups of bunnies, or grasshoppers were sold on Plastic Fashion Jewellery, (PL LTD.) cards for a few pence. (What was yesterday's "Novelty" jewelry is today's collectable kitsch.) A classic Bakelite and brass bracelet with a powder compact mounted on top found its counterpart in France, (made by Flamand) where powder or lipstick were worn on the wrist.

English version of the Flamand French compact bracelet for Josephine Baker. Midnight blue Bakelite on brass cuff with portable mirrored compact. Stamped "Made in England", 1930. Courtesy of the author. Photo by Sandro Moro

Ten frogs a-leaping, all "carved" Bakelite, except for the pink and white clips which are moulded Celluloid. Bracelets, dress clips and lapel pins all mounted on copper, Thirties. *Courtesy of the author and Joanne McPherson. Photo by Robert Weldon*

Plastic scotties (one with movable heads), bunnies and crickets photographed atop vintage Bakelite compacts. Marked "Made in England", or "Plastic Fashion Jewellery". Thirties. *Courtesy of Joanne McPherson and the author. Photo by Robert Weldon*

Thirties handbags with hand-carved butterscotch Bakelite elephants and crocodiles, and white Celluloid elephants inlaid in navy blue Celluloid. The bags are leather or silk, all marked "Made in England". *Courtesy of the author. Photo by Robert Weldon*

Reverse painted Lucite butterflies, parrots, and a lizard, post-war Britain. *Courtesy of Joanne McPherson, Santa Monica, CA. Photo by Robert Weldon*

Real amber (carved and faceted,) necklace and bracelet with ebony beads or clear amber spacers. *Courtesy of the author. Photo by Robert Weldon, courtesy of the G.I.A.*

During the war, Britain's full attention was turned towards defending her soil against the Germans. The jewelry centers in Birmingham (where much of the work was still executed in units of six each in terrace houses,) and London were destroyed by bombs. Base metals were reserved for airplane parts and shell casings. Children and prized possessions were shipped to cousins in the West country for the duration. After the war, in the Forties, the English reverse-painted Lucite butterflies, parrots, and lizards to restore color to their drab wardrobes. These were often hand-crafted at home, available in individual kits, as well as mass-produced by unknown companies.

Handbag decorations and clasps were a novelty that was enthusiastically embraced by the animal-loving English. Carved Bakelite elephants (simulating amber) competed with inlaid Celluloid elephants (faux ivory) for the affections of women who loved jewelry on their leather handbags. Carved Bakelite baby crocodiles served as fastenings for black silk clutch bags. Large two-toned Bakelite compacts were carried in these handbags to repair the ravages.

Meanwhile, the much-imitated natural plastic, amber, native to Britain, was faceted for necklaces and bracelets, alternating clear and opaque golden amber for effect.

In the late 19th-early 20th century, Peking glass was produced in Northen China, and exported to the West. The Peking palette was distinctive; pastel pink, green, blue, and yellow. Imperfectly formed opaque glass beads were lamp-worked on rods or bamboo, with large holes and frequent bubbles. There were two qualities of beads: the crude version intended for the masses and export which was hastily formed with insufficiently hot melted glass; and the more perfectly round beads which were used for the Mandarin court chains during the Manchu and Qing dynasties (1644-1911).[8] The officials of the Imperial court in Peking, and their families were required to wear beads of different colors for each occasion. Glass beads were made to simulate jade, turquoise, carnelian, tourmaline, and agate, as well as the Peking palette of pastels. When the Chinese Revolution of 1911 toppled the despised Manchus, the strands of court chains were broken up and sold individually, or strung with enamelled pendants. These were exported, and were especially popular in Britain and France in the Twenties. Fashionable department stores like Fortnum and Mason and the Galeries Lafayette sold them as sautoirs. British naval officers brought them home to their wives from Shanghai after the Opium Wars. Eventually, the Bohemian glass-makers were busy reproducing "Peking glass" in Gablonz.

By the Fifties, the French idea of *bijoux de couture* was happily accepted in London, as French haute couture clothes were copied and sold on Oxford street. Paste and faux pearls had been timidly used in Edwardian jewelry, set in silver to imitate the elaborate pieces worn by Edward VII's swan-necked wife, Alexandra. Now the English version of rhinestones was boldly splashed on gilded metal. "Paste" is an unattractive word used in England since the 18th century for imitation jewels, (derived from a word meaning "fusible stone", paste is also the English translation of *pâte*). The stones were imported from Murano, or Gablonz, and mounted in London in silver or silver gilt. The quality of the 19th century glass was superior to the ordinary bottle glass used until Swarovski began machine-cutting demi-crystal. Sometimes ordinary glass was fused to crystal stones, foil-backed, and collet mounted. Mirror-backed flat bottomed stones were even brighter.

In the Fifties, costume jewelry imitations of real jewelry were sold by Fior, and Ciro. Fior, which imported quality costume jewelry from America and Europe, as well as Attwood & Sawyer from Wales, was established in Burlington Gardens right around the corner from the Bond Street fine jewelers. Also known for real-look-

Delicate necklace of "Peking glass" pink and green beads with strass rondelles in original Fortnum & Mason box. *Courtesy of Tadema Gallery, London*

ing faux were the Ciro shops on Old Bond St. (and Madison Ave., NY.) Ciro evolved from Técla, famous in Paris in the Twenties for its imitation pearls (see Chapter One, for vintage Twenties ad). Both Fior and Ciro are still going strong. Extensive use was made of the cubic zirconia synthetic diamonds, nicknamed "CZ" in the trade, which were the perfect stone for the 1980s; only the experts could tell the difference and the price was right.

Mitchel Maer, a transplanted New Yorker, settled in London at the end of the Thirties. He founded a company called "Metalplastic", and hired Horace Attwood from Birmingham to cast his jewelry designs. When their business grew, thanks to an inexpensive gold-toned line for Woolworth's, the firm moved to Wales where new centrifugal casting techniques could be developed in a larger factory. After the war when the firm's name was changed to Mitchel Maer, the style changed as well, aiming for a more sophisticated clientele. Maer was inspired by romantic Georgian jewelry, with delicate garlands and feminine paste flowers tremblers. Alun Roberts joined the staff to collaborate on the model execution, where he continues to work as an Attwood & Sawyer designer.[9]

In 1952, Christian Dior commissioned Maer to produce costume jewelry for him from Parisian designs. All the Fifties Dior pieces are crafted with hand-set paste in prong mountings, and are signed "Christian Dior by Mitchel Maer". These were named after French *châteaux* to give an added Gallic charm, and featured 18th century touches like bows, flowers and hearts. Besides the Georgian parures, there were necklaces inspired by Moghul jewelry, using colored *champlevé* enamel, faux pearls and emerald paste with lavish fringes of metal, or simulated Ceylon rubies and faux turquoises and moonstone with pearl drops. Brooches were fanciful unicorns, horns of plenty dripping pearls, and cupids holding enamelled music boxes.

Eastern-style necklace with faux moonstones, Czech "Peking" glass, faux Ceylon rubies, and pearls with glass turquoise drops by Mitchel Maer for Christian Dior, early Fifties. *Courtesy of the author. Photo by Sandro Moro*

Reverse of Mitchel Maer necklace showing signature. *Photo by Robert Weldon*

Despite the success of the Dior line (perhaps it was too labor-intensive and costly to produce), Maer went bankrupt in 1956. One year later, Horace Attwood with a sleeping partner, Sawyer, set up their own firm, Attwood & Sawyer, and concentrated on classically designed fine costume jewelry, executed as always by Alun Roberts. These were largely adaptations of real jewelry and were exported abroad to be proudly worn by "Miss World", and other beautiful women.

London-Sixties

The Swinging Sixties burst on the fashion scene like an errant rocket..wham! Shazam! The Brits went bonkers. Everything was youth-oriented, larger-than-life, beyond outrageous. Exaggerated makeup demanded exaggerated clothes and accessories: the mini-skirt went as far as it could go..up; the bouffant hair styles went as far as they could go..out; the pendant earrings went as far as they could go..down.

At the center of this uncontrolled mayhem was stoic London, and her two happening streets: King's Road in Chelsea where Mary Quant launched her mini-skirt; and Carnaby Street, a psychedelic alley full of shops selling bell-bottoms in day-glo colors, granny glasses, hippie jewelry, and drug paraphernalia (all this in the shadow of the imposing Liberty's of London. What would William Morris have thought?) Thongs were in, for sandals as well as ethnic pendants. Ancient Rome was plundered yet again for slave bracelets above the elbow, and wide gladiator cuffs sprouting dangerous spikes matching gladiator boots.

Those of us living in France who were lucky enough to make the Sixties scene, abandoned staid old Paris for the Friday night ferry across the English Channel. Oh wow! How could you beat the Beatles, cheap Wallis copies of Cardin and Yves Saint Laurent fashions, and Saturday morning at Portobello Road in search of antique jewelry? Barbara Hulanicki's trendy dress shop, Biba, on Kensington Church Street revived Art Deco fabrics and decor which screamed for vintage jewelry. Butler and Wilson's stand at Antiquarius, the antiques mall that opened in 1970 on King's Road, was a favorite pit stop for French Art Deco jewelry.

Nicky Butler and Simon Wilson found most of their vintage Art Nouveau carved horn, and Art Deco chrome and Bakelite pieces at the Marché aux Puces flea market in St. Ouen. When the hard-to-find originals sold out, they copied the old designs and mass-produced the faux, all of which was gloriously hyped by the fashion magazines *Nova* and *Vogue*. In 1972, Butler and Wilson moved to larger quarters on Fulham Road, and went into the glitz business, Big Time. They had an adventurous eye; classic designs of lizards, snakes, big cats, bows, and medal decorations of exaggerated proportions were interpreted in diamanté (the British term for pavé rhinestones.) Everybody wanted one, even Princess Diana who set the fashion for costume jewelry, as Princess Alexandra had done for pearl parures, 70 years before her.

Butler and Wilson had time for romantic jewelry, as well. In 1975, they designed a line of Pierrot bracelets, brooches, and necklaces in pink, plum, or black and white plastic. In the early 80s between bouts of glitz, they produced discreetly chic grey, beige, and pink shagreen bangles and earrings in an Art Deco mood. Shagreen (taken from the French *chagrin*) is the skin of a ray fish found in the Indian ocean. Called sharkskin in America, and *Galuchat* in France (after Jean Claude Galuchat who made boxes and objets of sharkskin for Louis XIV,) shagreen was polished, dyed, and inlaid with ivory for Art Deco luxury items in England and France. Butler and Wilson substituted white plastic strips for the ivory inlay in their Neo-Deco designs.

English *Vogue* covers of the late Sixties- early Seventies featured underfed and underage models like Twiggy, Jean (Shrimp) Shrimpton, Veruschka (all 6 feet of her) and the petite Penelope Tree in a towering wig, modelling Pucci palazzo pants with shoulder-length sequined ping-pong ball earrings with rings to match, or hipsters with a jewel in the exposed navel. Breasts were first camoflaged, then exposed. In the Fifties, women wore bullet bras or falsies; in the Sixties, bras were burned by the Feminists, and body jewelry was molded to famous naked torsos.

English film and theater were exploring the common man. Richard Burton played an "Angry Young Man" on stage, but wore a

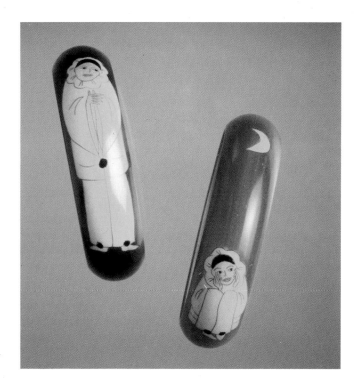

Pierrot bracelets of etched and painted Galalith by Butler & Wilson, 1975. *Courtesy of Jill Spalding Collection, NY. Photo by Richard Marx*

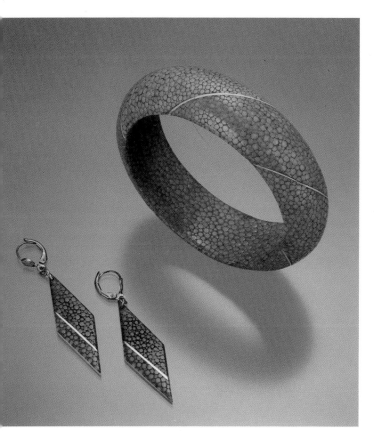

Neo-Deco pink and beige shagreen bracelet and earrings (with white plastic strips imitating the ivory insets) by Butler & Wilson, 1983. *Courtesy of the author. Photo by Robert Weldon*

Two nickel-plated wire neckpieces with reversible plastic ovals. Unsigned Sixties. *Courtesy of private collection, Los Angeles. Photo by Robert Weldon*

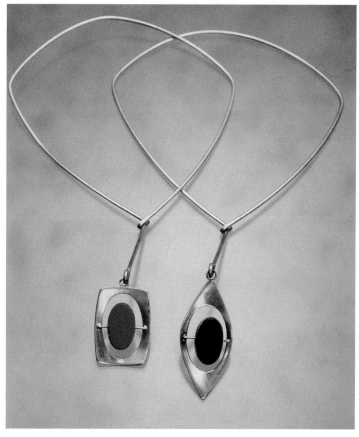

Nehru jacket and uni-sex pendant after the show. The movie *Blow-up* was typical of the times. Jewelry was blown up so large, it had to be light, i.e. plastic, wood, or hollow metal. The Counter-culture was against everything that the cautious, overprotected Fifties represented. For the politically engaged, the anti-war movement proclaimed "flower power". The daisy was a favorite, showing up in fabrics, necklaces, and earrings.

In 1969, Man went as far as he could go..to the moon, which inspired spaced-out, futuristic fashions with satellite dish jewelry to match. "Outta sight". "Far out!" White metal wire collars were hung with spinning plastic pendants that could switch from red to black to match the outfit. Op Art showed up in black and white plastic accessories. "Mod" became "Sci-Fi". But living for the moment produced ephemera. Very little has endured from that demented, disposable decade. Throwaway paper dresses and jewelry disintegrated, as they were meant to. The love beads that the hippies on a spiritual quest brought back from the Indian ashrams broke and scattered. Turkish puzzle rings fell apart, never to be reassembled. British Rock stars collected ancient amber Berber necklaces bought on trips to North Africa (in search of desert serenity or the perfect pot-pie.) These were copied in chunky plastic for those who "tripped out" at home. A recent request for Sixties Peace symbol pendants at local flea markets was met with the innocent question: "What's a Peace symbol?"

For the first time young people could be who they really were, not who they were supposed to be. There was hope in the air. In the 90s, the Sixties/Seventies fashions were back, but the original energy was gone. (Mary Quant even opened a store in Carnaby Street in 1988.) The rebellious, experimental spirit was missing, leaving a listless rehash. What had been an exuberant self-expression was now just fashion. Waif models were entangled in knee-length Hippie love beads, and Punk was called Grunge this time around. In 1995, Glamour made a welcome comeback.

Sixties and Seventies costume jewelry firms mass-produced quantities of inexpensive lines. "Miracle" (by the Birmingham-based A. Hill & Co.) made bead necklaces for the Youth Cult as well as their faux Scottish agate brooches for tourists touring the Lake Disrict in search of the Loch Ness monster. Recently, since Scottish/Celtic jewelry is hot again, Miracle is reissuing their interpretations (cast or stamped) for those who can't afford the originals. Adrien Mann (established in 1945) signed his name to Sixties imitations of the Byzantine *pâte de verre* and pearl brooches that Robert Goossens had reinvented for Chanel ten years earlier.

The bell bottoms and hand-made (by amateurs, mostly) jewelry lasted well into the Seventies when, once again, street fashions launched by Rock groups (Sid Vicious in the lead) promoted Punk. Everything turned black. Black leather, black rubber jewelry, black boots, black gloves, black bikes, black stockings, black lipstick, black nailpolish, and black eyes were flaunted by young men and women with spiky collars who longed to be pit bulls. Safety pins were worn on torn clothes not to hold them together, but as shock jewelry, even more effective when worn sticking out of one's face.

Interesting variations on the Punk rubber/metal jewelry fad are still surfacing in the 90's. Socialites show up at parties dressed in dominatrix chains and boots by Vivienne Westwood, who was cracking the same bondage whips in her dress shop in the late Seventies when it was shocking. Vulcanized rubber, (Charles Goodyear's 1838 discovery) had been synthesized by the Germans during the first World War, but not with jewelry in mind. The Mods and Punks thought they were the first to don rubber jewelry. Not so; in the Twenties and Thirties, rubber bangles and anklets were worn to the beach with mad rubber bathing turbans topped with Carmen Miranda rubber fruit. These accessories were waterproof, and expensive.[10] Picture a Punk with a rubber duckie!

Several talented artists appeared on the Sixties scene who made limited-edition jewelry, working with alternative materials.

Wendy Ramshaw was born in Sunderland, England in 1939. She studied illustration and fabric design at Newcastle-upon-Tyne and Reading University from 1956-61. A self-taught jeweler, in the Sixties she produced both linear and three-dimensional forms with inlaid plastic, or folded paper for Something Special. Ramshaw's Origami paper jewelry kits of psychedelic butterflies could be assembled and taped to paper dresses at rock concerts while grooving to the Beatles or the Stones. Perspex was printed and hand-polished for black and white geometric Op Art. In the Seventies, she created a send-up of the King's Road Mohawk haircut with her own silver-gilt version made with emu feathers.

Wendy Ramshaw has since passed the exacting exams demanded by the Worshipful Company of Goldsmiths, to become a Freeman, then a Lady Liveryman in 1986. (The standards for joining this modern medieval Guild are very high indeed). One-Woman shows followed at the Pace Gallery, and the Victoria and Albert Museum. Ramshaw's husband, David Watkins (1940-), who also studied at Reading University in 1960, produced plastic pieces in the Seventies by bending perspex rods into unusual shapes, or coating steel wire necklaces with neoprene. He is now working uniquely in precious metals. Both Ramshaw and Watkins jewelry can be found in the collections of major international art museums.

In 1990, Wendy made an extraordinary series of jewelry inspired by Picasso's portraits of women. "Amongst the women with whom Picasso had emotional relationships, I looked for the images that would inspire a piece of jewelry.. a sense of rythmn, the

Celluloid glasses with "Blue Swirl" earrings an extension of the temples curling around the ears, by Stanley Unger of Tunbridge Wells, England. Fifties design became Sixties Op Art. *Courtesy of l.a. Eyeworks Collection, Los Angeles*

form or flow of lines, and the power of color."[11] She made a necklace of nickel alloy and Colorcore (plastic), and sets of silver rings inlaid with yellow agate, enamel, or black resin, stacked on their own matching stands. For Picasso's "Woman with a Flower", she produced cufflinks, earrings and a brooch of gilded metal and enamel in an edition of 200. The enamel is fired on the piece, then polished flat (a demanding process) and gold-plated. Though originally conceived as adornment for Picasso's women, a Cubist profile is not obligatory for the modern wearer!

The Seventies were pretty slim pickins in London as well as the rest of Europe, although some designers kept up their Sixties head of steam. The price of gold rose at the end of the decade to $800 an ounce, as the boring gold chain fad embraced by successful women suffocated creative imagination. But defiant Punk Rock fans stalked King's Road in black leather, their shaved heads bristling with Commanche Indian ruffs, with safety pins and real dog collars their only adornments.

Zandra Rhodes, designer of diaphanous chiffon dresses and beaded evening wear, as well as costume jewelry and accessories, was born in 1940 in Chatham, Kent. She studied textile design at the Royal College of Arts in London, 1961-64, graduating just in time to offer her unique talents and original eye to Swinging London. She designed and printed fabrics for her own shop as well as for Mary Quant and Roger Nelson and Foale and Tuffin. By 1969 she was featured in English *Vogue*, and designing costumes for the theater. She borrowed the Punk ideas for her couture dresses, declaring that "chains and safety pins are just alternative, non-traditional decorations for the Seventies".

Zandra asked Mick Milligan to create jewelry for her Seventies collections. Mick, another Royal College of Arts alumnus, was the first student to show his jewelry collection with a fashion show at

Inspired by Picasso's "Woman with a Flower" (La Fleur), the brooch, earrings and cuff links were hand-enamelled in five colors, then polished and gold-plated, by Wendy Ramshaw, 1990. *Courtesy of Electrum Gallery, London. Photo by Bob Cramp*

the Royal College. In the Sixties, Mick was known for his chrome and diamanté Walt Disney characters and prose jewelry for the Mr. Freedom Boutique. For Zandra, he devised coiled and crinkled gilded metal pins, dubbed the "magic head", as well as earrings like mobiles, and hair ornaments. Another design was the "torn" brooch, which was a freeform shape to accessorize Zandra's hand-printed dresses. (These were sold as works of art, signed and numbered.)

Andrew Logan, (1945-), who graduated from Oxford in 1970, was a sculptor who worked with mirrored pieces on a large scale. Twenty years after Line Vautrin's Talosel resin, he constructed miniature sculptures, using fragments of mirrors and colored glass set in resin. For Zandra's "Indian Collection" of 1982 (following their trip to India where mirrored jewelry is common) he designed his uncommon "Third Eye" brooch of mirrors, and pink glass. For the "Egyptian Collection" he plucked the star off Zandra's fabric and covered it with mirrors for earrings, and fashioned a pink mirrored cap for the Queen of the Upper and Lower Thames. Logan plated resin with 22 ct. gold for glittering glass bangles and pagoda earrings from his Burmese collection in 1986.

Zandra Rhodes also designed her own jewelry, using Swarovski crystals in 1987. The "Lilly" range was comprised of a metal bracelet, earrings, necklace and brooches, and the "Egyptian" line showed gilded metal acanthus pins, bracelets, necklaces and earrings, accented with blue and clear crystals.

In the Eighties, British Fashion designers (Jean Muir, Vivienne Westwood, etc.) attracted international buyers in large numbers, with a corresponding rise in demand for accessories. Artist-jewelers (who had learned to adopt costume jewelry materials and methods in the Sixties,) were comfortable with the lower prices charged which made their work accessible to a wider public. Art School graduates (Valerie Robertson, Julia Mannheim, Linda Atkinson and others) found commercial outlets for their work in specialty shops like Aspects, and Detail. The Victoria and Albert Museum Metalwork department in conjunction with Design Gap has held costume jewelry exhibitions. The venerable Worshipful Goldsmiths'Company holds annual competitions and frequent "Loot" shows featuring inexpensive silver crafts, and Goldsmiths Fairs for costume jewelry. Both the Crafts Council and the Design Center encourage the sale of non-precious jewelry.[12] The line between artist-jewelers and costume/fashion jewelers is increasingly blurred in England as it is in the rest of Europe.

1. Leah Margulies Roland, "Liberty Jewels Merge Artistry and Industry", *Jewelers' Circular-Keystone, Heritage*, Radnor, Pa. Chilton Co., August, 1993, pg. 121.
2. Graham Dry, "Liberty & Co.'s "Nola" Metalwork: Art Nouveau Nickel-Silver Jewellery from Pforzheim," in *Journal of the Decorative Arts Society*, Nr. 14, London, 1990, pg. 40.
3. Vivienne Becker, *Art Nouveau Jewelry*, E.P. Dutton, NY, 1985. pg.178.
4. Anne Pyne, "George Hunt, Art Jeweller," *The Antique Collector*, National Magazine Company LTd., London, February, 1990, pg. 55.
5. Elyse Zorn Karlin, *Jewelry and Metal Work in the Arts & Crafts Tradition*, Atglen, PA., Schiffer Publishing, 1993, pg.46.
6. Vivian Swift, G.G., "Victorian Scottish Jewelry: Highlander Style with a British Twist", *Jewelers Circular Keystone*, Heritage, Radnor, PA., November, 1992, pg. 59.
7. Leonard Griffin, Louis K. and Susan Pear Meisel, *Clarice Cliff, The Bizarre Affair*, New York, Harry N. Abrams, Inc., 1988, pg.54.
8. Peter Francis, Jr., *Beads of the World*, Atglen, PA., Schiffer Publishing Ltd., 1994, pp. 85-85.
9. Vivienne Becker, *Fabulous Fakes, The History of Fantasy and Fashion Jewellery*, London, Grafton Books, 1988, pg. 164.
10. Jody Shields, *All That Glitters*, New York, Rizzoli, 1987, pg. 50.
11. Wendy Ramshaw, "Jewels for Picasso's Ladies" *The Antique Collector*, London, National Magazine Co. Ltd., London, March 1990, pp. 58-61.
12. Jane Stancliffe, *Costume and Fashion Jewellery of the Twentieth Century*, Victoria & Albert Museum, London, n.d., pg. 122.

Crinkled gilt metal "Magic Head" ornaments by Mick Milligan for Zandra Rhodes, 1979. *Courtesy of Zandra Rhodes, London. Photo by Grant Mudford*

Gilded brass pin with Swarowski crystals from the Egyptian Collection by Zandra Rhodes. A necklace, earrings and bracelet of the same lotus leaf completed the parure, 1980's. *Courtesy of the author. Photo by Sandro Moro*

"Egyptian" portrait of Zandra Rhodes wearing glass and resin earrings and pink mirrored skullcap by Andrew Logan, 1983. *Courtesy of Zandra Rhodes. Photo by Robin Beeche*

Chapter 4:

Austria

The Legacy of the Vienna Secession and the Wiener Werkstätte

The Austro-Hungarian Empire (1867-1918) was an improbable stew of Slavs, Germans, and Magyars in an area slightly smaller than Texas. Austria included Bohemia and Moravia (until 1918 when it became Czechoslovakia, since broken up again into two separate nations) and Galicia (now part of Poland) as well as the northern provinces along the coast of what we knew as Yugoslavia.

To add to the confusion, Hungary included Croatia, Slavonia, and Transylvania (now northern Romania.) At the heart of this glorious pot-pourri were the Hapsburgs in Vienna, capitol of the Austro-Hungarian Empire.

"To Every Age Its Art, To Art Its Freedom": this motto of the Viennese Secessionists was emblazoned in gold letters across the facade of Joseph Maria Olbrich's 1898 exhibition building. The Secessionists were a group of painters, designers, and architects who broke with the conservative Künstlerhaus which sponsored art exhibitions in *fin de siècle* Vienna. Their publication *Ver Sacrum* (named after the ancient Roman "Sacred Spring" rites) symbolized the birth of the Secessionist artists who wanted to create avant-garde art and architecture to please themselves, not the conformist art patrons who supported the antiquated faux-Gothic and Baroque ambience of the Ringstrasse which encircled Vienna.

For the architect, Olbrich (1867-1908) whose amazing golden cluster of leaves atop his Secessionist building was like an immense jewel, it was only a question of downscaling to become an artist/jeweler. He left Vienna to devote his life to designing for the Darmstadt Colony in 1899. The rare jewelry he designed there was executed by the German firms F. Zerrener and Fahrner in Pforzheim.

The Secessionist group broke up after a surprisingly successful first exhibition which introduced The Glasgow Four to the Viennese. The architects Koloman Moser and Josef Hoffmann founded the Wiener Werkstätte in 1903 to promote and retail the jewelry, fashion, objets, and decorative arts of the Secessionist designers. The painter Gustav Klimt (whose sensual art decorated the exhibition building) went his own way, depicting with relish in gold leaf and mosaics the suppressed eroticism of the decadent Viennese socialites who were his willing models.

A cleansing wind blew in from the north to support the Viennese Workshop artists. The British Arts & Crafts movement hopscotched across Europe, touching down in Scandinavia and Holland before placing one foot firmly down in Darmstadt, Germany and the other in Vienna. Ironically, what was essentially a backward-looking movement in turn of the century England proved to be the springboard for avant-garde design in the Austrian Wiener Werkstätte, 1903-1932, and subsequently the rigorous design community of the German Bauhaus in the Thirties.

The dynamics of the two movements were, however, very different. The Viennese artisans and apprentices who realized the sketches in the Viennese Workshops were skilled craftspeople, whereas in England they were largely self-taught. Nor were the economics the same. Birmingham and London suffered the worst effects of the Industrial Revolution, but in the more rural Austro-Hungarian Empire, the glass and ceramics centers were in the distant provinces (Bohemia and Moravia), leaving Vienna and most of Austria free of industrialization even to this day. Lacking the concentrated jewelry manufacturing centers like Birmingham and Pforzheim, the Austrians developed a highly efficient system of provincial applied art technical schools *(fachschule)* funnelling into the Kuntsgewerbeschule (Arts and Crafts School) in Vienna which

Opposite
Fashion designs by Maria Likarz-Strauss showing Poiret's influence of pantaloons, and aigrettes. Originally pictured on Wiener Werkstätte post cards in 1912-1914, and reproduced as *Kunstkarten* by Edition Christian Brandstätter, Vienna, 1991. *Courtesy of the author and Edition Brandstätter. Photo by Robert Weldon*

trained artisans to create their own jewelry, or graphic arts. These students and Viennese silversmiths executed the jewelry designs of the architect founders of the Wiener Werkstätte, Koloman Moser and Josef Hoffmann. The students' names were not marked on the finished pieces, but Moser and Hoffmann's initials did appear alongside the intertwined WW monogram.[1]

The utopian goal in England to involve the common folk in the crafts movement didn't work because the high-priced handicrafts were beyond their means. In Austria, Hoffmann and Moser wisely focused on designing for the well-to do Viennese cultural elite (usually the liberal Jewish upper-middle class), many of whom were their financial backers. In fact, the Wiener Werksätatte could not have survived without the patronage and support of wealthy industrialists like Adolf Stoclet, Fritz Wärndorfer and Otto Primavesi. When Hoffmann and Moser founded the Viennese Workshop in 1903 with the backing of Wärndorfer, they proclaimed the need for a *Gesamtkunstwerk*, a total art work uniting all the decorative arts in a cohesive style as if it emanated from a single sensibility. The wallpaper, objets, and furniture promised to be of the same harmonious design as the architecture. The clothes worn on this stage set (the Viennese being very theatrical) were styled from modern textiles, and the jewelry complemented the dress, shoes, and handbag. All of these separate parts were designed and executed by the Wiener Werkstätte artists and artisans who were well compensated, and given considerable creative freedom. Unique in Europe, the Royal Arts & Crafts School professors encouraged hands-on execution of students' designs as well as providing a commercial outlet for their products. (Early ambivalence regarding the use of the machine was resolved by referring to it as a helper, not a tyrant.) The Artists' Workshops provided an invaluable support system for the artists and craftsmen who eventually numbered around 200.[2]

Josef Hoffmann (1870-1956) contributed to all branches of the arts and crafts. Trained as an architect, and painter, he also designed jewelry, ceramics, glass, furniture, and textiles. He was a walking *Gesamtkunstwerk*. His brooches were rectilinear silver or silver gilt frames setting off his signature plump heart-shaped leaves, and mother of pearl flowers. As a founding member of the Secession which scorned fusty Austrian historicism, Hoffmann had enthusiastically welcomed the Arts & Crafts work of Charles Ashbee, and the pure austerity of the Scot, Charles Rennie Mackintosh, at a Secession exhibit in 1900. Hoffmann's use of the cube, and openwork squares in black and white contrasts (called Zebradecor) in his metal work, and belt buckles, was reinforced by Mackintosh who had been working along the same lines. For both, it was "back to square one." Hoffman's distinctive black leather wallets and pochettes were gold-tooled with abstract leaves and flowers. Hoffmann's jewelry, however, was more sensuous. He designed each piece, following through the execution of his sketches with the artisan. Anton Pribyl, a Czech goldsmith who had his own workshop in 1913, executed designs for Hoffmann in gold or silver-gilt and moonstones which bore his benchmark, "A.P."

Koloman Moser (1868-1918) was a multi-talented painter, graphic artist, and furniture designer who also created jewelry. A Vienna Secessionist member, his style in art and ornament became linear and abstract following a brief flirtation with floral Art Nouveau for his enamelled belt buckles (produced by Georg Anton Scheid.) He used cubes and spirals effectively in black and white checkerboard enamel on brass brooches, as well as in silver pendants. Moser left the Workshop in 1906 (convinced that noone could avert a financial failure) but continued to teach at the Vienna Kuntsgewerbeschule until his death.

1907 was a major turning point in the Werkstätte aesthetic. Berthold Löffler (1874-1960) and Michael Powolny reintroduced the Cupid and curlicue motifs when they founded the Wiener

Silver pendant with mother of pearl attributed to Hoffmann. *Courtesy of Ilene Chazanof Collection, New York, NY. Photo by Richard Marx*

Brooch of plump golden heart-shaped leaves and spirals with a moonstone flower. One of the many variations of a Josef Hoffmann design executed by Anton Pribyl, in gold or silver-gilt. Stamped "A.P.", 1914. *Courtesy of Bel Etage, Vienna, Austria*

Black, white, and grey enamelled pin with flower attributed to the Wiener Werkstätte in the style of Kolo Moser. *Courtesy of Ilene Chazanof, NY. Photo by Richard Marx*

Brooch, enamelled blue, with cupids and garlands, Viennese-style, ca. 1912. *Courtesy of Ilene Chazanof, NY. Photo by Richard Marx*

Keramik. Löffler produced silver wire-work jewelry unadorned by stones. Carl Otto Czeschka (1878-1960) was a talented artist (wallpaper, textiles, and lithographs) who transformed his two-dimensional graphics into three-dimensional openwork spirals and leaves in high relief for opulent pendants and brooches set with black opals or mother of pearl. Anton Pribyl executed many of his sketches. Czeschka designed the first jewelry for children when he enamelled silver brooches with rabbits, birds, or fish. He designed for the Wiener Werkstätte between 1904-08, then accepted a teaching assignment at the Kuntsgewerbeschule in Hamburg. He continued to contribute ideas to the Workshop, however, from Germany.

Unidentified Viennese artists, not directly associated with the W.W., painted cherubs with bouquets on porcelain medallions or enamel brooches in 1912, in the same spirit as Powolny's ceramic figurines. Animals and birds nestled in gold painted spiral motifs; parrots with splendid tails, and grinning salamanders perched in arabesque branches were decorative porcelain pendants and brooches produced by an independent manufacturer.[3]

Students under the tutelage of Hoffmann and Moser were encouraged to use alternative materials like textiles, chenille, painted wood, glass beads, or ceramics for commercial designs. Ostentatious pieces or rare materials were out of the question in training classes, so the WW distinctive style evolved partly out of deprivation.[4] Even though Hoffmann initially objected to machine production, he licensed their designs to outside manufacturers like Oskar Dietrich, who produced and sold the merchandise to the public.

Anton Hofer (1888-), a student of Moser's between 1909-1911, made decorative pieces of chenille, felt, and ribbons or cord, weaving these simple black and white materials into unusual cape and shawl tassels, hair ornaments and hatpins.

In 1915, decoration switched from the geometric, subdued Moser influence to the playful fantasies of Dagobert Peche (1887-1923). His forms defied function in a world of enchantment. His creative genius as manager of the Workshops was contagious, permeating the graphic and applied arts. Textiles and table ornaments of painted tin or silver erupted into an exhuberant froth of exotic vegetation. Peche carved ivory floral tiaras, which were elegantly figurative. Hoffmann, who found Peche's ideas amusing and inspirational, approved the move away from the original strict style principles of the Workshop.

The need for a coordinated look of clothing to be worn in the new Viennese interiors was implemented by the Fashion Department of the Workshops in 1911. Eduard Josef Wimmer-Wisgrill (1882-1961) designed clothes, textiles, and glass, as well as silver belt buckles and rings which bore his monogram "EIW", alongside that of the trained jewelers who executed his designs. Wimmer directed the Fashion Department between 1910 and 1922. (His double-barrelled name has been the source of historical confusion;

Three overglaze painted porcelain brooches and one pendant with parrots and a grinning chameleon perching on golden spiral motif branches. The pendant, far left is signed "PBG", Vienna, ca. 1912, from *Porzellanschmuck*, Munich. *Courtesy of Graham Dry. Photo by Robert Weldon*

Putto cupid, hand-painted overglaze porcelain pendant with spirals and flowers, Vienna, c. 1912, from "Porzellanschmuck," *Die Kunst und das schöne Heim*, Munich, Germany. *Courtesy of Graham Dry. Photo by Robert Weldon*

Black and white chenille shawl tassel by Anton Hofer, 1910. *Courtesy of the Hochschule für angewandte Kunst, Vienna*

he was one man, not two different designers.) Fabrics and outfits were also designed by Maria Likarz, Fritzi Löw, Lotte Calm, and Hilda Jesser and illustrated in *Mode Wien*, a limited-edition portfolio of hand-colored linoleum prints (1914-15). There was a refreshing awkwardness about the artists' designs, who were not trained dressmakers and knew very little about couture construction. At first imitating the Poiret harem pyjamas, French fashion was disdained during the war and the Viennese Mode emerged triumphant even as the Austro-Hungarian Empire collapsed in 1918. The large quantity of lithographed postcards which promoted the fashion designs and accessories before and after the war testify to the success of the department.

Accessories became a thriving cottage industry. Hatpins were needed for the hats, shoe buckles for the shoes, and beaded bags, compacts, and belts complemented the clothes. Venetian *conterie* glass beads were coiled around balls of wood or papier-mâché and woven into vari-colored geometric patterns by Wiener Werkstätte artists Felice Rix and others. Peche designed beaded belts. Unidentified artists made beaded cravate necklaces and "sausage" bracelets with abstract designs.

Austrian petit-point embroidered compact, ca. 1920. *Courtesy of Annie Forcum, Berkeley, CA. Photo by Robert Weldon*

Black Deco design on Austrian grey beaded *conterie* cravate necklace. Twenties. *Courtesy of Marie-Hélène Laurens Collection, Venice, Italy. Photo by Pierre Higonnet*

Beaded bag picturing a dog on a pillow with personalized inscription (dedicated to a royal engineer) pre-WW 1. *Courtesy of Ages Ahead, Palo Alto, CA. Photo by Robert Weldon*

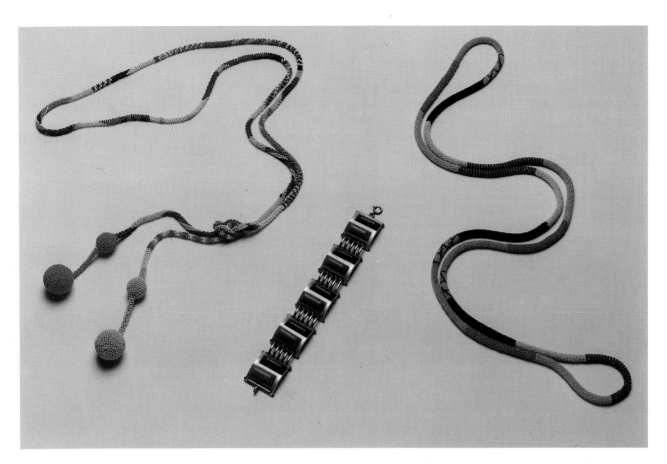

Conterie seed-beaded sautoirs in contrasting colors and patterns with glass beaded balls by Wiener Werkstätte artists, ca. 1910-1912, and an Art Deco aluminum and brass bracelet with green and black Bakelite bracelet, marked "Made in Austria", Twenties. *Courtesy of Wiener Interieur, Vienna. Photo by Helmar Dankl*

"Sausage" beaded bracelet with Austrian Deco pattern. Twenties. *Courtesy of Marie-Hélène Laurens Collection, Venice. Photo by Pierre Higonnet*

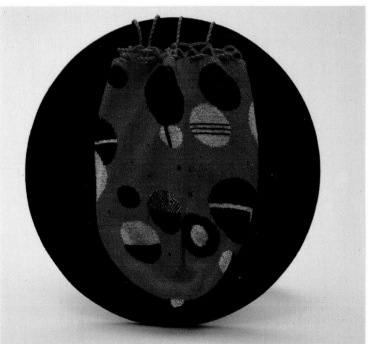

Twenties drawstring Tango-orange beaded bag with black and grey circles, and a kid leather lining, attributed to Maria Likarz, Wiener Werkstätte. *Courtesy of Historical Design Collection, New York, N.Y.*

In the Twenties, the war, premature death, and a virulent flu epidemic felled the male creative leaders of the Artists' Workshops. Talented women designers took the helm of the fashion and ceramic departments acting as stylists who determined the direction of the Werkstätte. (Eduard Wimmer had relinquished his directorship to teach at the Chicago Art Institute in 1923.) Male chauvinist critics scornfully blamed the women for the decline of the W.W. principles, even though it was Peche, Löffler, and Czeschka who had steered the Workshops away from the original pure aesthetics.[5] In fact, these artists' "little art" (*Kleinkunst*) was playful and original, and the ceramics by Gudrun Baudisch, Susi Singer, and Vally Wieselthier are avidly collected today, as is their jewelry which is rare.

Black and white silk scarf "Whisky", designed by Maria Likarz in 1929, and a gold embossed black leather purse by Hoffmann; both are new Wiener Werkstätte editions produced by the Vienna Osterreichisches Museum für angewandte Kunst, 1991. The ceramic redhead with the pink cheeks by Walter Bosse (1904-1979) is typical of the playful style of his Kufstein workshop, active between 1923-1937. *Courtesy of the author. Photo by Robert Weldon*

Maria Likarz (1893-) was a student of Hoffmann's at the Kuntsgewerbeschule from 1911 to 1915. Before and after the war she was active as a graphic artist, designing postcards, textiles, wallpaper, glass, and ceramics. For the Fashion Department at the W.W., she created hats, beaded bags, silk scarves and layered costumes for women featured in *Die Mode*, 1914/15. Aigrettes à la Poiret, enamelled bracelets and beaded bags were among the accessories that Maria sketched for her clientele. In 1922, when Wimmer moved to America, Likarz and Max Snischek took over the fashion and textiles divisions, the most successful branch of the Werkstätte until 1932 when it closed.

Hilda Jesser (1894-), another Hoffmann student (1912-17), taught graphic design at the Kuntsgewerbeschule from 1922 till 1967, continuing the evolutionary cycle of student/teacher which kept the Wiener Werkstätte ideas alive for decades. She contributed postcard and textile designs and woodcut or linoleum cut fabric designs to the *Wiener Mode* and *Das Leben Einer Dame* portfolios from 1914 t0 1916. Her jewelry was executed by Oskar Dietrich (1853-1940) who also executed the jewelry designed by Peche and other WW members who were not jewelers by training. Dietrich participated in both the 1900 and 1925 Paris Expos, and closed his atelier in 1931.

The Viennese excelled at *cloisonné* enamelled jewelry in the Twenties and Thirties. Cut off from the glass making center of Gablonz (renamed Jablonec nad Nasou) which was now in the newly formed country of Czechoslovakia, Austrian artists designed abstract enamel on copper brooches, belt buckles, and necklaces. One Art Deco necklace, stamped MADE IN AUSTRIA, was composed of eleven convex spheres each enamelled a different colored geometric design. Separate green and gold abstract enamel sections were threaded on a gold ribbon for a bracelet in the Thirties, and abstract opaque *cloisonné* rectangles intersected white metal rectangles in an interesting pattern, circa Forties.

Wooden beads were hand-painted, each a different pattern, orange and grey, possibly by Wiener Werkstätte artists. Bakelite bracelets, mixed with either aluminum or brass links were pro-

Woodcut textile design by Hilda Jesser for *Die Mode*, 1914/15 showing the spiky leaves characteristic of the Wiener Werkstätte at the time. *Original print courtesy of the author. Photo of print by Robert Weldon*

Eleven convex copper circles, each enamelled a different geometric design, alternating with square black enamelled elements, stamped "Made in Austria," ca. 1930. *Courtesy of the author. Photo by Robert Weldon*

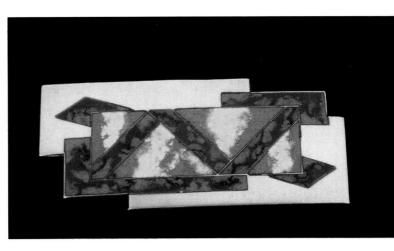

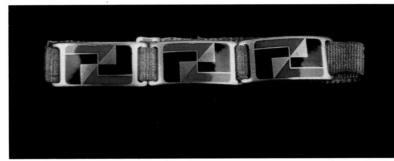

Brooch of matt *cloisonné* enamel rectangles intersecting a white metal brooch, ca. 1940, and a bracelet of green, black, and gold *cloisonné* enamel on copper sections threaded on a gold ribbon, each section stamped with illegible maker's mark, 1920's. *Courtesy of the author. Photo by Robert Weldon*

Two enamel brooches on copper, ca. 1920, a *cloisonné* enamel belt buckle, 1925, and a necklace of grey and orange hand-painted wood beads, ca.1920. *Courtesy of Wiener Interieur, Vienna. Photo by Helmar Dankl*

duced on a small scale in Austria with a German Deco look. A Bakelite clip in the shape of an Austrian Tyrolian hat with a painted feather and a suede ribbon was made in the Thirties. Handbags were multi-colored pouches of beaded Celluloid with Bakelite frames. Pressed cobalt blue glass segments were alternated with gilded brass elements for an Art Deco necklace and brooch set (shown here with a Hagenauer mirror, nickel-plated from the Thirties.) These are stamped "Made In Austria."

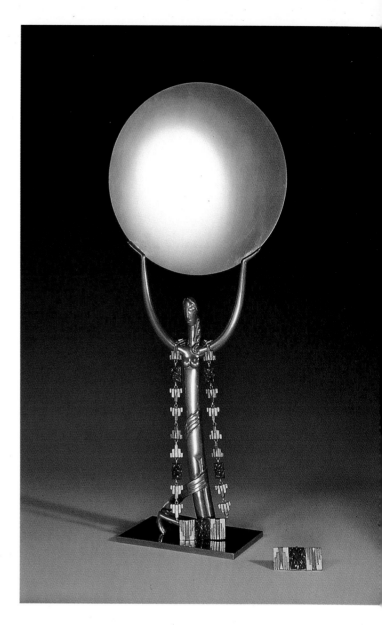

Black Bakelite clip of a Tyrolian hat with a jaunty painted feather and green suede ribbon, 1930. *Courtesy of the author. Photo by Robert Weldon*

Necklace of cobalt-blue Czech pressed glass alternating with Art Deco gilded brass elements, with a matching brooch, Twenties. Stamped "Made in Austria." *Courtesy of Carri Priley collection, St. Paul, MN.* The stylized woman wearing the necklace is a nickel-plated mirror by Hagenauer, stamped "Made in Austria", ca. 1930. *Courtesy of the author. Photo by Robert Weldon*

Two pouch plastic beaded bags with polka dots and stripes. One bag frame is ivory Bakelite, Thirties. *Courtesy of Wiener Interieur, Vienna. Photo by Helmar Dankl*

The Werkstätte Hagenauer metalworkshop (1898-1956) was founded by Carl Hagenauer. His son Karl joined his father in 1919. This Viennese family of sculptors produced outstanding brass, nickel or chrome-plated brass and wood sculptures ranging from 2" high cavorting animals to sleek, stylized masks, busts, and statues of African or Art Deco motifs. Nickel-plating was invented in Germany in 1932, and was adopted by Hagenauer as a non-tarnishing reflective surface. From the Thirties to the Fifties, small editions of bright metal brooches were produced figuring birds and other creatures amidst flowering branches which were influenced by the Wiener Werkstätte. These were stamped on the reverse with the "WHW" marks or "Atelier Hagenauer Wien", and "Karl". The Hagenauer workshop also executed silver designs by Hoffmann and Otto Prutscher.

Tyrolian-cut crystal beads and stones have been a major Austrian export since the turn of the century. Crystal balls and amber glass beads made attractive sautoirs in the Twenties. Long necklaces of clear and amber faceted crystal were still popular in the Eighties. A dazzling necklace of foiled Tyrolian-cut crystals prongset in five graduated clusters mounted on a rhodium-plated chain stopped traffic in Hollywood and Vienna before the war. (An almost identical necklace with the same clusters belonged to actress Carole Lombard. [6])

Daniel Swarovski (b. 1862) revolutionized the industry when he patented his stone cutting machine in 1892. One of many Sudeten Germans working in Bohemia, Swarovski recognized the importance of mass-producing calibrated stones of uniform size in any color for the international costume jewelry market. In order to keep his invention safe from imitators, Swarovski moved to the village of Wattens in the Austrian Tyrol mountains in 1895 where superior hydro-electric power was available.

Beginning with the popular round cut stones (called *châtons*), Swarovski expanded his repertoire to include fancy cuts, coating the back of the stone with a silver film which augmented the reflected light. Exported to Paris, these Tyrolian-cut stones (the label *pierre taillée du Tyrol* was mistaken for a proper name in America; *pierre* meaning "stone") were set in cast or stamped mountings and exported to North and South America. During the two World Wars, the factory was machine-tooled for munitions. In 1955, Manfred Swarovski (the founder's grandson) introduced the famous "Aurora Borealis" stones. (These were named after the Northern Lights,

Faceted clear and amber crystal necklace, ca. 1980. *Courtesy of private collection, Los Angeles. Photo by Robert Weldon*

Long sautoir of amber glass, crystal balls, and strass rondelles, Twenties. *Courtesy of the author. Photo by Robert Weldon*

Necklace of foiled Swarovski Tyrolian-cut crystals, (oval, round and tear drop) prong set in five graduated clusters mounted on a rhodium-plated chain, ca. 1940. *Courtesy of the author. Photo by Sandro Moro*

nature's light show of shimmering blue and green produced by electrically charged electrons entering the oxygen of the earth's atmosphere, visible in the Far Northern skies between November and May.) These "A.B." stones seemed to change color with the light, and were enthusiastically utilized by all the costume jewelry designers. (The Josef Riedel firm of Gablonz was experimenting with the process two years earlier.[7]) The iridescence was produced by coating the glass surface with a metallic sheen by vacuum-plating, which interfered with the light reflections.

In the late Fifties, Schiaparelli used Aurora Borealis stones to simulate watermelon tourmalines. Countess Zoltowska worked with the blue/green shifting shades for her elaborate necklaces and brooches, and devised floral designs for the unusual Swarovski square-cut glass slices of the Sixties. Coppola e Toppo loved the iridescent scalloped "daisy" stones which were so effective in pendant earrings and necklaces.

Who can forget the novelty "Mood Rings" of the late Seventies which changed colors with the wearer's temperature? Swarovski's secret was a heat-sensitive film applied to the stone's surface, which mysteriously betrayed the wearer's hidden anger, or passion.[8] (These are collectible again for $3 each, following the 1993 movie, *My Girl*, which featured mood rings.)

The Swarovski Company can economically make use of off-cuts from the company's lead crystal optical glass production which assures top quality faux gemstones unmatched by other companies.[9] Their stones in 67 colors continue to be widely used for costume jewelry and *bijoux de couture* as is amply illustrated in this book.

1950s thru 1980s

In the Fifties, after the Kuntsgewerbeschule became the Hochschule für angewandte Kunst (School of the Applied Arts), the tradition of enamel, bead and metalwork was continued. Werner Schmeiser (1940-) alternated deep purple transparent enamel over an engraved ground with shiny silver segments of the same triangular shape in 1959. Lacy hair ornaments for pony tails of gilded brass wires were designed by Anna Storno and Elisabeth Weish (1934-). Bandeaux and barrettes of wire daisies (1956) were light and easy to wear.

Karin Byrne-Laimbock (1940-) was a Hochschule student of Franz Hagenauer for metalwork, and Hilda Jesser for graphics from 1959 to 1965. There were further studies in gold and silversmithing in Innsbruck, and at the Academy of Applied Arts in Neugablonz, Austria. In 1967, Karin designed some stunning tie necklaces which she says "represented the transition from ladies' to men's jewelry". At first these spectacular pendants were of orange, cranberry, and lime green Plexiglas segments studded with large Swarovski crystals, "stitched" together with nickel-plated loops. Later, in '69, the pieces she designed specifically for men were a more subdued black and white Plexiglas and crystal because she felt that "they would match better with a smoking jacket or turtle-neck sweater". They were no less spectacular.

Karin had a contract with Swarovski to experiment with crystals, strass, and Plexiglas at the same time as she was teaching in the Sixties. She put together a collection of strass pieces and went to Paris to see if she had developed an internationally recognized style. She was personally received by Pierre Cardin. Her flexible strass collars were asymmetrical ruffles, completely hand-crafted. Disappointed because she couldn't survive on jewelry sales alone, Karin turned to teaching in Innsbruck where she still lives.

Asymmetrical lariat of colored strass with a black and white ringed stone. *Courtesy of Karin Byrne-Laimbock*

Bracelet of purple *basse-taille* enamel alternating with silver triangular segments by Werner Schmeiser, 1959. *Courtesy of the Hochschule für angewandte Kunst, Vienna*

Lacy gilded brass wire barrette by Elisabeth Weish, 1956. *Courtesy of the Hochschule für angewandte Kunst*

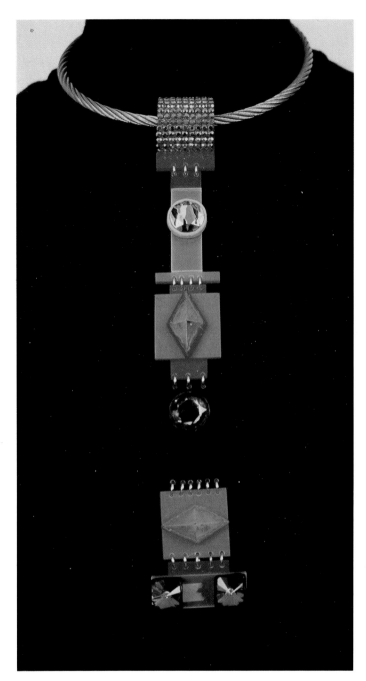

Tie necklace of orange, cranberry and lime green Plexiglas segments studded with Swarovski crystals, stitched together with nickel-plated loops, 1967 by Karin Byrne-Laimbock. *Courtesy of the Hochschule für angewandte Kunst, and the artist*

"Distinguished Order Decoration Medal" of engraved copper by Andrea Halmschlager, 1988. *Courtesy of the Hochschule für angewandte Kunst*

Two enamelled copper "Star" brooches with silver spikes by Kristine Böhmig, 1989. *Courtesy of the Hochschule für angewandte Kunst*

Vienna in the 80's was decorated with donuts; not made of flour and water, but copper and enamel. Andrea Halmschlager (1961-) studied at the Hochschule from 1980-'86, then at the Rietveld Academy in Amsterdam with Onno Boekhoudt. In 1988, Andrea made a series of witty "Distinguished Order Decoration Medals" of engraved and enamelled copper rings with brass decorative "ribbons".

Kristine Böhmig (1965-) was a student at the Hochschule in 1985, and exhibited at several art shows in Linz and Vienna, and New York. Her "donuts" were copper brooches with daunting spikes around them, called "stars".

The beaded jewelry tradition has been carried on by Greta Freist (1904-). Between 1924-1930 she was an art student in Vienna.

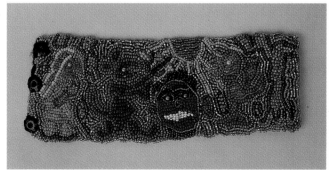

Beaded bracelet of seed beads and faux stones by Greta Freist, 1989. *Courtesy of the Hochschule für angewandte Kunst*

In 1936, she settled in Paris, soaking up and contributing to the Surrealist and Abstract art movements. She has exhibited at international shows from Paris to Cairo. Fantastic animals and faces captured in beaded bracelets and glass stones were a product of her imagination at the age of 84.

Jacqueline Lillie (1941-) was born in Marseilles, but was educated in Vienna at the Hochschule metal workshop with Hagenauer from 1962-65. Beginning where the Wiener Werkstätte left off, Jacqueline evolved her own exacting technique in fine beadwork. She was aware of the extreme fragility of the WW beaded ropes mounted on unknotted cotton thread which deteriorated with time and use. Jacqueline painstakingly knots each of the 25,000 tiny beads necessary to make a necklace under high magnification. Her magic is seen in the patterns, the subtle colors and the extraordinary workmanship of both the glass *conterie* and metal beads.

Jacqueline acknowledges indebtedness to the Russian Constructivists, the Bauhaus for its functional simplicity, and the African beadwork of the Yoruba and Masai tribes. Given the changing role of women in society, Jacqueline's work had to be aesthetically pleasing as well as sturdy enough for the working woman. "Jewelry has to adapt to the wearer, as an extension of her character and a reflexion of her attitude towards the environment. The basic principle is of straightforward flexibility with an unobtrusive clasp."

Jacqueline's pieces include an exquisite cravate of knotted beads folded over and finished with a silver clasp; 2 graceful pins of glass beads and sea snails; and a nest of shimmering glass filaments punctuated with elements of multi-colored glass. A superb necklace was made in Austria for the Corning Glass Museum, endowed by the Rakow Commission, 1992. Jacqueline Lillie's work is a fitting celebration of the enchanting jewelry of the Wiener Werkstätte, exceeding her mentors in making the complicated seem simple.

Folded flat necklace of 25,000 individually knotted glass beads with a silver clasp by Jacqueline Lillie, 1992. *Courtesy of the artist and Rosanne Raab Associates, New York, New York*

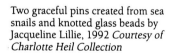

Two graceful pins created from sea snails and knotted glass beads by Jacqueline Lillie, 1992 *Courtesy of Charlotte Heil Collection*

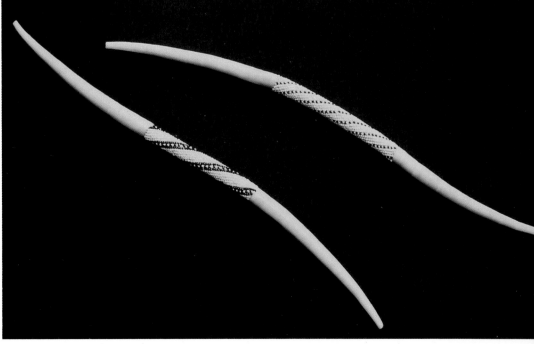

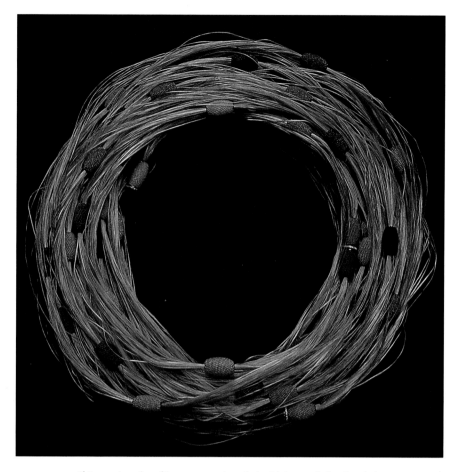

Shimmering glass filaments are threaded with knotted glass beads in a synthesis of light from two different forms of glass by Jacqueline Lillie for the Corning Glass Museum, 1992. *Courtesy of the artist and the Corning Glass Museum, NY*

Continuing in the Viennese enamel tradition, the Emailstudio Steinböck hand-painted silver and gold Klimtian spirals on black enamel bracelets and brooches in the 1980's. These were sold in Vienna and at the Museum of Modern Art in New York. They are marked "Handmade in Austria, Steinböck, Wien. (The *steinböck* (ibex) is the studio trademark.) Ironically, the 20th century in Austria ends where it began, with a bow to the artist, Gustav Klimt, who so outraged the Viennese with his controversial art in 1900.

1. Gerda Buxbaum, "The Opulence of the Poor Look" in *Jewels of Fantasy, Costume Jewelry of the 20th Century*, New York, Harry N. Abrams, Inc. New York, 1992, pg. 106.
2. *Ibid.* pg. 69.
3. Graham Dry, "Porzellanschmuck," *Die Kunst und das schöne Heim*, München, Juli, 1982. pg. 492.
4. Werner Schweiger, *Wiener Werkstätte, Design in Vienna, 1903-32*, New York, Abbeville Press, 1984, pg. 212..
5. Jane Kallir, *Viennese Design and the Wiener Werkstätte*, New York, Galerie St. Etienne/George Braziller, 1986, pg. 108.
6. Harrice Simons Miller, *Costume Jewelry; Identification and Price Guide*, 2nd edition. New York, Avon Books, 1994, pg. 164.
7. Nancy Schiffer, *Rhinestones!*, Atglen, PA., Schiffer Publishing, 1993, pg. 47.
8. Edward Schweiger, "The History of the Production of Ornamental Stones in Tyrol," *Jewels of Fantasy*, pg. 378.
9. Jane Stancliff, *Costume and Fashion Jewellery of the Twentieth Century*, London, V. & A. Album, Victoria and Albert Museum, pg.114.

Black enamel pins and bracelet with gold and silver motifs inspired by the sensual gold decorations in Gustav Klimt paintings, ca. 1985. Marked "Handmade in Austria-Steinböck, Wien". *Courtesy of the author. Photo by Robert Weldon*

Chapter 5:

Hungary

The Fausse Renaissance

Vienna was elegant and prosperous, a neo-Baroque magnet for artists and musicians. Budapest was the romantic "second city" of the Austro-Hungarian Empire, sharing with Vienna the same monarch, Franz Josef, and a passion for the arts. Hungary, however, had its own constitutional government and pursued its own distinctive style. Hungarians lived in a neo-Renaissance ambience which was echoed in their jewelry and decorative arts.

Hungarian jewelry from this Empire period was inspired by the 15th and 16th centuries when the royal courts of King Corvinus and King Ladislav II were renowned for splendid garments and jewels. Noblemen swash-buckled in castle courtyards with swords and daggers encrusted with square-cut diamonds and precious stones, while their ladies cheered showing off lavish corsage and hair ornaments, with gold rings on every finger set with rubies, pearls, and emeralds. The distinctive Transylvanian enamel technique of tiny colored brushstrokes over white glossy enamel had evolved in the mid-17th century to punctuate the Baroque belt buckles and brooches of goldsmiths who had survived centuries of Turkish domination in the protective shadow of the Transylvanian Alps.[1] Under the Hapsburgs in the 18th century, the influx of Italian and German craftsmen brought new techniques, but the fashion for the characteristic Hungarian enamel endured.

Nineteenth century Budapest, however, was a pretend-Renaissance. Instead of gold and diamonds, semi-precious stones like tourmaline, amethyst, and pyrope garnets from Bohemia, were combined with fresh-water pearls and commercial grade pale emeralds and aquas in elaborate silver-gilt settings. These were evocative of Russian Renaissance court jewels, and were worn with great style by the Hungarian nobility through the reign of Franz Josef. The women wore feathery open-work silver-gilt necklaces, fragile pins and earrings with dangling pearl drops, and bracelets with faceted stones around moonstone cabochons. Parures of the palest aqua and seed pearls were charmingly feminine. Belt and shoe buckles were open-work Renaissance design set with faceted garnets and turquoise cabochons and mother of pearl, or filigreed silver overlaid with enamelled tulips and tourmalines. Winged cherubs were scattered among the stones, which were sometimes real, sometimes faux. What did it matter, this was the Austro-Hungarian masquerade! Silver rings with elaborately embossed shanks were delicate bouquets of garnets, opals, seed pearls, and minuscule white enamelled petals.

The men wore short velvet jackets (*disz-magyars*) trimmed with sable, and pearl and enamel buttons in two to four rows down the front. The buttons were as elaborately decorative as rings. Wearing their sable hats and tasseled boots with spurs, Hungarian horsemen made a dashing picture, as they galloped across the Great Plain of Hungary.

Silver-gilt bracelet and ring with moonstone cabochons and faceted tourmalines and topaz. Early 20th century. *Courtesy of private collection, Los Angeles, CA. Photo by Robert Weldon courtesy of the G.I.A.*

Opposite
Vintage print of Hungarian nobles dancing the *csarda*, fuelled by fine Hungarian wine. (Watch those spurs!) The vests and sable-lined jackets were adorned with rows of silver-gilt buttons set with garnets and mother of pearl. *Courtesy of Mrs. George Pal Collection, Los Angeles, CA. Photo of print by Robert Weldon*

Belt buckle of openwork design and winged *putti* set with garnets and mother of pearl. Late 19th century. *Courtesy of European Antiques, Los Angeles. Photo by Robert Weldon*

Silver ring with embossed shank set with opals, moonstone, rhodolite garnets, pearls, and black, white, and green enamelled petals, ca. 1920. Illegible silver marks. *Courtesy of the author. Photo by Robert Weldon*

Fine turn of the century belt buckle converted to a brooch decorated with enamelled tulips, (the symbol of Hungary,) baroque fresh water pearls, and almandine garnets. The mauve and green enamel leaves and pink tulips are laid over a silver filigreed background. *Courtesy of European Antiques, Antiquarius, Los Angeles, CA. Photo by Robert Weldon courtesy of the G.I.A.*

Silver-gilt necklace and matching brooch set with pale aquas and seed pearls in neo-Renaissance style, early 20th century. *Courtesy of private collection, Los Angeles. Photo by Robert Weldon courtesy of the G.I.A.*

Vintage (ca. 1900) print of a Hungarian nobleman wearing the sable-lined jacket with jewelled silver buttons, and flowers jauntily tucked in his hat. Detail of two garnet and pearl silver buttons with blue and white enamelled tulips, photographed on the print. *Courtesy of private collection, Los Angeles, CA. Photo by Robert Weldon*

Openwork neo-Renaissance silver pendant and chain with blister pearls, emeralds, and glass "emeralds" with pearl and "emerald" fringe. Bearing French silver import mark. A silver embossed ring is set with pearls and pyrope garnets. *Courtesy of the author. Photo by Robert Weldon, courtesy of the G.I.A.*

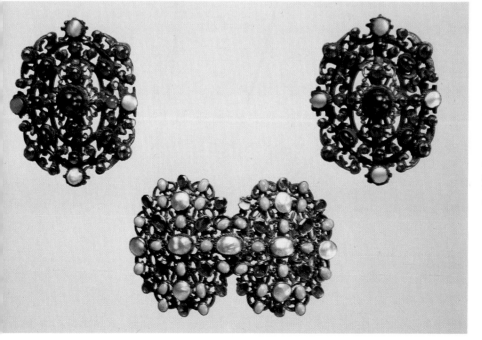

Openwork shoe buckles with "ruby" and "emerald" stones and blister pearls, and a belt buckle with turquoises, garnets and blister pearls. Early 20th century. *Courtesy of Rita Sacks Collection, New York, NY. Photo by Richard Marx*

Matching silver gilt pin and earrings with amethysts, emeralds and pearls. This set is elaborately layered with leaves and scrolls as well as faceted stones. With dog's head silver mark. *Courtesy of Gail Freeman Antique and Estate Jewelry. Photo by Robert Weldon, courtesy of the G.I.A.*

Neo-Renaissance brooch, silver-gilt with pale square-cut emeralds, rubellite tourmalines, baroque pearl drops, and hand-painted white enamel petals. Illegible silver mark. *Courtesy of the author. Photo by Robert Weldon, courtesy of the G.I.A.*

Silver-gilt bracelet with amethysts, emeralds, pearls and enamel. Bearing Hungarian silver mark. *Courtesy of Gail Freeman Antique and Estate Jewelry, Los Angeles, CA. Photo by Robert Weldon, courtesy of the G.I.A.*

Large openwork silver bracelet with pyrope garnets and turquoise cabs. Early 20th century. *Courtesy of Rita Sacks Collection, NY. Photo by Richard Marx*

Apart from heirloom pearls, the main adornment of the lower classes was embroidery. During the long winters, the women covered jackets, vests, and skirts with blue, red, and yellow stitched flowers and tassels. The design varied with the province.

Variations on the Renaissance theme were played in Hungary thru the Twenties. Enamel accents of tiny green and white petals added a delicate charm, typical of the jewelry of this period. From 1867 to 1922, the silver hallmark, when found, was the Austrian head of Diana, or the dog's head. After World War I, when Hungary became a republic, the letter "P" was added, and "Hungary" was stamped on the clasp. The styles of the Viennese Secession and the Jugendstil of Prague, never took firm hold in Budapest, where the jewelers whipped up their delightful froth until the peasants revolted in the Twenties, and Socialism made aristocratic excesses inadvisable. In this semi-feudal state, where there was widespread poverty, intellectuals and peasants alike thought the costumes and jewelry of the nobility were "comic opera" and decadent. With World War II, the German and Russian occupations brought artistic activity to a halt.

A rare exception to the Renaissance rule was Oskar Huber. His silver gilt pendants were a subdued German Jugendstil form with *cloisonné* enamel in deep blues and reds, set with Bohemian garnets. His jewelry was displayed at the Turin International Exhibition in 1902.

Other Hungarians who made their mark outside their country, in France in the Twenties and Thirties, were the sculptors Gustave Miklos and Béla Voros, who also designed jewelry. Countess Cissy Zoltowska, of Austro-Hungarian parentage, made her astonishing pieces for the French couturiers in the Fifties and Sixties. More about them in the chapter on their adopted country, France.

1. Carolyn Benesh. "Baroque Splendor." *Ornament,* vol. 18, no. 1, Autumn, 1994, pg. 22.

Wide hinged cuff with turquoise (?) cabochons and enamel decorations of uncertain age and origin. (The Hungarian Countess Zoltowska thinks it is a fairly recent interpretation.) *Courtesy of Kerry Holden Collection, Santa Monica, CA.*

Chapter 6:
Bohemia/Czechoslovakia

The Bohemian province of the Austro-Hungarian empire was the center of the glass-making industry. French jet, Egyptian revival scarabs, Art Nouveau and Art Deco molded glass pins and belt buckles, Art Deco enamelled belt buckles, faceted glass beads, as well as wooden beads, Celluloid jewelry, and pyrope rose-cut garnets all originated in Bohemia. Gablonz, or Jablonec nad Nisou (the German or Czech pronunciation of the town depending on the political orientation of Bohemia), was the center of this fecund artistic activity. Located in the Jizera mountains on the Nisou River, there was plentiful hydro-electrical power. Natural resources abounded: garnets; quartz; and the industrious crafts-people of the region. Largely anonymous, they have been the source of much of the world's costume jewelry for centuries.

Czechy (the native name for Bohemia) was one of the most powerful kingdoms in Europe. There was a large Sudeten German population, which may have advanced their artistic culture beyond that of the other Slav nations. The Germans and Jews made significant contributions to the glass, jewelry, and manufacturing trades. The German-speaking workers tended to live and work separately from the Czech Bohemians, preserving their nationalist identity, but creating tensions with the Czech majority. When Bohemia and Moravia in the north joined with the southern Slavic territory of former Hungary in 1918, Czechoslovakia made great advances in agriculture and industry. The Elbe River carried their products to Hamburg and the North Sea, and the Danube linked up with the Black Sea.

The art of glass-making was encouraged by the various emperors from the 16th century till 1918. Competing with Venice for exports to Europe, Gablonz enjoyed a period of fruitful activity, growing from a village to a city, which by 1940 supported 70,000 people cutting glass in their homes. The Art Nouveau movement (which was so enthusiastically embraced in Prague, the "third city" of the Austro-Hungarian Empire) was celebrated in Bohemian glass, as was Art Deco. The independant workshop production of the skilled craftsmen was augmented by a large cottage industry of farmers and their families who worked through the cold winters in their kitchens assembling jewelry in quantities which obviated the need for factory assembly lines.

"French jet" was neither French nor jet. It was faux Whitby jet simulated in black glass. The real thing was fossilized wood, related to coal, which was found and fashioned in Whitby, Yorkshire. Originally made into mourning jewelry, it received a terrific boost from Queen Victoria's missing her beloved Prince Albert. When demand exceeded supply, the Gablonz alternative was highly polished black glass. The moulded and faceted pieces were fused to a blackened metal base, or soldered to black wires. Complicated, lacy necklaces of interlocking pieces were light and easy to wear. At the

A delightfully rare and delicate French jet necklace of moulded and faceted elements made in Bohemia at the turn of the century. All parts are separately mounted, so the piece is light and supple on the neck, 6" long. *Courtesy of the author. Photo by Christie Romero*

Opposite

Hand-colored *pochoir* print by Georges Lepape from the *Gazette du Bon Ton*, January, 1914. *"Le Collier Nouveau"*, shows the "New Necklace", a long sautoir of Czech red and green glass beads that Poiret introduced with his lampshade tunic to be worn with a matching headband and tassels. *Courtesy of the author's collection, photo by Robert Weldon.*

Two French jet machine-faceted shoe buckles, with hand-painted enamel dot decoration, circa Twenties, and a spiderweb-light jet wire ornament for hair or hat, 1900. *Courtesy of private collection, Los Angeles. Photo by Robert Weldon*

A large French jet hat ornament (over 4" long) with drops, soft-soldered to black wires to be worn on the high crowned, wide brimmed hats of 1890-1910. *Courtesy of the author. Photo by Robert Weldon*

Two 1900 cape clasps; one with faux turquoises and cut steel, the other with faux amethysts and rhinestones, made by Gablonz metalsmiths. *Courtesy of private collection, Los Angeles. Photo by Robert Weldon*

turn of the century, the European ladies were smothered in jet from head to toe. Hair ornaments, hat pins (some were elaborate ornaments 4" long, including drops, to adorn the enormous wide-brimmed hats), buttons, appliqués for dresses and belts, muff chains, and shoe buckles were all made from jet which was faceted or painted with enamel designs. In the Twenties, long sautoirs and pendant earrings adorned the flappers, who carried French jet handbags. Not to be left out, men wore jet watch chains to match jet cravate pins and shirt studs.

Metalworkers in non-precious metals like tombac (85% copper to 15% zinc), and brass (63% copper to 37% zinc), were specialized for two centuries in the fabrication of shoe and belt buckles, and jewelry. They were called *gürtler*, or belt makers, in Gablonz. (Belts were still called "girdles" in the nineteenth century, before the supporting undergarment adopted the archaic name for another purpose altogether.) The *gürtlers* also made cape clasps, adorning them with faux turquoises or amethysts. Designs were cut by engravers in metal, then stamped by machine to simulate the technically difficult gold filigree wirework or embossed designs for bracelets and brooches. The separate stamped elements (a choice of tens of thousands of available styles) were taken from common factory pools, the *estamperies*, then soldered or riveted into three-dimensional brooches and bracelets. The metal was gilded, and enamelled accents were added. The moulded or faceted colored glass stones were prong or bezel-set by hand. Great care was taken to finish the reverse side of the jewelry with filigree stampings.[1]

The Renaissance revival in Czechoslovakia was not as elaborately conceived as in Hungary. While the Hungarians recreated Renaissance gold and gemstone jewelry in silver-gilt and semi-precious stones, the Czech *gürtler* went one step further using only faux gemstones set in copper and brass elements for the mass market. Gablonz enamelling was limited to simple white, green, or black strokes, never the delicate brushwork of the Hungarian petals. The effect was romantic but not as lush.

Belt buckles were produced in prodigious quantities in Bohemia. In 1900, flowers and vegetables were cast in metal or silver, and decorated with colored stones. Lillies and the cardoon, a Mediterranean vegetable related to the artichoke, were popular designs for the French market. Sensuous three-dimensional tulips and poppies in Art Nouveau pastel enamel were also cherished by the French. (The tulip was imported to France for Henri IV's exotic *Jardin du Roi* in the 17th century where it was much admired, and translated into jewelry motifs.) Stylized *cloisonné* enamelled flowers were applied to an open-work copper base in the Twenties.

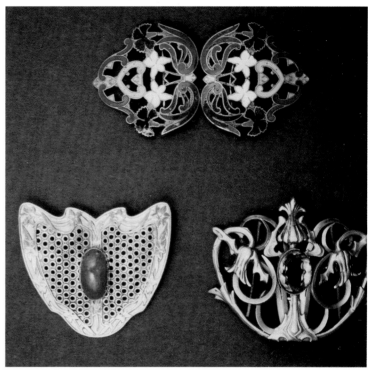

Renaissance revival bracelets, Czech *gürtler* style:. The top one consisting of multiple layers of stamped filigree and colored rhinestones and pearls; the middle one with large faceted "sapphires" and enamelled leaves; and the lower bracelet with blue glass cabochons and white enamel were made circa the Thirties. *Courtesy of Diane Keith Collection, Beverly Hills, CA. Photo by Robert Weldon*

Early Twentieth Century belt buckles. The top one is of *champlevé* enamel. The clasp on the second row left has a faux lapis cabochon. *Courtesy of Christie Romero, Anaheim, CA.* The buckle on the right is a fine Art Nouveau *gürtler* depiction of the cardoon, (related to the thistle) with an "amethyst". *Courtesy of the author. Photo by Christie Romero*

Three ornate Bohemian brooches, with layers of faux filigree and prong-set faux turquoises, amethysts, emeralds, and other colored rhinestones. The clip on the top right is an example of the flower petal technique produced by the Neiger Company in the Thirties in Gablonz. *Courtesy of Diane Keith Collection. Photo by Robert Weldon*

A truly sumptuous Art Nouveau belt buckle, with subtly shaded 3-dimensional enamelled tulips. *Courtesy of Rita Sacks Collection, New York. Photo by Robert Weldon*

Geometric Art Deco designs in vivid *cloisonné* enamel were exported world-wide to serve as belt buckles or necklace clasps mounted with Czech glass stones. Moulded glass belt buckles (some with simulated marcasite sections electro-plated silver) were produced in the Twenties and Thirties in a thousand different patterns and colors with glass clips and press-moulded buttons to match. Literally tons of these accessories were exported to America and France. A black and scarlet glass clasp was mounted with jet and garnet-colored beads. (Even though pyrope garnet was plentiful and inexpensive in Bohemia, faceted faux garnet beads were exported on a large scale.) Novelty items like Twenties hand-blown reversible beads (a caricature of Josephine Baker(?) on both sides) were mounted with glass lampwork flowers and leaves at a later date.

Two *cloisonné* Art Deco patchwork red and blue enamel clasps, mounted with pink iridescent and red faceted "garnet" beads; and clear crystal and blue beads with blue rhinestones. *Courtesy of the author. Photo by Robert Weldon*

A red and black moulded glass buckle, stamped Czechoslovakia, mounted with faceted cranberry red and black glass beads. *Courtesy of private collection, Los Angeles. Photo by Robert Weldon*

Another Art Deco gold enamel *basse-taille* patchwork clasp mounted with "topaz" glass beads and Venetian foiled beads. *Courtesy of the author. Photo by Robert Weldon*

10 press-moulded glass bracelets, royal blue, orange, and French jet painted with gold, silver (simulating marcassite) or black geometric designs, one Egyptian revival, mounted on elastic. Thirties. *Courtesy of the author. Photo by Sandro Moro*

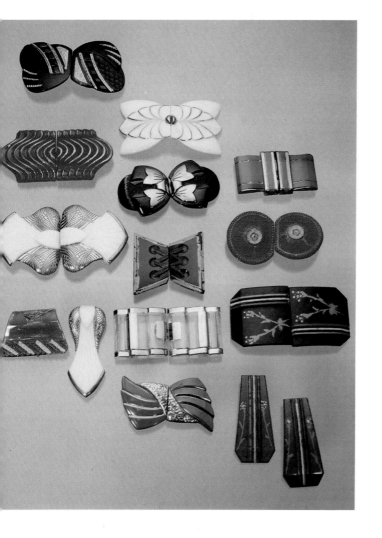

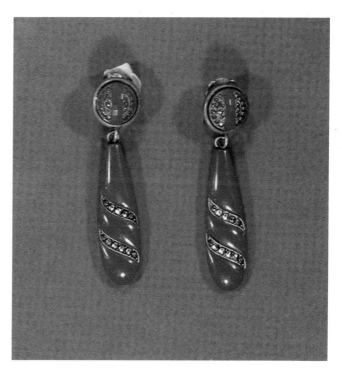

Pair of ear clips of press-moulded red glass painted with silver to simulate marcassites. Thirties. *Courtesy of the author. Photo by Sandro Moro*

A collection of 12 press-moulded glass Art Deco buckles, with 4 matching dress clips, typical of Thirties Gablonz production. Thousands of these pieces were mass-produced for export, some with hand-painted flowers, or simulated marcasites (painted silver.) *Courtesy of private collection, Milano, Italy, and Joanne McPherson, Santa Monica, CA. Photo by Robert Weldon*

Necklace of hand-blown black 1920's reversible beads (Josephine Baker caricatures?) mounted with lampwork oranges and leaves at a later date. *Courtesy of the author. Photo by Robert Weldon*

Four Egyptian revival motifs of press-moulded glass used for clips or earrings, with painted verdigris in the crevices. Three *pâte de verre* extendable bracelets of a gold-painted spider in its web, and silver electro-plated blue sections, mounted on elastic for the French market. A gold lace belt with mirror-backed stones and a faux filigree buckle set with colored rhinestones. All from the Thirties. *Courtesy of the author. Photo by Robert Weldon*

The same firm that produced the 1937 Paris Expo moulded glass bracelets made extendable *pâte de verre* bracelets featuring a gilded spider in its web, or silver-plated facets on royal-blue glass circles. These were mounted on elastic and exported to France. (Each section has the "*Importé de Tschecoslovaquie*" mark in the mould.) An amazing amount of these Deco pieces survive today, considering that they were made of such fragile material.

There were numerous Egyptian revivals celebrated in costume jewelry. Napoleon's campaign on the Nile in 1798 spawned the first one. Then in the 1890s, Lalique and Alphonse Mucha (who was Czech) designed dramatic Egyptian jewelry for Sarah Bernhardt, who revelled in the bizarre. Mucha's countrymen produced cheaper glass versions of the *plique-à-jour* and gold originals. When the tombs of Nefertiti and Tutankhamon were excavated in the Twenties, an avalanche of winged scarabs, hieroglyphics, animal deities, and noble Egyptian profiles were immortalized yet again, in glass and enamel on silver or brass, or Celluloid. The original carnelian, lapis, coral, and turquoise stones were imitated by glass cabochons. Red and blue cameos of Nile princesses and scarabs were antiqued with a pale green wash (which simulated verdigris and the ravages of burial in the Sahara sands) and mounted into necklaces and clips by the *gürtler* for export to France and America.

Egyptian revival brooches from the Twenties and Thirties: the top one is painted Celluloid; gilded metal (the one with a real Brazilian beetle and strass eyes was put together in France). *Courtesy of Christie Romero Collection, Anaheim, Ca. Photo by Christie Romero*

A cheerful selection of Czech stained, or hand-painted wooden beads in floral designs. The painted faces and hats dangling from the brooch represent four different nationalities. *Courtesy of Joanne McPherson Collection. Photo by Robert Weldon*

As in Oyonnax, France, but on a smaller scale in Gablonz, Celluloid and Galalith simulated ivory and the natural plastics horn, amber, and tortoiseshell for necklaces, bracelets, and pins. These were soldered with metal "exotic" motifs and set with stones in the Twenties and Thirties.

Wherever there was a strong folk-art tradition and abundant forests (i.e. Czechoslovakia and Finland), there were wooden beads. Stained red or painted, the gaily colored jewelry was as playful and naive as children's toys. The beads were shaped like flowers and flower pots, hats and hand-painted faces, bells and stars. Colorful combinations were strung on cord for necklaces, and wooden wedges were stacked on elastic string for bracelets. Wreaths of wooden beads made pretty pins, and wood was carved to simulate walnuts. These were exported to Europe and America from the Thirties to the Fifties. (Even Yves Saint Laurent showed a belt of wooden beads in his 1970 summer collection designed by Roger Scemama.) Clutch handbags were also made out of brightly colored wood beads in the Thirties and Forties.

Two stained and carved wood necklaces, the walnuts hanging from Celluloid leaves, and a large wreath brooch with wood flowers. *Courtesy of Mario Rivoli collection, Denver, Co. Photo by Robert Weldon*

Frames for Twenties embroidered bags were enamelled over filigree elements, and metal handbag clasps were stamped with faux marcasite and set with shimmering yellow satin glass cabochons. The Thirties handbag pictured here is imitation crocodile leather, and a faux marcasite and faux amber clasp, stamped "Made in Czechoslovakia".

Two Thirties clutch bags: one a colorful clutch of wooden beads; and the other a genuine faux alligator leather creation with a metal clasp of stamped faux marcasites and a satin glass cabochon with amber pretensions. Clasp is marked "Made in Czechosovakia." *Courtesy of private collection, Los Angeles. Photo by Robert Weldon*

Satin glass, made by mixing transparent and opaque glass in one cane, was very effective in brooches and beads. It came in white (faux moonstone), pink, green, and yellow (which was supposed to imitate amber but could not approximate the warm touch or waxy texture of the real thing). Other fancy beads were made with silver foil "windows" in lampwork beads which were reheated in a little gas lamp furnace with overlaid crystal to fuse the colors together. The "eyes" of the peacock feather, the popular Art Nouveau motif, were marvelously recreated in silver-foil fused with green and blue glass to be mounted in belt buckles and pins in Austria, Germany, and France.[2]

Two necklaces of silver-foiled beads: one with grey/green and mauve glass; and the other Venetian *lattimo* opaque white beads with cinnamon trailings, and iridescent "porcelain" pressed glass beads from Gablonz. *Courtesy of the author. Photo by Robert Weldon*

A pretty pastel necklace strung with blue Czech crystal beads, blue rhinestone balls, green satin glass pressed beads from Gablonz, raised eye "landmine" and lampwork foiled beads from Venice. *Courtesy of private collection, Los Angeles. Photo by Robert Weldon*

"French" opaline glass, pale and translucent, was moulded or cut into round or oblong beads from the Twenties on. The addition of cobalt to the clear glass gave it the dreamy milk-glass look. Porcelain-look beads was fired in a kiln, and used for buttons. A novelty bead was created using *ballottini* (tiny glass spheres from Venice) to encrust the blown glass surface with an unexpected grainy texture and luster.[3] These are dubbed crumb glass by the trade.

A long sautoir of opaline translucent milk glass beads, press-moulded, entwined with the foiled beads. The shape and color (achieved by adding cobalt,) were popularized by Lalique in France in the Twenties, and reproduced in Gablonz. *Courtesy of private collection, Los Angeles. Photo by Robert Weldon*

A striking Fifties combination of three rows of hot pink satin-coated glass beads, Bohemian black pressed glass beads, pink "ballottini" or "crumb" blown beads which were rolled in crushed glass, and Venetian orange foiled lampwork beads. *Courtesy of Rialta, Venice, Italy. Photo by Robert Weldon*

This array of typical Art Deco necklaces was made in Bohemia of press-moulded glass in the Thirties. *Courtesy of Christie Romero Collection. Photo by Christie Romero*

"Rhinestones" were originally quartz pebbles carried down from the Alps by the Rhine and deposited in the valleys. Called *cailloux du Rhin* in France, the Rhine pebbles displayed a natural pink and blue iridescence. The magicians of Gablonz lost no time in imitating the real rhinestones in glass. (The "Aurora Borealis" of the Fifties created by Swarovski and adopted by Cis, Schiaparelli, and Dior bore a strong resemblance to these stones.) In America, rhinestone is the generic term for an imitation gemstone made of either clear or colored glass, no matter what the country of origin. In Gablonz, and the surrounding villages, hundreds of simple Art Deco rhinestone necklaces were fashioned for the French and German market in the Thirties. (These trinkets were denigrated by Hitler when the area was annexed by the Third Reich in 1938.) More sophisticated designs were produced post-war, by Bohemian craftsmen who had resettled in Neugablonz, Bavaria.

There was a wide range of designs produced in Bohemia up until World War II: pressed glass for inexpensive Art Deco buttons, necklaces, and bracelets were painted with silver or gold. Faceted faux gemstones set in Neo-Renaissance stamped brass filigree were decorated with enamel and chain garlands. One imaginative piece was created using the same filigree findings for two clips and a pendant chatelaine with glass balls. Multicolored rhinestone rings were also produced, but few have survived. Pressed glass animal figurals and Oriental buddhas were worked into earrings, brooches, and charms. In the Forties, the Czechs even copied their own Art Deco peach faceted glass pendants in moulded Lucite which was lighter to wear on the ear.

Four Thirties bracelets: the top one is Galalith imitating ivory set in Deco gilded brass links for the German market; a white press-moulded glass bracelet, enamelled, and hand-painted gold; an orange press-moulded bracelet; and a commemorative 1937 Paris Exposition bracelet, the orange medallion depicting the Expo entrance gates, marked "*Importé de Tschecoslovaquie*." All three *pâte de verre* bracelets were intended for the French market. *Courtesy of the author. Photo by Robert Weldon*

A fine set of colored rhinestones in a pendant necklace and faux filigree bracelet, Thirties style. These were possibly made in the Fifties by *gürtler* who settled in Neugablonz. *Courtesy of Diane Keith Collection, Beverly Hills. Photo by Robert Weldon*

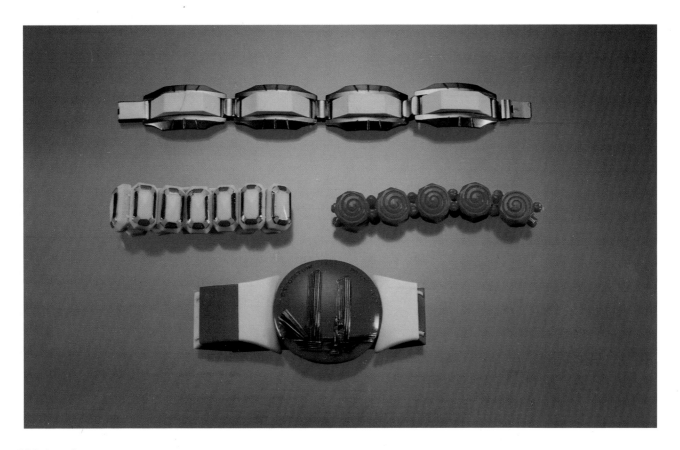

Press-moulded blue over pink glass bead bracelet, four earrings of moulded Oriental motifs, one multi-colored satin-glass earrings, and peach Lucite faux glass earrings. *Courtesy of Rita Okrent Collection, Los Angeles. Photo by Robert Weldon*

Collection of glass figural animals, parrots, turtles, and ladybugs destined for earrings or charm bracelets. *Courtesy of Rita Okrent Collection, Los Angeles, CA. Photo by Robert Weldon*

This unusual piece is composed of the same stamped filigree pattern used for two clips (on opposite lapels) and a chatelaine pendant with glass beads on chains. The foiled rhinestones are bezel set. The ring is stamped brass filigree with multicolored "gemstones". *Courtesy of Davida Baron Collection, co-editor of Vintage Fashion and Costume Jewelry Newsletter. Photo by Robert Weldon*

Gold-lined hexagonal blown glass beads from Morchenstern, Bohemia, mounted with turquoise glass beads for three bristling bracelets and earrings. Ca.1930. *Courtesy of Diane Keith collection, Beverly Hills, CA. Photo by Sandro Moro*

An ornate Neo-Renaissance necklace of stamped brass filigree with prong-set faux amethysts, bezelled green rhinestones, and turquoise painted enamel leaves. The garlands of chains are the added touch which gives this Thirties piece distinction. *Courtesy of Davida Baron Collection, Fresh Meadows, NY. Photo by Sandro Moro*

Carré-cut pink crystals were exported to France to be made up into sautoirs in the Thirties and Fifties.

Nineteenth century Bohemian glass beads were lined with toxic mercury (quicksilver) and lead solutions which were sucked into the beads, poisoning the workers. (These workers could be recognized by their blackened skin.) Dr. Weiskopf, a chemist with the Fabrik Morchenstern, introduced a silver solution for lining the beads which saved thousands of lives.[4] A gold solution was used in the Twenties and Thirties for blown glass beads which could effectively be worn in copious clusters because they were so light weight.

When the 3 million Sudetan German-speaking Czechs were expelled by the Czechs in 1945 (with only a day's notice!), they left their workshops and many tools behind, but with great determination applied their skills anew in the Neugablonz communities reborn in Bavaria (Kaufbeuren) and Austria (near Linz). Many of the old techniques and products had a new life, making up for the curtailment of exports from Communist Czechoslovakia in the Forties and Fifties. The market is opening up again for the new Czech Republic, where Western merchants and dealers have descended to plunder the antiques and jewelry that have remained in peasant hands since the end of World War II.

1. Sibylle Jargstorf, *Baubles, Buttons, and Beads*, Atglen, PA., 1993, Schiffer Publishing, pg. 84
2. *Ibid.*, pg. 146
3. *Ibid.*, pg. 107
4. *Ibid.*, pg. 37

Carré-cut unfoiled pink crystals make up a long, sparkling sautoir/pendant which was mounted up in France. Stamped "Made in France" on metal setting. *Courtesy of Peregrine Gallery, Santa Barbara, CA. Photo by Sandro Moro*

Chapter 7

Italy

La Falsa Fantasia

The great period of Italian costume jewelry began post World War II when the designers of Milan and Florence emerged from the oppressive Fascist years with characteristic Italian *brio*. There was an initial boost from the mutually advantageous collaboration with the French Haute Couture. The Parisians provided the elegant clothes and the Italians the complementary theatrics, using their native materials: glass, ceramics, and coral. In the Fifties and Sixties, the Italian *Alta Moda* came into its own. Instead of copying French models, designers like Emilio Pucci, Sorelle Fontana, and Valentino showed their collections in Italy with Italian costume jewelry to international buyers. Milan was the headquarters of Coppola e Toppo, Giuliano Fratti, Ken Scott, Emma Pellini, Ornella, Canesi, and Ugo Correani. In Florence, where the collections were shown in the Sala Bianca at the Palazzo Pitti, Bijoux Fiaschi, Bijoux Cascio, and Bijoux Elfe were prominent jewelry firms providing the pizazz for the models. Rome was home and atelier to Luciana, who designed for the international jet set. Cinema accessory designers, Nino Lembo, and Guattari created dramatic pieces for Italian and American stars shooting at the Cinecittà film studios in the Eternal City.

The Italians draw a great divide between the North and the South of their country. Milan represents wealth and intellect, and Venice, sophistication and beauty. The South is rich only in history and passion. If an artist from the South is to succeed commercially, the message has always been: "Go North, young man!"

The Italian custom of family corporate bonding (unique in Italy) goes back to the Renaissance, when each family member had a job to perform in the family enterprise. In modern times, this has produced the Fendis, the Missonis, and the Versaces, whose fashion statements also include jewelry and accessories.

Milan, the commercial hub

Emma Caimi Pellini founded her company in Milan in 1947, the first of three generations of women designing for the French couture and Milanese boutiques. In 1950, when her creations were shown at the Palazzo Pitti, she received orders from the American buyers. Pellini used only Venetian glass furnished by Barovier and Venini of Murano. Multi-rowed necklaces and earrings of *pâte de verre* floral petals were popular items. Balenciaga and Dior bought her designs in the Fifties.

In 1960, Emma retired, passing the glass baton to her daughter Carla, who opened a store in Milan. She designed real-looking jewelry for the American market. In 1972, Carla's daughter,

Donatella took over the creative duties of the firm, leaving the administrative production to her brother, Ernesto. In the Eighties she collaborated with Fendi- her bracelets looking like diamond-studded coal were shown with full length Fendi fur coats. Valentino, Armani, and Versace have also shown Pellini jewelry with their Italian couture.

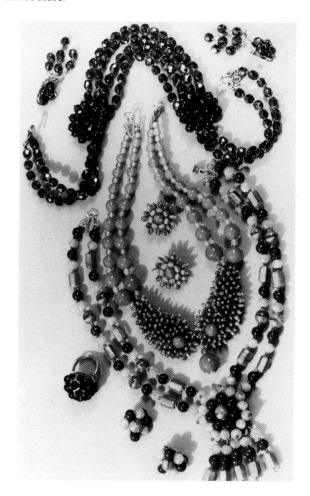

By Emma Pellini, 1950s. Pink and white Murano glass beads. Periwinkle blue and green glass beads, and pastel bead necklace, earrings and ring. *Courtesy of Donatella Pellini, Milan, Italy*

Opposite
Vintage 1920 *pochoir* print by Mario Cito, showing the pervasive influence of the Ballets Russes style in Italy with the turban, aigrette, and sautoir. Cito was a set and costume designer for the Teatro alla Scala Opera in Milan. *Courtesy of the author*

Donatella Pellini's Rhodoid stars with multi-colored mosaics, 1991. *Courtesy of Pellini Bijoux, Milan*

Necklaces in clear or bright blue Perspex, 1985 by Donatella Pellini. *Courtesy of Pellini Bijoux*

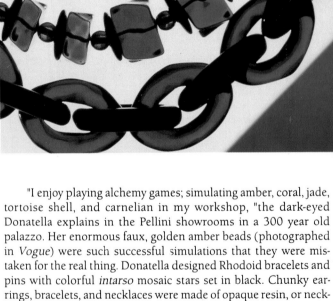

"I enjoy playing alchemy games; simulating amber, coral, jade, tortoise shell, and carnelian in my workshop, "the dark-eyed Donatella explains in the Pellini showrooms in a 300 year old palazzo. Her enormous faux, golden amber beads (photographed in *Vogue*) were such successful simulations that they were mistaken for the real thing. Donatella designed Rhodoid bracelets and pins with colorful *intarso* mosaic stars set in black. Chunky earrings, bracelets, and necklaces were made of opaque resin, or necklaces in brilliant blue or clear Perspex, an acrylic resin first used in the Thirties. In 1985 her Triennale sets resembled birch bark or taffy candy, while the Pellini 1991 collection was of "granulated gold" resin. She is currently creating models for Christian Lacroix's *prêt-à-porter* 1994-95 collections in colored resins. The company logo is a round silver plaque stamped "Pellini, Milano".

Granulated gold resin bracelets and beads by Donatella Pellini, 1991. *Courtesy of Pellini Bijoux*

"Triennale" sets of bracelets and earrings made of resin, resembling birch bark or taffy, 1985 by Donatella Pellini. *Courtesy of Pellini Bijoux*

Giuliano Fratti entered the fashion world in the late Thirties by making belts, an accessory that was part of his repertoire into the Sixties. This evolved into jewelry design which was curtailed by the outbreak of war. War-time jewelry was, of course, limited by lack of materials, funds and customers. After two years spent in a German POW camp, Fratti returned to his shop where he catered to conservative post-war tastes. In the Fifties he imported jewelry prototypes from France and adapted them for sale in chic department stores. Fratti designs were mostly traditional; pearls with a large hardstone clasp, and bracelets with baroque pearl drops and discreet rhinestone accents. A Fifties vivacious necklace of glass fruits was a takeoff on the popular American bakelite pears and cherries necklaces of the Thirties.

Interviewed by the Italian newspaper, *Il Giorno*, in December, 1963, Fratti delighted in having finally conquered the Italian aristocracy: "Contessa M. has capitulated and bought a costume jewelry necklace that complements her blue-tinted hair. Today, it's always the most elegant person who owns real jewels who understands the amusing bizarreness of costume jewels." The fashion for clothes was at that point extremely simple, so costume jewelry took on a role of prime importance, on the same level with beautiful material and fine workmanship. Fratti had "great luck with belts, which are like real jewels" draping them with gold and pearl chains, or decorating them with one large cabochon as the sole elegant ornament for an evening at La Scala. In 1972, Fratti closed his shop, unhappy with the direction Italian *Alta Moda* was taking.

Lyda Coppola of Coppola e Toppo left her personal imprint on glass bead jewelry. She probably did more for the glass industry of Murano and Bohemia, and crystal from Austria than any other Italian designer of the period. She fashioned ties, scarves, bibs and chokers, bracelets and earrings, pins, bags, and even umbrella handles out of glass beads. Her work is immediately recognizable, with multiple rows of glass, crystal or plastic beads falling in cascades of subtle hues.

PERLE E STRASS

1 - *Le clip a fiore* di perle e strass con pietra colorata al centro: si portano generalmente a coppia. G. Fratti alta moda, Milano.

2 - *Gemelli da sera* di perle con montatura di strass, per bluse di cady e di chiffon: 5 mila lire. Sonia Petroff per P. L. Tricò.

3 - *Perle a goccia* sul collare a un filo: nella spilla con montatura di strass e nel bracciale a gocce barocche. Creazione alta moda di G. Fratti, Milano.

4 - *Perle a frangia* nel bracciale a polsino, guarnito di strass. Si trovano in vendita da G. Fratti a Milano.

5 - *A sautoir*, la collana formata da un filo di strass e uno di perle, uniti dal « medaglione della nonna» di smalto nero. E' una creazione alta moda di Giuliano Fratti.

6 - *Grosse perle* nel bracciale a cinque fili, chiuso da un fiore di perle e strass. Da assortire alle clip in alto. Giuliano Fratti.

Jewelry by Giuliano Fratti: 1) pearl and strass clips. 3)pearl drops for a necklace, pin and bracelet. 4) pearl fringe on a bracelet with strass. 5) sautoirs, strass and pearls with a black enamel medaillon. 6) bracelet of 5 rows of pearls to match clips. *From Amica, December 1964. Courtesy of the author*

Lyda Coppola was the designing half of a business partnership with her brother, Bruno. She opened a shop in Milan in 1946, but international recognition didn't come until May, 1948 when French *Vogue* featured an article and photo of her faux pearl sautoirs with ornate clasps for French couturier Robert Piguet. In the same year she designed coral and jet jewelry for her fellow countrywoman, Schiaparelli, who had defected to Paris.

In 1952-'54, there were elaborate necklaces and bracelets of alternating rows of pearls and glass for Jacques Fath's boutique in Paris.

In 1952, The European fashion magazine, *Marie Claire*, declared a "definite *addio* to the single perfect strand of real pearls so dear to our mothers". Too boring. *Addio*, also, to discreet jewelry. Lyda Coppola blew the lid off all that. *Ciao* to the solitaire diamond ring and hello to the shamelessly *falso*!

Lyda (her married name was Toppo) tempted her clients with wonderful colors: burnt brown sugar; peach; apricot; lemon-yellow and mint green - looking good enough to eat. She was well acquainted with the exigencies and tastes of the French, Italian, American, and German markets, altering the design to adapt to each country. Her brother, Bruno Coppola, showed several collections a year in New York. In 1959, *Woman's Wear Daily* quoted astonishingly low wholesale prices at $15 to $35 a necklace, with matching earrings available. Later the same year, Lyda designed clutch bags covered with glass beads, umbrella handles, key chains with glass balls, and pillboxes with glass bead lids. These were all available gift items in the Coppola e Toppo boutique in Milan. In 1960, she covered sponge balls with clear crystal beads, which, because they were so light, could be strung by the dozens on one necklace. (It took 40 minutes to make each ball. Somebody counted.) By 1962, Lyda's necklaces were retailing in America for $55-$100 at Neiman Marcus. In 1964, she was appointed artistic

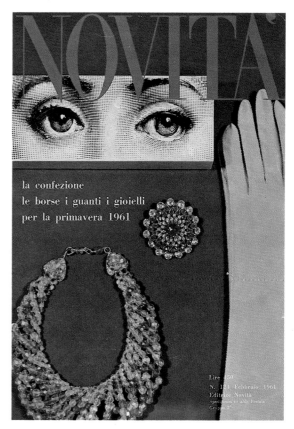

Cover of *Novità*, a magazine devoted to Italian fashion until it was bought by Condé-Nast to become *Vogue-Italia* in 1965; featuring a Coppola e Toppo blue and green crystal necklace, and a box by Piero Fornasetti. *Courtesy of the author*

Opposite
Cascades of crystal beads subtly shaded from clear to deep blue. 1960's necklaces, signed Coppola e Toppo. *Courtesy of the author and Norman Crider Antiques, NY. Photo by Victor de Liso*

Coppola e Toppo pearls with ornate glass bead clasps or pendants. 1948-51. photo Fortunati, Milano. *Courtesy of the author*

Bracelet of smoky glass and ruby red beads, with fringe, and earrings to match; another bracelet, 4 rows of red glass; a pair of earrings shading from pink to red, in the popular Coppola e Toppo paisley shape; and blue and aqua leaves of glass for another pair of earrings, bottom row. All signed Coppola e Toppo, 1960's. *Courtesy of the author. Photo by Robert Weldon*

A set of clear crystal beads: a necklace of 5 rows looped around a gilded brass crescent; matching earrings; and a bracelet of beads clustered over a gilded brass cuff. Coppola e Toppo Sixties. *Courtesy of the author. Photo by Robert Weldon*

Four faceted crystal bead necklaces: the top one of pomegranate iridescent beads and pink and orange lampwork *sommerso* drops; a 4 row blue and aqua necklace, a 4 row emerald green beads with a pearl clasp, and 4 rows of graduated deep blue to pale aqua with a royal blue beaded pendant. All Coppola & Toppo, Sixties. *Courtesy of the author. Photo by Robert Weldon*

Opposite
A shaggy bracelet of long smoky and clear crystal beads; and a collar of Swarovski "daisy" crystals and beads the color of winter mist in Milan. Coppola e Toppo, 1960's. *Courtesy of Norman Crider Antiques, NY. Photo by Victor de Liso*

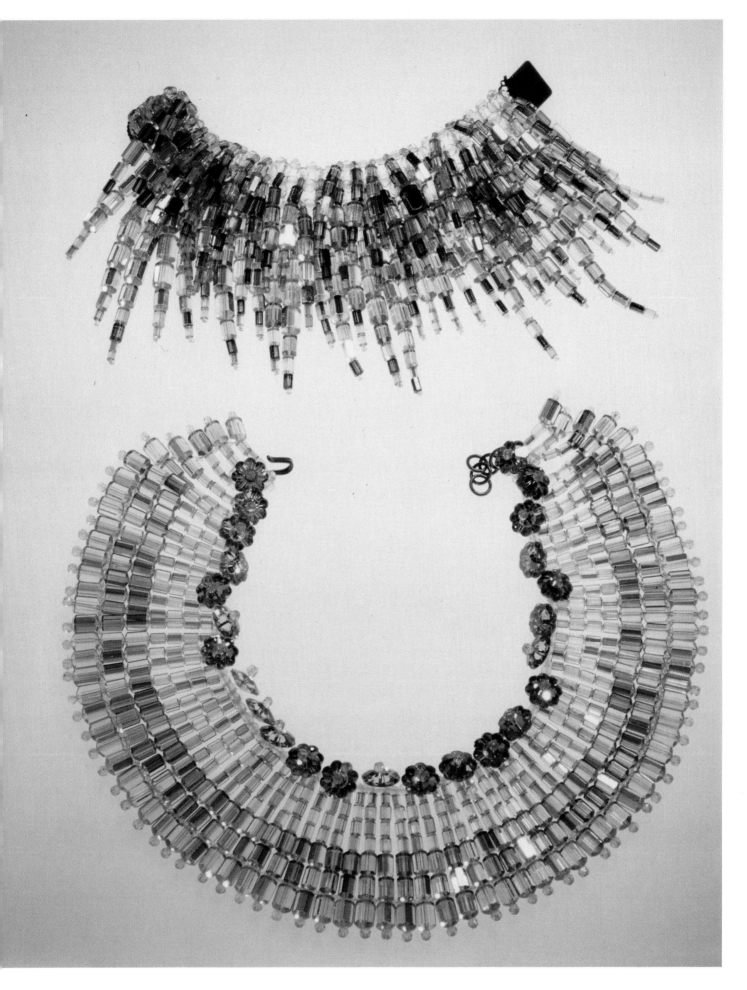

A large creole double hoop earring of silvered glass beads photographed on a 1935 original woodblock print, *Une Belle de Palaos*, by Paul Jacoulet. *Courtesy of the author. Photo by Robert Weldon*

Aqua plastic beads on cylinder pendant earrings, 1966; and a necklace of midnight blue iridescent glass beads shading down to aqua, around a midnight blue bowtie. Coppola e Toppo, Sixties. *Courtesy of the author. Photo by Robert Weldon*

consultant to Swarovski of Austria, making generous use of the new "daisy" beads, and other specialty faceted stones from the Wattens company. In the Sixties, faceted plastic beads were substituted for or mixed with glass when the earrings or necklaces were so ornate that glass or crystal beads would have been intolerably heavy.

In 1963, Lyda announced, "I don't bother with private clientele much." She didn't have to. Most of her production of 60 models a year went abroad. (This is still the case; the rediscovery of vintage Coppola and Toppo jewelry in the 1980s in America and Europe, has not made a ripple in Lyda's homeland, where Italian collectors prefer Forties and Fifties American pins by Eisenberg and Trifari. "The glass is always greener"..).

There were three Italian couturiers who collaborated successfully with Lyda: Emilio Pucci; Ken Scott; and Valentino. "Pucci is the Italian Chanel," she announced. Each necklace was expressly created to repeat the hues of his house models. The collaboration was very close; the jewelry carefully coordinated with the neckline and cut of the dress. Coppola e Toppo necklaces were also a natural choice for the floral prints of Ken Scott.

"My jewelry requires enormous amounts of time and labor, and a vast choice of colors and hues. Of course, not everyone understands this jewelry, which does not imitate real jewels. It has a precise decorative function and must be aggressive, outrageous and fantastic. This is appropriate not only at La Scala opera openings, but chic with sweaters in the mountains or at the seaside. Naturally I have a more sedate line which is adaptable to all women."[1]

Lyda concocted elaborate frothy pieces for Valentino in the late Sixties. Using a new long tube-bead in a V pattern, inspired by the pheasant feather print that was Valentino's hallmark, she made supple necklaces, handbags, earrings and bracelets. Wrap-around body jewelry of metal faux bamboo and coral curled around the waist, arms and wrist, also for Valentino in 1969. Lyda Coppola Toppo died in 1972, but the firm actually closed its doors in Milan in 1986.

Valentino Garavani was born in 1932 near Milan, where he studied fashion design. From 1949-51, in Paris, he learned cutting at the Chambre Syndicale de la Couture, and design at the Ecole des Beaux Arts, 1949-'51. He was assistant to Jean Dessès, 1950-55, and Guy Laroche until 1958. With his partner, Giancarlo Giammetti, the House of Valentino was founded in Rome in 1960.

Opposite
Six rows of blue crystal looped thru brass rings, covered with beads; and a tapestry of blue- green and smoky beads woven over the shoulders, to swing free from the throat. This was a new technique used by Coppola e Toppo in the mid-Sixties. *Courtesy of Norman Crider Antiques, NY. Photo by Victor de Liso*

A bright green version of the crystal leaves sautoir with gold beads, to be worn long or looped around the neck. Coppola e Toppo, 1964. *Courtesy of the author. Photo by Robert Weldon*

Wraparound bracelets in pink and red glass with gold beads, and swinging pendant earrings of colored rhinestone balls, worn with Ken Scott floral print. Coppola & Toppo for Ken Scott, November, 1969. *Courtesy of Ken Scott archives, Milan, Italy*

Opposite
Crystal and plastic beads mounted by hand on a circular weft of plastic beads, (measuring 6 inches across), hung from long glass bead chains. Red, blue, olive green and yellow blossoms from the Coppola e Toppo garden for Ken Scott in the Sixties. The flower pendant in the upper right *Courtesy of the author*, the other two pendants *Courtesy of Norman Crider Antiques, NY. Photo by Victor de Liso*

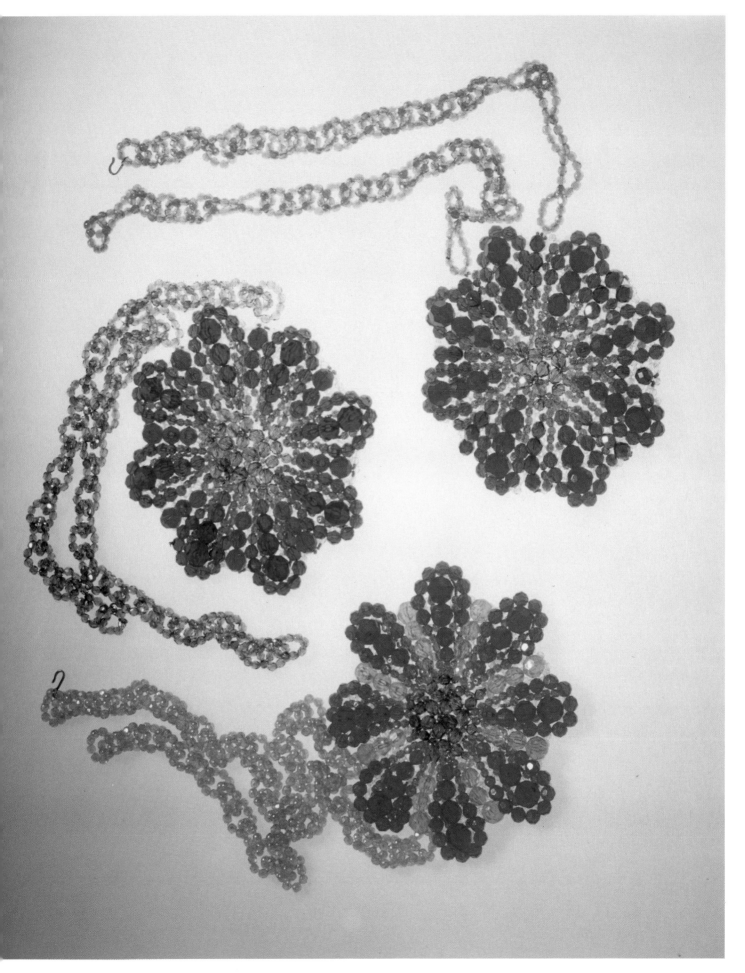

The magnificent "Thirtieth Anniversary of the Founding of the House of Valentino", held in Rome, then in New York at the Armory in October, 1992, displayed 300 dresses (some with vintage Coppola e Toppo jewelry) and divulged the sources of his inspiration. These included Gobelin tapestries, Persian miniatures, Hoffmann's work for the Wiener Werkstätte (for his Op Art collection late Sixties), and even a Sienese door knocker. His Ideal Woman was graceful and feline, (Valentino was one of the first to play with wild animal fabric prints), and above all, elegant. The jewelry he chose to show with his lush creations reinforced this utterly glamourous image. Coppola e Toppo provided the perfect complement.

Ken Scott (-1991) an American in Milan, was infatuated with flowers. He splashed them everywhere: on fabrics, stockings, scarves, palazzo pants, caftans, suitcases and jewelry. Born in Indiana, and trained at Parson's School of Design, he began his expatriate life in Paris in the Forties. He chose Milan as his design workshop because of the accessibility of factories, fabric printers and accessory manufacturers. His boutiques on the via Corridoni and Manzoni were frequented by the fashionable women and film stars of the Sixties and Seventies. His models wore jewelry by Coppola e Toppo and Luciana in the rosy palette he favored for his clothes. A huge floral pendant of woven beads hanging on a long beaded chain was like a blowup of the flowers on his fabrics, interpreted by Coppola e Toppo, who also made earrings of shiny balls swinging on long chains. Scott's own design of geometric painted leather pendants was his contribution to the ethnic jewelry trend of the late Sixties.

Vermillion tube-bead in V patterns, (inspired by Valentino's pheasant feather prints), with glass flower petals, and rows of rhinestones. A matching bracelet and necklace set for Valentino, late Sixties. *Courtesy of Norman Crider Antiques. Photo by Victor de Liso*

Two sumptuous Coppola e Toppo tube-bead necklaces with gold or silver leaves and rhinestones; one of black tube-beads and glass petals, for Valentino. Featured in Italian *Vogue*, September, 1968. *Courtesy of Norman Crider Antiques, NY. Photo by Victor de Liso*

Piero Fornasetti (1913-1988) was an industrial designer and painter, who had nothing whatever to do with fashion. He was expelled for insubordination from the only art school he ever attended. He collaborated with Gio Ponti from the Thirties on in furniture, glass, and ceramics design. He was an illusionist who played with fantasy and reality, creating *trompe l'oeil* masterpieces. He was obsessed with the sun, and a woman's face, using these themes in endless variations. The face he chose from a 19th century illustrated magazine (though he kept her identity a secret). This mysterious, enigmatic face was framed, disguised, distorted, and dissected in 500 variations on dinner plates, scarves, boxes, and finally, jewelry. He returned to his primary simple image, unadorned this time, for tiny porcelain pins, buttons and cufflinks in the Eighties. His son, Barnaba, designs the same motifs.

Fornasetti's famous woman's face on a porcelan pin, 1980s, surrounded by a 1950s sun theme coaster, and a bejeweled arm toasting femininity by Fornasetti. *Courtesy of author. Photo by Robert Weldon*

Ugo Correani (1936-) was professionally born with the first ready-to-wear collections in Milan in 1973, when he designed jewelry and belts for Walter Albini's collection. In 1976, besides his own line, he accessorized for Valentino and Fendi in Rome, and began a long, fruitful association with Gianni Versace in Milan. In Paris, his highly original work for Karl Lagerfeld was appreciated by Chloé and Chanel clients. Christian Lacroix, another couturier who is always receptive to new ideas, also commissions Correani's designs.

Correani is well known in Europe for his jewelry of the future. He mixes materials in an unexpected way, bending resin and enamelled metal into intriguing shapes for sculptural bracelets and necklaces.. unmistakably Ugo Correani. These are not created for the Establishment, he is anti-bourgeois. "I like to help women be beautiful, daring, and self confident, so why not be noticed!" he exclaims. The chances of any woman wearing Correani jewelry going unnoticed are very slim indeed.

A wild eruption of sea shells encrusted with red rhinestones and coral for Gianni Versace couture, spring/summer 1991. *Courtesy of Ugo Correani, Milan*

Hinged baroque cuff of gilded metal swirls studded with faux gems by Ugo Correani. *Courtesy of Ugo Correani, Milan*

Gianni Versace (1948-) was born in Calabria, in the impoverished toe of the Italian boot. His work is marked by the conflicts and contrasts of northern vs. southern Italy. He trained in his mother's atelier, then moved to Milan in 1972 where he contributed designs to Mario Valentino and Genny. In 1978 he launched his own label, aided by his brother Sandro, and his sister Donatella. Versace's daring designs feature asymmetrical draping and wildly colorful combinations. He experiments with different materials, introducing metal chain mail for evening (out of fashion since the crusades!). He also used embossed silks, inspired by Kandinski and Pop-Art, and pressure-cast moulded leather. "I am constantly seeking new materials, treatments, and effects," he explains. (Sonia Delaunay was his last inspiration for vivid fabrics and accessories, looking as modern in 1994 as she did 80 years ago.) Ugo Correani was the answer to his search for a jewelry designer as fearlessly creative as he. Donatella and Gianni collaborate with Correani on jewelry for his collections. Cult couturier to Cher, Sting, and Elizabeth Taylor (Versace outfitted Elton John's last world tour), he welcomes his stage work which releases him from fashion's commercial restraints.

A necklace of enamelled mesh jungle flowers with a golden bird of Paradise by Ugo Correani for Gianni Versace autumn/winter collection, 1990. *Courtesy of Ugo Correani, Milan*

In addition to his outstanding fashion line, Versace designed costumes for the Maurice Bejart ballet "Evita". Correani did the accessories for this, as well as Robert Wilson's production of "Salome" at the La Scala Opera. The amazing necklaces he has created for Versace, and his own Ugo Correani line, are works of art, twisting metal mesh and enamelled metal into fantastic jungle flowers that twine around the neck. One is the nest for a gilded bird of paradise. His bracelets are also larger than life, baroque cuffs of gilded metal that curl 5" up the arm.

Domenico Dolce (1958-) from Sicily, and Stefano Gabbana (1962-) from Venice, like all ambitious Italian designers, set up their atelier in bustling Milan in the early 1980s. Determined to design "what they liked, the way they liked it", they created patterns and accessories with complete freedom, producing their own collections and fashion shows in 1985 and 1986. They opened their first Dolce & Gabbana boutique in Milan in 1990, via Sant'Andrea, and are fashion consultants for Complice.

Dolce & Gabbana's clothes are fresh, young, sensual and charismatic. There is a strong Meditteranean look to their designs,

Jewelry from Ali Baba's cave by Dolce & Gabbana for their spring/ summer 1993 collection. Brass chains and coins and an enamelled red and turquoise belt to wear with their ribboned vests. *Courtesy of Dolce & Gabbana, Milan*

whether it be Sicily, the Middle East, or Morocco. Their jewelry, which they design themselves to accessorize each collection, is a mix of ethnicity and elegance, piled on in happy profusion from chokers and chains down to the fantastic elaborate belts.

For the spring/summer 1993 collection, Dolce & Gabbana raided Ali Baba's cave and brought back a treasure of brass coins hanging from chains, Persian pendants with tassels, and an enormous red and turquoise enamelled belt to complement their ribboned vests. Multi-colored buttons covered their high crowned hats, and embroidered flowers were strewn across their jackets. For the winter '94 collection, the treasure was purloined from the Topkapi harem in Istanbul; silver rings and collars with faux turquoises, and Byzantine pendants on chains to be worn with Kashmir shawls and patchwork jackets. A skull cap of black jet beads formed bangs, and long, swinging tresses. Cameos on pretty ribbons, and tons of pearl sautoirs contributed to the romantic look of their chiffon dresses for the spring/summer collection.

The multimillion dollar knitting empire of Rosita and Tai Missoni began in 1956 with four knitting machines. The Missonis are a prime example of the family cottage industry which is the backbone of Italian commerce. At first, Tai created the unusual colors and textures which looked vaguely Peruvian or was it Indonesian? Noone was sure, but they were altogether Missoni. Rosita designed the fluid clothes which had to be simply cut, as the fabric was so complex. Today, son, Luca, designs the fabrics on a computer; Vittorio handles promotion, and daughter Angela is in sales, besides designing her own dress line. They are a close knit family. Missoni jewelry is colorful, of course, in Rhodoid plastic, or moulded matt glass which takes off from the *mosaico* of Venetian trading beads, or repeats the knit patterns for beaded necklaces and bracelets. Large (2") round red or green plastic earrings had chrome dome centers in the Eighties.

Booty purloined from the Topkapi harem in Istanbul; silver rings and Byzantine pendants for the winter 1994 collection by Dolce & Gabbana. *Courtesy of Dolce & Gabbana*

Venice- a "stroke of the enchanter's wand" (Lord Byron)

Anyone who has ever floated on the shimmering lagoon of a lazy summer evening has carried a piece of Venice away with her; a mixture of mist, light, and water captured in glass - a souvenir, *ricordo*, of magical moments spent in *La Serenissima*.

Venice was founded a thousand years ago on the lagoon island of Torcello by hardy folk fleeing from barbarians who, happily, were not seafarers. 500 years later the glass makers left Venice, "Queen of the Seas", to settle on Murano far out in the lagoon, because there was a real fire hazard from the furnaces burning in the glasshouses. Centralization of the industry also facilitated protecting the glass products from the prying eyes of rival glassmakers. By Doge's decree, revealing the secrets of the trade to Bohemia or France was punishable by death. By the 16th century, however, Venetian émigrés glassmakers roamed over Europe, bringing their secrets with them. The 17th and 18th centuries were marked by an European preference for English and Bohemian glass. In the mid-19th century Venetian glass was back in style, and the ancient techniques of *murrine* and foiled glass were reinvented for vases and beads. The 20th century master glassmakers like Salviati, Venini, Flavio Poli, Barovier and Toso etc. have been responsible for a modern Renaissance in glass design.

The Società Veneziana per L'Industria della Conterie e Cristallerie was originally composed of 17 different companies which have produced *conterie* (seed beads) since its formation in 1898. (A crystal-producing plant in Gablonz was acquired in 1920 which introduced crystal beads to the Venetian market in competition with Swarovski.) From 1960 into the Seventies, the Società also manufactured inexpensive costume jewelry of different sized beads for sale to department stores and costume jewelry manufacturers in Europe and America. Sold by the pound, thousands of multi-strand twisted glass bead necklaces which had been laboriously strung by the working class *impiraresse* in their homes, were shipped unfinished to avoid import taxes. In the foreign markets, the beads were assembled with catches and company trademarks. The best quality beads were used by Milanese designers Coppola e Toppo, Ornella, Emma Pellini, Ken Scott, and Bijoux Bozart, as well as Roberta di Camerino in Venice.[2] A change in fashions and competition from the Japanese forced the Società Veneziana to cease production of finished jewelry and iridescent beads in 1985.[3]

Antique and vintage beads used individually or together were not incorporated into the unimaginative necklaces for the tourists and department stores. These are now the object of dedicated search by collectors and Bead Societies in America.

To make a necklace of Venetian beads, a delicious menu is presented for the collector's delectation. One can incorporate any of the following beads into a personal work of art:

Sommerso, or overlay bead; starting with a plain opaque glass base which is decorated with floral designs or leaves of silver and gold foil which is then submerged under a layer of clear glass.

Closeup of *sommerso* or overlay beads with silver foil and a touch of gold under a glass layer. *Courtesy of Marie-Hélène Laurens Collection, Venice, Italy. Photo by Pierre Higonnet*

Perle al lume, lampwork (or lamp-wound) beads; the previously drawn glass cane is reheated over a gas flame in a small furnace and wound around a copper wire which is later removed by acid. The cottage workers are paid by the bead rather than by the hour for this process which allows room for infinite variety of expression as decorative layers are superimposed. Care must be taken that the different glass layers are compatible, or the bead will crack as it cools. This expertise is paid accordingly, though few tourists recognize the hours of work that this process requires when they choose their Venetian souvenirs.

Al lume or lampwork beads; turquoise glass and gold leaf alternating with gold overlay beads, 1920. *Courtesy of Marie-Hélène Laurens Collection. Photo by Pierre Higonnet*

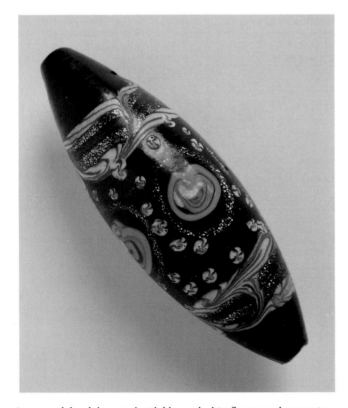

Lamp-work bead decorated with blue and white flowers and aventurine trailings, from the Twenties. *Courtesy of M.-H. Laurens Collection, Venice. Photo by Pierre Higonnet*

Pater noster, "our Father," in Latin; originally prayer beads, they have a wooden core around which long rows of tiny seed beads (*conterie*) have been strung thru a hole with a needle.

Pater noster beads of different colors and design, 1900-1920. Tiny beads are strung through the hole in the wooden bead with a needle. *Courtesy of Marie-Hélène Laurens collection, Venice. Photo by Pierre Higonnet*

Conterie, term referring to the ensemble of glass seed beads, usually minuscule, cut from long slender canes measured in millimeters widths. The origin is probably Spanish or Portuguese (*contar*), when in colonial times they were used as money beads for barter. Another use was for rosary beads; from the God Mammon to God Almighty, their use now is primarily commercial. They were exported all over Europe for embroidery purposes and were made into cushions, handbags, and sautoirs in the Twenties.

Conterie, minuscule seed beads used here in Twenties handbags for the purse, fringe, and drawstrings. *Courtesy of Marie-Hélène Laurens Collection. Photo by Pierre Higonnet*

Rosetta or *chevron*; invented in 1497 by Maria Barovier, this was a five to seven-layered bead with a terracotta and white rick-rack design on a deep blue ground. The cog-shaped layers were successively moulded before the tube core was drawn (stretched out). Tube drawing is now done by machine, replacing the old process using two men pulling at the opposite ends of the tube.[4] When the round end section is sliced off, the rosetta design is exposed and polished. *Rosetta*, in Italy, applies to a single slice and the whole bead itself, and is known as a chevron bead among American collectors. The antique seven-layered bead fetches the highest prices. The more layers there are, the higher the price. In a version of the chevron process, intermediate colored layers were composed of pencil-thin yellow, red, or blue rods producing a stretched oval pattern on long, black beads drawn in the Thirties.[5] (Robert Liu, editor of *Ornament* magazine says, "The secret is in the grinding of the bead ends after moulding.")

Necklace of large (almost 2" long) black beads, the intermediate colored layers are composed of pencil-thin rods; six with yellow layers, the center bead with five different colors. From the Twenties and Thirties, here strung with faceted Bohemian jet beads. Similar beads, a variation of the chevron process, were in the Moretti family collection in Venice. *Courtesy of the author. Photo by Robert Weldon*

Rosetta chevron beads of terracotta, white, and dark blue star pattern adorn this Twenties sautoir of *lattimo* chalk white seed beads twisted with a long fringe tassel. *Courtesy of the author. Photo by Pierre Higonnet*

Millefiori, or a thousand flowers; beads of this type were found in the ruins of ancient Egypt, 100 B.C. Different colored canes are arranged in a circle. The negative spaces in between are filled with contrasting color, and the whole element is fused and stretched. This can be repeated many times so that any number of flowers are contained in the design. They were found frequently in African trading beads as well as in paperweights.

Mosaico Africano or African trading bead; usually a deep yellow with red, white, and green mosaic designs on a black or cobalt blue core, they were used as trading beads first in North Africa, then exported all over the world. Spurned by 19th century wealthy clients who thought they were intended for trade with "savages", they were enthusiastically embraced in the Sixties by the hippies and flower children who found their "ethnicity" and vivid floral motifs very appealing. West Africans, who have used them in their tribes for generations for barter, have been persuaded by African dealers to part with antique beads for sale abroad to Bead Societies and collectors. These are replaced by new trading beads.

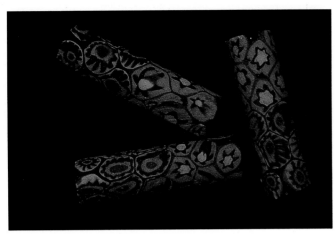

Mosaico Africano. A detail of the African trading beads first used for barter in North Africa, then exported worldwide.
These are the yellow, terracotta, blue, and white *millefiori* variety popular for centuries. Circa 1910-1920. *Courtesy of Signora Moretti-Giusi private collection, Venice, Italy. Photo by Pierre Higonnet*

Murrine, beads and decorative elements which had their origin in ancient Roman *millefiori*. One of the oldest expressions of art in glass, they were used in miniature glass portraits. This was an artistic achievement mastered by very few Muranese craftsmen. It's basically the same technique as the *millefiori*, except that the separate elements assembled must have subtle shadings to create the likeness of the subject. This ensemble is then fused and stretched. In the lamp-blown method, the melt is rolled with a rod and then blown for glassware. A *murrina* slice of an extremely complex cane by Vicenzo Moretti in 1870 portrayed Garibaldi or the rooster (the symbol of Murano independence). An exhibition of Moretti masterpieces by Vicenzo, Luigi, and Vederico (1870-1930s) were displayed 100 years later at the Doge's Palace in 1990.

Murrine are one of the oldest expressions of miniature glass art, requring subtle shadings for portraits. The rooster is a symbol of Murano independence. *Courtesy of Signora Moretti-Giusi's private collection, Venice. Photo by Pierre Higonnet*

Avventurina; aventurine or goldstone, is glass mixed with copper crystals, simulating the sparkling mica of aventurine quartz. The etymology is derived from *avventura* (chance, or adventure) because producing the correct glass/copper formula was such a risky business. A chrome-aventurine variety produces silver sparkles, instead of gold.

Avventurina; aventurine or goldstone glass pendant simulating the sparkling aventurine quartz. This one is a two-color inlay. *Courtesy of Marie-Hélène Laurens Collection. Photo by Pierre Higonnet*

Pizzo or lace; a layer of contrasting color is laid over a bead in a lacy pattern.

Pizzo lace-work. A layer of contrasting color over a glass bead makes a lacy pattern of black on aventurine, and black on white in these 2 necklaces mounted with blue iridescent crystal and jet beads. The black bead with white swirls holding the tassel is a *fenicio* combed bead. Circa 1950s. *Courtesy of the author. Photo by Robert Weldon*

Mosaico; an ancient technique dating back to Byzantium. The mosaic tiles in the glorious Basilica di San Marco in Venice were the inspiration for these glass beads.

Stellatine; beads with starred mosaic patterns.

Stellatine; or starred mosaic patterns in black and white beads, strung on a necklace with conterie tassels. Twenties. Courtesy of M.-H. Laurens Collection. Photo by Pierre Higonnet

Soffiati; hand-blown beads that are hollow inside.

Soffiati; or hand blown turquoise beads, (2" long) strung with aventurine beads. Circa 1950. Courtesy of the author. Photo by Robert Weldon

Pannochie; long *pater noster* beads shaped like corn cobs.

Pannochie or corncob Pater noster beads strung with black beads. 1920. Courtesy of M.-H. Laurens Collection. Photo by Pierre Higonnet

Fenicio, or combed; a design formed in the molten glass when striated filaments are pulled down with an instrument making a dip in the pattern.

Fogliato, or foiled; a bead with gold or silver leaf between layers of glass. This foil technique has the virtue of permanence which coated beads do not.

Filigrana; filigree threads applied to overlay beads.

Filigrana, or filigree gold threads on blue lampwork beads, and gold fogliato 1920s beads, mounted recently. Courtesy of M.-H. Laurens Collection. Photo by Pierre Higonnet

Strisca, or *stricá* are striped beads.

Stricá or striped beads of different colors. *Courtesy of Marie-Hélène Laurens Collection. Photo by Pierre Higonnet*

Lattimo; opaque white glass beads simulating milk glass or porcelain.

Woven necklace of blue and white beads on a red Fortuny cushion. *Courtesy of M.-H. Laurens Collection. Photo by Pierre Higonnet*

There are many different ways of mounting the beads besides the obvious one of stringing different elements on a long thread of silk or nylon:

doppia or *treccia*; braided into 2 or three ropes.

Long sautoir/belt, (1 meter and a half long) of black *Pater noster* beads strung on *doppia* double strands of beads with a long lustrous tassel. 1920s. *Courtesy of Marie-Hélène Laurens Collection. Photo by Pierre Higonnet*

torchon; 2 ropes of beads twisted together.

al telaio, on a loom, or woven like a tapestry for making into handbags, long *sautoirs* or belts.

strangolino, a daunting name for the dog collar (*collier de chien* in French) worn tight around the neck circa 1900 to 1925.

Al telaio beads woven into sautoirs or handbags. Pink sautoir from the Twenties. *Courtesy of Marie-Hélène Laurens collection. Photo by Pierre Higonnet*

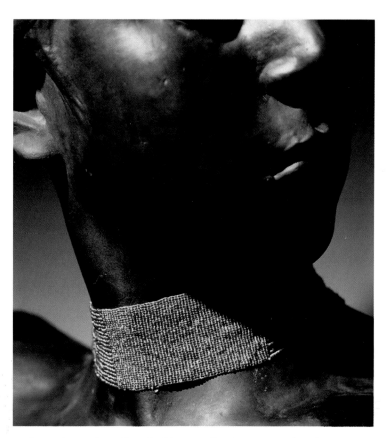

Strangolino or dog collar, of gold *conterie* beads. Twenties. Photo by Pierre Higonnet. *Courtesy of Marie-Hélène Laurens Collection*

Another time-consuming method of mounting was to sew long loops of *conterie* seed beads onto a strip of cotton cloth, which was then twisted to form a necklace with the beads hanging down in festoons.

Necklace made with strings of beads sewn onto a cotton cloth, then twisted. *Courtesy of M.-H. Laurens Collection. Photo by Pierre Higonnet*

Dog collar of silver seed beads. Twenties. *Courtesy of Marie-Hélène Laurens Collection. Photo by Pierre Higonnet*

Collection of necklaces of olive shaped, or cane glass beads, each strung individually on copper wire, with tiny metal drops which caught the light. For the Fifties tourist trade. *Courtesy of Joanne McPherson Collection, Los Angeles, CA.. Photo by Robert Weldon*

There were three methods of making the beads: **Winding** the molted glass from a large pot around a conical rod (like winding pasta around a fork); **cutting** the beads (*conterie*) from long hollow canes (up to 20 meters long) that had been previously drawn and were then cut into one meter lengths for wholesale, (this was a faster, more efficient method); or **hand-blowing** the beads.

A clever glassmaker or bead stringer could combine any number of the techniques or beads above into a unique necklace, bracelet, or belt.

Bright clown faces were "painted" on wide plastic cuffs and pins in 1986. These bear the orange fabric tag "MISSONI". The moulded lampwork matt glass earrings and purple, yellow, and orange, a new direction for Venetian glass in 1990 for Missoni.

Three contemporary Venetian glass rings, with a 1950s delicate glass perfume bottle by Sergio, Venice. *Courtesy of the author. Photo by Robert Weldon*

Pietra dura inlay of an insect with malachite and agate wings set in a silver-gilt ring, ca. 1910, and three micromosaic pins of scarabs and flowers, 1910-1950. *Courtesy of Joanne McPherson, Santa Monica, CA. Photo by Robert Weldon*

Micromosaics are made using an ancient glass technique originating in Byzantium and Rome. The magnificent Byzantine mosaics of San Vitale in Ravenna, and the Basilica of San Marco in Venice are examples of the marvels created from thousands of inlaid pieces of minuscule opaque glass cubes. The glass *smalti* came from Murano, though the jewelry production came to be associated with Rome. Portraits and landscapes were faithfully reproduced in glass, especially popular in the 19th century. The smaller the elements, and the more shadings represented, the finer the portrait. Subtle gradations of each color produced a *pointilliste* picture in glass for brooches and pendants. The technique coarsened in the 20th century when souvenir pieces of classical tourist attractions were produced in vast quantities, using larger glass segments, compound-fused, and roughly assembled. Wax was often used to fill in the holes between the separate elements after the mosaic design was polished down. Flower bouquets and insects in modern jewelry are left rough without wax fill to save time, but at the expense of quality and artistic finesse.

Florence, Modern Style in a Renaissance setting

The combination of technical expertise and artistic imagination which has fired the Italian creative spirit for centuries is especially prolific in Tuscany. The province is also blessed with clay deposits for ceramic and terracotta products, which were used in jewelry. Fine craftsmanship has been a proud tradition passed from generation to generation. Individual designers and a thriving cottage industry to support them, have always been in abundant supply.

In 1966, the elements showed no mercy for the Florentine genius. The usually tranquil Arno River engulfed the Ponte Vecchio and surrounding medieval streets where goldsmiths had had their workshops for 500 years. The bust of Benvenuto Cellini, father of all goldsmiths, was torn from the old bridge and buried in the mud. Archives, prototypes, gems and findings were lost or destroyed. The damage from the tragic devastation of the priceless artworks and paintings of Florence has not been completely restored despite international efforts.

Italian fashion came to world attention in 1951 when the Marchese Giorgini presented the first fashion show by Italian designers for international critics and buyers. Among those participating were Emilio Pucci, Sorelle Fontana, Marucelli, Simonetta, and Jole Veneziani. In 1952 the designers moved to the elegant Sala Bianca in the Palazzo Pitti to celebrate Italian craftsmanship and flair, having successfully thrown off the couturiers' tyranny north of the Alps. The new fashions in bright colors and bold prints required accessories and jewelry with punch and personality. Viva "Made in Italy"!

Marchese Emilio Pucci (1914-1992) was heir to one of the oldest Florentine families. He resided and worked in the ancient Palazzo Pucci, which was restored by the Renaissance artist, Brunelleschi. Educated at Reed College in Oregon and the University of Florence, his intention to follow a diplomatic career was interrupted by World War II. For 14 years he was a career officer.

An enthusiastic sportsman, he wore a ski outfit of his own design on the slopes in 1947. This prompted a *Harper's Bazaar* photographer's request that he design women's skiwear for a story on European winter fashion. In 1949, his designs in Capri for a friend became an instant success with elegant women on the French and Italian Rivieras. The Casa della Alta Moda Emilio Pucci was born.

With the first presentation of Italian High Fashion in Florence in 1951, Pucci launched his spectacular sports collection. Using the vivid colors of Capri and Sicily, he introduced a new palette to Italian fabrics: Emilio pink, geranium, and almond green were swirled in modern designs over simply constructed silk jersey shirts and dresses, underwear and handbags. After 35 years in the fashion business, he was still designing 3 collections annually of 250 models each, plus the accessories and jewelry until his recent demise. His collaboration with Coppola e Toppo has already been described, but Bijoux Elfe and Bijoux Fiaschi also contributed accessories. Unfortunately, jewelry archives prior to the 1966 flood have been destroyed, so one must be content with vintage fashion magazine clippings for provenance.

Emilio Fideli, a Florentine jeweler, in partnership with Cesari di Roma, created jewelry in the Fifties for Hollywood epic historical films shot at the Roman film studio, Cinecittà (*Quo Vadis* and *Ulysses*). When the Italian Alta Moda began its ascendance, Fideli opened a Bijoux Elfe showroom on the Ponte Vecchio (a glittering

Orange and raspberry crystal swirls for Emilio Pucci by Coppola e Toppo, 1963. *Courtesy of Norman Crider Collection, NY. Photo by Victor de Liso*

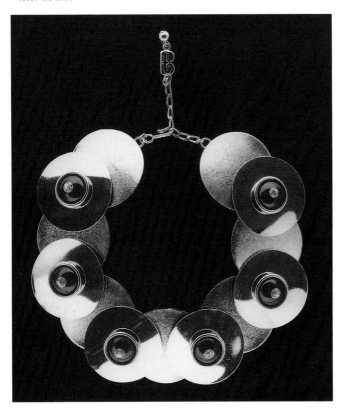

The flying saucer necklace for Pucci of alternating shiny and textured nickel-plated brass disks with black plastic and strass centers. By Bijoux Fiaschi, 1967. *Courtesy of Bijoux Fiaschi archives*

Gaetano Cascio tempting Claudette Colbert in the Fifties with a Bijoux Cascio bracelet. Photo by Levi. *Courtesy of Bijoux Cascio archives*

display of faux which was a shock to that centuries old bastion of traditional goldsmiths). He established a long working relationship with Emilio Pucci in the Sala Bianca. The Bijoux Elfe lines ranged from "Hollywood-Roman" to high fashion. In the Sixties, a wide range of materials was used, ranging from the native Italian ceramics and glass paste to plastic beads and woven raffia. Since 1963, more than half of the Elfe pieces were exported abroad to Europe and the United States, where they can be recognized by the metal label stamped "Bijoux Elfe".[6]

For over forty years, Bijoux Cascio has been synonymous with style in fashion jewelry. In 1948, Gaetano Cascio began his enterprise with 2 employees. He took part in the first showing of Italian Alta Moda in Via de' Serragli, and at the Sala Bianca where Bijoux Cascio accessorized the creations of Pucci, Capucci, Marucelli, Lancetti, and Ferragamo. In 1955, the best department stores in America (Bonwit Teller, Bloomingdale's, Lord and Taylor, and Henri Bendel,) opened a Bijoux Cascio showcase. At the same time a shop on the exclusive Via Tornabuoni in Florence sold the house creations to the public, with an additional boutique added at the corner of the Ponte Vecchio three years later. Gaetano Cascio designed massive bracelets, hoop earrings, and important chains in gilded metal, nickel silver, and tombak, inspired by the ancient Roman and Etruscan art of his country. In 1970, Riccardo Cascio took over from his father, expanding modern jewelry production and introducing franchising Bijoux Cascio to 50 boutiques in and around Italy by 1992.

Opposite
Rhinestone star necklace and earrings with pearl drops, and label, for Sorelle Fontana by Bijoux Fiaschi. 1959/60. *Courtesy of Bijoux Fiaschi archives*

Nickel-plated brass necklace with a hoop pendant and mesh chains. 1965/66. *Courtesy of Bijoux Fiaschi archives*

Unlike Bijoux Elfe and Cascio, Giancarlo Fiaschi lacked the extensive commercial distribution network of the larger firms, so he began by selling his models exclusively thru them. The Fontana sisters (Sorelle Fontana) of Rome bought one of his first (1959-1960) creations, a necklace of strass stars with simulated pearl drops and earrings to match. By 1965 he had his own establishment, via della Faggiola, where Bijoux Fiaschi continues jewelry production today. His laboratory and archives were destroyed in the flood, but he reprised one lovely necklace of 7 rows of pearls around a centerpiece of green and blue rhinestones in late 1966. His success with the ready-to-wear boutiques emboldened him to create designs with modern materials like nickel-plated brass and plastic. His flying saucer necklace for Pucci in 1967, and other space-age metal ring necklaces with masses of chains dangling from them contributed to the new look in Europe. Bijoux Fiaschi won the Oscar del Bijoux in 1969, and gold medals were regularly bestowed upon Giancarlo by the industry. In the Seventies he returned to elaborate necklaces and earrings of gilded brass with crystal drops, or frosted glass paste and gold sunburst elements which suited his elegant clientele.

Fashion and costume jewelry in the Eternal City

The history of Rome, both ancient and modern, put a different spin on Italy's fashion and jewelry. Milan had strong commercial ties with boutiques and department stores in Paris, London, Berlin, and New York. Florence challenged her fashion rivals among the French couturiers. Venice provided the world's designers with mass-production glass beads. But Rome was more aloof and elegant; the city where Europe's aristocracy had settled or vacationed for centuries. There were old ruins, old families, and old money. Bulgari was and is their favorite jeweler for precious stones set in gold. Luciana di Roma was the alternative source for costume jewelry.

Luciana Aloisi (1906-) the aristocratic designer for the aristocracy, was born in Rome, educated in London, and studied art in Florence, where she "fell madly in love with a Baltic Russian Baron." They were married within a month, and moved to Paris where they lived for 15 years. Luciana's husband, Max de Reutern, was the director of Chanel and Paquin. She went yachting with Coco, and lived the elegant life of a *mannequin de ville*, who was given couture clothes to wear to social events as publicity for the house. Luciana was a correspondent for the Italian fashion magazine, *Bellezza*, in the Thirties. In postwar Rome, 1947, she began designing jewelry to divert women's thoughts from the grim war years, for Elizabeth Arden and Gucci. In 1951, for the first Italian fashion show in Florence, her chic, timeless jewelry was shown with Simonetta Visconti's clothes.

Interviewed recently in Rome, Luciana remembers: "In the Fifties, Italian Moda had the effect of a bomb on American fashions. It was all surprising and fun! All my jewelry was done by hand in my workshop, which enabled me to design large but very light pieces. As for Schiaparelli, she was delighted and ordered madly for her boutique. I never designed for her couture, specifically, but Luciana pieces were sold at Schiaparelli on the Place Vendôme." In the late 60's Luciana designed flexible "fish scale" brushed metal bracelets and necklaces with metal fringes for Ken Scott in Milan.

When everyone else was wearing bright gold metal jewelry, Luciana developed a satiny matt surface on her gilded brass pieces, which made the others look garish. The textured look was dubbed "Florentine", because it was first shown with the Italian Alta Moda in Florence, then widely copied by other jewelers in America where the Italian look was so popular. "Noone else was doing this brushed

finish at the time. Each piece had to be striated or *satiné* by hand," Luciana recalls.

Luciana's shop on the via della Vita was frequented by the international jet set (Jackie Kennedy among them) who appreciated her seamless, elegant style. Ignoring current fashion trends, her inspiration was rooted in extensive research in Etruscan and Roman art history. "When you live in Rome, you become accustomed to being part of the centuries. One is practically on top of the other, as anyone discovers who decides to dig a well."[7] Her layering of expertise resulted in a supple design of matt gilded brass elements superimposed like the overlapping of terracotta tiles on Mediterranean roofs. Each piece was individually hand-wrought, the sections curving into a smoothly flexible unit. Bracelets and necklaces were encrusted with colored glass stones.

Luciana sold her jewelry to the Parisian couturiers Dior, and Cardin, as well as to the finest department stores: Harrod's in London; and Bergdorf Goodman and Bonwit Teller in New York. "I even designed collections for Cartier, N.Y. in 18kt. gold, but they were stolen twice, so I stopped." Her fame as an art historian brought Luciana the assignment of creating all of Elizabeth Taylor's personal jewelry for *Cleopatra* in 1963. "I firmly think nothing ever should be copied", Luciana declares. "An idea can be taken from a horse's stirrup, for instance, but most antiques jewelers were so repetitious." Now, "a jolly 88 years of age", she has taken up painting again in Rome.

Roberto Capucci, born in Rome in 1930, was not represented at Giorgini's fashion show in 1951, but showed independently to American buyers. In 1953 he joined the designers at the Palazzo Pitti, to become known as the "clothing sculptor". Two years later he had his atelier on the via Gregoriana in Rome. Capucci was one of the many Italian designers who showed his clothes with Coppola e Toppo accessories.

The Sorelle Fontana sisters, Zoe, Nicol, and Giovanna (born 1911, 1913, and 1915 respectively) opened their first atelier in Rome in 1943. They were included in the first Florence fashion show in 1951, and got into the cinema loop by designing clothes for Ava Gardner as the unforgettable *Barefoot Contessa* in 1953. (Giuseppe Canesi designed her necklace of four wings of faux pearls and strass which complemented her Fontana strapless satin dress.) Jacqueline Kennedy wore a Fontana dress at her wedding. The Fontana sisters had their own jewelry line in the Sixties to create the Total Look adopted by all the couturiers by that time.

The Cinecittà film studio in Rome was a magnet for beautiful women in the *Dolce Vita* days of the Fifties and Sixties. Italian movie stars like Sophia Loren and Gina Lollobrigida may have worn sexy, off-the-shoulder torn peasant blouses in their films, but at night on the Via Veneto they were dripping with spectacular jewelry (duly captured by the *paparazzi*) which gave a great boost to the industry. Coppola e Toppo and Bijoux Fiaschi decorated their plunging necklines with "Made in Italy" creations. Elizabeth Taylor wore an asp belt and bracelets by Joseff of Hollywood in 1963, as *Cleopatra*, but Luciana was responsible for her elaborate earrings, pectoral collars and headresses. Guattari (who started out as a camera man) designed the costume jewelry for the other actors, and Lani e Rodo accessorized the extras in this film as well as many others produced in Italy.[8]

Nino Lembo and his wife, Eva Serrao, furnished costume jewelry and accessories for theater, television, and film productions from the Sixties to the present. Lembo created historical interpretations of jewelry for Luchino Visconti's films *Il Gattopardo* (*The Leopard*, 1963) and *Ludwig* (1973, the story of "mad King Ludwig

Matt Florentine gold metal cuffs set with faux turquoises and citrines, and a turquoise bib with matching earrings. A collar covered with ruby red cabochons, "topaz" and pearls, and a matt gold hair ornament with topaz and pearls, all worn by Contessa Luisa della Noce for Luciana's collections, 1961-63. She is holding a textured matt gold powder box in the shape of a tomato, also by Luciana di Roma. *Vintage photo courtesy of Contessa Luisa della Noce Collection, Rome, Italy*

Gilded brass flexible layered necklace set with "topaz" and "citrines" by Luciana for Ken Scott and her Rome boutique in the Sixties. *Courtesy of private collection, Milan, Italy*

of Bavaria") as well as *The Bible* (1966, starring Eva Gardner) and Pasolini's *Medea* (1969, starring Maria Callas). The name of the company was changed to L.A.B.A. (Lembo Antonio Bigiotteria Artistica) when Lembo died.

Jewelry and accessories were created by L.A.B.A. for Fellini's *Fred and Ginger* and *E la Nave Va* (*And the Ship Sails On*, 1984), Terry Gilliam's *Adventures of Baron Munchhausen*, and the *Age of Innocence* (1993, starring Michelle Pfeiffer, Daniel Day Lewis, and Winona Ryder). This film inspired the Romantic look, with *fin de siècle* black velvet dog collars and delicate Edwardian silver brooches dripping with articulated strass and pale amethyst drops which trembled on the bodice, cameo brooches, and rings worn on the index or middle fingers. We can look forward to seeing L.A.B.A jewelry in *Catherine The Great* and adorning Demi Moore in *The Scarlet Letter*. Like Joseff of Hollywood, L.A.B.A. rents out their commissioned pieces after the films' completion to other productions. Unlike Joseff of Hollywood, their jewelry is unsigned, though a photocopy of each piece rented bears the trademark "L.A.B.A., Serrao Eva-Roma" with a crown and scepter. The jewelry is not commercially available in boutiques, but costume jewelry copies inevitably follow in the wake of a film's release.

For the tourist trade in Italy, there was always a choice of glitz-free, typically Italian adornment. *Pietra dura*, a hard stone pattern constructed from inlaid sections of lapis, malachite, aventurine, and jasper has been a Florentine specialty for centuries. Portraits, flowers, and insects are popular subjects. *Intarsia* is mosaic work of glass inlaid to simulate the hard stones. These pieces are by unknown artists, and, as is the case with the micromosaics produced in Rome, the quality of 20th century workmanship is inferior to the earlier jewelry; quality being sacrificed to quantity and sloppy execution.

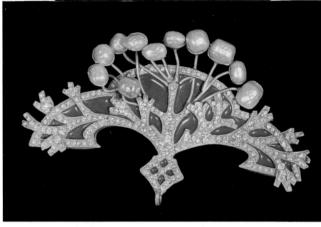

Two Art Nouveau blue enamel brooches, gold-plated, with faux pearls for the 1984 Fellini film *E la Nave Va* (*And the Ship Sails On*) created by L.A.B.A. *Courtesy of Gioielli L.A.B.A., Eva Serrao, Rome, Italy*

Two contemporary L.A.B.A. recreations of Edwardian brooches, rhodium-plated, set with pavé strass and pale amethyst articulated drops (*en pampilles*) for the Martin Scorsese film, *The Age of Innocence*, 1993. Worn by Michelle Pfeiffer. *Courtesy of L.A.B.A., Rome*

Precious coral necklaces: two red hand-faceted coral beads with carved coral cameo gold clasp (ca. 1900), and one of pale coral beads with crystal, 1920. *Courtesy of private collection, Los Angeles. Photo by Sandro Moro*

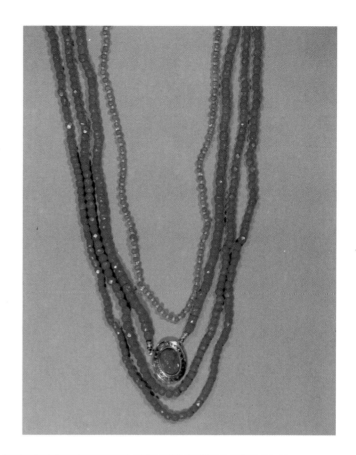

Precious coral, which grows on both sides of the wide Mediterranean, has long been a decorative Italian item. South of Naples, in Torre del Greco, there is a unique school specialized in cutting and carving coral and shell cameos. Workshops have been in Torre since the 18th century developing the world monopoly of the craft which presently employs 5000 workers (often several generations of one family toil together in the ancient Italian tradition). An apprentice must work five years to master his art. Up until the Thirties, coral beads were still hand-faceted, and coral cameos were carved to be set in gold brooches or clasps. Cameos were also carved from male helmet shells which were thick enough to carve through the layers, leaving a sharp profile in relief. The cameos can be dated from the profiles, which were Neo-classical Greek busts with long tresses in 1900. As the century progressed, both the hair-style and the nose became shorter, as Aphrodite was replaced by Grace Kelly as the ideal beauty. Contemporary cameos range in price from $50 to $400, with elaborate ones fetching as much as $3000.[9]

Hardstone cameos were usually carved in Idar-Oberstein, the gem-cutting center of Germany (this is now being done ultra-sonically). In the Twenties there was competition from Gablonz, Bohemia, which produced moulded glass cameos, followed by plastic imitations for tourism or export. As with the micromosaics, and *pietra dura*, the quality deteriorated with mass-production.

The mutual appreciation and similarity of Italian and Californian resort life-styles brought palazzo pyjamas and Capri pants to Palm Springs and Malibu (the latter launched by Audrey Hepburn in *Sabrina*, 1954). Novelty jewelry was crafted on both sides of the Atlantic from natural materials with coral branches crocheted into bibs with gilded leaves, and earrings made of woven raffia were set with glass stones. These looked smashing with the black turtleneck sweaters in vogue at the time. Once the fashion magazines had convinced their readers that costume jewelry should not be imitation Cartier, but a liberating alternative to the real thing, there was no stopping the Italian imagination.

1. Maria Pezzi, "Il Falsi Raffinati della Fantasia," *Il Giorno*, Milan, December, 1963.
2. Chiara Padovano, "Venice," *Jewels of Fantasy*, New York, Harry N. Abrams, 1992, pg. 298.
3. Peter Francis. Jr., *Beads of the World*, Atglen, PA. Schiffer Publishing Ltd., pg. 68.
4. *Ibid.*, pg.56
5. John and Ruth Picard, *Chevron and Nueva Cadiz Beads, Beads from the West African Trade*, volume VII. Carmel, CA., Picard African Imports, 1993.
6. Nicoletta Bocca, *Jewels of Fantasy*, pg. 303.
7. *Washington Star News*, clipping in Luciana's archives, n.d.
8. Nicoletta Bocca, *op.cit.*, pg.293.
9. Anna Miller, *Cameos-Old and New*, New York, Van Nostrand Rheinhold, 1991, pg. 84.

Hand-crocheted gold yarn bib hung with gilded metal leaves and real coral bits in the late 1940s style using natural materials which were popular in Italy and California. *Courtesy of the author. Photo by Sandro Moro*

DE
TOEGEPASTE KUNSTEN
IN NEDERLAND

EEN REEKS MONOGRAFIEËN
OVER HEDENDAAGSCHE
SIER- EN NIJVERHEIDSKUNST

SIERADEN

DOOR JKvr Dr. C.H. de JONGE

MET 87 AFBEELDINGEN

UITGEGEVEN BIJ
W.L. & J. BRUSSE'S
UITGEVERS MIJ
TE ROTTERDAM

Chapter 8:

The Netherlands

Amsterdam School

Jewelry in Holland in 1900-1914 was a Dutch take on the English Arts and Crafts movement. The scale was small (discretion was the better part of design) and the stones were modest. This may have had something to do with the rigorous morality of the Calvinistic Dutch character. The principal foreign influence, however, was not Celtic or Japanese, as with the English, but Indonesian. The Dutch East Indies exported exotic spices and Javanese batiks to Holland, which had a strong influence on its cuisine, textiles, book-binding, ceramics, carpets, jewelry, and architecture.

The Amsterdam School (1918-1940) jewelry was crafted in hammered copper or silver settings, (the hammer marks were either authentic or stamped), turquoise, moonstone, coral, or carnelian. The Dutch did not adopt the flamboyant Art Nouveau of their Belgian neighbors to the south. Their style was more akin to the disciplined, angular Jugendstil of the Germans.

Bert Nienhuis (1873-1960) began as a ceramicist (one of the dominant crafts in Holland). From 1905-1912 he designed jewelry for Hoeker Silversmiths in Amsterdam. He was especially adept at enamel techniques in geometric abstractions. He took his forms from nature.

Frans Zwollo Sr. (1872-1945) pioneered a break with tradition. He studied metalwork in Brussels, Haarlem, and Hagen, Germany. His talents were diverse in copper and silver in the applied arts. His silver open-work brooches of 1912 had a harmony of movement, gracefully incorporating the turquoise stones with a sculptural sweep.

Zwollo's son, Frans Jr. (1896-) studied Arts and Crafts techniques in London, and brought the intense blue and mauve enamels back with him to Holland for his brooches and pendants. He worked with his father in *champlevé* and *cloisonné* designs in the Twenties.

Jan Eisenloeffel (1876-1957) was deeply involved in the applied arts, producing coffee and tea sets in silver, and brass lamps. He studied *niello* enamelling in St. Petersburg and Moscow, applying his expertise to boxes and jewelry in square and rectangular elements. His later designs in the Twenties were like Moorish mosaics, with complex enamel linear rhythmns constructed around a central cabochon. He fought against the excesses of turn of the century furniture in his interior designs, and was just as innovative with his jewelry and belt buckles.

An enamel brooch by Zwollo Sr. and Jr., 1920. From *De Toegepaste Kunsten in Nederland: Sieraden*; by Dr. de Jonge, 1924. *Courtesy of Willemijn Betrams Collection, Amsterdam*

Enamelled buckles and brooches showing Moorish influence by Jan Eisenloeffel, 1923-4. From *Sieraden*, op.cit.
Opposite
The Applied Arts in the Netherlands, "Jewelry," by Dr. C.H. de Jonge with 87 illustrations. Rotterdam, W.L. & G. Brusse's Uitgenersmaatschaffs 1924 (with monographs of each artist). *Courtesy of Willemijn Bertrams, Amsterdam*

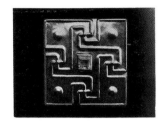

A silver belt buckle and two silver brooches with chalcedony and citrine, by J.L.M. Lauwericks, 1914. From *Sieraden*, op.cit.

J.L.M. Lauweriks (1864-1932) shared an architectural atelier with De Bazel, where they collaborated on interior design. In 1904-1916 he taught at the Kuntsgewerbeschule in Düsseldorf. From Germany, he adopted the geometric compositions of the Darmstadt School for his silver belt buckles and brooches. He was a fine graphic artist, designing posters and one stunning cover for *Wendingen*, the principal design source magazine in Europe (1918-1931). He taught a course in Theosophy, the trendy philosophy which directed the "awakened spiritual eye" towards designing by mathematical systems and an awareness of the beauty of the cosmos. This course was attended by the avant-garde artists in Amsterdam who formed the Amsterdam School, and was the spiritual motor behind the movement.

Jac.A. Jacobs (1885-1968) used hammered silver mixed with smooth surfaces for his belt buckles and pins. His smooth plastic forms were larger in size than other contemporary designs, but were still refined and elegant. Shape was essential to his vision.

Cor Vos from Utrecht, studied with Jacobs, but went off on an independent tack, working in naturalistic forms. Shells, fish and other sea-life were worked in a rough surface, looking like silver fragments that washed up on the beach. His technical skill was so great, that he might have been a successful sculptor.

Jan Kriege (1884-1944) was a self made man. His technical skill at chasing and embossing was evident in tin, silver, and copper trays, and vases. In 1923, he devised scalloped silver brooches and bracelets and a hairband around moonstones and agate, probably spontaneously conceived at the jeweler's bench without benefit of a sketch.

Chris Agterberg (1883-1948) modelled kneeling or seated women (some in Indonesian costumes) holding amethyst, opal or moonstone cabochons for his Twenties silver pendants and pins. By 1930 his candelabra and tea services were very streamlined and Moderne.

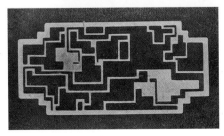

A hammered silver pendant with opal, and silver brooches with agate, and niello enamel brooch by Jac. A. Jacobs, 1924. From *Sieraden*, op.cit.

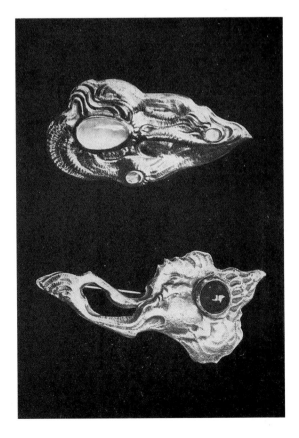

Sculptural brooches in silver with moonstone and agate by Cor Vos, 1923. From *Sieraden*, op.cit

Silver pendants, brooch, hairband, and bracelet with opal, moonstone, and agate by Jan Kriege, 1924. From *Sieradem*, op.cit.

Stylized figural brooches in silver with amethysts and opals, by Chris Agterberg, 1924. From *Sieraden*, op.cit.

Roelf Gerbrands (1891-1953) was moved by a different spirit. His hammered round brooches in tomback copper, were highly decorated with overall embossing in muted brown hues. Occasionally he would add an opal to reflect the light, but the overall effect was of discreet bas-relief.

Jan Toorop (1858-1928) a Symbolist artist, was born in Java. His paintings incorporated Indonesian gestures and motifs into Art Nouveau painting. He shared a missionary idealism with other Mannerists who were bent on improving Man's way of life. The heavy-lidded, melancholy women that he painted, 1890-1900, were usually in a trance. (The science of dream-interpretation was developing at the time.) Toorop's posters and graphic designs became increasingly abstract, until he abandoned his decadent style, to become a devout Catholic in 1905. He embraced a different symbol; the cross, which he made in red and blue enamel in 1920.

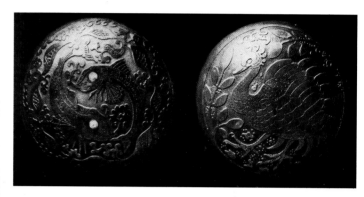

Two embossed tomback brooches by Roelf Gerbrands, Haarlem, 1922. From *Sieraden*, op.cit.

An enamelled red and blue cross by Jan Toorop, 1920. From *Sieraden*, op. cit.

An Art Deco earring, French style, in onyx and enamel, 1920, by J. Steltman. From *Sieraden*, op. cit. All above black and white photos from *De Toegepaste Kunsten in Nederland: Sieraden*, 1924 (Applied Arts in the Netherlands: Jewelry). *Photos by Robert Weldon*

Johannes Steltman (1891-1961) was a silver and goldsmith who trained in Hanau, Germany in 1910, opening his own shop in Den Haag in 1917. The Hague was, and still is, a cosmopolitan city, where diplomats attached to the foreign embassies reside. (Scheveningen, the seaside suburb, was the fashionable meeting place on the North Sea.) Steltman's Art Deco designs, with a strong French flavor, were destined for this clientele. One year after the discovery of King Tut's tomb, his brooches bore Egyptian lotus leaves. Long pendant earrings in onyx and enamel were typical of his elegant designs.[1]

Of Fons Reggers, Conrad Fehn, and J. Peters, very little is known. This is unfortunate, because they designed some of the most interesting pieces of the Twenties and Thirties. Frans Leidelmeijer, whose book, *Art Nouveau en Art Deco in Nederland* is a fine source for this period, reports that Reggers was one of two brothers working in Amsterdam (their benchmark is RR 4) from 1923 to 1934. His masterful merging of coral or moonstone in organic brooches was complemented by carefully orchestrated hammer marks.

Organic silver shapes by Fons Reggers (top and bottom left), and Conrad Fehn (right), 1920s. *Courtesy of Frans Leidelmeijer Gallery, Amsterdam. Photo by Eric Hesmerg*

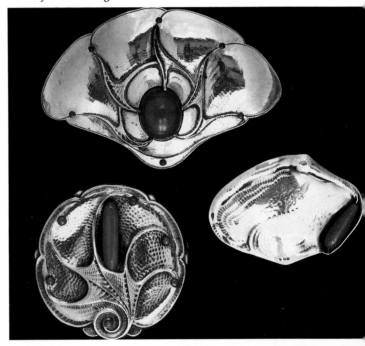

A large machine-hammered silver brooch with amazonite, signed "JJ" (Jacobs?), 1920s. *Courtesy of Gail Gerretsen collection. Photo by Robert Weldon, courtesy of the G.I.A., Santa Monica*

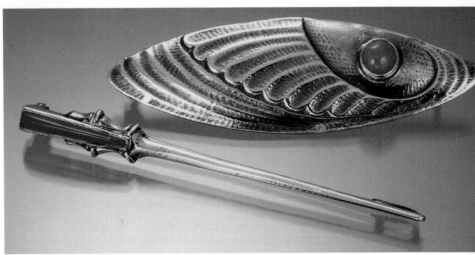

A bar pin by Fons Reggers, silver with coral, and the benchmark RR 4, and a silver shell pin with coral, 1920's. *Courtesy of the author. Photo by Robert Weldon, courtesy of the Gemological Institute of America, Santa Monica, Ca.*

Silver sea shell brooches with coral and moonstones with hammered and chased surfaces defining the shells, by Fons Reggers, 1920s. *Courtesy of the Frans Leidelmeijer Gallery, Amsterdam*

Conrad Fehn worked in Haarlem in the Twenties, specializing in hammered copper objets and silver jewelry. J. Petersen eschewed the oval shapes of his compatriots and embraced an angular Art Deco approach, which was uncommon in Holland. His command of the geometric style remained, however, quintessentially Dutch.

The years following WW II were a fallow period in Holland for jewelry. In the Fifties, the traditional Dutch restraint regarding personal adornment was not conducive to innovative ideas. Gold and diamonds in a safe setting were as conservative as the art in the galleries.

The Sixties in Western Europe, like America, was a time of ferment; there was political reassessment and social reflection. The middle-aged were prospering, but the young were impatient and rebellious. The strict rules of conduct of the Fifties Establishment were intolerable, so in Holland the Provo youth movement protested against the royal family, the church, their elders and the status quo. This upheaval of new ideas was expressed in the Arts, and spread to the technical schools, galleries, and theaters. Silversmiths and goldsmiths welcomed the break with tradition, and two schools of creative thought emerged. One rejected the use of gold, silver, and precious stones as capitalistic status symbols, enthusiastically experimenting with aluminum, plastics, wood, and geometric forms. The other school remained loyal to precious metals, but espoused a liberated approach towards design. The first found the second group bourgeois, and the latter accused the constructivists of being too intellectual and restrictive.

Anneke Schat, who chose the precious metal route, said in a recent interview in Amsterdam, "By the late Sixties and early Seventies, teachers in the art schools who taught gold and silver techniques were slowly eased out of their positions, and students were discouraged from finishing their projects if they weren't composed of wood, paper, or base metals. Art shows were closed to them. The Socialist atmosphere was intolerant of any views but   its own." Undaunted, Anneke, following her five years at the Gerrit Rietveld Academy in Amsterdam, opened her own workshop in 1964. The gold and silver metals may have been traditional, but her designs

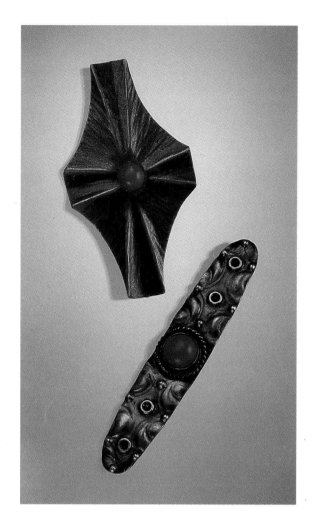

Two copper brooches with faux coral cabochons. ca. 1930. These were made in large numbers to be sold very cheaply. *Courtesy of the author. Photo by Robert Weldon*

Five silver brooches with moonstone and coral in a personal Deco style by J. Peters. Twenties and Thirties. *Courtesy of Frans Leidelmeijer Gallery, Amsterdam. Photo by Co-Press Studio*

Silver pendant "Bamboo" by Anneke Schat, 1976. *Courtesy of Anneke Schat, Amsterdam. Photo by Thesi Geesink*

A sweep of silver; a ring called "The Wind" by Anneke Schat. *Courtesy of Anneke Schat, Amsterdam. Photo by Thesi Geesink*

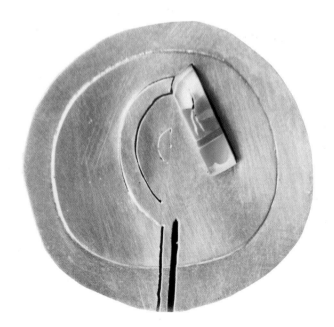

Silver and Perspex pin by Onno Boekhoudt, 1967. *Courtesy of Onno Boekhoudt, VM de Hoeve, Holland*

were not. Travels in the Balkans produced jewelry inspired by nature, and Anneke incorporated rough, uncut crystals in her designs until 1972.

Japanese calligraphy, which Anneke studied for ten years, became an important influence; the control, movement and balance necessary in the ink brushwork was applied to brooches, earrings and rings, one discipline enriching the other. A voyage to Japan stimulated further experiments. The "bamboo" brooch in 1976 is a three dimensional piece using matt and polished curved surfaces to balance the vertical bamboo.

Inspired by Miyamoto Musashi's *Book of Five Rings*, which is a seventeenth century Zen-based essay on personal strategy and Kendo self-discipline, Anneke created a ring portraying the essence of each chapter. The drawn circle (ring) is a Zen-Buddhist symbol.[2] In 1987, her series of five silver rings representing water, fire, earth, wind, and the void are a simplified design with oriental symbolism. The "wind" ring represents the vagaries of the wind, and the need to bend with it like bamboo so as not to break.

Onno Boekhoudt (1944-) worked primarily in silver, but used alternative materials as well. He trained at the Technical School in Schoonhoven (1963-66) and at the Staatliche Kunst und Werkschule in Pforzheim (1966-68), becoming adept at traditional techniques. The tiny scale of German contemporary jewelry was rejected by Boekhoudt, who wanted to feel free to experiment with form and Thinking Big. "In the Sixties, Amsterdam was a completely different story from Pforzheim, where many of us studied. There was no tradition of metalwork or goldsmithing in Holland. The interest was Design. When we used Perspex and steel, new and futuristic materials, it was never to shock. It was simply because we LOVED it!"

In 1967 and 1968, Boekhoudt designed round (but not perfectly round) silver brooches, 3" wide, with colored Perspex, and silver rings with Perspex drops taking the place of stones. His rectangular brooches of the early Seventies combined silver with steel, an unusual combination. He has had one-man shows at the Galerie RA and the Rijksmuseum in Amsterdam, and the Electrum Gallery in London, and participated in numerous international group shows from Italy to Australia. Since 1974 he has been teaching metalwork and silversmithing at the Gerrit Rietveld Akademie, the Royal College of Art in London, and the Rhode Island and Parsons Schools of Design, encouraging his students "to express themselves, and

Silver ring with a Perspex tear, 1968, by Onno Boekhoedt. *Courtesy of Onno Boekhoudt, Holland*

A revolutionary collar of aluminum by Emmy Van Leersum, on dress of Thai silk made to order, 1967. Shown in the Stedelijk Museum, Amsterdam. *Courtesy of Gijs Bakker, Amsterdam. Photo by Matthijs Schrofer*

An unusual combination of steel and silver in a pin by Onno Boekhoudt. *Courtesy of the artist*

use their skill and knowledge to create a form. That is the big thing in my life!" Boekhoudt has been turning out sets of objects and jewelry, ranging in materials from heavy lead alloys to the lighter and brighter silver.

Emmy Van Leersum (1930-1984) and her husband Gijs (pronounced Hayss) Bakker (1942-) were leaders in the movement away from traditional methods and shapes. Both artists studied at the College of Arts and Crafts (now the Rietveld Akademie) in Amsterdam, and the Konst Fack Skola in Stockholm in the early Sixties. In 1966 Emmy became Mrs. Bakker, and they opened a jewelry atelier in Utrecht. They worked with cool, grey metals like aluminum and stainless steel, and Acrylic, which did not carry the onus of status symbols for the wealthy. In the late Sixties, Van Leersum and Bakker constructed large, uncompromising, aluminumn collars, turned up or ruffled, which had to be worn with clothes that were made for them. These turned out to be limited-edition, hand-crafted pieces, though the original intention was

to launch an Industrial Look, available to the masses, as opposed to the "ladies who lunch". Bracelets (1966-1967) of point-welded stainless steel, aluminum, free-form Acrylic (Perspex) or wood were made in larger editions. Bakker had fun with a stovepipe, making a necklace and bracelet set out of his kitchen equipment.

In the Eighties, Bakker played with PVC plastic, laminating a photograph of an 18th century necklace as a satirical jab at bourgeois tastes, and calling it his "Pforzheim 1780" collar.

Other modern takes on the Elizabethan ruff were PVC laminated silk prints, and a delicate collar of hand-painted petals, called "Chrysantium". The most original piece was "Embrace", a laminated photo of a man with his arms around (your?) neck, which could be slipped over the head for a little portable "t.l.c.". In the Eighties, Bakker inserted one tiny diamond into his PVC creations, an audacious mix of the precious and the banal.

Bakker and his wife, Emmy, favored undecorated geometric shapes, aiming for a major impact with a minimum cost. Bakker

Collar of flexible nylon in two hues of red, blue, or yellow by Emmy Van Leersum, 1982. *Courtesy of Gijs Bakker. Photo by Jos Fielmich*

Photograph of an 18th century necklace, laminated in PVC, "Pforzheim 1780", by Gijs Bakker in 1985. *Courtesy of Gijs Bakker, Amsterdam. Photo by Jos Ruijssenaars*

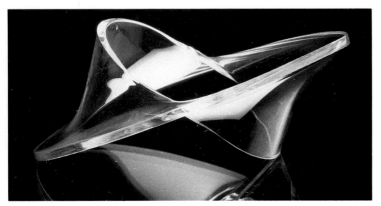

A freeform Acrylic (Perspex) bracelet by Gijs Bakker for the Sixties rebel, 1967, by Gijs Bakker. *Courtesy of Gijs Bakker, Amsterdam, Holland. Photo by Rien Bazen*

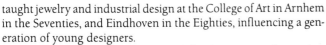

Painted petals captured in PVC by Gijs Bakker, "Chrysantium," 1985. *Courtesy of the artist. Photo by Jos Fielmich*

taught jewelry and industrial design at the College of Art in Arnhem in the Seventies, and Eindhoven in the Eighties, influencing a generation of young designers.

A commercial outlet was needed for the avant-garde jewelry, so Hans Appenzeller (1949-) who had studied at the Rietveld Academie, opened the first gallery for experimental jewelry in the Netherlands in 1969. In 1975 it closed. (The Galerie Ra opened a year later to fill the need.) Appenzeller constructed brass latticed bracelets in 1978 which Josef Hoffmann would have applauded. He experimented with new materials for about ten years, then abandoned the severe formality of the post-Sixties to return to precious metals. (He had a shop in New York City in the Eighties.) In 1985 Appenzeller's work was displayed at the Stedelijk Museum in an exhibit entitled "As Far As Amsterdam Goes".

Several talented Dutch women designers worked with alternative materials in the 1960s-'80s. Nel Linssen constructed her jewelry from folded strips of colored paper which were then linked to make pleated bracelets and necklaces. Lam de Wolf (1949-) created wearable art from textiles and wood, and Marion Herbst (1944-) played with paper mâché collars or necklaces of silver and Acrylic. What continues to distinguish "Dutch School" jewelers is an open mind to new ideas, while retaining their own strongly individual character.[3]

Two pairs of silver and marcasite Art Deco earrings: one with faux amethysts mounted upside down; the other, orange enamel and onyx, and a carnelian and onyx silver tie pin created with vintage parts by Jorge Cohen, 1990's, Amsterdam. *Courtesy of the author. Photo by Robert Weldon*

A pair of Art Deco silver earrings with marcasite trim, and pink and etched clear glass vintage stones by Jorge Cohen, 1990's, Amsterdam. *Courtesy of Jorge Cohen*

Jorge Alberto Cohen (1941-1993) turned a treasure trove of antique Art Deco moulded glass, Galalith, and enamel elements found in Paris into retro designs, seamlessly mounting the vintage pieces with modern silver, onyx, chrysoprase, paste, or marcasites. His workmanship was so fine, the jewelry is often mistaken for vintage in Paris and London antique shops. Jorge was born in Argentina, and studied painting at the Academy of Arts in Santa Fe (Argentina) exhibiting paintings in Buenos Aires galleries. In 1970, he turned his attention to jewelry design, fascinated by the Art Deco style. In 1976, he moved to Amsterdam, making his living by constructing tiny art object boxes which he sold to antiques shops. In 1982, he opened a shop on a 17th century canal, specializing in Art Deco-style jewelry. Jorge's silver earrings and pins bear the Dutch silver hallmark, the sword, as well as his "JAC" benchmark. He died suddenly in 1993, but his associate, Ilja de Bruin, will continue his work, using designs and materials that he left her.

1. Door JKVR. Dr C.H. de Jonge, *De Toegepaste Kunsten in Nederland, Sieraden*, Rotterdam, The Netherlands., W.L & J. Brusse's Uitgeversmaatschaap, 1924. The source for the biographical information on the above "Amsterdam School" artists, pp. 3-21.
2. Monique Mokveld, *Anneka Schat, Edelsmeedkunst- Modern Jewelry*, Amsterdam, Ploegsma, 1987, pg. 89.
3. Evert Roderigo, *Dutch Jewellery, 1967-1987*, Amsterdam, Rijksdienst Beeldende Kunst, 1987, pp. 7-23.

Geometric design silver bracelet and earrings with green and black onyx, 1990's by Jorge Cohen. *Courtesy of Jorge Cohen*

Chapter 9

Belgium

Of Two Minds

Belgium is a country of two cultures living in relative harmony: the French-speaking Walloons of the south; and the Flemish (whose language Rubens and Breughel spoke) in the north. This ethnic structure, combined with their geographic location, has infused Belgian decorative arts with an intriguing Latin sensuality and an Anglo-Saxon discipline.

Belgium was the cradle of the Art Nouveau movement, and together with France, created its quintessential best. The flamboyant curves of Victor Horta's architecture existed side by side with the more measured abstractions of organic themes created by the protean Henry van de Velde (1863-1957) who was a member of the avant-garde artists' group, *Societé Les Vingt*. Van de Velde was an important link betweeen the English Arts & Crafts movement across the Channel, the French Symbolists, the German Jugendstil, and the Wiener Werkstätte. (His genius flowered in Germany, where he spent most of his productive years.) He embodied the best of many styles; a distillation which brought a rare harmony to his architecture, furniture, and applied arts. The limited production of Van de Velde's jewelry made in his Ixelles workshop in 1900 were of gold and semi-precious stones, and his dramatically swooping belt buckles were oxidized silver curves;[1] all very different from the work of Belgium's answer to Lalique, Philippe Wolfers (1858-1929) who made extravagant, bizarre pieces with precious stones and diamonds set in gold.

Unlike Germany, England, and Austria, where architects were also sculptors and jewelers, the Belgians (apart from Van de Velde) were specialized in one field. Unknown jewelers designed Art Nouveau buttons, hatpins, and belt buckles in non-precious metals and Bohemian glass, but the dog collars and pendants worn by the affluent Bourgeoisie were gold and *plique-à-jour* enamel.

Ivory was used extensively by all artists in *fin de siècle* Brussels, as large shipments of elephant tusks were imported from the

Art Nouveau buckle of cast white metal with a large faux sapphire center stone, turquoises and strass, 1900. *Courtesy of the author. Photo by Robert Weldon*
Opposite
"Primevere" poster, 1926, by René Magritte. The Belgian Surrealist designed fashion posters in the early Twenties to support himself and his new young wife, before a complete change of style when he joined the Surrealists in Paris. *Courtesy of Pat Kery Fine Arts, NY, and Wolfgang Ketterer, Munich, from Art Deco Graphics, reprinted Courtesy of Harry N. Abrams, 1986.*

A hand-carved cuff from Belgian Congo ivory in the shape of an African bust for the International Colonial Exposition in Paris, 1931. *Courtesy of the author.* Black Bakelite grotesque Oriental pin, *Courtesy of Joanne McPherson. Photo by Robert Weldon*

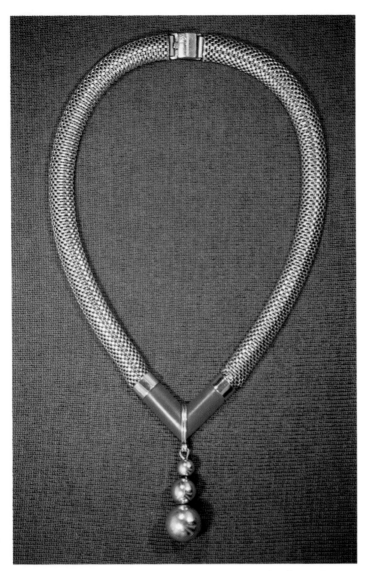

A nickel-plated mesh and coral Bakelite necklace, with a three sphere pendant, Thirties. *Courtesy of Arts 220, Winnetka, IL. Photo by Sandro Moro*

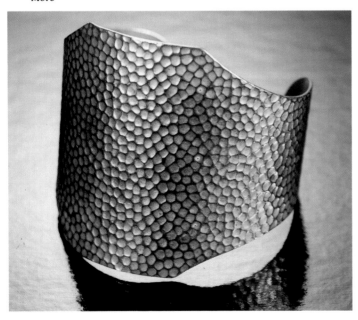

Hand-hammered nickel-plated cuff, ca. Thirties. *Courtesy of private collection, Los Angeles. Photo by Robert Weldon*

An Art Deco necklace of chrome links and peach glass links, with matching moulded peach glass link bracelet. *Courtesy of the author. Photo by Robert Weldon*

Belgian Congo. King Léopold II encouraged craftsmen and sculptors to work with the colonial ivory,[2] and proudly displayed the statues, decorative objets, and carved ivory jewelry at the International Exhibitions in Brussels (1885) and Paris. (No thought was given to the decimation of the elephant population.) An unknown artist carved an solid ivory cuff in the shape of a Negro head in profile for one of the Thirties Expos in Paris. Exotic woods imported from Africa were another product from the Congo which was promoted by the King, and utilized by furniture designers, sculptors, and jewelers in Belgium, France, and Germany.

Antwerp, in the north of Belgium, is a major diamond cutting center, so gold and platinum have always been favored over silver and the base metals for precious stone settings by Belgium's numerous, highly trained goldsmiths. Costume jewelry design was not regarded as a "serious" enterprise.

In 1905, work was begun on the extraordinary Palais Stoclet, a "total artwork" residence created by the Wiener Werkstätte in Brussels. It was commissioned by the Belgian industrialist, Adolf Stoclet, who had admired Josef Hoffmann's work in Vienna. Every detail harmonized with the whole, down to the doorknobs and silverware. Hoffmann insisted that even the clothes worn in his interiors should match the decor (and the jewelry had better follow suit!). Since Gustav Klimt designed the sumptuous friezes in the dining room, using real gold and jewels in the mosaics, Mme. Stoclet might have presided over dinner wearing the silver-gilt embossed cuff with mother of pearl designed by Georg Klimt, the painter's brother.

Costume jewelry enjoyed a brief spurt of popularity. Art Nouveau belt buckles of cast antiqued white metals were set with strass and large Bohemian glass stones. Belgium's taste in Art Deco jewelry was a synthesis of French and German styles. A nickel-plated mesh rope was combined with bakelite and three spheres. Chrome links with flesh-colored *pâte de verre* glass links moulded to match were a typical Deco necklace and bracelet set. A Machine Age necklace of hollow chrome tubing and a hinged spiral pendant, and a wraparound chrome bracelet with a decorative ball are reminiscent of Naum Slutzky and the Bauhaus influence. A hammered metal bracelet needed no stones for effect, since the Belgian aesthetic is characterized by restraint.

Marcel Wolfers (1886-1976) who succeeded his father, Philippe, in 1929, as head of the prestigious fine jewelry firm, Wolfers Frères (with his brother, Lucien) was a sculptor and lacquerer. He made bangle bracelets of exotic African wood which were lacquered and inlaid with eggshell (in the style of Jean Dunand). Most were lacquered a rich dark brown on the inside. This fashionable color was called *tête de nègre* (negro's head) and replaced the black and white color scheme for a time, coinciding with the Colonial Expos. (Jean Patou's 1931 collection was entirely designed around this newly popular color.) Wolfers set his bangles with coral cabochons in eggshell lacquer. These were signed in gilt MARCEL/WOLFERS in the late Twenties, early Thirties.

There was a small production of unsigned costume jewelry in Belgium with *pierres du Rhin* rhinestones imitating the real thing, but since quantities of jewelry were imported from France, it is almost impossible to establish a provenance. (The patent mark "déposé" was used in French-speaking Belgium as well as in France.) Belgian women in the Fifties and Sixties wore *bijoux de couture* signed by Christian Dior, Balenciaga, or Pierre Balmain, if they could be lured away from their gold heirlooms.

Chrome-plated hollow tube necklace with ball pendant, and chrome wraparound cuff with chrome ball. Thirties. *Courtesy of the author. Photo by Robert Weldon*

Wooden bracelet set with six coral cabochons in an eggshell lacquer ground. The interior is dark brown *tête de nègre* lacquer. Signed in gilt, "MARCEL/WOLFERS", ca. 1929. Béla Voros carved the Belgian Congo ivory bracelet in shallow relief with two abstract female heads in 1931 to celebrate the Paris Exposition Coloniale, signed "VB". *Courtesy of Sotheby's, New York. Important 20th Century Decorative Arts, Nov. 1987*

One creative Fifties aberration developing out of the French poodle skirt fad was a life-like poodle purse entirely embroidered with black or white glass beads (standard and toy sizes.) These were designed and hand-made by Walborg, whose imagination soared out of the prevailing conventional Belgian mode. Whatever they cost at the time, it could not have been the $800, and $1800 they fetched at a 1994 collectible auction in New York. (Not since the quirky stuffed animals of Dagobert Peche in Vienna, had such delightful creatures been seen.) French poodle jewelry was enormously popular in America and France, but these handbags may have been the only canine accessories available in Belgium in the Fifties.

In the Seventies and Eighties, Belgians remained conservative in their tastes and faithful to fine jewelery, though exceptions were made for the occasional authentic Art Deco pieces which showed up in antiques shops. An extraordinary collection of American "Retro" jewelry in a boutique in the Place du Grand Sablon was appreciated mostly by foreign collectors.

1. Vivienne Becker, *Art Nouveau Jewelry*. New York, E.P. Dutton, 1985, pg. 197.
2. Annelies Krekel-Aalberse, *Art Nouveau and Art Deco Silver*, New York, NY. Harry Abrams, Inc., 1989, pg. 95.

Two delightful French poodle purses made in Belgium (standard and toy sizes). They are entirely embroidered with black or white pearlescent beads, complete with embroidered features, gold collars, leashes, and fluffy tails, but no ears. Both with label: "Made in Belgium by hand, Walborg." A pure Fifties fantasy. *Courtesy of WM. Doyle Galleries, New York. "Couture, Antique Clothing, Accessories & Costume Jewelry", April 27, 1994*

PART II

SCANDINAVIA *AND* FINLAND

Preface

The major sources of jewelry design for the Scandinavians were Norse and Crusader legends. The Finns merged the Viking motifs with the Eastern Baltic culture from which they sprang. European art movements had little impact on these lands separated by the Baltic Sea and Gulf of Finland from the Continent. Art Nouveau hardly made a ripple, but the Art Deco geometric influence could be seen in the work of Swedish designers Wiwen Nilsson and Sigurd Persson. There was no fashion jewelry *per se* in Scandinavia, although in the Fifties and Sixties jewelry was specifically designed for exhibitions in department stores in Stockholm and Helsinki. Avant-garde art galleries in the capital cities held regular exhibitions, and the national museums and crafts societies of each country actively supported the artists by purchasing, as well as exhibiting, their work. The prestigious Lunning Prize, established by Frederick Lunning (director of Georg Jensen in New York) was awarded to two outstanding young industrial or jewelry designers from Scandinavia or Finland each year between 1951 and 1970, facilitating further study in foreign lands.

The material of choice was silver in Scandinavia, although the best trained jewelers also worked in gold, cast bronze or oxidyzed metal. Porcelain was popular in Denmark and painted wood in Finland was made into colorful jewelry. Quartz, jasper, and spectrolite stones native to the area were widely used; rhinestones were never in the Scandinavian taste, but Acrylics were welcomed in the Sixties. Silver manufacturers produced the work of both the independent and in-house designers for the prosperous middle class in Denmark. Bronze replicas of ancient folk jewelry were worn in the country with the local costumes and are still being produced and worn in Norway and Finland today.

Since the apprentice system is especially strong in the Nordic countries, the various trade schools and workshops that the artists attended are important steps in their development. Most of the artists were also artisans who conceived and executed their own jewelry, and those who were not worked closely with artisans in their designs. The Fifties and Sixties were a time of exhuberant originality in Scandinavian and Finnish industrial and jewelry design which was displayed in international craft fairs fuelling a renaissance in the applied arts. Professional metal-working in general suffered in the Seventies, replaced by industrial design and amateur handicrafts. This was rectified in the Eighties by a revival in metal workshops, with the challenging courses offered in trade schools for the new generation and the opening of the Museum of Applied Arts in Finland to display the work of the older established artists. Silver was combined with alternative materials and once again experimentation was encouraged.

The Viking dragon ships carried the Norse Warriors to the forefront of European history in the 9th century. *Courtesy of The Consulate General of Sweden, Los Angeles. Painting of ships and runic inscriptions by Sven Olaf Ehrén from "Vikingar pa Frimarken" cover.*

Danish cover with unusual (from Denmark) Art Deco design by Sven
Brasch, poster artist, of *Tik Tak* magazine, 1926. *Courtesy of Pat Kery
Fine Art, NY, from Art Deco Graphics, reprinted Courtesy of Harry N.
Abrams, 1986.*

Chapter 10:

Denmark

The Danish Silver Adventure

The Danish telescoped version of what we know as the Arts and Crafts and Art Nouveau movements was called *skønvirke*, meaning aesthetic endeavours. During this creative period 1900-1925, many artists were equally at home in sculpture, graphics, architecture, or jewelry design. The founders of the Museum of Decorative Art supported the Danish artists with purchases and exhibitions, and arranged exhibitions of foreign artists like René Lalique and Charles Ashbee. The work of these fine artists was admired, but never slavishly emulated. *Skønvirke* in Denmark had a style of its own, despite the French and British influences, as well as the extensive training received at German trade schools. There was a desire to make more popular things, but at the same time jewelry that was artistically pleasing and well made, and able to reach a larger public. *Skønvirke* was a working combination of British social commitment and the Danish roots in industry and craftsmanship.[1]

Where the Norwegians used enamel, the Danes preferred semi-precious stones or decorative porcelain plaques. For the Royal Copenhagen Porcelain Manufactory, porcelain elements were modelled and mounted up as hatpins by Anna Pedersen, and belt buckles by sculptor Christian Thomsen in 1900. At both the 1900 and 1925 Paris Expos, Danish porcelain won prizes, which encouraged porcelain exports.

The workshops founded in 1900 by Mogens Ballin, Evald Nielsen, and Georg Jensen provided the craftsmen and women with an outlet for their new ideas. A major source of inspiration was Japanese art and *tsuba* sword handles, not French Art Nouveau. As in Holland and England, Danish craftsmanship progressed from a preference for a smooth silver surface to the handcrafted hammered look, then to the inevitable machine-stamped or press-molded faux hammer marks which minimized serial-production costs. These were of commercial not aesthetic value. Silver and jewelry manufacturers like A.Dragsted, A. Michelsen, and Bernhard Hertz (which

Porcelain hatpin modelled in the shape of a dragonfly, and underglaze painted by Anna Pedersen in 1900 for the Royal Copenhagen Porcelain Manufactory, Copenhagen. Photo from *Porzellanschmuck* by Graham Dry. *Courtesy of Graham Dry and the Thiemig Verlag, Munich, Germany*

Two splendid *skønvirke* silver brooches. Top left: silver and lapis signed "E.V." for Evald Nielsen, 826S. Lower right brooch with green onyx is stamped "D.A." for Dansk Arbejde. *Courtesy of Ilene Chazanoff, New York City. Photo by Richard Marx*

Signatures on verso of owl pin showing the D.A. stamp with the hammer within the shield for *Dansk Arbejde*, or Danish Handicraft. *Photo by Robert Weldon*

Four silver pins showing the range of the *skønvirke* period. Top left: the dove pin, (original design by Møhl-Hansen in 1904), had many different variations. This one from 1915 is still in production, and bears the early "GJ" Jensen mark. *Courtesy of Christie Romero.* Top right: brooch with foliage and grapes design is signed "A.C.P" (not officially registered), with the silver mark 826 S. The wise old owl with chrysoprase eyes is stamped "H.P.K." for H.P. Kreiberg, Nykøbing F. (officially registered from 1893-1967) and the *Dansk Arbejde* "D.A." stamp. The Art Nouveau brooch on the bottom bears the two towers stamp for silver plate, and illegible makers initials. The stones are real and faux amber. *Courtesy of the author. Photo by Christie Romero*

began as workshops) produced the jewelry designed by independant artists as well as in-house jewelers, providing the necessary supportive continuity and exports to mass markets in Sweden, Norway, and Europe.

An important point in establishing provenance in Scandinavia should be noted. In 1908, an association of artists who promoted Danish Trade stamped their work with "D.A." for "Dansk Arbejde" (or Danish Handicraft) within a shield with a hammer separating the initials. This stamp was used until 1940. There has been some confusion on this point with the Norwegian silver marked "D-A" for David-Andersen, even though the silver stamp indicates another Scandinavian country.

Denmark's neutral status during World War I was an economically profitable decision. The Danes exported quantities of canned goulash to the Germans with one hand, and with the other provided the British with goods imported from America. By the end of the war, the sale of the Danish colonies in the West Indies to the U.S. made Denmark one of the few prosperous countries in wartorn Europe. Numerous talented artists tapped into this positive energy to animate the decorative arts, and there was an abundant supply of customers to purchase their wares. Jewelry was exhibited at the national and international expos and was eagerly acquired by the prosperous middle-class to be worn in the many restaurants and theaters, and in the lively Tivoli Gardens in Copenhagen.

In Scandinavia and most Northern European countries, the apprentice system is regulated by law. In Denmark, to be a skilled silversmith or goldsmith one must study four years, including five school periods of 45 weeks together. The rest of the apprentice period is spent in a workshop where an education contract must be established between the apprentice and the atelier. Those who pass the two year practical exam are journeymen. The apprentice payment starts at $8 an hour. The course of a young jeweler's career can be shaped by the workshop he chooses for study.

When the subject of Danish silver comes up, the first name mentioned is usually Georg Jensen. That company has dominated

This sculptural brooch by Georg Jensen displays his sensually organic style of 1905. Green agate cabochons surrounded by the acanthus foliage are balanced by four amber pendants. *Courtesy of Kunstindustrimuseet, Copenhagen*

the XXth century silver jewelry and holloware market in Denmark and worldwide. Jensen (1866-1935) was apprenticed at 14 to a goldsmith in Copenhagen, followed by several years in a technical school. He put all this training on the back burner for 12 years while he earnestly studied sculpture and ceramics. Unable to earn a good living at either, he hired on as a journeyman with the Mogens Ballin workshop in 1901. By 1904 he had decided to sculpt in silver, so he opened his own workshop, and successfully exhibited jewelry in Copenhagen and Germany. Soon he was exporting to London and Paris. The gold medal at the Brussels Expo in 1910 was all that was needed to secure his international renown.

Jensen was an astute businessman, hiring skilled designers and craftsmen who contributed to the *skønvirke* style, adding their individual interpretations. Jensen's personal treatment of silver in lush high relief was warm and tactile. Sterling (925/1000) was not used until 1928-30 in Jensen jewelry. Amber, coral, garnet, carnelian or lapis stones were contrasting elements which nestled or burst from silver leaves in sensual swirls. Jensen, and those who succeeded him after his death, continually renewed the company inventory with innovative designers and fresh ideas which have kept the name of Georg Jensen at the top of the heap. Jewelry comprises only one quarter of the silver output of the company (the same Jensen designers also turn out holloware and flatware) and is certainly the most inspired. But Jensen was not the only game in town.

Two silver bracelets by Georg Jensen. The stylized charms representing a hedgehog, horse head, birds, and fish are from 1938. *Courtesy of Ed Forcum Collection, Berkeley, Ca.* The floral bracelet is from the Forties. *Courtesy of Bette Evans Collection, Santa Barbara, Ca. Photo by Robert Weldon*

Silver brooch by Georg Jensen featuring moonstone and sapphire cabochons, ca. 1910. *Courtesy of Terrance O'Halloran Collection, Los Angeles. Photo by Robert Weldon, courtesy of G.I.A.*

Silver wreath pin with garnet cabochons, pre-WW I, Georg Jensen. Stamped Georg Jensen and number 49, 828 S, and the early "GI" (for GJ) signature. *Courtesy of the author. Photo by Robert Weldon, courtesy of G.I.A.*

Three silver Jensen brooches: the brooch on left with green agate, ca. 1925. The center brooch is set with opals and labradorite with a labradorite pendant, ca. 1921. The third is the all silver version (ca. 1935 with "GJ" hallmark) of the flower basket brooch which was first designed in 1908 with amethyst, agate, and moonstone cabochons. *Courtesy of Rosebud Gallery, Berkeley, Ca. Photo by Robert Weldon*

Two Jensen brooches, one with spectrolite cabochons (ca. 1945) and the other with amazonite cabochons, ca. 1933 with "GJ" hallmark. *Courtesy of Rosebud Gallery, Berkeley. Ca. Photo by Robert Weldon*

There were many superbly talented silversmiths in Denmark. The same designers worked simultaneously for Jensen and other smithies, or maintained their own workshops. The generally superlative quality of workmanship and design associated with Danish silver was shared by many, spanning both the *skønvirke* style of the early 1900s and the Functionalism of the Twenties and Thirties, followed by the completely new identity given to Danish jewelry and design in the Fifties. The fineness of silver used until the Twenties was generally 825 or 830 S (the S is stamped on most Scandinavian silver). The sterling 925 was standard after the Twenties.

Responding to the flood of costume jewelry that was imported into Denmark from Germany, France, and England in the Twenties and early Thirties, the Danes began to realize the power of Functionalism. Artist-jewelers accepted the need for machines and the lower production costs which would make it possible to target a larger market than just the prosperous middle class which had formed the *skønvirke* clientele. Brass, nickel and steel jewelry was made by Astrid Wessel (1904-1961) and Carla Rasmussen mixed copper with silver, unheard of in the late Twenties. Craftsmen like Harald Nielsen, Arno Malinowski, Karl Gustav Hansen, and Just Andersen designed serially produced silver jewelry that the shop girls could afford.[2]

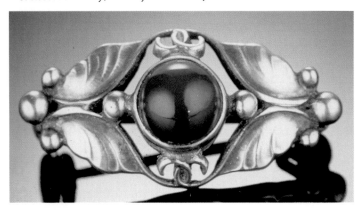

Silver brooch with chrysoprase cabochon, ca. 1945, Georg Jensen. *Courtesy of Terrance O'Halloran. Photo by Robert Weldon, courtesy of G.I.A.*

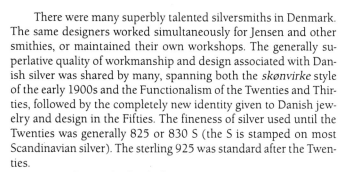

Reverse of Jensen pin with oval Georg Jensen hallmark. Sterling Denmark, with number 224. *Courtesy of Terrance O'Halloran. Photo by Robert Weldon, courtesy of G.I.A.*

Harald Nielsen (1892-1977) was one of the first to design mass-produced silver brooches and belt buckles to be sold at reasonable prices. He had the courage to break with the traditional naturalist themes to create downright Deco or "Funkis" pieces to successfully compete with the imported costume jewelry. He apprenticed with his brother-in-law, Georg Jensen, working up to artistic director of the firm.

Frantz Hingelberg founded his workshop in 1897 in Arhus. In the late Twenties he hired silversmith Svend Weihrauch (1899-1962) as artistic director. Weihrauch had designed for Jensen, and brought the style and craftsmanship learned there to Arhus. The Hingelberg firm became a prosperous enterprise under his leadership. His quirky floral rings and brooches showed the Jensen influence in the Thirties, becoming a more simplified form for his bright enamelled silver brooches of the Forties. The benchmark "F.H." was a sign of quality on all Weihrauch's designs. Hingelberg is now owned by Andkjaer & Aaquist who have no early archival information.

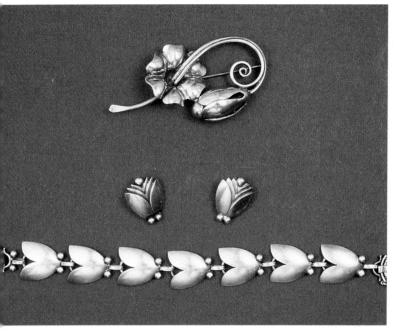

Silver bracelet and earrings by Harald Nielsen for Georg Jensen, ca. 1930, with floral brooch, Jensen, USA, post-war. *Courtesy of the author. Photo by Christie Romero*

 1904-1908

 1909-1914 Used together

 1915-1930

 1925-1932

 1933-1944

Since 1945

Two *skønvirke* silver rings: one signed "F.H." for Frantz Hingelberg, (probably a Svend Weihrauch design); the other stamped "E.L.", an unknown maker. The "Future" line ring, and pin on the left are Functionalist designs by Karl Gustav Hansen for his father, Hans, in 1932. Stamped "HaH", they did indeed prefigure future Danish design. *Courtesy of the author's collection. Photo by Robert Weldon, courtesy of G.I.A.*

HaH hallmark, Karl Gustav Hansen for Hans Hansen, for "Future" line, 1932 until the late 1940s. *Photo by Robert Weldon*

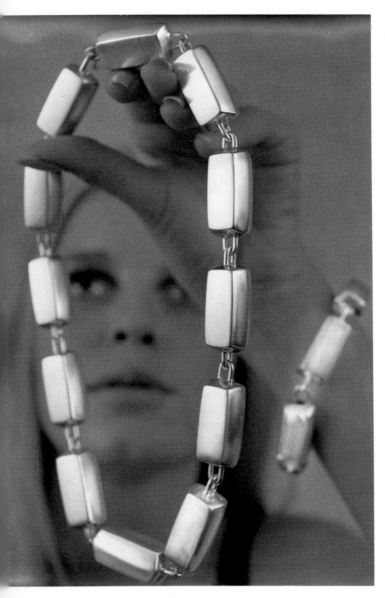

Hans Hansen (1884-1940) started his workshop in 1906 in Kolding on the Jutland peninsula, where it still exists. He produced mostly holloware until he was successful enough to take a chance on jewelry design. He asked his 18 year old son, Karl Gustav (1914-) to design a "Future" line for him in 1932. This collection of 50 rings, pins and earrings was unlike anything designed in Denmark at the time, and was undeservedly given the pejorative label "Funkis" (for funky Functionalism) but was successfully sold into the late Forties. (The "HaH" benchmark was used in these years, often accompanied by the script Hans Hansen mark.) Karl study-travelled in Italy in 1939, returning home to head the Hans Hansen workshop in 1940. From the Fifties, he concentrated mostly on holloware production, leaving the jewelry design to Bent Gabrielsen Pedersen. From 1962 he was artistic director. Hansen exhibited at the 1937 International Expo in Paris, at the World's Fair in New York in '39, the Nordisk Handcraft Exhibit in Paris, 1958 and '65, and in London in the Danish Design Show at the Victoria and Albert Museum, 1968. His work is represented in the major museums in Europe and New York. The Hans Hansen firm was taken over in 1991 by Royal Copenhagen (which also acquired Georg Jensen) so future collections will be much smaller.

Bent Gabrielsen Pedersen (1928-) studied at the Danish College of Jewelry and Siversmithing which formed all the major artists in Denmark from its inception in 1952. He designed smooth silver "boomerang" style bracelets and earrings, then "atomic" jewelry with enamel for Hans Hansen in the Fifties, taking over the jewelry design department for Karl Gustav in 1953. His variation on the circle form of the late Fifties was a necklace of connected links hung with a pendant that evoked Thor's hammer. The beautiful necklace he designed for Georg Jensen in 1953 transformed the natural form of sycamore seed pods into a symmetrical ornament of identical links. In 1962 his bracelet simulating interlaced silver fingers gripping the wrist followed his winning the Gold Medal at the Triennale in Milan. Major exhibitions of Modern Scandinavian Jewelry in New York, Paris, and London in the Sixties established his name worldwide. His early designs for Hans Hansen Silversmiths A/S are still represented in their collection. He dropped Pedersen from his signature, and has been known as simply Bent Gabrielsen in recent years.

A necklace and bracelet of silver cylinders by Karl Gustav Hansen for Hans Hansen, 1969. *Courtesy of Guldsmedefagets Bibliotek, Denmark. Photo by Reventlow*

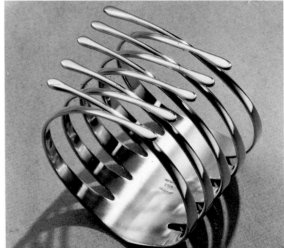

Cuff of silver interlaced "fingers" by Bent Gabrielsen for Hans Hansen, 1962. Script signature. *Courtesy of Guldsmedefagets Bibliotek. Photo by Jonals*

Silver cuff with elongated ends by Bent Gabrielsen for Hans Hansen, late Fifties. This bracelet was available with or without enamel, and is still in production. Hans Hansen script signature. *Courtesy of Christie Romero. Photo by Robert Weldon*

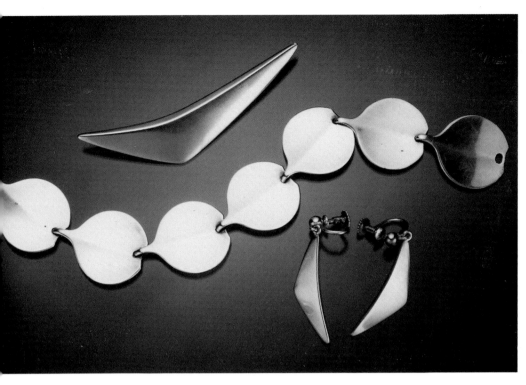

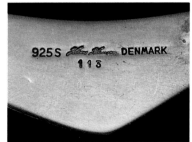

Silver boomerang brooch and earrings, and bracelet with leaf-shaped links designed in the late Fifties by Bent Gabrielsen for Hans Hansen. These classic pieces are still in production, signed with script Hans Hansen. *Courtesy of Christie Romero Collection. Photo by Robert Weldon*

Reverse of a Hans Hansen boomerang brooch, showing script signature. *Photo by Robert Weldon*

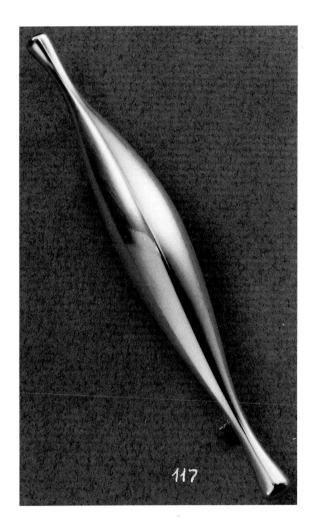

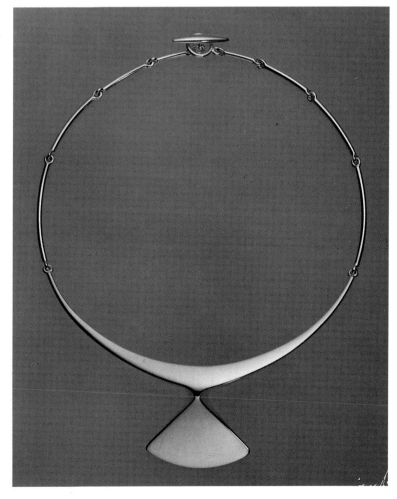

Silver brooch of elliptical elegance by Bent Gabrielsen for Hans Hansen, script signature. *Courtesy of Guldsmedefagets Bibliotek*

Bent Gabrielsen's cool version of Thor's hammer necklace for Hans Hansen, 1958. Stamped with Hans Hansen script signature *Courtesy of Guldsmedefagets Bibliotek. Photo by Jonals Co.*

Bent Knudsen (1924-) joined the Hans Hansen workshop in 1946, where he developed a distinctive style. He opened his own Kolding workshop in 1956 with his wife, Anni, who shared his ability to express a minimalist style with simple amethyst, malachite, or hematite cabochons accents. The line was unfailingly elegant and wearable. In 1969 he produced a bracelet of stacked square rings with a ring to match which broke with the deceptively simple style of the Fifties. He used the benchmark "Bent K" to identify work by his wife and himself.

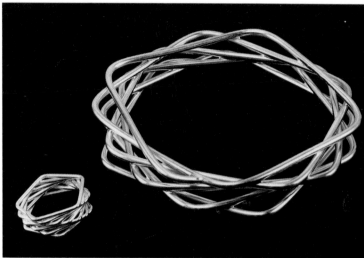

Silver earrings and bracelet by Bent Knudsen, ca. 1956. Signed Bent K. *Courtesy of Thanks for the Memories. Photo by Robert Weldon*

Stacked silver squares form a bracelet and ring set by Bent Knudsen, 1969. Signed "Bent K." *Courtesy of Guldsemedefagets Bibliotek. Photo by Hanne Richter*

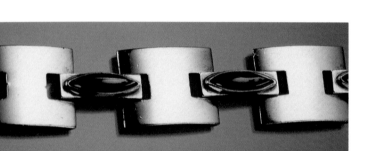

Danish craftswomen made a major contribution to Danish design in the Fifties. In addition to Anni Knudsen, Nanna Ditzel worked with her husband, as did Tove Kindt-Larsen. Karen Strand, and Gertrud Engel worked alone. Strand (1924-), along with Bent Gabrielsen, was one of the first to take advantage of the classes at the Danish College of Jewelry and Silversmithing. In '53 she won First Prize in the Jeweler's Competition, and joined the A. Dragsted workshop in Copenhagen, eventually becoming its director. A 1956 parure based on the lyre was a popular design, followed by a much more elaborate necklace of two rows of silver petals. She also designed brooches for A. Michelsen, based on the the ancient paisley symbol.

Handsome bracelet of silver links with hematite cabochons by Bent and Anni Knudsen, Kolding, ca. 1965. Signed Bent K. *Courtesy of Rosebud Gallery, Berkeley, Ca. Photo by Robert Weldon*

Parure of necklace, bracelet, clips, and earrings of lyre design by Karen Strand for A. Dragsted, 1956. *Courtesy of Guldsemedefagets Bibliotek. Photo by Struwing*

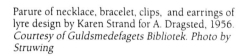

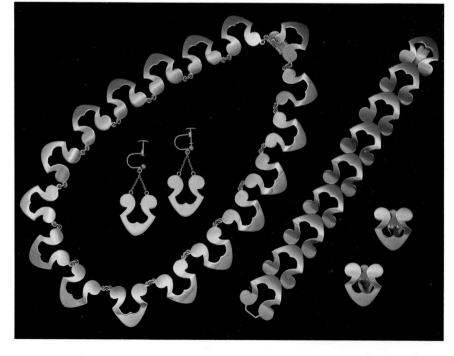

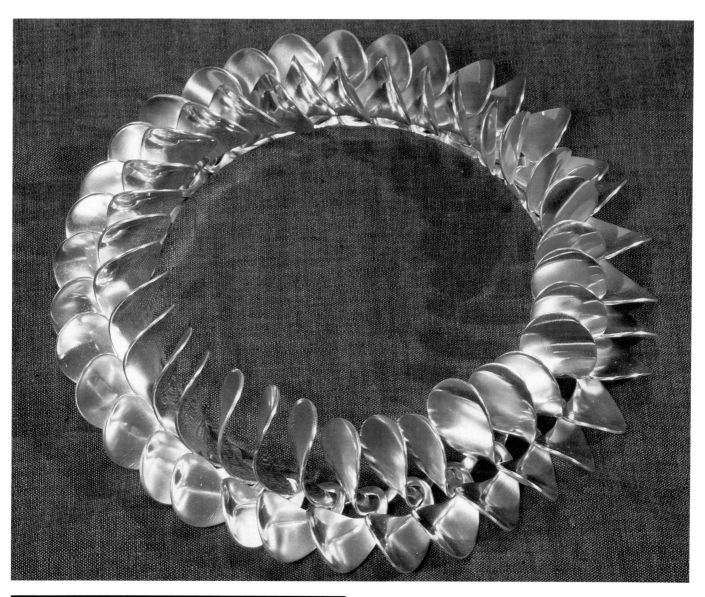

Double rows of silver petals by Karen Strand. This necklace won first prize in 1956. *Courtesy of Guldsmedefagets Bibliotek. Photo by Erik Hansen*

A silver brooch based on the Persian palm motif updated in 1953-55 by Karen Strand for A. Michelsen. *Courtesy of Thanks for the Memories, Los Angeles, CA. Photo by Robert Weldon*

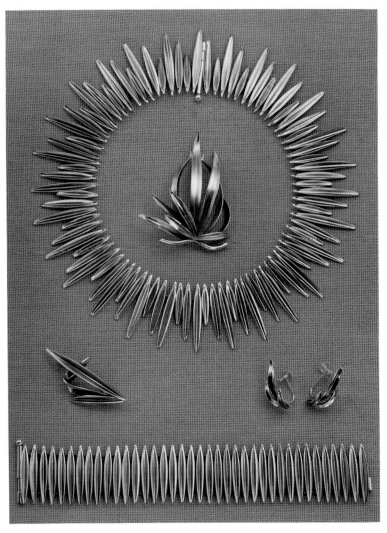

Parure of silver necklace, brooch, clip earrings, and bracelet, "Grass" design by Gertrud Engel for A. Michelsen, 1952. *Courtesy of Guldsmedefagets Bibliotek. Photo by Jonals*

Silver parure with necklace, bracelet, earrings, and pin in naturalistic plant motif by Gertrud Engel, 1960. *Courtesy of Guldsmedefagets Bibliotek. Photo by Jonals*

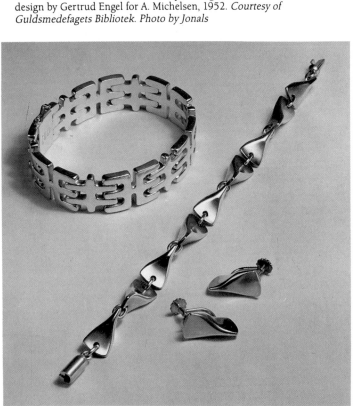

Gertrud Engel worked from nature, and produced two parures for A. Michelsen in the Fifties, both based on plant-life found along the Danish coast.

Tove Kindt-Larson (1906-) and her husband Edvard (1901-1982) met at the Royal Academy School of Architecture, married in 1937 and designed together from that time for Georg Jensen and A. Michelsen. They were leaders in a movement away from Functionalism, and, casting about for new ideas in an economy devastated by war and the German occupation of Denmark, turned out some original enamel jewelry on free-form heart necklaces for A. Michelsen. Kindt-Larsen's work for Jensen in the Fifties returned to the more classic shapes of that period.

Articulated silver bracelet, and silver link bracelet with earrings to match by Edvard and Tove Kindt-Larsen, 1953 for Georg Jensen. *Courtesy of Guldsmedefagets Bibnliotek*

Nanna (1923-) and Jørgen Ditzel (1921-1961) studied at the School of Arts, Crafts, and Design. From 1946 their working relationship and marriage were fruitful and mutually stimulating. Although trained as furniture designers, the transition to jewelry craftsmanship was easily made. Beginning with a stunning red striped enamel brooch for A. Michelsen in 1953, and continuing through a series of seminal pieces for Georg Jensen in the Fifties and Sixties, the Ditzels inspired a generation of silver designers. The 1956 necklace of a waterfall of silver petals, and the swooping lines of their bracelets, earrings and pins were as carefully crafted as racing yachts. Nanna Ditzel felt that: "Clarity of mind and dress are needed to wear this jewelry."[3] She has continued her clear vision of design dynamics in London, where she has lived and worked since 1970.

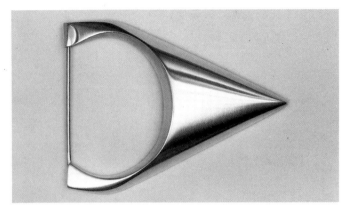

Silver brooch by Nanna and Jørgen Ditzel, 1956, for Georg Jensen. *Courtesy of Guldsmedefagets Bibliotek. Photo by Junior*

Another silver brooch with the pure lines the Ditzels did so well for Georg Jensen, 1956. *Courtesy of Guldsmedefagets Bibliotek. Photo by Junior*

A cascade of silver petals graces this lovely silver necklace by Nanna and Jørgen Ditzel for Georg Jensen, 1956-7. *Courtesy of Nordenfjeldske Kunstindustrimuseum, Trondheim, Denmark. Photo courtesy of Guldsmedefagets Bibliotek*

Sculptural cuff bracelet with earrings of similar cool design. Nanna and Jørgen Ditzel, 1955, for Georg Jensen. *Courtesy of Nordenfjeldske Kunstindustrimuseum. Photo courtesy of Guldsmedefagets Bibliotek*

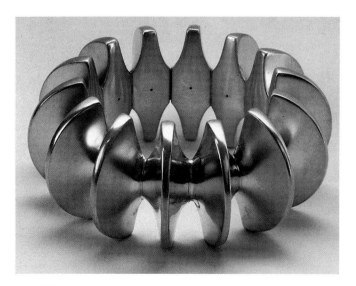

Beautifully structured bracelet by Nanna and Jørgen Ditzel, for Georg Jensen, 1960. *Courtesy of Guldsmedefagets Bibliotek. Photo by Erik Junior*

Erik Magnussen (1884-1960) was a self-taught silversmith. He briefly studied chasing at the Kunstgewerbeschule in Berlin in 1907, but was too independent to be accepted by a workshop. He created extraordinary naturalistic silver-gilt and porcelain brooches of insects in 1905-15, only to sell off his work in 1925 to try his luck in America. Gorham Silver Co. hired him as artistic director, where he worked in unaccustomed luxury till the 1929 crash. A shop he opened in New York failed, but an impulse to adorn the movie stars proved a successful venture in Los Angeles in 1933. Returning to Denmark in 1939 just in time for WW II, Magnussen crafted jewelry with a nationalistic theme. A red enamelled open work fish is post-war, signed with the "EM" monogram, as well as Volmer Bahnen, a sculptor (1912-) who had a workshop in Denmark.

Verso of Erik Magnussen fish brooch with artist's monogram and Volmer Bahner signature.

Red enamelled silver fish blowing bubbles by Erik Magnussen. ca. Forties. *Courtesy of Peacock Alley. Photo by Robert Weldon*

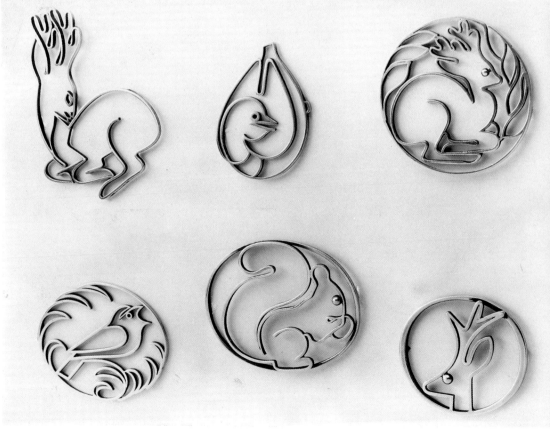

Silver wire brooches of animals by Ernst Hansen, 1945, for Evald Nielsen (celebrating the German withdrawal from Denmark.) *Courtesy of Guldsmedefagets Bibliotek*

Evald Nielsen (1879-1958) was apprenticed to a Copenhagen goldsmith in 1893. Ten years later he traveled for two years as a journeyman in Germany and Paris, absorbing continental techniques and styles. When he returned to his wife and child in 1905, he was ready to work industriously for other workshops until he could establish his own. A lucrative deal with a manufacturing company for the exclusive rights to export his lush *skønvirke* silver thruout Scandinavia assured him of a steady income. He used the usual lapis or chrysoprase cabochons favored by the Danes, with sumptuous settings in the Jensen style. In 1925 his pin depicting a gold bee sucking honey won a Grand Prix at the Paris Expo. The relief shared by all Danes when the Germans began their retreat in 1944 was celebrated by his "Mood" collection of jolly silver stick figures playing sports or musical instruments. In 1945 Ernst Hansen (1892-1968), a graphic artist, sketched some line drawings of animals which translated by Nielsen into silver broches. In both cases silver wire and balls were used cheaply for maximum affect and serial production.

Another Nielsen, Jais (pronounced Yayss, 1885-1961) was a painter/ceramist who began his creative life on a trip to Paris in 1911, where he rode the Cubo-Futurist waves until the outbreak of WWI sent him back to Copenhagen. There he exhibited with the Den Frie Udstilling group, for which he designed a poster in 1916. Ceramics gradually took precedence over graphic art. He was good enough to win the Grand Prix for ceramics at the 1925 Paris Expo. His ceramic jewelry plaques were produced by the Royal Copenhagen Porcelain Manufactury for A. Dragsted in the early Forties. Pastel glazed porcelain heads, plants, and animals in stylized Moderne plaques were mounted in silver bracelets and pins.

Porcelain, enamel, and brass were three of the inexpensive options open to jewelers for serial production in the Thirties and Forties. Brass was used for neo-African necklaces sold in department stores. Enamel, which was long the material of choice for Norwegian jewelry, was a new concept in Denmark. The immensely popular "Marguerite" design of enamelled daisies on silver gilt that commemorated Princess Margrethe's birth in 1940 was a best seller for A. Michelsen for decades. (Marguerite means "daisy" in French.) Enamel was effectively used in the pierced brooches by Arno Malinowski, Svend Weihrauch, and Erik Magnussen, but became more than mere decoration in the hands of Henning Koppel in the late Forties and Fifties.

Porcelain plaque with blue glaze by Jais Nielsen mounted in silver by A. Dragsted, 1942-45. And an enamelled silver-gilt daisy brooch, commemorating the birth of Princess Margrethe in 1940. *Courtesy of Christie Romero. Photo by Robert Weldon*

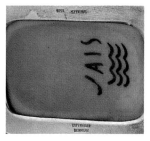

Verso of Jais Nielsen brooch showing Jais signature in ceramic and the silver mark "AD" under the crown for A. Dragsted.

Silver dancing links bracelet displaying the sculptor's mastery of form and movement (incorporating the clasp) by Henning Koppel for Georg Jensen, 1947. Five brooches making an art form of the amoeba shape by the abstract pools of brown, black, or blue enamel, 1940s-'50s. Stamped with Henning Koppel's HK monogram and Georg Jensen silver marks. *Courtesy of Christie's, Geneva. 20th Century Scandinavia, Decorative Arts, May 7, 1989*

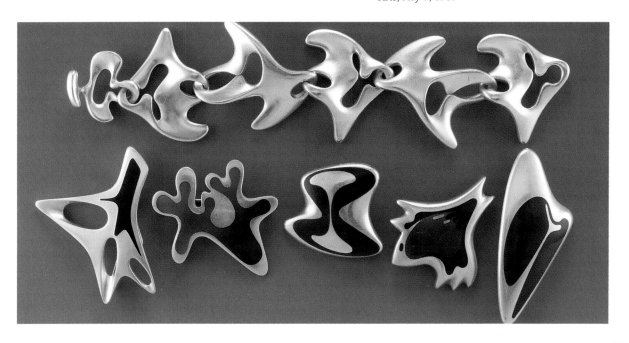

Henning Koppel (1918-1981) was trained as a sculptor at the Royal Academy of Fine Arts in 1936-37. He spent the war years in Sweden, where he designed some jewelry. Returning to Denmark in 1945, he joined the Jensen workshop as a designer, even though he had never worked with silver jewelry. (He was not the first sculptor at Jensen's to turn his talent to jewelry design.) Koppel combined the craftsman expertise he learned at the workshop with his own command of the plastic arts to forge original concepts in 1945-47. His bracelets were like dancing vertebrae, an enchanting blend of form and movement. His brooches played with the current free-form amoeba shapes, and glowing blue or brown enamel gave each piece an individual energy. Jewelry by Jensen stamped with Henning Koppel's monogram fetch the highest prices at auction.

Koppel's inlaid shapes and the Ditzels' work were quickly adapted by Danish costume jewelers into Fifties free-form brooches which were layered Bakelite with pewter, or exotic woods with chrome-plated metal, or silver. The barriers between artist vs. artisan, and the use of precious vs. alternative materials were dissolving at a time when graduates of the new Danish College of Jewelry and Silversmithing were eager to express themselves, whether it be for established smithies like Jensen, or in independent workshops.

Since successful Georg Jensen vintage designs are still being produced and sold at Jensen shops in Europe and America, it would be wise for collectors to check the model numbers (which are in sequence) and style with the New York Georg Jensen shop before bidding at auction. It often happens that collectors bid high prices for a piece which is available for less in a Jensen store.

Three designers who contributed to the Sixties were Ole Bent Petersen (1938-) and Jens Andreassen (1924-) and Thor Selzer (1925-). Petersen's work in 1958 looked like folded Japanese origami in silver. His bracelet of 1966 was simply two inter-connected links. Andreassen designed notable necklaces in tiers of silver petals for A. Dragsted in 1960. Thor Selzer's silver and gold rings set with semi-precious cabochons were conservative Fifties, but the Sixties found him designing a tangled nest of silver wire for a most unusual bib.

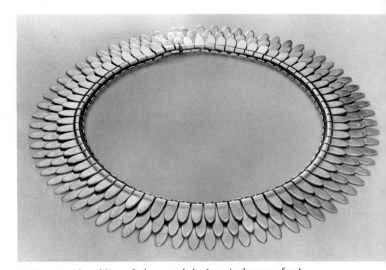

A three-tiered necklace of silver petals by Jens Andreassen for A. Dragsted in 1954. *Courtesy of Guldsmedefagets Bibliotek. Photo by Schleifer*

Two linked elements form a bracelet by Ole Bent Petersen in 1966. *Courtesy of Guldsmedefagets Bibliotek*

Silver wire nest of "scrambled eggs" by Thor Selzer, 1968. *Courtesy of Guldsmedefagets Bibliotek. Photo by Bent Kroyer*

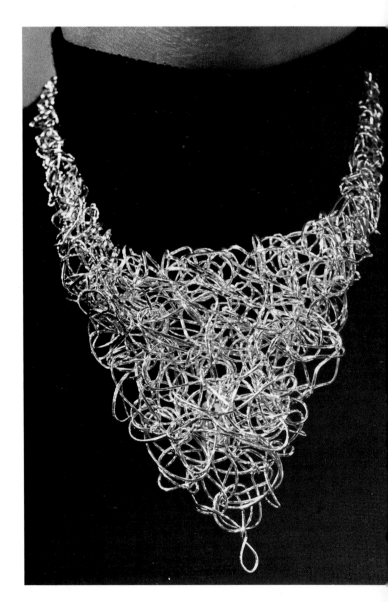

The N.E.From Silversmithy was founded in 1931 as a small workshop for jewelry repair. A wholesale production company was established in the late 1940's which joined in the generally lucrative period of Scandinavian design prosperity of the Sixties. For the past twenty years N.E. From has exported 50% of its total production to Western Europe, the U.S. and Japan.

In the Seventies, Astrid Fog (1911-), who also designs clothes to be worn with her jewelry, turned out classic silver spiral jewelry for Jensen, as well as green onyx rings and bracelets with pendant clusters of long silver drops. Mikala Naur (1960-) recently brought an original touch to Danish design. Her silver rhomboid bracelet featured Acrylic tubes filled with red plastic kitchen sponge. In Germany, or Holland, it would have been made with chrome or nickel, but the Danes remain faithful to their silversmithing tradition, even for the most "utilitarian" costume jewelry designs.

1. Jacob Thage, *Danske Smykker, Danish Jewelry*, Komma & Clausen Bóger, pg. 60. This book is the best source for biographical details on Danish designers up until 1960.
2. *Ibid.*, pp. 130-131.
3. *Ibid.*, pg. 167.

Silver bangle with malachite cabochon, and silver ring with faceted rock crystal center stone by N.E. From, circa 1965.
Courtesy of Christie Romero Collection. Photo by Robert Weldon

Verso of bracelet showing N.E. From signature and Sterling, Denmark.
Courtesy of Christie Romero Collection. Photo by Robert Weldon

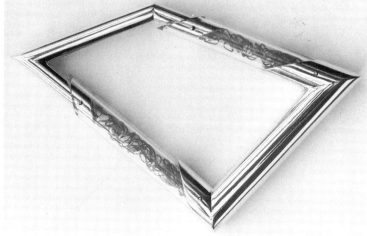

Silver bracelet with Acrylic tubes filled with red plastic kitchen sponge by Mikala Naur, Eighties. *Courtesy of Guldsmedefagets Bibliotek. Photo by Ole Woldbye*

Spiral silver necklace and earrings designed by Astrid Fog, 1986 for Georg Jensen, Royal Copenhagen. Signed by maker's mark and silver mark. *Courtesy of Guldsmedefagets Bibliotek*

10th century pagan amulets, Thor's hammer, replaced by the Christian cross in the 12th century Crusades; motifs which have been endlessly reinterpreted through the centuries in ancient and modern Scandinavian jewelry. *Courtesy of Antikuarisk - Topografiska Arkivet, Stockholm, photo by Süren Hallgren. Reprinted from* Viking Ways.

Opposite

Sølje brooches, cast in silver or bronze, were ancient Viking or medieval designs adapted over the centuries to be worn with traditional clothes in rural Norway by children and adults. Mass-produced, they are worn today as folk costume jewelry with everyday clothes in the villages and towns, by Norwegians of all classes. From the book *Draktsølje* by Jorunn Fossburg. *Courtesy of Universitetsforlaget, Oslo, Norway. Photo of cover by Robert Weldon*

Chapter 11

Norway

Berserk in Scandinavia

The Vikings (pronounced "weeking" in Norway) were Scandinavian sea warriors who in the 9th and early 10th century overran the British Isles, Burgundy and the Rhinelands. Because they were cruel invaders, the literature of the lands they occupied naturally described them as destructive and uncivilized. The Viking side of the story is largely unwritten. Norse literature recounts an enthusiastic battle madness (*berserkgangr*) which propelled the pirates through nearly 200 years of devastating conquests.

"Berserk" entered the lexicon, and Norse legends bequeathed their lore to posterity. Archeological remains are the primary source for their culture. Jewelry and objects were unearthed and served as in inspiration for modern jewelry design in Norway, Sweden, Denmark and Finland. The ancient runic script was Nordic graffiti inscribed on memorial stones (later employed in 13th century Iceland heroic poetry and devinations) which turned up in Scandinavian jewelry of the Sixties as symbols for the "spiritual warriors."

Norway is especially rich in Viking folklore. Medieval excavations disgorged some gold and many bronze and silver pieces. Tor's hammer was a popular motif. Tor, or Thor, the warrior god of Norse mythology, was the protector of the Cosmos. Thor's hammer was an iron or silver amulet pendant (usually cast) worn as protection by the pagans, endowing the wearer with strength and courage, (until it was replaced after the 11th century Crusades by the cross.) This very simple, powerful shape has been adapted by Scandinavian jewelers through the centuries into elegant silver pendants and earrings.

Medieval jewelry was worn only by the upper classes, as signs of luxury were suppressed among the peasants by the government. Silver, which was believed to provide protection against evil or to have healing powers, was nevertheless more widely worn by the peasants in Norway than elsewhere in Europe.

Sølje, meaning silver, was the term applied to all silver accessories, be it belts, shoe buckles or brooches. By the 18th century, silver rural jewelry was quite different from the urban gold. Silver gilt bridal headdresses and bodices twinkled with trinkets. Filigree (which was cast in bronze or silver in the Middle Ages) was influenced by European fashions and handwrought of delicate "real" filigree wire by the 18th century. Called *bolesølje*, silver brooches became very elaborate as silversmiths evolved different styles to be worn with traditional festive folk costumes (*bunad*) from different parts of the country.[1]

These brooches are still worn today. The *bolesølje* brooch from Telemark has six cast roundels decorated with animal heads in between. A ring-shaped brooch (common in Europe in the Middle Ages) has a large hasp prong in the middle, and is universally worn today by children and adults of all classes. The heart-shaped brooch with pendants and ornaments hanging from it, is from the eastern provinces. The rose *sølje* brooch, which was worn all over Scandinavia in the Middle Ages, is still popular, though its original rose design is almost buried under numerous glittering saucershaped pendants.[2]

Bolesølje brooches range from 6 to 9 cm. in diameter, and are worn in profusion down the front of the peasant bodice, or *bunad*. Silver pieces were mounted on girdles and collars. In a high wind, all these twinkling pendants from head to waist were a spectacular sight.

The *bunad* national dress differed from district to district, as did the jewelry. *Draktsølje* is the name given to silver jewelry formerly used on traditional costumes, which is now worn on everyday clothes as well. (Costume jewelry with a history.) Clasps for cloaks, tunics, and collars have survived the centuries.

Cast silver "Saga" ring, a replica of an embossed ring found in the grave of a well-to-do couple in 300 A.D., and a sky blue *guilloché* enamelled sterling bracelet for the upper arm, Twenties, with early stamp, both by David-Andersen. *Courtesy of private collection, Los Angeles.* An abstract Sixties silver brooch by an unknown maker, stamped sterling, Norway. *Courtesy of Carri Priley Collection. Photo by Robert Weldon*

Turquoise *guilloché* enamelled silver bar pin with floral design, with early David-Andersen hallmark from 1930. *Courtesy of author's collection. Photo by Robert Weldon*

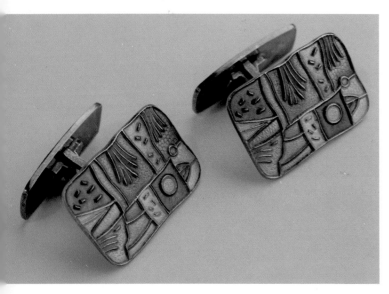

An abstract landscape decorates silver cufflinks with pressed enamel by Thor Lie-Jørgensen, ca. 1960. Signed with maker's mark and silver mark. *Courtesy of Tadema Gallery, London.*

The dragon ring has ancient origins. The dragon, possibly of pre-Christian origin, can be seen in the wood entrelac carvings of medieval stave churches still extant in Norway.[3] When the Historicism revival of Viking and medieval origins developed in the late 19th century in Scandinavia (about the same time as Celtomania gripped the British Isles), the dragon motif popped up again in jewelry, metalwork, weaving, and architecture. Like the snake, the dragon adapted well to the Art Nouveau whiplash, and was often pictured in combination with other ancient motifs. The political repercussions of the Historicism revival fueled the nationalist movement, which in 1905 resulted in Norway's breaking away from her union with Sweden.

Lori Talcoatt, jeweler and lecturer, who apprenticed in Telemark, Norway points out that: "There is a big difference between the medieval "Saga" cast silver replicas reproduced in large numbers by David-Andersen and others, and the actual folk costume jewelry which has its roots in the Middle Ages but has evolved over the centuries as a living tradition. People will still save their pennies to buy an original *sølje* piece."

The David-Andersen Co. founded in 1876, is a fourth generation family-owned enterprise. The founder, David Andersen was the son of a Norwegian tenant farmer. Apprenticed at 19 to a silversmith in Oslo, he studied enamelling techniques which he incorporated into designs made for English firms in London. By the time he died in 1901, his Christiana (as Oslo was then called) workshop was producing holloware, flatware, and jewelry which was exhibited at international expos in Europe.

Norwegian enamelling techniques rapidly evolved under the artistic direction of Gustav Gaudernack (1865-1914) at David-Andersen. A Bohemian who trained in the enamel workshops of Vienna, he constructed fragile standing dishes of *plique à jour* enamel which filtered the light like miniature stained-glass windows. *Plique à jour*, so beautifully adapted to Art Nouveau forms, was too delicate for the more robust modern shapes of the Thirties. *Guilloché* enamel, first used in the 18th century in France, was a hardy substitute. An incised wavy ground was overlaid with layers of transparent enamel in clear reds, blues and aqua. This quickly became the preferred enamel technique in Norway and was utilised for objects and jewelry right up to the present day.

When David Andersen's son, Arthur, took over the firm he hyphenated his father's name, adding it to his own. He produced prize winning designs until he was 90. Ivar David-Andersen studied sculpture in Paris, becoming director of the firm in 1952. He perfected technical and artistic techniques until 1972. Today, Jon David-Andersen is head of retail operations. Over 80% of the company's production is flat and holloware.

Fine modern jewelry designers have worked for the company since 1927. Guttorm Ganges used large topaz stones in sober rectangular designs. He also produced less expensive pendants, replacing stones with lush enamel. Thorbjørn Lie-Jørgensen designed geometric enamel pieces from 1927 until he died in 1961. The later pieces were composed of large fields of contrasting color in pressed enamel. In 1957, his necklace of identical enamelled peanut-shaped disks was intended for large serial production, a first for the company.

Harry Sorby, from 1946 to 1970, concentrated on jewelry whose artistic value was superior to the market value of the stones. In other words, inexpensive stones in elegant settings. Bjørn Sigurd Østern joined the David-Andersen stable in 1961, and designed some of the most original pieces in the '60s. His graceful harp pendant of 1966 has ribs of silver over brilliant aqua enamel. Unusual pendants were stylized shapes of birds, arcades, a cross with enamelled squares, a rune, and variations of Tor's hammer. An openwork silver brooch set with enamel and a pearl center was made ca. Sixies. Østern is now designing for his own workshop in Oslo.

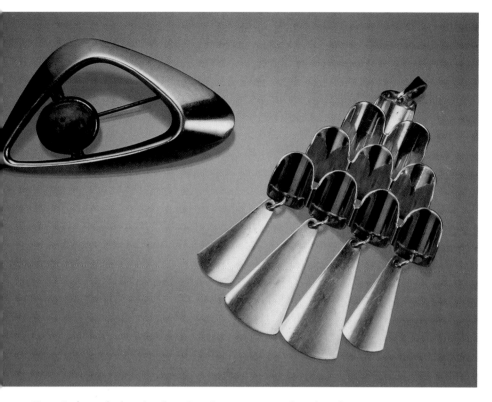

Harry Sorby made this silver brooch with an amazonite cab in the Fifties for David-Andersen. It is stamped "INV. H.S." 1962. INV (Inventor, meaning designer) was used with identifying artists' initials. The unusual sterling pendant with four triangular dangles is by David-Andersen, no INV. stamp, 1972. (The spoon dangles are an ancient Nordic motif.) *Courtesy of Christie Romero Collection. Photo by Robert Weldon*

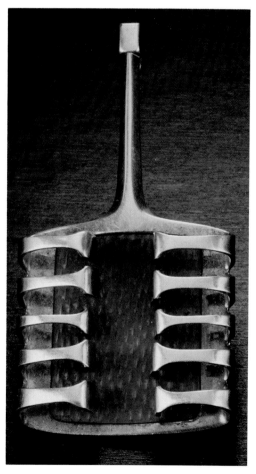

Thorbjørn Lie-Jørgensen created highly original pieces in the Fifties for David-Andersen with pressed enamel. This one, called "Rock Carving", is also stamped Nora G. *Courtesy of Dena McCarthy Collection, Sherman Oaks, Ca.* The purple, yellow, and black enamel sterling owl, ca. 1977, was produced in the Sixties in monochrome colors by David-Andersen. *Courtesy of Christie Romero Collection, Anaheim, Ca. Photo by Robert Weldon*

The sterling silver "harp" pendant with turquoise *guilloché* enamel, 1966, with "INV. B.S.Ø." stamp of Bjørn Sigurd Østern for David-Andersen, with sterling silver mark. *Courtesy of the author. Photo by Robert Weldon, courtesy of G.I.A.*

A three dimensional silver convertible pendant (can be worn upside down with loops on both ends) with enamel over grooved ground in autumn colors by B. S. Østern, Sixties, with maker's and silver marks. Worn on a silver neck ring by Hans Hansen, "DSD" of same vintage. *Courtesy of the author. Photo by Robert Weldon*

Three elegant sterling pieces by Bjørn Sigurd Østern: "Silver Bird" brooch on left has cobalt blue enamel center. The middle pendant is a stylized Thor's hammer. The "Silver Palette" pendant on right has a teal green *basse-taille* enamel center. All bear "INV. B.S.Ø." for David-Andersen, mid-Sixties. *Courtesy of Christie Romero Collection. Photo by Robert Weldon*

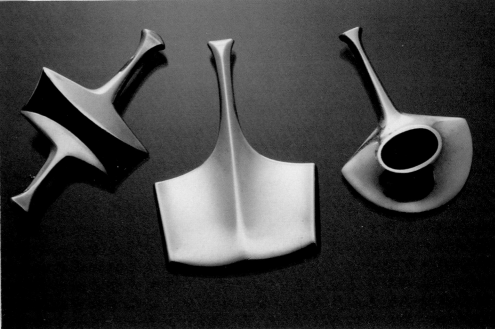

Reverse of above pendant with "INV. B.S.Ø." mark and David-Andersen sterling marks. *Photo by Robert Weldon*

Openwork silver brooch with green and red enamel and a pearl center by Bjørn Sigurd Østern, Sixties. With maker's mark. *Courtesy of Gail Gerretsen, Los Angeles. Photo by Robert Weldon*

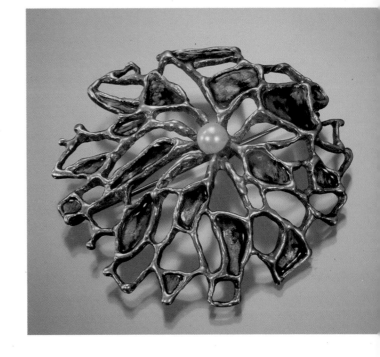

Uni David-Andersen, Ivar's daughter, also left in the '70s to strike out on her own very individual path, selling directly to shops. Marianne Berg, whose troll and knipling series were produced as earrings, necklaces and pins for David-Andersen in the '60s now designs for Uni. The prices for these original silver and enamel pieces were a reasonable $40 to $50.

Owl and fish brooches were produced first in one or two colored enamels in the Sixties, then in three colors. In the '70s, mass-produced silver butterflies, hearts, ladybugs, and bracelets and necklaces in alternating striped enamel lacked the originality of the earlier years, and were phased out by 1980.

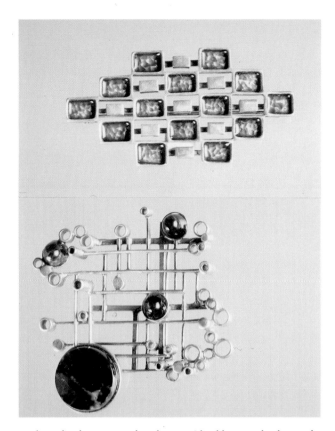

Two brooches by Uni David-Andersen: "Silverklang" with white and turquoise-blue enamelled mosaics in a silver grid; and a modern geometric combination of circles and squares with labradorite cabochons. Mid-Sixties for David-Andersen. *Courtesy of Ilene Chazanoff Collection. Photo by Richard Marx*

Silver hoop earrings and bracelet with black enamel by Aksel Holmsen. *Courtesy of Christie Romero* Silver brooch with white *guilloché* and black enamel stamped with Aksel Holmsen crossed bench tools mark, and Norway sterling marks. *Courtesy of the author. Photo by Robert Weldon*

David-Andersen used 830 S fineness silver mark alone until 1939, when the scales mark was added. From 1940, 830 S was replaced by the sterling 925 S mark in conjunction with the scales stamp.

The Aksel Holmsen Smithy in Sandefjord since 1932, designed enamel floral brooches in the Fifties, and abstract silver pins with enamel in the Sixties. The firm used a crossed bench tool stamp before changing to the "A.H.S." stamp for Aksel Holmsen Salg A/S, 1969 in Oslo.

Norwegian maker's marks: The three-pronged fork stamp was used by David-Andersen from 1888. This is the version from 1924-30s. The 1955 crossed jeweler's tools mark of Aksel Holmsen A/S, Sandefjord was changed to "A.H.S." for Aksel Holmsen Salg, Oslo in 1969.

Pale blue *basse-taille* enamel on vermeil flower brooch, and a black enamel on sterling abstract modern brooch, both by Aksel Holmsen, Sandefjord. Ca 1955-60. Stamped with crossed jeweler's tools maker's mark. Red *basse-taille* enamel on sterling abstract bow pin marked with "H" in a circle, and Norwegian silver marks. *Courtesy of Christie Romero. Photo by Robert Weldon*

The J. Tostrup workshop, known for its beautiful 19th century *champlevé* and *cloisonné* objects, turned to *plique à jour* for the Paris Expo of 1900. The Prytz family has been involved in the art direction of Tostrup from the beginning; the father specialized in Art Nouveau, and Jakob, who was the director in 1912, also taught Functionalism at the School of Art and Design. (The David-Andersen artists applied his theories to mass-produced objects.)

In the 1950s, Grete Prytz (1917-) designed unusual free-form enamel and silver jewelry, larger and more dramatic than her contemporaries. Her highly original ideas were enthusiastically supported and executed by the Tostrup firm from 1945. Educated in France, and at the Art Institute in Chicago, she was awarded the Lunning prize in 1952, the first of many prizes and gold medals. She married the architect Arne Korsmo, and later Kittelsen, signing these names to her designs. In the Fifties, Paolo Venini hand-made colored glass elements in Murano which Grete mounted into silver necklaces in Oslo. This successful Norse-Venetian collaboration abruptly ended with Venini's death. Grete continues the fine craftsmanship established by her great-grandfather, J. Tostrup.

Sigurd Alf Eriksen (1899-1991), painter and metalwork designer, was another Tostrup alumnus in 1921. He studied at Hanau, and Pforzheim in Germany, followed by work with various ateliers in Vienna, Paris and Rome. A major figure in Norwegian enamel art, he returned to Tostrup to head the enamelling atelier from 1926 to 1946, when he left to establish his own workshop. He specialized in painted and relief enamel pins and buckles inspired by Norse saga myths and nature, and Byzantine enamels admired in Italy. He won the Prix d'Honneur at the Milan Triennale in 1954. Curious, almost primitive shapes, characterized his very original work.

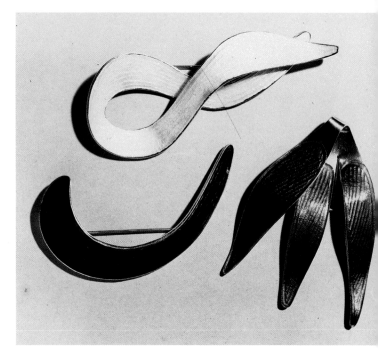

Three *guilloché* red and white enamel brooches engraved free-hand by Grete Prytz Kittelsen, 1953-55. *Courtesy of Kunstindustrimuseet, Oslo, Norway*

Norwegian/Venetian collaboration of Grete Prytz with Paolo Venini colored glass pendants, 1958. *Courtesy of Museum of Applied Art, Oslo*

Gilded silver and enamel "Medieval Age" brooch, 1955, and gilded silver and enamel "Snake Dance" brooch, 1968 by Sigurd Alf Eriksen. *Courtesy of Museum of Applied Arts, Oslo*

Regine Juhls designs jewelry in Norwegian Lappland in the town of Kautokeino. In her workshop above the Artic Circle, she makes both traditional jewelry based on ancient lore, and contemporary pieces. Her husband Frank works with her. The "JUHLS" stamp is accompanied by the 830 silver mark.

Tone Vigeland (1938-) studied at the National College of Art, Crafts, and Design in Oslo in 1955, and Technical College in '57. Tone explained in Oslo that the apprentice system requires four years of training with a master jeweler, which she did in the old fortified town of Fredrikstad at Norway Silver Design. "First, you take your practical exam and become a jeweler (journeyman) and two years later you take your commercial exam for mastercraftsman, which I did in 1962, so you can have the possibility of having people work for you in silver and gold, and can open a jewelry store."

Tone had a fresh, original approach to design from the very beginning. She foil-backed her enamel pieces, to make them shimmer, and turned out "atomic burst" hair ornaments and pendants with a modified geometric theme, and graceful earrings with moonstone pendants in 1960. By 1975 she was teaching at the National College of Art, having exhibited widely in traveling exhibitions of Norwegian Arts and Crafts in the U.S.A. and Europe. She observed that small workshops would have to become larger factories in order to keep prices down, but that the need to comply with the demands of the middleman, whose aims were commercial, rather than artistic, was stultifying to the artist-craftsperson. Tone Vigeland remained an independant woman and artist, conforming only to her own very high standards of craftsmanship.

"Harmony between the jewelry and the body is very important for me. The wish for something adjusting to and moving with the body led to working with chainmail. Even when putting many small parts together, I want the impression to be of sculptural and harmonious shapes. Jewelry must be beautiful and have an artistic value of its own. The obvious, matter-of-fact simplicity combined with personality, is what I'm aiming at."

Large Celtic Cross pendant with ring dangles by Regine Juhls, Kautokeino, Finnmark (Lappland.) Marked "*haandarbeide*" or hand-crafted. *Courtesy of Christie Romero. Photo by Robert Weldon*

Reverse of pendant with "JUHLS" mark and silver marks. *Photo by Robert Weldon*

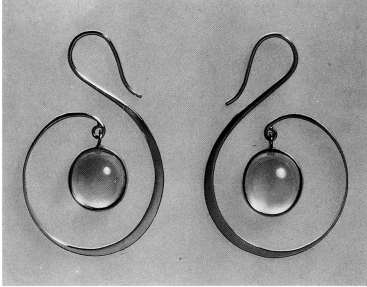

Gold earrings with moonstone pendants by Tone Vigeland, Oslo. *Courtesy of Tone Vigeland*

Feathered steel neckpiece with gold clasp by Tone Vigeland, Oslo, 1986. *Courtesy of Tone Vigeland*

Steel feather on gold pin, 1981, by Tone Vigeland. *Courtesy of Tone Vigeland*

Tone has worked mostly in silver, oxidyzed to a smoky grey and artistically stacked like shakes on a roof into dramatic necklaces and wide cuff bracelets. In the Eighties she worked wonders with dark iron or steel combined with dramatic touches of gold. Her silver belt of chainmail and scales coils around the waist like a snake. The elegant pin and necklace made with a burst of steel feathers, fastened with a minimalist gold catch look daunting but are wearable art. A square collar of oxidized silver segments and a bracelet of chainmail links interlaced with wrought metal nail heads could have been worn by the samurai. (These pieces do not have fastenings, but slip over the head or wriggle down the wrist of their own weight.)

In early 1994, Tone's slim sterling bangles worn in sets of 34 or 60 were photographed on models in fashion magazines (selling for $2000-2400 the set). Tone Vigeland's work is avidly collected in Japan, and represented in the National Museum of Modern Art in Tokyo, as well as the major art museums in London, New York, Pforzheim, Oslo and Stockholm. Shops specializing in artists/jewelers carry her work in New York and Europe. A 1995 exhibition of Tone Vigeland's work at the Applied Art Museum in Oslo will travel to the U.S.A. in 1996.

1. Jorunn Fossburg, *Draktsølje: Norwegian Folk Costume Jewellery*, Oslo, Universitetsforlaget AS, 1991, pg. 190.
2. *Ibid.*, pg. 191.
3. *Ibid.*, pg. 191

Square collar of oxidized silver squares which slips over the head, 1989, by Tone Vigeland. *Courtesy of Tone Vigeland*

Oxidized silver belt/necklace by Tone Vigeland, 1986. *Courtesy of Tone Vigeland*

Oxidized silver chainmail bracelet with wrought metal nail heads, 1991, which falls down the wrist without a fastening by Tone Vigeland. *Courtesy of Tone Vigeland*

Outstanding silver neckpiece set with chalcedony and rose quartz by
Sigurd Persson, 1965. Signed "SIGP" with Swedish silver marks. *Courtesy
of Sigurd Persson. Photo by Sandahl*

Chapter 12:

Sweden

Cool and Controlled

The deeply conservative tastes of the Swedish people in the first two decades of the XXth century did not welcome innovations. Georg Jensen was admired, but from afar. The Art Nouveau and Deco influences of Europe were ignored until Wiwen Nilsson broke the silence. A basically agrarian society, with no royal or aristocratic patrons, Sweden's traditionalist designs were evident at the 1900 Paris Expo, but by the 1925 Arts Décoratifs Expo there were stirrings of modern silver design.

Wiwen (pronounced Veeven) Nilsson (1897-1974) was the catalyst. The most outstanding Swedish artist in holloware and jewelry, his work was a triumph of simplicity. He used outsized emerald-cut, rock crystal stones, soberly set in silver. He had studied at Hanau, Copenhagen, and Paris, where exposure to German Expressionism and abstract art confirmed his geometric style. Squares, cubes, rectangles, and circles, pure in concept and gracefully interpreted, empowered his style in the Thirties. In 1928, after receiving a gold medal in Paris, he was appointed court jeweler in Sweden. In Paris, the Black and White fashion was discreetly created in diamonds and black onyx or enamel. Nilsson's pins and pendants were large scale stark contrasts of clear crystal and black onyx set in stepped silver mountings. Malachite, lapis, and moonstones, always austere and stoic, were joined with perfectly proportioned silver shanks.

Nilsson's workshop was nestled next to a Romanesque church in Lund, Sweden. He derived tranquility and power from this location. The silver that he designed for church services was "monumental", his adjective for describing the place and his reaction to it. Altar crosses of large clear crystals, especially cut for him, were so effective that he adapted them into pendants for costume jewelry, starting a secular fashion. In the Fifties, his style changed completely, inspired by oriental tapestries and woodcuts. Flying cranes, dragons baring their fangs, and slender fish were created in etched silver gilt brooches, unadorned with stones. His workshop was a very personal place, with only 30 craftsmen or apprentices toiling at any one time. His was the strong hand guiding the operation, and his spirit charged each piece that evolved entirely by hand.

Nilsson declared: "The only artistic effect which I strive to achieve is to make the rhythmic relationships inherent in the proportions come to life."[1]

Sigurd Persson (1914-), jeweler and industrial designer, studied the 18th century filigree technique used in folk jewelry with his father, F.S. Persson, from 1928 till 1937. He qualified for the journeyman's diploma in the same year. He enrolled in the Akademie für angewandte Kunst in Munich for two years, making

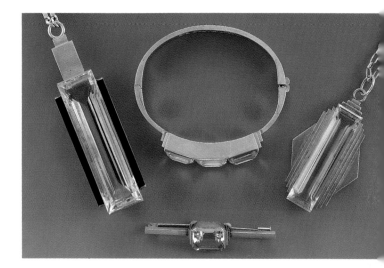

Silver-mounted rock crystal pendant with onyx baguettes and silver chain, Wiwen Nilsson. Stamped with maker's marks and Swedish silver mark for 1939. A silver hinged bracelet with three square cut faceted rock crystals, stamped with maker's marks and Swedish date letter for 1945. A rectangular cut rock crystal pendant in a stepped mount with silver chain, stamped with maker's marks and silver mark for 1933. A gold bar pin with rectangular cut aquamarine, stamped with Nilsson's maker's marks and date letter for 1933. *Courtesy of Christie's, Geneva, 20th Century Scandinavian Decorative Arts, May 1989*

Three classically cool silver pieces with malachite plaques by Wiwen Nilsson, 1939-41. Matching pendant, ring, and bracelet with stepped sides supporting square or rectangular cut stones. Signed "Wiwen Nilsson" script signature, with the Swedish three crown silver mark and date letters. *Courtesy of Knutsson Antik Gallery, Stockholm, Sweden*

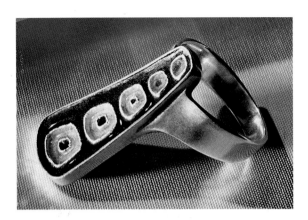

Silver ring with yellow, blue, and green enamel, 1951, by Sigurd Persson. Signed "SIGP", with Swedish silver marks. *Courtesy of Sigurd Persson, Stockholm, Sweden. Photo by Sundahl*

All by Sigurd Persson, a silver bracelet with two silver gilt wire-work globes, stamped with maker's marks and Swedish silver mark for 1964. Five high standing rings: from left, a silver ring mounted with a large smoky topaz, stamped with maker's marks and silver mark for 1964. A gold ring mounted with square cut quartz stones, stamped with maker's mark and silver mark for 1962;

and, in the center, a gold ring set with large citrine, stamped with maker's marks and silver mark for 1962. A silver ring with the eye of gilt wire-work, stamped with the maker's marks and silver mark for 1964. Gold ring in a pierced mount holding a faceted rock crystal, stamped with maker's mark and silver mark for 1965. These were made for the Nordiska Companiet department store exhibitions featuring the Hand, Arm, Ear, and Throat. *Courtesy of Christie's, Geneva, 20th Century Scandinavian Decorative Arts, May, 1989*

innumerable trips to the Glyptotek where the Egyptian and Greek ornamental arts displayed there inspired him to "Think Big", particularly in ring design. This ran counter to current Swedish taste. "I cannot deny that my studies at the Glyptotek were of decisive significance. It was a revelation to me that one could create large on a small scale".[2]

Back in Stockholm in 1942, wartime rationing of silver forced a changeover from large objets to jewelry in Erik Fleming's Atelier Borgilia, where Persson was employed. Here the first exhibition of modern jewelry designed by Sigurd Persson made a great impact. (The reduced allocation of precious metals inspired one designer, Estrid Ericson, to show gilded pewter instead of silver.) The Stigbert Atelier with jewelry by Stig Engelbert showed designs influenced by Nilsson. Persson broke away from the naturalistic Swedish preference, for a more sculptural approach. The exhibition was so successful that it was repeated in '44 and '45, stimulating interest in fine Swedish craftsmanship. In the early Fifties, travel in Europe culminated in working with *cloisonné* enamel at the Monastery of St. Martin near Poitiers, France, where Braque, Rouault and Chagall also worked.

In the early Sixties, for the large department store Nordiska Kompaniet (NK), Persson devised jewelry around four thematic exhibitions: the Hand; the Arm; the Ear; and the Throat. His rings for the first exhibition were high standing silver and gold mounts of large faceted rock crystal, citrines, or smoky quartz, specially faceted for him by G. Carlsson. One ring was like a silver eye with the iris fashioned of radiating gilt wires. The "77 Rings" show was so successful it was shown at Liberty's of London in 1961. A silver bracelet for the second NK exhibition in 1963, supported two globes of wound silver gilt wire. The mini-skirt was in style, so Persson sketched a silver knee bracelet with a gold bow to draw attention from the ugliest joint in the human body. The ear jewels for the 1964 show curled up above and around the top of the ear, and swooped inside it, avoiding the traditional lobe fastening. In the same year, Georg Jensen in New York held an exhibit of Persson's jewelry, bringing international recognition. The last thematic show in 1965 for NK was devoted to necklaces. One was in the shape of filigree epaulettes perched on each shoulder; another was a gondola of silver with rose quartz and calcedony stones balanced on either side of the neck.

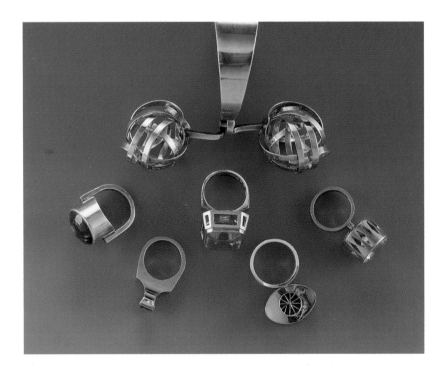

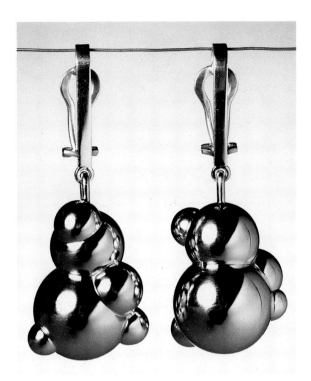

Silver "soap bubble" clip earrings by Sigurd Persson, stamped with maker's mark and silver date mark 1974. *Courtesy of Sigurd Persson. Photo by Sundahl*

Persson was busy blowing soap bubbles in the Seventies, transforming them into fragile silver clusters looking ready to pop, on bracelets, earrings, rings, and onyx and agate brooches . He attached cast plastic seashells in bright yellow or red to silver bracelets and rings, or hung a shiny black plastic shell from a gold wire finished with a fresh water pearl on the other end. He has found time to design glass for Kosta, as well as industrial design objets, cutlery, and sculpture in the Eighties. He celebrated his Golden Wedding Anniversary with Silver in a 1987 expo in Stockholm.

Persson believes that: "The need to disguise oneself, not only for a masquerade, is basic to the human psyche--the decoration of one's body is a function which moved from a must to a wish."[3]

photocopy of Sigurd Persson maker's mark, Swedish three crown silver mark, and date letter K9 for 1960.

Hair ornament of orange and red plaque with silver center by Sigurd Persson, 1984. Stamped with maker's and silver marks. *Courtesy of Sigurd Persson*

Space Age bracelet made of a red plastic disk with silver cone on a silver band by Sigurd Persson, 1974. Stamped with maker's and silver marks. *Courtesy of Sigurd Persson*

Seashell of cast red plastic mounted on a silver band bracelet by Sigurd Persson, 1974. Stamped with maker's and silver marks. *Courtesy of Sigurd Persson*

Silver wire necklace with portable holder for exchangeable flower by Sigurd Persson, 1982. With maker's marks and silver marks. Courtesy of Sigurd Persson

Silver geometric pendant on silver wire by Sigurd Persson, 1991. *Courtesy of Sigurd Persson. Photo by Sundahl*

Vivianna Torun Bülow-Hübe (1927-) studied at the National College of Art, Craft and Design in Stockholm, opening her studio there in 1951. On a trip to Paris in 1956, she was excited by the primitive artifacts at the Musée de L'Homme, and designed necklaces with Egyptian amulets. Torun decided to stay and work in France. She married an African-American painter, Walter Coleman, and through him became friends with the expatriate Black community. She designed silver necklaces with rutilated quartz and moss agate pendants and matching pendant earrings for Billy Holiday. Billy wore these "performance sets" during her singing engagements at the Mars Club and other European jazz clubs in the late Fifties. From 1954-'68, Torun's jewelry was displayed at the Galerie du Siècle in St. Germain-des-Prés. Because she repeated some of the same designs later for Georg Jensen, some of Torun's jewelry bears the Danish hallmarks, and others the French and Swedish hallmarks.[4]

One day while collecting pebbles on a Mediterranean beach after a storm, she was observed by a short, bald man with intense black eyes. He asked her what she was going to do with all those pebbles. She explained that she was going to mount them in a silver necklace. The stranger was so impressed with her imagination (her good looks could not have escaped his artist's eye) that in 1958 she was given an exhibition in the Picasso museum in Antibes. Torun had not recognized the painter on the beach.

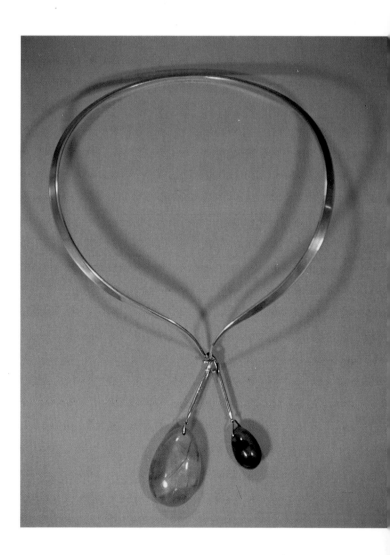

Sterling neck ring (numbered 169) with a tongue from which two pendants could be hung separately or together; one moss agate numbered 128, the other a rutilated quartz, numbered 101. All three are stamped Georg Jensen, 925 S, and signed "TORUN". Billy Holiday was pictured wearing a similar silver neck ring and pendant with matching rutilated quartz earrings in Paris in 1957. These were produced by Jensen ca. 1968. *Courtesy of Peregrine Gallery, Montecito, CA. Photo by Sandro Moro*

Torun opened a workshop in Biot, in the South of France, eventually working with five assistants in the ten years she spent there. Her work was sculptural body art, silver mobiles for the neck and shoulders. A 1959 design snaked around her throat, with a rutilated quartz carefully balanced on each end. She set a large chunk of overlay glass by Edward Hald of Orrefors into a silver bracelet. In 1960 she won the Lunning prize. From 1968-78 she moved her studio to Wolfburg, Germany, where she worked as a free-lance designer for Georg Jensen. Invited to teach young people jewelry techniques in Indonesia, Torun opened yet another studio in Djakarta in 1978. In her latest adopted country, Java, she is known as Vivianna, and prowls the beaches looking for shells and objets for her jewelry. She uses only natural materials like horn and mother of pearl, always searching for that "little smile that radiates " from an inspirational source. Torun expressed best the force behind the Scandinavian artist-jewelers: "Jewelry is a mystical not a fashion thing."

For a recent retrospective of her 40 years as an artist (20 of them designing for Georg Jensen), she uses the life-giving form of the spiral as a symbol of eternal movement. She is "fascinated by the double spiral movement which permeates the universe, the galaxies, and the smallest atom. The vortex symbolizes for me the great vibration of life, the infinite, and heavenly creation."[5] In her earrings and bracelets, the spirals are like two lovers who have become one.

Silver bracelet with hinged stone of overlay glass by Edward Hald, Orrefors, signed TORUN (visible) with Swedish silver mark for 1966, by Torun Bülow-Hübe. *Courtesy of National Art Museum, Stockholm, Sweden*

Double spiral silver earrings, "Vortex", a symbol of infinity by Vivianna Torun Bülow-Hübe, 1987, for Georg Jensen, 1968. *Courtesy of Guldsmedebladet and Georg Jensen, Copenhagen*

The double spiral theme translated into a graceful silver bracelet by Vivianna Torun, 1988, for Georg Jensen. *Courtesy of Guldsmedebladet and Georg Jensen*

Birger Hagelund (1918-) was apprenticed at 16 to mastercraftsmen in Koping, then worked four years with Erik Fleming at the Atelier Borgila. He had his own atelier during the war, but always independent, he gave it up to make his fortune in South Africa. He returned in 1952, appalled by apartheid, and started all over from scratch. He constructed a pendant of a bird's golden plumage encrusted with gems that can be seen in the Nationalmuseum in Stockholm. But Sweden in the politicized late Sixties was inhospitable to silver and goldsmiths (luxury items for the upper class were roundly denounced there, as in Holland). Haglund again left his homeland, this time for Afghanistan, where he was struck by the essential simplicity of the copperware by native artisans. He returned in 1976 a changed man (and craftsman). The Swedish perfectionist now allowed the rough edges to show, while still keeping the design basically simple. In 1982, he designed a necklace of two blades of silver which played with the reflection of light. This could not have been further removed from his earlier elaborate pieces.

In a Foreword to a book on contemporary Swedish design, Helena Dahlbäck-Lutteman writes: "One hopes that Swedish character is not only manifested by dismal discretion. We have never been particularly bold or flamboyant. We have worked with poise and moderation, but also, we hope, with an element of inspiration."[6] The work of the above artists certainly attests to her evaluation, although the inspiration is often sought outside of Sweden.

Swedish hallmark of 3 crowns and date letter for 1960.

Benchmark of silversmith Wiwen Nilsson.

Opposite
Necklace of two blades of silver reflecting the light, by Birger Haglund, 1982. *Courtesy of Swedish National Art Museum, Stockholm*

1. Kersti Holmquist, *Silver Smeden, Wiwen Nilsson*, Lund, Sweden, 1990, pp. 244-245.
2. Sigurd Persson, "Foreword," *Sigurd Persson Smycken*, Seelig & Co., Stockholm, Sweden, 1980.
3. S. Persson, *Ibid.*
4. Ann Westin, *Torun: Conversations with Vivianna Torun Búlow-Hübe*, Sweden, Carlssons Bøkforlag, 1993, pg. 58
5. Chantal Bizot, *Les Bijoux de Torun*, Musée des Arts Décoratifs, Paris 1993.
6. "Foreword," *Contemporary Swedish Design*, Swedish Society of Crafts and Design, Stockholm National Museum, Sweden.

The sources of Finnish design date back to the 6th century in the Eastern Baltic where bracelets were forged and embossed (pictured on the left,) to Viking Age bracelets (on the right) which were cast in the far north wilds of Finland. Bracelets were worn several on the wrist and were used as payment for furs. Rings were a symbol of union. The chain necklaces were first worn in bronze in the 9th century. Modern Finnish jewelers, working with museum experts, have adapted these ancient designs in bronze, silver and gold, adding creative touches of their own and the native spectrolite, jasper, or granite stones. *Courtesy of Kalevela Koru, Helsinki, Finland. Photo by Reijo Nykanen*

Chapter 13

Finland

The Fantastic Finns

The Finns are people of the fens, or marshes. They were agrarian; hunters, not traders and sailors like the Scandinavians. The Finno-Ugrian ethnic group is made up of the Baltic and Volga Finns (the latter were Magyars from the Urals in Russia, so there is a connection with Hungary). Their language is not slavonic, with its own structure and vocabulary (and spelling; the liberal use of double consonants and vowels is not a typographical error). The Finns are, therefore, independent of both Europe and Scandinavia-racially, linguistically, and artistically.

Finland was ceded to Russia by Sweden in 1809 as a semi-independent Grand Duchy. She became independent after the Revolution in 1917. There were large numbers of Finnish jewelers in St. Petersberg and Moscow who had worked with Fabergé and other fine goldsmiths, who returned to Helsinki in 1917. Some, like Alexander Tillander, established a shop there (which continues manufacturing fine *objets d'art* and gold jewelry today, directed by Alexander's great-granddaughter, Ulla Tillander-Godenhielm.) Before World War II a cooperation existed between artists and shops, but in 1940 they were faced with the double dilemma of shortages of precious metals and craftsmen. Wedding rings and heirlooms were sacrificed for the national defense. Base metals were also melted down, fashioned into new pieces and plated. The native Finnish stones; Lapp jasper, smoky and rose quartz, uncut rock crystal, and spectrolite were abundantly available after the war. In the Thirties and Forties, brightly painted wooden beads, a cheap substitute for silver, were exported to America, where a crafts industry embarked on its own production of painted wood necklaces.

Nationalism was applauded, and as in Norway, the largest jewelry company, Kalevela Koru (established in 1935 and named for the Finnish national epic *Kalevela*) began producing replicas of Viking and crusader jewelry. The company became a major force in modern Finnish jewelry, holding jewelry design competitions in the Forties to reward new ideas in a post-war market that had become stultifyingly conservative. Continuing its important link to the adornments of the ancient past, Kalevela Koru reproduced a cast bronze pendant (numbered on the back) with a stylised Thor's hammer, characteristic little knobs (which are the simplified versions of Scandinavian animal heads) and dangling charms. Round and horseshoe brooches which were worn by men and women originally during the Crusades of the 11th century to fasten their cloaks or veils are still being cast. Made in cooperation with the Finnish National Museum, these are Finnish folk costume jewelry pieces in bronze or silver worn by the modern day Finns, and exported to Sweden, Norway and Germany by the thousands.

Gaily painted wooden beads strung on plastic or cord were exported to America and Europe from the forests of Finland in the Thirties. (Americans were also busily painting their own necklaces for wartime accessories.) *Courtesy of private collection, Los Angeles. Photo by Robert Weldon*

Cast bronze replica of legendary Thor's hammer pendant with knobs and dangling pendants by Kalevela Koru, still worn today in Finland. *Courtesy of the author. Photo by Robert Weldon*

Finnish ingenuity was sorely tested during the war. Tuula Poutasvo, in her article "Finnish Silver; From the Second World War to Postmodernism," reports that when even glass stones and beads were hard to obtain in 1945, that the Kupittaan Kulta workshop, in the town of Turku, melted down colored pin heads for jewelry accents, and Finnish granite was upgraded to a precious stone.[1] Tough times indeed!

Henry Tillander, in 1948, initiated an artistic competition (a fine Finnish tradition) for quality souvenir boxes and jewelry for the Olympics to be held in Helsinki in 1952. Tapio Wirkkala (1915-1985) won first and second prizes, the first of many awards won by this multi-talented designer of glass, porcelain, silver, and wood sculptures. He designed silver earrings and a pendant of flexible concentric circles in the Fifties, but Wirkkala is known principally for his industrial designs.

The Finnish arts renaissance of the Fifties was led by Bertel Gardberg (1916-) who excelled at transforming scrap silver into rings and brooches. These were rejected as being too avant-garde, so he turned to industrial design, and sold brass objects and silverware to the Artek Gallery, a Helsinki shop which markets furniture by Alvar Aalto, and other avant-garde designers. Later in the Fifties, Artek sponsored Avant-garde Exhibitions which featured Gardberg's hinged "orange" bracelet. Gardberg's fine craftsmanship and industrial design won him many international prizes and commissions in the Sixties. A five year stint as artistic director of an Irish design workshop awakened in him a love of stone sculpture to which he devoted most of his energy upon returning to the Finnish countryside in 1971. He made time, however, for individual jewelry commissions, as industrial design was phased out.

Hinged silver bracelet "Orange" by Bertel Gardberg exhibited at Artek Avant-garde show in 1958. With silver stamp, date letter, and bench mark BRG. *Courtesy of Museum of Applied Arts, Helsinki, Finland*

"Silver moon" earrings and pendant of concentric silver circles designed by Tapio Wirkkala in 1970, (unusual examples of jewelry by this industrial designer.) In production by Kultakeskus Oy in the Seventies. These bear the Finland silver punch: a crown within a heart, "NW", and the silver date letters for 1972, '73. *Courtesy of Carri Priley Collection, St. Paul, Mn. Photo by Robert Weldon*

The Kupittaan Kulta jewelry workshop was established in 1945 by Elis Kauppi (1921-). Rejecting the popular Forties naturalistic flower and leaf designs, he was one of the first to use the native Finnish stone, spectrolite, in modern spring-clip bracelets. Spectrolite is related to labradorite, a feldspar which is quarried and cut in Ylamaa. A dark, shimmering blue stone with an iridescent schiller, its qualities are spectacularly displayed in silver settings. Exhibited at international expos in the Fifties, spectrolite excited interest in Finnish jewelry, world-wide. Kauppi's exquisite "Mountain Stream" necklace of cascading bubbles of rock crystals and spectrolite is an example of his original craftsmanship. The anvil benchmark beside the Turku town stamp are identifying marks for this designer, and his company.

The Kaunis Koru shop, established in 1954, employed young designers like Paula Häiväoja and Björn Weckström, who ten years later were established artists on the international scene. The Kaunis Koru stamp was two K's back to back. Kalevela Koru bought the company in 1989.

Sparkling "Mountain Stream" pendant by Elis Kauppi, made by Kupittaan Kulta Oy in Turku, 1975, with rock crystal bubbles over spectrolite "pebbles". Signed with Turku city stamp, and the anvil stamp for Kupittaan Kulta. *Courtesy of Museum of Applied Arts, Helsinki*

Two silver rings, one with a carnelian ball by Elis Kauppi, both made by Kupittaan Kulta with anvil mark, Sixties. *Courtesy of Thanks for the Memories, Los Angeles, CA.*

Reverse of amethyst brooch showing: anvil stamp for Kupittaan Kulta, Finland Crown stamp, silver fineness 813 H, Turku city stamp, and date letter for 1966. *Photo by Robert Weldon, courtesy of G.I.A.*

Silver brooch with jasper stone with "HN" benchmark, Kaunis Koru, 1962. *Courtesy of Joanne Adler Collection, Los Angeles. Photo by Robert Weldon*

Reverse of jasper brooch with bench mark "HN", Crown silver mark, fineness silver mark 916H, LI for town of Lahti stamp, I7 date mark for 1962, "Kasityo" meaning handcrafted, and the KK back to back mark for the Kaunis Koru workshop. *Courtesy of Joanne Adler. Photo by Robert Weldon*

Silver pendant with jasper center, marked Finland, and a necklace and bracelet set of abstract design with winged hammer stamp, Turku city stamp and date letter S7 for 1971. A two tiered silver pendant stamped with Kupittaan Kulta anvil mark. *Courtesy of Carri Priley Collection. Photo by Robert Weldon*

Silver brooch with rectangular cut amethyst with silver marks for Kupittaan Kulta, city mark, and date letter for 1966. *Courtesy of the author. Photo by Robert Weldon, courtesy of G.I.A.*

Dramatic "Wing Ring" by Saara Hopea-Untracht to be worn across three fingers. Designed in 1959, the ring was made in silver with enamel and gold accents, by Ahlberg at Hopea. Stamped with "OH" in rectangle for Ossian Hopea firm, the crown punch within the heart, 830 silvermark, Porvoo heraldic coat of arms, and date letter. *Courtesy of Oppi Untracht, Porvoo, Finland. Photo by Oppi Untracht*

Saara Hopea-Untracht (1925-1984) played an enthusiastically active part in the creative renaissance that enlivened all fields of design in post-war Finland. She grew up in Porvoo, the oldest town in Finland, where the medieval and Empire quarters have long sheltered an artistic community of writers and artisans. Leaving these strong roots behind, she traveled extensively with her writer/artist husband, Oppi Untracht, applying and adapting themes and colors from foreign cultures into her work. She began in furniture and interior design in Helsinki, created glass in Nuutajärven, enamelling in New York, textiles in India, and jewelry in Porvoo.

Hopea means "silver" in Finnish. Saara came from four generations of goldsmiths but she found contemporary jewelry uninspired and graduated from the Central School of Applied Arts in interior design. Working with Kaj Frank, an internationally recognized designer, she contributed to the practical needs of the post-war years with her space-saving stacking glasses, which won a silver medal at the Milan Triennale in 1954. Her father's death four years later thrust her into a new métier which she approached with characteristic thoroughness and imagination. The intimate collaboration between designers and artisans was highly developed in Scandinavia, and Saara found an ally in goldsmith Göran Ahlberg who encouraged her startling ring designs which spread silver wings across three fingers, or regally extended beyond the first finger joint. These rings survived the initial shock to the consumer and were produced from 1958-1970s in limited editions of 20 or so.

When she returned from an extended stay in India, Saara incorporated the traditional knitted silver chains she had seen there into her necklace and pendant designs, meticulously knitting the chains herself from specially drawn wire. In his book *Saara Hopea-Untracht*, her husband, Oppi, describes the long hours of hand labor required for knitting these silver chains: "It was Saara's philosophy to make these chains available to as many people as she could. Hand knitting caused severe pain in her fingers because of the need to pull each loop tightly to make them uniform. The leather finger-guards she devised only partly helped the problem. The satisfaction she derived from this work must have been enough, because she only asked token payment for her work."[2]

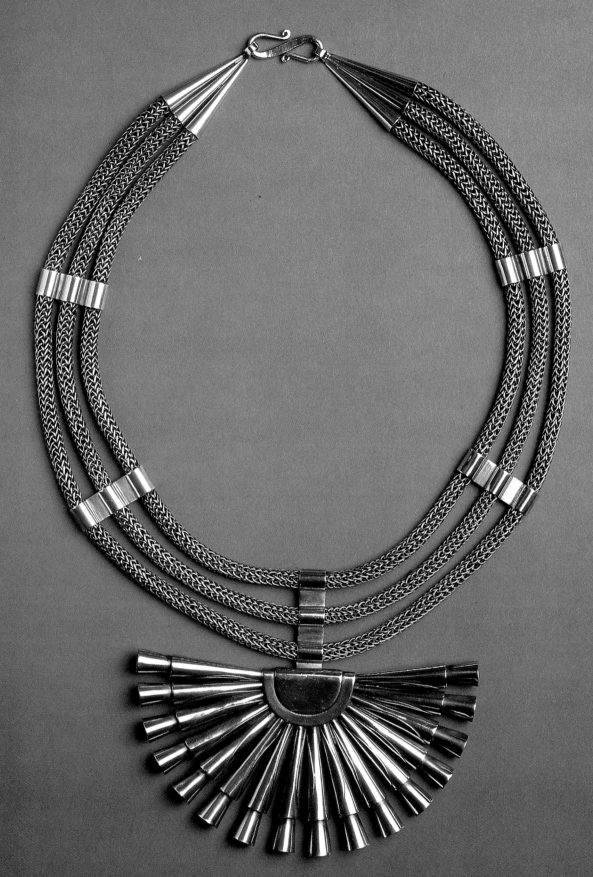

Silver necklace of three chains hand-knitted by Saara (an old Nepalese and Indian technique) and an abstract pendant fabricated by Ahlberg, designed by Saara Hopea-Untracht, 1977. Stamped with "OH", crown, Porvoo place, and date marks. *Courtesy of Aki Hopea collection, Porvoo. Photo by Kari Haavisto*

Cluster of semi-precious stones gathered in her travels to India set in gold brooch by Saara Hopea-Untracht, 1969. A collection of chalcedony, tourmaline, topaz, hawkeye, smoky quartz, carved Indian topaz, rose quartz, moonstone and citrine stones mounted with gold shot to fill the negative spaces. With usual "OH, crown, Porvoo and date marks. *Courtesy of Harriet Fersh Collection, Finland. Photo by Arto Hallakorpi*

Stunning silver pendant on hand-knitted chain of two birds holding a garnet cabochon in their gilded beaks. Their outspread wings are patterned with twisted silver strands, and flattened knitted tubes, 1980. Bearing "OH", crown, 925, Porvoo, and date letter marks. *Courtesy of Oppi Untracht. Photo by Kari Haavisto*

Creating the elaborate silver pendant, "Two Birds", symbolically sharing a garnet berry in their gilded beaks was as much a tribute to a symbiotic marriage as an artist's tour de force. These were made of sheet metal, flattened knitted tubes, and twisted silver wires. Saara's early design predilection for geometric shapes, domes, and pyramids, had been reinforced by the similar patterns in Indian architecture, mughal mosaics, and chakla textiles. She also incorporated the antique engraved stones she found in India into her semi-precious stone mosaics for rings and brooches of 1970.

In 1983 Saara was asked to design serial production jewelry to ornament Marimekko hand woven dresses. Her oxidized silver heart pendants with gold-plated roses were mounted on black, green, or shocking pink Japanese silk cord, and are still available at the Marimekko shop in Helsinki. It was to be Saara'a last assignment. She died the following year.

Oxyidized silver heart pendant with gold-plated rose hand finished strung on green, black, or shocking pink silk cord, with sliding tube length adjustor and back heart counterpoise, ca. 1983. This was Saara Hopea-Untracht's last assignment before she died. It was serially produced for the Marimekko Esplanade boutique in Helsinki, where it can still be found. Illustrated in *Saara Hopea-Untracht* by Oppi Untracht, pg. 276. *Courtesy of Marimekko, Oy, Finland*

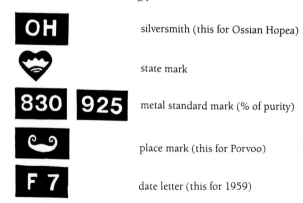

Silversmith's benchmark and Finnish silver hallmarks in rectangular blocks (gold marks are ovals).

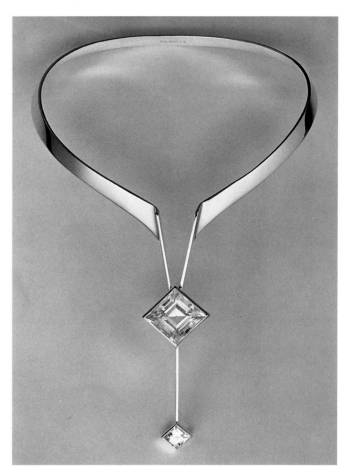

Silver neckpiece with square-cut crystal pendants, late Sixties, by Paula Häiväoja. With Finnish silver marks, boat for Helsinki stamp, and KK for Kalevela Koru. *Courtesy of Kalevela Koru Oy, Helsinki. Photo by Studio Wendt*

Wire necklace with pendant squares by Paula Häivöja made by Kalevela Koru in the Sixties. With Finnish silver marks and KK for Kalevela Koru. *Courtesy of Kalevela Koru Oy, Helsinki. Photo by Pietinen*

Paula Häivöja (1929-), another of the many talented women artists in Finland, graduated from The Institute of Industrial Arts in 1953 where she studied fashion design. Kaunis Koru hired her in 1957. She produced silver and onyx rings for them, structured and uncomplicated. In the free- spirited Sixties, her bracelets for Kalevela Koru spiraled up the arm, the separate parts moving with the wearer, reflecting the clear Nordic light. An elegant line of large square-cut crystals set in a pyramid in rings, and hanging from slender silver links was very different from a stabile of myriad squares casually hooked around the neck; both designs from the Sixties.

In 1967, Paula opened her own shop where she could fully display her talents as a fashion and jewelry designer, selling knits and silver cuffs and amazing rings with satellite parts. In the Seventies she concentrated on teaching at the University of Industrial Arts and freelance designing. A 1983 exhibition of her jewelry triggered a new crafts revival. Her new brooches were like silver space craft with slender wires curled around them, bold yet delicate, and like all her other pieces, highly original.

High standing silver ring with square-cut pyramid crystals by Paula Häiväoja, late Sixties. With silver and city marks. *Courtesy of Kalevela Koru Oy. Photo by Studio Wendt*

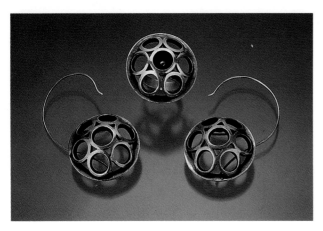

Earmuff silver earrings and openwork ring by Aarikka. Signed "AAJ" with date letters for 1968 and '69. *Courtesy of Christie Romero. Photo by Robert Weldon*

Reverse of Aarikka piece showing signature, and Finnish silver hallmarks and date marks. *Photo by Robert Weldon*

Clean lines and clasp for a silver bracelet by Börje Rajalin for Kalevela Koru, Fifties. With corresponding silver marks. *Courtesy of Kalevela Koru*

Kaija Aarikka (1929-) graduated from the Industrial Arts school in textile design, and manufactured wooden buttons from the endless Finnish forests to go with her fabrics. This evolved into functional wood and silver jewelry which was a great success in Sweden, and, eventually, jewelry using silver shot which was hand-made for her by two silversmiths. For one daring set in the Sixties she curled pierced silver earrings on a wire around and into the ear like earmuffs, with a ring to match. The Aarikka shop continues its industrial and handmade lines of jewelry and objects today in Helsinki.

Pekka Piekäinen (1945-) designed a simple, straightforward line for Kaunis Koru in the late 60's that was unusual for the time. Moving to Turku for Auran Kultaseppä, the second oldest silver factory in Finland, he ventured into silver holloware, and rings and brooches using odd cuts of amethysts in high relief silver settings. His commissions for gifts of State and industrial concerns make him the leading silver designer in Finland today.

Börje Rajalin (1933-) studied art metalwork with Bertel Gardberg. He became chief designer for Kalevela Koru in 1956 where he made all the prototypes for serial production. In 1958, he, Elis Kauppi, Bertel Gardberg, and Eero Rislakki participated in an avant-garde exhibition which received enthusiastic press and eventually international recognition for the artists. Sigurd Persson, the noted Swedish silversmith, wrote; "Since the war, Finnish industrial arts have acquired global recognition. However, jewelry was never included in their international showings for the simple reason that no real work had been done in that field. Now this has all been changed at Helsinki's Galerie Artek." Tuula Poutasuo quotes Rajalin as saying: "Our pieces were pure line, with attention focussed on materials and function. Their design even extended to the closing devices, and many novel techniques were invented." Rajalin's contributions were the simplest possible twists of silver around the neck and a handsome hinged silver bracelet with a large spectrolite stone. In the Sixties his style changed dramatically, when he produced bracelets of large clusters of smoky and rose quartz cabochons and faceted garnets, very decorative and "unfunctional".

Lappland stones smoky and rose quartz, garnet and topaz adorn this handsome gold bracelet by Börje Rajalin produced by Kalevela Koru, Sixties. *Courtesy of Kalevela Koru Oy. Photo by Otso Pietinen*

Simple silver twist necklace by Börje Rajalin for Kalevela Koru, ca. Fifties. With silver marks and the boat stamp for the city of Helsinki. *Courtesy of Kalevela Koru Oy. Photo by Otso Pietinen*

Silver bangle bracelet with crystal stone, 1972, and sterling dome ring, 1957 by E. Granit & Co. And a sterling ring with concave hemispheres around a high-domed amethyst, with Kupittaan Kulta anvil stamp. *Courtesy of Christie Romero. Photo by Robert Weldon*

Erik Granit (1930-1988) opened his silversmith's workshop E. Granit & Co.in Helsinki in 1956. He continued working there until his death. A bangle bracelet with a rock crystal center, and a high domed ring with silver granulation are typical of his work over those 30 years.

In the Sixties, cast silver and gold jewelry was developed by two extraordinary artists, Pentti Sarpaneva (1925-1978) and Björn Weckström. This was an ideal method for large production of rough-surfaced or sculptural jewelry which did not need extensive polishing or refining. (The Sarpaneva name is well-known in Finland, Timo and Pi, Pentti's brother, and sister-in-law design glassware for Iittala.) Pentti was a graphic artist into his thirties, when he began assembling his original jewelry of *objets trouvés*; bits of birch bark, zippers, embroidery, and boat rivets which he enamelled. These were regarded as outrageous and unwearable by the general public. Tamed, but only slightly, he cast high relief pins in silver and bronze which looked like frozen lava with rough, uncut smoky quartz centers, and small hanging chains. (These decorative chain elements can be seen in ancient Viking ornaments.) His Finnish folklore pendants, cufflinks, and brooches for Kalevela Koru in the late Sixties were barbaric shapes in silver and bronze. For the Turku firm of Turun Hopea, Pentti cast romantic lace jewelry from plastic molds of Rauma lace, even carrying the theme to his candlesticks and silverware. Sarpaneva was a fine example of the fertile Finnish imagination.

High relief cast silver brooch with rough uncut smoky quartz center stone and silver dangle rings by Pentti Sarpaneva, Fifties. *Courtesy of the author. Photo by Robert Weldon, courtesy of G.I.A.*

Reverse of Pentti Sarpaneva brooch, showing signature. *Photo by Robert Weldon, courtesy of GIA*

Reverse of E. Granit piece showing firm signature, the Helsinki boat stamp and date letter. *Photo by Robert Weldon*

Cufflinks of rough and smooth silver elements by Pentti Sarpaneva for Kalevela Koru, late Sixties. With appropriate silver marks. *Courtesy of Kalevela Koru. Photo by Studio Wendt*

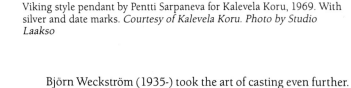

Viking style pendant by Pentti Sarpaneva for Kalevela Koru, 1969. With silver and date marks. *Courtesy of Kalevela Koru. Photo by Studio Laakso*

Björn Weckström (1935-) took the art of casting even further. He wanted to train as a sculptor, but family opposition turned him in another direction. Encouraged by his relative, Bertel Gardberg, he studied at the Goldsmith school in 1956. As a master-craftsman, he set up his own workshop and Lapponia Gallery in Helsinki, selling his work as well as that of Gardberg and Sarpaneva. His cast pieces using raw gold nuggets won first prize at an international competition in Rio de Janiero in 1965. His Lapponia jewelry caught on, and Weckström's reputation was further enhanced by winning the Lunning prize three years later. Weckström's sculptural cufflinks and rings played with volumes and surfaces, alternating the light reflections on shiny and matt silver.

Weckström has successfully balanced his artistic career between the monumental (sculpture) and the miniature (jewelry). His rings, bracelets, cufflinks, and necklaces are "tiny sculptures and miniature landscapes" created from figurative silver and Acrylic. They are dramatic, mystical, and unforgettable. "Technically," he explains, "when making a work of small size, one must overdramatize the forms. Jewelry is a miniature sculpture to me, but because a woman is going to wear it, it gets a quite specially sensual, mystic-erotic charge. So many forces and symbols can be concentrated in it!" Weckström divides his time between Italy, where he produces astonishing bronze statues from mythical sources, and his Helsinki gallery. In Finland, "nature is present as a very dominant element. The language of form starts from an organic basis in nature, whereas people are the central factor in Italy."

Cast "crumpled" silver cufflinks by Björn Weckström, 1970, with silver marks and "BW" signature. *Courtesy of the author. Photo by Robert Weldon*

Reverse of cufflinks showing Lapponia stamp,"BW" signature for Björn Weckström, and sterling, Helsinki, and date marks for the above piece. *Photo by Robert Weldon*

Helsinki   *Hämeenlinna*   *Turku*

A –1810	O 2–1847	B 4–1883	O 5–1919	B 7–1955
B –1811	P 2–1848	C 4–1884	P 5–1920	C 7–1956
C –1812	Q 2–1849	D 4–1885	Q 5–1921	D 7–1957
D –1813	R 2–1850	E 4–1886	R 5–1922	E 7–1958
E –1814	S 2–1851	F 4–1887	S 5–1923	F 7–1959
F –1815	T 2–1852	G 4–1888	T 5–1924	G 7–1960
G –1816	U 2–1853	H 4–1889	U 5–1925	H 7–1961
H –1817	V 2–1854	I 4–1890	V 5–1926	I 7–1962
I –1818	X 2–1855	K 4–1891	X 5–1927	K 7–1963
K –1819	Y 2–1856	L 4–1892	Y 5–1928	L 7–1964
L –1820	Z 2–1857	M 4–1893	Z 5–1929	M 7–1965
M –1821	A 3–1858	N 4–1894	A 6–1930	N 7–1966
N –1822	B 3–1859	O 4–1895	B 6–1931	O 7–1967
O –1823	C 3–1860	P 4–1896	C 6–1932	P 7–1968
P –1824	D 3–1861	Q 4–1897	D 6–1933	Q 7–1969
Q –1825	E 3–1862	R 4–1898	E 6–1934	R 7–1970
R –1826	F 3–1863	S 4–1899	F 6–1935	S 7–1971
S –1827	G 3–1864	T 4–1900	G 6–1936	T 7–1972
T –1828	H 3–1865	U 4–1901	H 6–1937	U 7–1973
U –1829	I 3–1866	V 4–1902	I 6–1938	V 7–1974
V –1830	K 3–1867	X 4–1903	K 6–1939	X 7–1975
X –1831	L 3–1868	Y 4–1904	L 6–1940	Y 7–1976
Y –1832	M 3–1869	Z 4–1905	M 6–1941	Z 7–1977
Z –1833	N 3–1870	A 5–1906	N 6–1942	A 8–1978
A 2–1834	O 3–1871	B 5–1907	O 6–1943	B 8–1979
B 2–1835	P 3–1872	C 5–1908	P 6–1944	C 8–1980
C 2–1836	Q 3–1873	D 5–1909	Q 6–1945	D 8–1981
D 2–1837	R 3–1874	E 5–1910	R 6–1946	E 8–1982
E 2–1838	S 3–1875	F 5–1911	S 6–1947	F 8–1983
F 2–1839	T 3–1876	G 5–1912	T 6–1948	G 8–1984
G 2–1840	U 3–1877	H 5–1913	U 6–1949	H 8–1985
H 2–1841	V 3–1878	I 5–1914	V 6–1950	I 8–1986
I 2–1842	X 3–1879	K 5–1915	X 6–1951	K 8–1987
K 2–1843	Y 3–1880	L 5–1916	Y 6–1952	L 8–1988
L 2–1844	Z 3–1881	M 5–1917	Z 6–1953	M 8–1989
M 2–1845	A 4–1882	N 5–1918	A 7–1954	N 8–1990
N 2–1846				

Finnish City marks (3), and date letters from 1810-1990 from the TTK. *Jalometallituotteet* Precious Metal Hallmark book *Tarkastusleimat Suomessa*, Helsinki, 1984.

The Lapponia Jewelry label has adapted easily to the Space Age. Literally. A necklace called "Planetary Valleys" (1977) was worn by Princess Leia (played by Carrie Fisher) in *Star Wars*. Weckström's fun with Acrylic and silver in a spaced-out ring called "Petrified Lake" was worn by Yoko Ono, deserving a close up on Dick Cavett's T.V. show in 1972. Lapponia sales went ballistic.

By the Sixties, silver jewelry and objets were as treasured a gift as art glass. The Finnish Society for Crafts and Design arranged local and international exhibitions. There was a dearth of modern silver jewelry in European countries, so Finnish and Scandinavian exports were successfully sold there for ten years until the usual problem of copies wrecked the market. In the Seventies the invasion of the dread gold chains further cut into sales. Happily, in the late Eighties there was a proliferation of silver and goldsmiths with intriguing ideas, and the galleries and handicraft centers to market them. The Finns have a talent for simplification which is displayed in all the decorative arts. Finland will continue to astonish us into the next century.

1. Tuula Poutasuo, *Finnish Silver From the Second World War to Post-Modernism*, Rauma, Finland, 1989, pp 48-83. This booklet was the source for most of the biographical details of the Finnish artists in this chapter.
2. Oppi Untracht, *Saara Hopea-Untracht: Life and Work*, Porvoo-Helsinki-Juva, Werner Söderström Osakeyhtiö, 1988, pg. 264.

The "Man from Mercury" adorns this Space cuff of crumpled cast silver, 1969, by Björn Weckström, bearing maker's marks and sterling and city marks. *Courtesy of Lapponia Gallery, Helsinki, Finland*

A cast sculptural ring with matt and shiny surfaces by Weckström, bears the "W", Lapponia and 925 silver marks, and date letter V7 for 1974. A high-domed silver ring also showing the alternating smooth and rough surfaces technique is stamped "E. Granit Co. Design Jewellery, the Helsinki city mark, and P7 date letter for 1966. *Courtesy of the author. Photo by Robert Weldon*

Epilogue

Over the past century we have seen jewelry evolve from the British and Dutch Arts & Crafts designs fuelled by the spiritualist revival, to modern Nordic pendants inspired by ancient amulets worn for their magic powers, to the "Power Jewelry" of the Eighties, status symbols which gave women confidence in a fiercely competitive world. From mystical to mythical to monumental.

The impact of the Old World designers cannot be overstated. Following the World Wars and Depression, there was a migration of artisans from the fine jewelry ateliers to costume jewelry or artists' workshops. Even more important was the emigration to the New World of gifted designers and craftspeople from Europe (Germans, Italians, French, and Austrians settled on the East Coast) and Scandinavia (Chicago and the Mid-West) where they contributed their extensive training and expertise to all facets of 20th century design. (A list of the top manufacturers and workshops in America is composed principally of jewelers of foreign birth.) They brought with them a sense of history which when combined with American verve and business knowhow produced an explosion of creative energy. In the 21st century, the new generation of artists which has emerged in Europe and America will be making history of its own. The millenium holds a promise of renewal; the year 2000 is both an end and a beginning.

Far-out ring, "Petrified Lake", of silver and Acrylic, showing the texture contrasts between the rough cast silver and the smooth transparent Acrylic bubble. Designed by Weckström in 1971, and worn by Yoko Ono in 1972. Presently out of production. Bearing the maker's marks, silver, city, and date marks. *Courtesy of Lapponia Oy Gallery, Helsinki*

"Planetary Valleys" designed in 1969, and worn by Princess Leia (Carrie Fisher) in *Star Wars*, 1977. Designed by Björn Weckström, and cast by Lapponia Oy Jewelry Gallery. With maker's marks and Finnish silver marks. *Courtesy of Lapponia, Helsinki*

Bibliography

Anscombe, Isabelle. *A Woman's Touch: Women in Design from 1860 to the Present*. New York, NY: Elisabeth Sifton Books - Viking. 1984.

Arwas, Victor. *Art Deco*. New York, NY; Harry N. Abrams Inc. 1980.

Baker, Lillian. *Twentieth Century Fashionable Plastic Jewelry*. Padukah, KY: Collector Books. 1992.

Ball, Joanne D. *Jewelry of the Stars*. West Chester, PA: Schiffer Publishing Ltd. 1991.

Battersby, Martin. *The Decorative Thirties*. New York, NY: Walker and Co. 1971.

_____. *The Decorative Twenties*. New York, NY: Walker and Co. 1969.

Becker, Vivienne. *Fabulous Fakes: The History of Fantasy and Fashion Jewelry*. London, England: Grafton Books. 1988.

_____. *Rough Diamonds: The Butler and Wilson Collection*. New York, NY: Rizzoli Publications Inc. 1972.

_____. *Art Nouveau Jewelry*. New York, NY: E.P. Dutton. 1985.

Bowman, Sara. *Fashion for Extravagance: Art Deco Fabrics and Fashions*. New York, NY: E.P. Dutton. 1985.

Brunhammer, Yvonne. *Le Style 1925*. Paris, France: Baschet et Cie. n.d.

_____. *The 1920s Style*. London, England: Paul Hamlyn. 1969.

Cartlidge, Barbara. *Twentieth Century Jewelry*. New York, NY. Harry N. Abrams Inc. 1985.

Damase, Jacques and Delaunay, Sonia. *Robes Pòemes*. Paris, France and Milan, Italy: Edizioni del Naviglio. 1969.

Delhaye, Jean. *Art Deco: Posters and Graphics*. New York, NY: Rizzoli Inc. 1977.

Davidoff, Corinne and Dawes, Ginny R. *The Bakelite Jewelry Book*. New York, NY: Abbevile Press. 1988.

Delaunay, Sonia. *Compositions, Couleurs, Idées*. Paris, France: Charles Moreau. 1930?

_____. *Nous Irons Jusqu'au Soleil*. Paris, France: Editions Robert Laffont. 1978.

Ellman, Barbara. *The World of Fashion Jewelry*. Highland Park, IL: Aunt Louise Imports. 1986.

Erté. *Things I Remember: An Autobiography*. New York, NY: Quadrangle/The New York Times Book Co. 1975.

Fahrner, Theodor. *Jewelry...Between Avant-Garde and Tradition*. West Chester, PA: Schiffer Publishing Ltd. 1991.

Farneti Cera, Deanna (editor, Italian ed.). *Jewels of Fantasy - Costume Jewelry of the Twentieth Century*. New York, NY. Harry N. Abrams Inc. 1992.

Flanner, Janet. *Paris was Yesterday*. New York, NY: Popular Library. 1972.

Fossburg, Jorunn. *Draktsølje*. Oslo, Norway. Universitetsforlaget. 1991.

Fry, Charles F. (editor). *Art Deco Designs in Color*. New York, NY: Dover Publications Inc. 1975.

Gabardi, Melissa. *Art Deco Jewellery 1920 to 1949*. Suffolk, England: Antique Collectors' Club. 1989.

Ginsberg, Madeleine. *Paris Fashions: The Art Deco Style of the 1920s*. London, England: Bracken Books. 1989.

Gordon, Angie. *20th Century Costume Jewelry*. New York, NY: Adasia International. 1990.

Griffin Leonard and Meisel, Louis K. and Susan P. *Clarice Cliff: The Bizarre Affair*. New York, NY: Harry N. Abrams Inc. 1988.

Hallmarks and Date Letters on Silver, Gold and Platinum. Colchester, Essex, U.K. N.A.G. Press Ltd. 1977.

Haslam, Malcolm. *Art Deco*. London, England: Macdonald and Co. Ltd. 1987.

Hammond, Bryan and O'Connor, Patrick. *Josephine Baker*. London, England: Jonathan Cape Ltd. 1988.

Hase, von, Ulrike. *Schmuck in Deutschland und Osterreich 1895-1914*. München. 1977.

Haslam, Malcolm. *Arts and Crafts*. London, England: Macdonald and Co. Ltd. 1988.

Hermanovits, Jean and Brunelleschi. *La Guirlande*. Paris, France: 3 Rue de Chaillot. 1er Fascicule.

Holme, Charles, editor. *Modern Design in Jewellery and Fans. Special Winter Number of the Studio, 1900-1902*. London, Paris, N.Y. Offices of The Studio.

Jargstorf, Sibylle. *Glass in Jewelry: Hidden Artistry in Glass*. West Chester, PA: Schiffer Publishing Ltd. 1991.

_____. *Baubles, Buttons and Beads: The Heritage of Bohemia*. Atglen, PA: Schiffer Publishing Ltd. 1993.

Kallir, Jane. *Viennese Design and the Weiner Werkstätte*. New York, NY: Galerie St. Etienne. 1986.

Karlin, Elyse Z. *Jewelry and Metalwork in the Arts and Crafts Tradition*. Atglen, PA: Schiffer Publishing Ltd. 1993.

Katz, Sylvia. *Early Plastics*. Aylesbury, England. Shire Publications Ltd. 1986.

_____. *Classic Plastics: From Bakelite to High-Tech*. London, England: Thames and Hudson. 1984.

Kelley, Lyngerda and Schiffer, Nancy. *Costume Jewelry: The Great Pretenders*. West Chester, PA: Schiffer Publishing Ltd. 1987.

_____. *Plastic Jewelry*. West Chester, PA: Schiffer Publishing Ltd. 1987.

Kery, Patricia F. *Art Deco Graphics*. New York, NY: Harry N. Abrams. 1986.

Krekel-Aalberse, Annelies. *Art Nouveau and Art Deco Silver*. London, England: Thames and Hudson Ltd. 1989.

Lanllier, Jean and Pini, Marie-Anne. *Five Centuries of Jewelry in the West*. New York, NY: Arch Cape Press. 1983.

Lanoux, Armand. *Paris 1925*. Paris, France: Bernard Grasset. 1975.

Lesieutre, Alain. *The Spirit and Splendour of Art Deco*. New York, NY: Paddington Press Ltd. 1988.

Lynam, Ruth (editor). *Couture*. Garden City, NY: Doubleday and Co. Inc. 1972.

Marcilhac, Félix. *Jean Dunand, His Life and Works*. English edition. New York, NY. Harry N. Abrams. 1991.

Martin, Richard. *Fashion and Surrealism*. New York, NY: Rizzoli Ltd. 1987.

Mauriès, Patrick. *Jewelry by Chanel*. Boston, MA: Little, Brown and Co. 1993.

McClinton, Katherine M. *Art Deco: A Guide for Collectors*. New York, NY: Clarkson N. Potter Inc. 1972.

McClinton, Katherine M. *Lalique for Collectors*. New York, NY: Charles Scribner's Sons. 1975.

Miller, Anna. *Cameos - Old and New.* New York, NY. Van Nostrand Reinhold. 1991.

Miller, Harrice S. *Costume Jewelry.* 2nd edition. New York, NY: Avon Books. 1994.

Mokveld, Monique. *Anneke Schat: Modern Jewelry.* Amsterdam, Holland: Ploegsma. 1987.

Montorgueil, Georges. *Rouge et Blanc, Dessins de Paul Iribe.* Paris, France: Etablissements Nicolas. 1930.

Morano, Elizabeth and Vreeland, Diana. *Sonia Delaunay: Art into Fashion.* New York, NY: George Braziller Inc. 1986.

Nadelhoffer, Hans. *Cartier: Jewelers Extraordinaire.* New York, NY: Harry N. Abrams Inc. 1984.

Neuwirth, Waltrand. *Weiner Gold- und Silberschmiede und ihre Pünzen 1867-1922.* (two vols). Vienna, Austria. 1977.

Poiret, Paul. *En Habillant L'Epoque.* Paris, France: Bernard Grasset. 1930.

Poutasuo, Tuula. *Finnish Silver.* Rauma, Finland: 1989.

Pullée, Caroline. *20th Century Jewelry.* New York, NY: Mallard Press. 1990.

Registrering Af Navnestempler For Arbejder Af Aedle Metaller 1893-1988. København, DK. Statens Kontrol med Aedle, Metaller. 1988.

Rheims, Maurice. *The Flowering of Art Nouveau.* New York, NY: Harry N. Abrams Inc. n.d.

Romero, Christie. *Warman's Jewelry,* Radnor, PA. Chilton Company, 1995.

Rudolph, Monika. *Naum Slutzky: Meister am Bauhaus Goldschmied und Designer.* Stuttgart, Germany: Arnold'sche. 1990.

Schiffer, Nancy. *The Best of Costume Jewelry.* West Chester, PA: Schiffer Publishing Ltd. 1990.

_____. *Costume Jewelry: The Fun of Collecting.* West Chester, PA: Schiffer Publishing Ltd. 1988.

Sembach, Klaus-Jürgen. *Style 1930.* New York, NY. Universe Books. 1971.

Shields, Jody. *All that Glitters: The Glory of Costume Jewelry.* New York, NY: Rizzoli Ltd. 1987.

Spencer, Charles. *The World of Serge Diaghilev.* Middlesex, England: Penguin Books Ltd. 1974.

_____. *Erté.* New York, NY: Charles N. Potter Inc. 1970.

Stancliffe, Jane, *Costume and Fashion Jewellery in the Twentieth Century,* the V. & A. Album, London, The Montfort Publishing Co., 1985.

Tardy, *International Hallmarks on Silver.* Paris, France. 1985.

Tarkastustleimat Suomessa Jalometallituotteet. (Precious metal marks). T.T.K. Helsinki, Finland. 1984.

Thage, Jacob. *Danske Smykker, Danish Jewelry.* Komma & Clausen Bøgero. 1990.

Untracht, Oppi. *Saara Hopea-Untracht: Life and Work.* Helsinki, Finland: Werner Söderström Osakoyhtiö. 1988.

_____. *Jewelry Concepts and Technology.* London, Robert Hale Limited, 1982.

Van De Lemme, Arie. *A guide to Art Deco Style.* Seacaucus, NJ: Chartwell Books. 1986.

Vautrin, Line and Mauriès, Patrick. *Line Vautrin: Sculptor, Jeweler and Magician.* London, England: Thames and Hudson Ltd. 1992.

Vogelsberger, Vera. *Emailkunst aus Wein 1900-1989.* Vienna, Austria: Tusch. 1990.

Weber, Christianne. *Schmuck: Der 20er und 30er Jahre in Deutschland.* Stuttgart, Germany: Arnold'sche. 1990.

Westin, Ann. *Torun: Conversations with Vivianna Torun Bülow-Hübe.* Sweden. Carlssons Bökforlag. 1993.

White, Palmer. *Elsa Schiaparelli: Empress of Paris Fashion.* New York, NY: Rizzoli Ltd. 1986.

White, Palmer. *Haute Couture Embroidery: The Art of Lesage.* New York, NY: Vendome Press. 1988.

_____. *Poiret.* New York, NY: Clarkson N. Potter Inc. 1973.

Wingler, Hans. *Bauhaus.* Boston, MA: MIT Press. 1969.

Zahle, Erik. *Skandinavische Kunsthandwerk.* München, Germany: Droemer-Knaur. 1961

Zezschwitz, von, Beate Dry. *Fahrner-Schmuck.* München. Ketterer Kunst Verlag. 1990.

Journals

Benesh, Caroline. Baroque Splendor. *Ornament.* Autumn, 1994. San Marcos, CA. p. 22.

Dry, Graham. "Liberty and Company's `Nola' Metalwork: Art Nouveau Nickel-Silver Jewelry from Pforzheim." Decorative Arts Society 1850 to the Present. no. 14. 1990.

Dry, Graham. "Porzellanschmuck." from *Die Kunst und das schöne Heim.* July, 1982. pp 491-493.

Gazettes du Bon Ton. Paris, France. Aux Editions Lucién Vogel. 1912-1925.

Greenbaum, Toni. "The Enduring Legacy of Mogul Indian Jewelry." *Heritage, Jewelers' Circular-Keystone.* vol.CLXIV. May, 1993. pp. 110-114.

Lael, Hagan. "The Retro Revival." *Heritage, Jeweler's Circular-Keystone,* Vol. CLXV, May, 1994, pp. 85-98.

Ramshaw, Wendy. "Picasso's Ladies." *The Antique Collector.* vol.61. March, 1990. pp.58-61.

Roland, Leah M. "Liberty Jewels Merge Artistry and Industry." *Heritage, Jewelers' Circular-Keystone.* vol.CLXIV. August, 1993. pp.116-123.

Sutton, Denys (editorial). "Poiret: Pasha of Fashion." Apollo. vol.XCIX. London U.K. *The Financial Times Ltd.* January, 1974.

Swift, Vivian. "Victorian Scottish Jewelry: Highlander Style with a British Twist." *Heritage, Jewelers' Circular-Keystone.* vol.CLXIII. November, 1992. pp.55-59.

Catalogs

Bizot, Chantal. *Les Bijoux de Torun,* Musée des Arts Décoratifs, Paris, 1993.

Björn Weckström. Retretti. Finland. 1986.

Catalogue des Verreries de René Lalique, Paris, René Lalique & Cie., 1932

Christie's. *Designer Costume Jewellery.* London, England. April 1, 1992.

_____. *Important Art Nouveau and Art Deco.* New York, NY. October 2, 1981

_____. *Important Twentieth Century Decorative Arts.* New York, NY. December 9, 1988.

_____. *Twentieth Century Scandinavian Decorative Arts.* Geneva, Switzerland. May 7, 1989.

Contemporary Swedish Design. Swedish Society of Crafts and Design. Stockholm National Museum, Sweden.

Delaunay, Sonia: A Retrospective. Albright-Knox Gallery. Buffalo, NY. February 2, 1980.

Delaunay, Sonia and Robert: Le Centenaire. Musée D'Art Moderne. Paris, France. May 14,1985.

Delaunay, Sonia et Robert. Bibliothèque Nationale. Paris, France. 1977.

Delaunay, Sonia and Robert. (photo album of sets and costumes made for 1926 film *Le P'tit Parigot*). 1926.

William Doyle Galleries. *Couture, Antique Clothing, Accessories, & Costume Jewelry.* New York, April 27, 1994.

Gioie di Hollywood: American Designers of Fashion Jewelry, 1920-1960. Venice Design Art Gallery. Venice, Italy. 1987.

Hommage à Balenciaga. Lyon, France. Musée Historiques des Tissus, 1985.

Illustrateurs des Modes et Manières en 1925. Galerie du Luxembourg. Paris, France. October 25, 1975.

Georg Jensen Silversmiths: 77 Artists - 75 Years. Washington, D.C. Smithsonian Institution Press. 1980.

Kalevala Koru. *A Pageant of Ancient Finnish Dress.* 1835 - 1985. Helsinki, Finland.

La Grande Vapeur. Musée du Peigne et des Matières Plastiques. Ville D'Oyonnax, France. 1987.

La Mode dans L'Art. Millon & Robert, *Commissaires priseurs associés.* Paris-Drouot Richelieu, 9 Juin, 1993.

Lajos, Németh. *Béla Voros Exposition.* Musée Belassa Balmut Estergom, Hungary. Corvina. 1972.

Lepape, Georges. *Les Choses de Paul Poiret.* Paris, 1911.

Lille, Jacqueline. *Perlenschmuck: Beads at Work.* Cooper-Hewitt Museum: The Smithsonian Institution's National Museum of Design. September, 1990.

Sotheby's. *Arts Décoratifs du XXe Siècle.* Monaco. October 11, 1987.

Sotheby's. *The Diana Vreeland Collection of Fashion Jewelry.* New York, October, 1987.

Sotheby's. *Important 20th Century Decorative Arts.* New York, November, 1987.

Tone Vigelund. Kunstindustrimuseet. Oslo, Norway. ca. 1992.

Value Guide

The following is a guide to the value of the jewelry described in this book. Prices are approximate, based not only on condition, uniqueness, provenance, craftsmanship, and quality of design, but on location and date of purchase. Generally, but not always, the piece can be found in the country of origin for the best price. Experts at the source, however, may place a higher value on a piece than a less knowledgeable dealer elsewhere. The jewelry of some artists and collectors (who prefer not to quote prices) are marked "n.a.", not available. Refer to art galleries, museum and specialty shops, as well as auction houses for current values. Average prices are not definitive and are subject to revision at a later date.

The left hand number is the page number. The letters following the page number indicate the position of the photograph on the page: T=top, L=left, R=right, TL=top left, TR=top right, C=center, CL=center left, CR=center right, B=bottom, BL=bottom left, BR=bottom right. The right hand column of numbers are the estimated price ranges in United States dollars.

Page	Position	Item	Value
frontispiece		necklaces: see corresponding chapters	
half title		brooch, "topaz":	300-400
4 Dedication		brooches, top:	500-700;
		bottom:	700-1000
9 frontispiece		Europe brooch:	3200-3500

Chapter 1: France

Page	Position	Item	Value
12	TL	pendants,	l: 2500-2800; r: 4500-4800
12		pendants:	1300-1500;
		brooch:	2200-2500
13	TR	pendant:	750-850
13	BR	pendants:	650-700; B: 800-850
14	TL	bracelets:	250-300
14	C	pendant:	450-550
14	B	barettes:	250-400;
		hair combs:	500-600
15	T	combs:	500-600
15	B	dragonfly:	1000-1200
16	TR	buckle:	700-800
16	BL	buckle:	450-550
16	BR	buckle:	300-350
17	TL	buckles:	350-450
17	TR	belt: (2 buckles),	500-600
17	B	belt (2 buckles):	600-700
18	T	buckle:(2)	50-100
18	B	scarabs:	75-175
19	T	pin:	500-600
22	TL	bar pin:	900-1000
22	TR	brooch:	800-850
22	B	silver collar:	2700-3000
23	TR	pins:	150-250
23	BL	buckles:	200-250
23	BR	sautoir:	400-500
24	T	cases:	500-600;
		holders:	250-300
24	BL	purse:	500-700
25	TR	brooches,	l: 150-180; r: 250-350
25	BL	necklace:	200-300
26	TR	necklace:	250-350
26	BR	necklace:	1000-1200
27	TR	combs:	300-350
27	BR	diadems;	1500-2000,
		earrings:	400
28	TL	combs:	350-500
28	TR	barettes:	130-180
28	B	buckles:	70-120
29	T	pins:	80-150
29	CR	barettes:	140-175 pair
29	B	pins:	80-170
30	T	Forties necklaces:	1000-1500;
		Thirties,	2500-3000
31	T	brooches:	400-500
31	B	brooches/ compact:	160-200
32	TR	necklace:	125-115,
		clip:	100-135
32	TR	hat pins:	150-180,
		brooch:	175
32	B	purses:	250-300;
		pin:	150-180
33	TL	necklace:	600-800
33	TR		n.a.
33	B	cigarette cases:	250-300
34	TL	earrings:	250-300
34	TR	bracelet/ brooch:	200-250 each
34	BL	pendant:	700-800
34	BR	pendant:	500-600
38	T	brooches:	150-200;
		bracelet:	200-300
38	BL	brooch:	800-1200
38	BR	necklace:	250-300
39	TR	set:	300-400
40	T	pendants/ buckle:	500-700 each
40	C	cigarette case:	600-700
41	TR	ring:	1200-1500
41	CL	bracelet:	3000-4000;
		rings:	1500-1800
41	BR	bracelet:	3000-4000;
		brooches:	2000-3000
42	TL	necklace:	10,000-15,000
42	TR	collar:	10,000-12,000
42	B	from l to r:	3000-4000; 4000-5000; 2500-3000: 1200-1500
43	TR	cuff:	400-500;
		rings:	200-250
43	BR	box:	2000-2500;
		brooch:	300-400;
		pendant:	250-300
44	TR	pendant:	1500-1700
44	CL	pendants:	1500-1800
44	BL	pins:	80-125;
		bracelets:	250-350
45	TR	brooches:	250-300;
		bracelets:	250-300
45	CL	bracelet:	450-650
45	BR	bracelet:	700-800
46	TR	watches:	150-250
46	CL	bracelets:	500-600
46	BR	bowtie:	100-150;
		cufflinks:	25-45
47	TL	necklaces:	450-550
47	TR	top:	250-350;
		bottom:	175-220
47	CR	pendants:	450-550
47	BL	bracelet:	250-300;
		brooch:	200-250
48	TL	necklaces, top:	400-550;
		bottom:	500-600
48	TR	buckle:	250-300
48	BL	brooch:	250-300;
		rings,	c: 300-350: r: 200-250
48	BR	brooch:	250-300;
		necklaces:	350-450
49	T	mirror, case, ring:	250-300 each
49	BL	earrings:	100-175
50	TL	top left set:	350-500;
		brooches:	250-300;
		bracelet:	500-700
50	BR	silver rings:	150-250;
		gold:	300-350
51	TR	necklace:	200-250
51	CR	bracelets:	250-300
51	B	bracelet:	150-200
52	B	purse:	300-400
53	TL	clip:	275-350
53	C	glasses:	150-200

No.	Pos.	Item	Price
53	B	glasses:	150-200
54	TR	necklace:	2000-2500
54	BL	necklace:	2000-2200
55	TR	necklace:	2000-2200
55	CL	necklace:	2000-2200
55	BR	necklace:	1800-2000
56	TL	necklace:	800-1000
56	TR	necklace:	800-1000
56	BL	necklace:	500-700
57	TR	necklaces, top:	500-700;
		c:	800-1000;
		brooch:	500-600
57	BL	brooch:	350-400
58	TR	necklace:	700-800
58	CL	necklace:	700-800
58	BR	brooch:	1000-1500
59	TR	cross:	n.a.
59	CR	pendnat,	n.a.
59	BL	necklaces & bracelets,	n.a.
60	TR	necklace:	n.a.
60	C	cross:	500-700;
		earrings:	250-350
60	BR	necklace,	n.a.
61	TL	brooches:	400-500 each
61	BL	earrings:	200-350 the pair
61	BR	brooch:	400-500
62	TR	pendant,	l: 300-400;
		brooch:	250-350;
			r: 300-400
62	CR	earrings:	75-150
62	BL	necklace:	500-700
63	TL	pendants,	l: 150-200;
			c: 250-350;
			r: 250-300
63	CL	pendants:	200-250
63	BR	necklace:	500-700
64	TR	necklaces:	300-500
64	BL	necklaces:	200-300
64	BR	necklaces:	150-300
65	CL	necklace:	600-700
66	TR	necklace:	350-450
66	BR	necklace:	800-900
67	TR	sautoirs:	500-600
67	BR	earrings:	250-275
68	TL	necklace:	500-600
68	TR	necklace:	700-900
68	BL	necklace:	600-700
69	FP	handbag:	4000;
		earrings:	200-300;
		bracelets:	600-800
70	TL	handbag:	3000;
		earrings:	550;
		bracelet:	1000
70	BL	belt:	300-400
71	TR	cufflinks, earrings:	150-200 the pair
71	CR	silver bracelet:	1500-2000
71	BL	brooch:	350-400
72	BL	brooches:	400-500
72	BR	set:	700-800
73	BL	brooch:	350-450
73	BR	set:	1500-1800
74	TR	necklace:	n.a.
74	CL	necklace:	450-550
74	BR	set:	450-500
75	TR	brooch:	350-450;
		necklace:	1500-1700
75	CL	bracelets:	150-200;
		bracelet:	150-200
75	BR	necklace:	1500-1700
76	TR	ornament:	1000-1300;
		buckles:	300
76	BL	necklace:	400-450
76	BR	ring:	300-400;
		bracelet:	600-800
77	TR	necklace:	1500-1700
77	CL	necklace:	450-600
77	BR	necklaces:	700-800 each
78	BL	necklace:	600-800
78	BR	set:	1000-1200
79	TL	necklaces:	1000-1500;
		brooch:	400-500
79	TR	set:	700-800
81	TL	bracelet:	2200-2400
81	TR	necklace:	900-1000
81	BR	necklace:	1500-1600
82	TL	bracelet:	700-800
82	BL	brooches,	l: 700-1000; r: 800-1000
82	CR	pendant,	top: 4000-6000;
	2nd row	brooches:	600-700; 1600-1800; 400-500;
	bottom row;		500-600; 800-900
83	TR	earrings:	200-250;
		brooch:	800-900
83	BR	hat:	150-250;
		glasses:	150-200;
		brooch:	200-250
84	TL	hand:	1200-1500
84	TR	brooch:	500-600
84	CR	set:	900-1200
85	TR	brooch:	600-900
85	B	set:	600-800;
		necklace:	450
86	TL	set:	650-750
86	B	set:	800-1000
87	TL	set:	800-1000; 600-700
87	TR	set:	700-800
87	BL	demi-parure:	1000-1200;
		necklace:	250-300
88	TL	earrings:	175-200;
		brooches:	350-450
88	TR	bracelet:	450-550
88	BL	bracelets:	250-350;
		earrings:	200-250;
		brooch:	300-350
88	BR	brooch:	600-800
89	TR	set:	800-900;
		bracelet:	250-300
89	BL	clockwise from top: brooch, (part lot) with earrings, 500-600; perfume pendant, 500-800; necklace, (part lot) with earrings, 500-600; bracelet (part lot) with earrings, 700-900; bracelet (part lot) with earrings &	
		necklace,	700-800;
		brooch (part lot) with necklace, bracelet, & earrings,	800-900
89	BR	bracelet,	250-300;
		necklace,	300-350;
		brooch,	300-350
91	TL	l: "Flamenco" brooch, bronze,	1300-1500;
		silver brooch/ pendant,	2700-3000
91	BL	rings:	200-250
91	BR	rings,	100-150;
		pendants,	300-400
92	TR	bracelet:	500-700
93	TR	necklace,	n.a.
93	BR	necklace:	300-400
94	TL	earrings:	300-400
94	CL	brooches:	300-400
94	CR	necklace:	300-400
94	BL	necklace:	350-450
95	TL	set:	400-500
95	TR	bracelets:	600-800
95	B	set:	1800-2000
96	TL	bracelet:	300-400
96	BL	bow:	250-300;
		pendant:	300-400
96	BR	bracelet:	350-400
97	TL	belt,	n.a.
97	CR	hearts & crosses:	400-500
97	BL	faucet necklace:	600-700;
		other:	300-400
98	TL	set:	1500-1800
98	TR	earrings:	300;
		bracelet:	300-400
98	BL	belt,	250-300;
		combs,	200-300
99	TL	hoops,	150-200;
		earclips,	200-250
99	TR	pendant,	300-350;
		set,	350-400
99	CL	necklace:	1000-1200
99	BR	earrings:	150-250
100	TL	set:	n.a.
100	BL	pendants:	500-700 each
101	TL	set,	n.a.
101	TR	necklace:	600-700
101	BL	necklace:	300-350
102	TL	sautoirs,	n.a.
102	BL	unique example:	10,000
103	TR	necklace:	4200-4500
103	CL	necklace:	4500-4700
103	BR	necklace:	4200-4500
104	TL	necklace:	1000-1200
104	TR	brooch:	1800-2000
104	CL	brooch:	1800-2000
104	CR	leaf set:	1000-1200;
		brooch:	1200
105	BL	cuff:	300-350;
		pendant:	300-350
105	TR	set:	400-500
105	CR	rings:	100,
		brooches:	150
106	TL	bracelets:	200-250 each
106	BL	foxes, depending on	

Page	Pos	Item	Price
		edition,	50-150
106	BR	rings:	25-50;
		bangles:	150-250
107	TR	pins:	75-150
107	BL	pins:	75-150
107	BR	pins:	50-150
108	TL	Bracelets, Deco:	150-175;
		translucent "lace":	300-350;
		stacked bangles:	300-350;
		layered cuffs:	200-250
108	BR	earclips, striped, fan:	50;
		pinwheel:	100
109	TL	pins:	50-150
109	BR	necklaces:	200-250
110	BL	brooches, compacts, necklaces,	n.a.
111	TL	leap-sheep:	1: 1200-1500; r: 700-900
111	TR	brooches:	1000-1500;
		bracelets, sautoirs:	900-1500
111	BR	necklace, brooches:	400-500, each
112	BL	choker:	1200-1500;
		earrings:	300-400;
		combs:	350-400;
		necklace:	1500-1600
112	BR	brooch:	300-450
113	TL	necklace:	800-1000
113	CR	bracelet:	350-450
114	TL	ensembles,	n.a.
114	BR	bracelet:	500-600
115		cuffs:	300-400;
		rings:	250-300

Chapter 2: Germany

Page	Pos	Item	Price
117	B	buckle:	600-900
118	TR	pendant:	3200-3500
118	BL	brooch:	600-800
118	BR	brooch:	800-1000;
		ring:	250-350
119	TL	parure:	2000-2500
119	TR	rings:	250-350;
		bracelet:	2200-2700
119	B	top brooch:	1500-1800;
		ring:	600-750;
		pendant:	1500-1800;
		brooch:	1000-1200;
		earrings:	300-400
120	T	bracelet:	750-850
120	CR	brooch:	300-350;
		pendant:	850-950,
		turquoise pendant:	350-450
121	TL	sautoir:	1000-1200
121	BL	galleon:	300-350
121	BR	porcelain:	150, 200-300(Wendler)
122	TL	porcelain pendant:	200-300
122	CL	porcelain:	200-300

Page	Pos	Item	Price
123	T	bracelet:	n.a.
123	C	pendant,	n.a.
123	BR	brooch,	n.a
124	TL	necklace,	n.a.
124	BR	chrome necklaces:	450-650
125	TL	chrome necklaces:	400-500
125	TR	chrome necklaces:	500-600
125	BL	bracelets:	250-300
125	BR	bracelets:	100-150;
		brooches:	200-250
126	TR	necklaces, chrome:	450-600
126	C	chrome/enamel set:	600-700
126	BR	necklaces:	450-550
127	TL	watch fobs:	60-100
127	CR	top bracelet:	600-800;
		clip:	160-200,
		bracelet:	150-200
127	BL	clip:	275-300
127	BR	ring:	250-300
128	TL	sodalite bracelet:	2200-2500
128	TR	gold mesh bracelet:	700-900;
		glass bracelet:	250-350
128	BR	narrow bracelets:	400-500;
		wide:	600-800
129	TL	cufflinks:	200;
		bar pin:	300
129	CR	necklace,	n.a.
129	BL	Galalith necklaces:	350-600;
		bracelets:	300-500
130	TR	necklace,	n.a.
130	CR	necklace:	500-600
130	BL	pin:	250-350;
		earclips:	200
130	CR	set,	n.a.
131	T	bracelet,	n.a.
131	B	bracelet, pendant,	n.a.
132	TL	pendant,	n.a.
132	CL	pendant:	250-350
132	BR	glass pendants:	250-300
133	TR	box:	600-800
133	BR	brooches:	35-65
134	TR	set:	700-800
134	BL	narrow bracelet:	300-400;
		wide:	400-500;
		polka dot:	200-250
135	TR	pendant:	200-250;
		bracelets: narrow:	300-400;
		wide:	400-500
135	CL	bracelets:	450-475
135	BR	pendant:	300-400
136	TR	necklace:	300-400
136	BL	necklace:	300-400
136	BR	necklace:	300-400
137	TR	necklace:	250-400
137	B	necklace:	400-500
138	T	necklace:	400-500

Page	Pos	Item	Price
138	B	earrings:	100-150
139		gold glass bib:	350-450
140	T	pendant:	500-600
141		beaded balls:	300-400

Chapter 3: Great Britain

Page	Pos	Item	Price
frontispiece		lizard:	250-300;
others,		see chapter 3, 6	
143	R	necklace,	n.a.
144	TL	pendant:	900-1200
144	BL	card case:	250-350;
		pendant:	350-450
145	TL	brooches:	600-800
145	CL	buckle:	900-1200
145	B	brooch:	500-700
146	TL	buckle:	400-500
146	BL	brooch:	500-800
146	BR	brooch:	700-900
147	TR	brooch:	150-200;
		pendant:	150-200
147	C	set	250-300
147	BR	brooch:	200;
		pendant:	250
148	TL	pendant brooch:	2200-2500
148	CL	ring:	2200-2400;
		brooch:	2000-2200
148	BL		800-1000
149	TR	pendant:	1200-1500
149	BL	silver belt:	350-450;
		silver buckle:	200-250;
		enamel buckle:	250-300
149	CR	enamel buckle:	300-400
150	TL	belt:	350-400
150	TR	ring, brooch:	n.a.
150	BR	buckles, pendant:	n.a.
151	TR	small brooches:	50-120;
		large brooch:	80-150;
		necklace:	75-100
151	BL	brooch:	300-400
151	BR	brooches:	60-120
152	TL		80-120
152	CR	Poole brooch:	250-350
152	BL	Cliff pendant:	400-500
153	TR	celluloid frogs:	175;
		bakelite:	250-350
153	CL	compact bracelet:	450-600
153	B	scotties:	75-175;
		crickets:	30-50;
		bunnies:	75;
		compacts:	150-175
154	TL	purses, elephants: bakelite,	300-350;
		celluloid,	200-250;
		crocodile:	150-200
154	BL	figurals:	75-125

154	BR	necklace:	300-400;
		bracelet:	200-300
155	TR	necklace:	900-1200
156	TL	necklace:	600-700
157	TL	bangles:	200-250
157	BL	bracelet:	200-250;
		earrings:	100-125
157	BR	pendants:	200-250
158	TR	glasses:	100-150
159	TR	ornament, n.a.	
159	C	pin:	150-250
159	BR	earrings, n.a.	

Chapter 4: Austria

162	TR	pendant,	n.a.
162	CR	(rare) gold brooch, moonstone:	18,000-20,000
162	CR	white enamelled brooch:	n.a.
162	CR	blue enamelled brooch:	n.a.
163	T	porcelain:	150-250
163	CR	porcelain:	150-250
163	BR	tassel,	n.a.
164	TR	compact:	250-350
164	BL	cravate:	250-300
164	BR	bag:	250-350
165	T	sautoirs:	2000-2500;
		bracelet:	500-550
165	BL	bracelet:	250-300
165	BR	bag:	600-800
166	T	purse:	75;
		scarf:	175
167	TL	enamelled necklace:	500-600
167	TR	brooch:	300-350
167	CR	bracelet:	250-350
167	B	necklace:	350-400;
		enamel brooches:	300-400;
		buckle:	300-350
168	TR	set:	350-400
168	CL	hat brooch:	250-300
168	B	bags:	100-125
169	TR	crystal:	250-300
169	CR	sautoir:	300-350
169	BL	necklace:	500-700
170	TR	bracelet:	250-300
170	CR	barette:	n.a.
170	BR	lariat:	400-500
171	TL	tie necklace:	1500-1800
171	TR	brooch,	n.a.
171	CR	brooches,	n.a.
171	BR	bracelet,	n.a.
172	TR	necklace:	n.a.
172	B	pins:	n.a.
173	T	glass necklace was a $5000 Rakow Commission endowment	
173	BR	set:	150-250

Chapter 5: Hungary

175	R	ring, bracelet:	n.a.
176	TL	set:	n.a.
176	TR	buckle:	500-650

176	CR	ring:	400-500
176	B	buckle:	600-700
177	TL	buttons:	250-350
177	TR	ring:	250-350;
		pendant:	350-400
177	B	shoe buckles:	700-900,
		belt buckle:	700-900
178	TR	amethyst set:	2500-2700
178	CL	emerald brooch:	500-600
178	BR	amethyst bracelet:	1500-1700
179	T	turquoise bracelet:	n.a.
179	BR	bracelet:	300-450

Chapter 6: Bohemia

181	R	necklace:	700-800
182	TL	ornament:	75;
		buckles:	150-175
182	BL	hat ornament:	300-350
182	BR	clasps:	175-250
183	TL	bracelets:	125-175
183	CR	buckles:	100-250
183	CL	clips:	250-300
183	BR	buckle:	900-1200
184	TL	buckles, mounted:	250-350
184	CR	buckle:	150-200
184	B	buckle, mounted:	250-300
185	T	bracelets:	100-250
185	BL	buckles:	100-150
185	BR	drop earrings:	150-175
186	TL	necklace:	500-700
186	TR	Egyptian motifs:	50;
		spider bracelets:	250-300;
		bracelet:	250;
		belt:	350
186	B	brooches, from top:	50, 75, 125
187	TR	bracelets:	65-150;
		pins:	75-125
187	B	brooch:	175;
		necklaces:	150-175
188	TL	clutch bags:	75-150
188	TR	necklace:	250-300
188	BR	necklaces:	150-250
189	TR	necklaces:	150-200
189	CL	necklace:	175-200
189	BR	necklaces:	100-125
190	TR	set:	475-500
190	B	bracelets, from top:	175-200, 75-100, 250-300
191	T	earrings:	20-50;
		bracelet:	50-75
191	B	earrings:	20-65
192	TL	chatelaine:	400-500;
		ring:	85
192	B	set:	150
193	TL	necklace:	300-400

193	BR	crystal necklace:	500-600

Chapter 7: Italy

195	R	necklaces:	n.a.
196	T	stars:	100
196	CR	necklaces:	150-200
196	L	gold resin:	n.a.
197	TL	birch resin:	75-175
197	R	clipping,	n.a.
198		crystal necklaces:	500-800
199	B	pearls:	250-450
200	TL	set:	325;
		bracelet:	175;
		earrings:	150-175
200	CR	set:	800-900
200	BL	necklaces:	450-550
201		necklace:	1400-1600;
		bracelet:	500-600
202		necklaces: top,	500-600;
		lower,	700-800
203	TL	hoops:	200-250
203	TR	earrings:	200-250;
		necklace:	350-400
204	L	bracelet, earrings:	n.a.
204	TR	necklace:	500-600
205		flower pendants:	700-800
206	TR	set:	2000-2500
206	CL	necklaces:	1800-2200
206	BR	pin:	150-200
207	TR	necklace:	1700-2000
207	BL	cuff:	500-650
208	T	necklace:	1400-1800
208	BR	necklaces:	400-500;
		belt:	500-600
209	BL	rings:	200-300;
		necklaces:	500-600
209	BR	necklace:	250-350
210	TL	necklace:	300-350
210	TR	beads:	45-75 each
210	BL	bead:	50
211	TR	necklace:	450-550
211	CL	sautoir:	700-900
211	TL	bead:	50-75
212	TR	pendant:	200-250
212	BL	murrine:	n.a.
212	BR	necklaces:	300-400
213	TL	sautoir:	400-450
213	TR	necklace:	600-650
213	BL	necklace:	400-450
213	BR	necklace:	300-350
214	TL	beads:	50 each
214	TR	belt:	800-1000
214	BL	necklace:	350-400
214	BR	necklace:	300-350
215	TL	necklace:	300-350
215	TR	dog collar:	200-250
215	BL	necklace:	250-300
215	BR	dog collar:	200-250
216	TR	necklaces:	150-200;
		bracelets:	50-75
216	BL	clowns:	150-200;
		earrings:	175

216	BR	perfume bottle:	450;
		rings:	50-75
217	TL	pietra dura ring:	200-250;
		micro-mosaics:	75-125
218	TL	necklaces:	450-600
218	CL	necklace:	500-600
219		set:	500-600
220	L	necklace:	n.a.
221	TR	necklaces:	500-600;
		bracelets:	250-350
221	BR	necklace (with earrings):	600-800
222	T	brooches,	n.a.
222	B	brooches,	n.a.
223	T	necklaces:	250-350
223	B	necklace:	150-200

Chapter 8: The Netherlands

note: the artists' prices date from contemporary sales

225	TR	brooch:	n.a.
225	BR	buckles, brooches:	n.a.
226	TL	buckle, brooches:	n.a.
226	BL	pendant, brooches:	400-500
226	BR	brooches:	n.a.
227	TL	pendants, etc.:	n.a.
227	CR	brooches:	350-450
227	BL	brooches:	n.a.
227	BR	cross:	n.a.
228	TL	earrings:	n.a.
228	CL	brooch:	350-450
228	CR	brooches:	500-800
228	BR	barpin:	300-400;
		brooch:	250-350
229	TL	brooches:	600-900
229	CR	brooches:	80-120
229	BR	brooches:	1500-1900
230	TL	brooch:	1400-1500
230	CL	ring:	1200-1300
230	BR	brooch:	250-300
231	TL	ring:	400-500
231	CL	brooch:	300-350
231	CR	collar:	500-600
232	TL	collar:	65-100
232	TR	PVC collar:	1400-1500
232	CL	bracelet:	125-150
232	CR	collar:	1200-1500
233	TL	earrings:	250-300
233	TR	tiepin:	150-250;
		earrings:	150-250
233	BR	bracelet:	400-450;
		earrings:	175-250

Chapter 9: Belgium

235	CL	buckle:	250-300
235	BR	brooch:	200-250;
		cuff:	400-500
236	TL	necklace:	450-600

236	TR	set:	600-700
236	BL	cuff:	250-300
237	TL	bracelet:	300-400;
		necklace:	550-650
237	B	lacquer bracelet:	2000-3000;
		ivory bracelet:	1500-2000
238		purses:	800-1800

Chapter 10: Denmark

For museum and artists' pieces marked n.a. (not available), refer to art galleries and specialty shops.

According to Michael von Essen of the Copenhagen Georg Jensen Museum: Georg Jensen silver was marked 826/1000 S fineness until 1912; 830/1000 S from 1912 to 1928-30, and after successful sales in New York and London, 925/1000 S sterling from 1930. The "S" after Scandinavian silver marks stands for *sólv*, silver. Vintage pieces are priced accordingly. Jensen models are numbered in sequence by category, i.e. necklaces; bracelets; rings; and earrings (the earlier ones fetching higher prices than later models), but there are exceptions. Prices range from Copenhagen (lower) to European auction and American dealer (higher.) "Georg Jensen Inc. U.S.A." is stamped on pieces produced ca. 1940-48 in U.S.A. not recognized or made by Jensen, Copenhagen silversmithy.

241	TR	brooches:	n.a.
242	TL	brooches:	
		top left:	150-175;
		right:	250-300;
		owl:	250-300;
		bottom:	250-300
242	BL	brooch with amber/agate:	8,500-9,000
243	TR	charm bracelet:	1200-1700;
		bracelet:	250-375
243	BL	moonstone/sapphire brooch:	750-900
243	BR	brooch (designed by Georg Jensen) 828 S:	600-800
244	TL	brooches:	
		green agate,	475-675;
		center, with opals/labradorite,	2500-3500;
		basket,	900-1200
244	CL	brooch, spectrolite:	575-875;
		amazonite brooch:	575-875
244	B	brooch, chrysoprase:	850-950
245	T	bracelet:	500-600;
		earrings:	200-250;
		brooch:	100-150
245	TL	bracelet:	700-800
245	B	skónvirke rings:	200-250;
		Future ring:	150-200;
		brooch:	200-250

246	TL	set:	n.a.
246	BL	bracelet:	200-250
246	BR	bracelet:	n.a.
247	T	brooch:	125;
		earrings:	125;
		bracelet:	175
247	BL	brooch,	n.a.
247	BR	necklace,	n.a.
248	TL	set:	250-350
248	TR	set,	n.a.
248	CL	bracelet, hematite:	2000-3000
248	BR	parure,	n.a.
249	T	necklace,	n.a.
249	B	brooch:	150-200
250	TL	parure,	n.a.
250	TR	parure,	n.a.
250	BL	earrings:	160-190;
		bracelets:	350-400 each
251	TR	necklace (most expensive ever made by Jensen):	4500-5000
251	TL	brooch:	350-400
251	CL	brooch:	350-400
251	BL	bracelet/earrings:	600-700
251	BR	bracelet:	350-450
252	TR	brooch:	250-350
251	B	brooches:	150-250
253	TR	porcelain:	150-175;
		daisy:	45-75
253	B	bracelet (this is the heavy version):	1400-1800;
		enamelled brooches:	600-1500
254	TR	necklace,	n.a.
254	BL	bracelet:	250-350
254	BR	necklace,	n.a.
255	TR	bangle:	85-100;
		ring:	65-85
255	BL	necklace:	375-400;
		earrings:	250-275
255	BR	bracelet,	n.a.

Chapter 11: Norway

note: for museum and artists' pieces marked "n.a.", refer to art galleries and specialty shops

257		brooch:	n.a.
259	TL	ring:	75-100;
		bracelet:	175-200;
		brooch:	150
259	CL	brooch:	250-275
259	BL	cufflinks:	150-200
259	TL	brooches:	l, 125-150;
			r, 75-100
259	BL	brooches:	75-100;
		owl:	50-75
259	BR	pendant:	300-350
260	TL	pendant:	400-500
260	C	brooch:	200-250;
		pendant:	150-175;
		pendant:	200-250
260	BR	brooch:	250-275
261	TL	brooches:	n.a.
261	BL	set:	125-150;
		brooch:	100-150

261	BR	brooches:	50-75
262	TR	brooches:	n.a.
262	BL	brooches:	n.a.
262	BR	necklace:	n.a.
263	TL	pendant:	125-175
263	BR	earrings:	n.a.
264	T	pin:	n.a.
264	B	necklace:	n.a.
264	TL	collar:	n.a.
265	TR	bracelet:	n.a.
265	B	belt/	
		necklace:	n.a.

Chapter 12:   Sweden

266	frontispiece	neckpiece/	
		chalcedony:	7000-8000
267	TR	pendant:	2000-2200;
		bracelet:	1500-1800;
		pendant:	1400-1600;
		gold bar pin:	1600-1800
267	BR	pendant:	1500-1800;
		ring:	800-1000;
		bracelet:	1800-2000
268	TL	ring:	800-1000
268	BL	bracelet:	1200-1500;
		rings, from left:	
		smoky quartz:	800-1000;
		gold:	1300-1500;
		eye:	700-800;
		gold:	1000-1200;

		center:	1300-1500
269	TL	earrings:	3000-3500
269	TR	hair	
		ornament:	1000-1200
269	CR	bracelet:	1200-1400
269	BR	shell bracelet:	1200-1400
270	TL	necklace:	4300-4500
270	TR	necklace:	4300-4500
270	BR	neckring/	
		pendants:	800-1700
271	TR	earrings:	275-300
271	CL	bracelet,	n.a.
272	T	bracelet:	450-500
273		necklace,	n.a.

Chapter 13:   Finland

274	frontispiece	silver bracelets:	
		bangles,	175;
		wide,	430-450;
		chain	
		necklace,	700;
		rings,	80-140
275		necklaces,	
		wood:	75-125
276	TL	bronze:	100-125
276	BL	set:	400-500
276	CR	bracelet:	n.a.
277	TR	necklace,	n.a.
277	CL	rings,	l.: 275-300;
			r.: 150-175

277	CR	brooch:	120-150
278	TL	pendant:	125-150;
		set:	275-300;
		pendant:	75
278	CL	brooch:	150-200
278	BL	ring,	n.a.
279		necklace,	n.a.
280	TL	brooch,	n.a.
280	TR	pendant,	n.a.
280	BL	pendant:	n.a.
281	TL	necklace,	350-450.
281	TR	necklace,	n.a.
281	BR	ring,	n.a.
282	TL	earrings:	100-125;
		ring:	100
282	CL	bracelet:	n.a.
282	BR	bracelet:	n.a.
283	TL	necklace:	n.a.
283	CR	brooch:	250-275
283	BL	bangle:	85-100;
		ring:	45;
		ring/	
		amethyst:	125
284	TL	pendant,	n.a.
284	TR	cufflinks:	150-175
284	BL	cufflinks:	200-300
285	CR	bracelet:	820-900
285	BL	rings:	l.: 75-100;
			r.: 200-250
286	TR	ring:	250-350
286	B	necklace:	1000-1500

Index